AF529132

SCHEDULED TRIBES AND DEVELOPMENT

SCHEDULED TRIBES AND DEVELOPMENT

Editors

H.S. Saksena
Vinay Kumar Srivastava
Sukant K. Chaudhury

SERIALS PUBLICATIONS
NEW DELHI

First Published - 2006

Reprint : 2013

ISBN : 81-8387-021-X

Published by

SERIALS PUBLICATIONS
4830/24, Ansari Road, Darya Ganj
New Delhi-110002 (India)
Phone : 91-11-23245225
Fax : 91-11-23272135
E-mail: serials@satyam.net.in,
serialspublications@vsnl.net
Website : www.seriealspub.com

Contents

Introduction

It is usually in terms of the concept of 'diversity' that we begin with our discourse on Indian society (Cohn 1971). In one of his interviews, the Cambridge professor, Alan Macfarlane (1991) says that when one speaks of India, one has in mind a cultural zone larger than Europe. Cultural differences among different communities in India are sometimes so strong, defined and glaring that one starts wondering how these communities have been able to live (and weld) together for time immemorial without any evidence of conflict between them and also, without their identity being blurred, effaced or lost. At the same time, in human history, several processes (such as, colonization, modernization, and now, globalization) have been unceasingly at work, which have created similarities between members of different communities. Some of these similarities are more in external features–for example, in dress patterns, kitchen utensils, house types, technology, manners of speech, etc – while others (for instance, education) have made a profound impact on the social morphology of people. Many studies have noted that among several factors, pilgrimage is one that brings people of different communities–sometimes nationalities–together, forging the bonds of fraternity among them (Cohn and Marriott 1958; Srinivas and Béteille 1964). It also creates certain long-lasting similarities between them, although each community tries to interpret the changes that are exogenously introduced in respect of its own reservoir of specific (or 'local') knowledge, which is regarded for the time being as beyond the pale of dispute and uncertainty (Geertz 1983).

Social systems may share similarities but are not identical. Studies of small-scale tribal and relatively complex rural societies, which are usually described as homogeneous, have time and again pointed out that each of these units comprises multiple–and contesting–perspectives on reality. Let us remember here what Parkin (1987) says that individuals spin 'endless perspectives' on reality from their 'cultural fleece' Fieldworkers have found that although we assume that the same dialect is spoken in a village, in reality, different castes have their special vocabularies and differ in terms of their styles of intonation, the use of honorific words and literary expressions (Gumperz 1958; Mandelbaum 1970: 321). In fact, just by listening to people on tape reorders, an experienced ethnographer of an area can quite correctly predict the caste and social background of the speaker. Studies have shown that it is incorrect to believe that lower castes share the same vision of caste system that the upper castes have, and this applies to all aspects of human living (Moffatt 1979; Quigley 1993).

Similarly, social reality is gendered, and one is expected to understand as clearly as possible the similarities and differences in male and female points of view with respect to each institution, custom, and practice (Moore 1988; Ortner 1996). Today, no anthropologist will regard the 'domestic' realm as 'female' and the 'extra-domestic', 'male'. Even when studying the social practices of obstetrics and pregnancy, which is regarded as exclusively a female domain, an anthropologist will also study what men feel about it, and how male perspectives on pregnancy interact and negotiate with that of the women. Equally sensitive are anthropologists today to the dimension of age–social reality as people of different age groups perceive and construct–and this has legitimately given rise to the anthropologies of children youths, and old peoples and centenarians.

Far from being a clear and an unequivocal picture, where different institutions fit well, without any ambiguity and conflict, social reality, including of those people who have been indisputably described in anthropological literature as 'simple', is an ensemble of contradictions, somehow co-existing. It may be conceptualized as a complex jigsaw puzzle, which is constantly being created and recreated, because of the unremitting interactions and negotiations that go on between different perspectives mediated by gender, age, social strata, and other socially and culturally recognized differences between people.

That people have their own interests, eternal tendencies to acquire, and wish to maximize their social and/or economic gain should not be forgotten, for this lies at the base of the ethno-political movements that have surfaced in all parts of the world. The idea of 'noble savage' that often figured in colonial anthropology is nothing but a figment of imagination of the classical evolutionists, who thought that the first human societies were non-acquisitive, non-accumulative, classless, stateless, and free from interests and one-upmanship, and that's why, they did not fight among themselves or with others. Studies have shown that without exception, all human societies have the notion of deriving 'advantage'–or, get the best–from a given situation or interaction. Bronislaw Malinowski was one of the first ethnographers who noted this in his work on Trobrinaders, and that's the reason why he is regarded as one of the precursors of transactionalism (Lewis 1976).

The contributors to this volume are well aware of the complexities of contemporary tribal existence in India, and show that it will be foolhardy to even think of a tribal society as 'isolated' (Mandal *et al.*, 2002). It seems that tribes in India have always been in contact with the outside world, including the communities described in anthropological literature as typical examples of isolated tribal existence; for instance, the Jarawa's use of iron in the last century shows their enduring relations with other people (Mishra 2002: 19). It is in the context of national and international social and economic systems that today the condition of tribal societies needs to be examined. Whenever a poor and debt-ridden country is in the grip of severe economic crises, it tries to overcome its problems whichever it can, by selling its precious natural resources, of which an important one is the forest wealth. Tribal communities dwelling for millennia in and eking out their subsistence from forests have been the worst sufferers. They are the ones thronging the streets of Ranchi as rickshaw-pullers, begging for tobacco in middle and south Andaman, working in middle and upper class households in Delhi as servants and maids, serving the contractors with labour for paltry sum. It is to the diversity of dismal tribal existence that this volume draws attention.

Many reasons have been given for why an overwhelming population of Indian villages, mostly belonging to lower castes and tribal groups, reels under the state of abject poverty and deprivation (Nanda 1994). Of them, an important cause of the vast disparities in levels of income and wealth is the age-old practice of bonded labour, which though legally abolished, continues to survive mightily (Hasnain 1982). A close relationship exists between land-alienation, indebtedness, and bonded labour (Roy Burman 1982). In fact, debt-bondage is an equivalent of slavery in the modern (and the post-modern) world. Every now and then, we read newspaper reports on the release of bonded labourers–*bandhua mazdur*, as they are popularly known in Hindi–with the active intervention of social workers and non-governmental organizations. At one time, it was thought that bonded labourers were confined to villages, but various surveys time and again have reminded us of the existence of this institution in towns and cities also. Known by different terms in different parts of the country, the institution of debt-bondage has certain typical characteristics–exorbitant interest rates and accounts manipulations, abysmally low wages provided to workers, and liabilities passed on to the family and successive generations. Many studies have shown that in contemporary India, a majority of tribal respondents know what debt-bondage is, and have also gradually gained knowledge of the law against it.

Many suggestions may be given for combating the system of debt-bondage, however two significant aspects emerge. First, though people may know this, it needs to be explained to them clearly and with emphasis that one of the most important reasons of their bondage is the customary practice of giving feasts on ritual occasions. If the community collectively resolves to cut down drastically on these feasts, the people will be less constrained to take loans beyond their capacity to repay. Second, people know how oppressive and exploitative the system of debt-bondage is, and they certainly want to emerge from it, but they cannot do so because the system at least ensures their survival. Since there does not exist an alternative economic arrangement for them, they are hesitant to leave the system of bondage. Therefore, it is extremely important that all agencies – governmental and non-governmental–think seriously in terms of the economic alternatives wherein the 'liberated bonded labourers' can be honourably rehabilitated. Also, the other economically weaker tribespersons are taken care of, especially during the lean months when they are forced to migrate, and are consequentially exploited in the system of contractual bondage at the hands of labour contractors

In addition, one of the main issues of tribal communities to which this volume addresses is that of poverty among tribesmen that the development programmes cause. The success stories of individuals from a few tribal communities (such as the Mina of Rajasthan, Christian tribespersons from central and north-east India, the families of tribal leaders who have acquired power in the democratic system) should not lead us to infer that the policy of compensatory discrimination and rapid development has elevated the economic status of a majority. On the contrary, the articles in this book document the perpetual conflict that exists between the national programmes of development on the one hand, and the interests of tribes, on the other, with the result that many tribal communities have become the 'victims of development', being drawn to the brink of a de-humanized existence, while many of non-tribal societies, located in towns and cities, have become affluent.

The national development programmes have included the setting up of large-scale industries, construction of dams for irrigation, systematic and intensive extraction of forest and mineral resources, establishing power projects for generating electricity, acquiring land at the outskirts of towns (generally inhabited by tribal people) for private housing projects, and also, reserving forests for regeneration. These development projects have invariably been undertaken in those regions that the tribes inhabit because of their richness in minerals and forest resources (Vidyarthi and Rai 1976 [1985]).

It was thought at one time that the programmes of development would facilitate the integration of tribal communities with what has come to be known as the 'mainstream of Indian society'. The basic difference between the tribal situation in India and in many other parts of the world has been in terms of the 'mainstream'; the Indian tribes are presumed to have one, whilst tribes in other parts of the world do not. So, the question of integrating tribes with the 'mainstream' has been of pivotal concern in India, and in this context, national development has been viewed as a cardinal step for bringing tribes in the national polity.

But, what has resulted is the opposite of what the national planners had thought of, i.e., the impoverishment and pauperization of tribes, the consequences of which for the psyche and self-esteem of tribal people have been disastrous (Saksena and Sen 1999). In an introduction to the book that he has edited, Joshi (1998: 14) writes.

> Our tribal development policies and programmes assumed that all the tribes will develop and will 'integrate' themselves with the so-called 'mainstream'. This has happened only in a symbolic way. Most of our researchers agree on this point that as a result of the planned tribal development, stratification on secular lines has taken place among tribals and only a small section has been able to take advantages of our tribal development programmes.

The impact of the policy of national development has been catastrophic to the basic resources of tribal societies – viz. water, land, and forest–on which the people have had usufructuary rights from time immemorial, bestowed to them by their tradition, their myth of origin, for which they did not need any bureaucratic sanction. The relationship of tribespersons with their ecological system was one of 'profound respectful dependence'. They used only that many resources and in only that much of quantity which they needed for their bare minimal survival. The notion of what is now called 'sustainable development' was in fact indigenously woven in the matrix of tribal culture. They did not need to be reminded of their posterity, the fact that they should cultivate an ideology of conservation–the conserver ethic–towards their ecosystem, so that their future generations could live well with dignity (Srivastava 2005a). For them, as the articles in this volume submit, the forest was not a commercial proposition, an 'uneven mishmash of trees that could be sold to the greedy world for revenue'; it was rather their 'way of life', an 'abode of their deities and ancestors', and the meaning of life for them was to live in 'harmony with nature' and 'venerate her for blessing people with all that they need for their existence.'

Development has led to a breakdown of this 'respectful' relationship between tribes and nature (Chaudhury 2004; Sah

2004). All over the world, tribesmen have witnessed the transformation of their nature from a 'way of life' to a 'commercial proposition'. Their ecosystems were overexploited, which they could neither stop from destruction nor to which could they register strong protests. And, when they raised their voice against the pillaging of their resources, their life-support system, the exploiters silenced it. Against this background, many tribal communities had no option but to flee to those areas where they could have a minimal level of freedom to live the way they would have liked to live. In fact, the isolation of tribes, which is usually regarded in anthropological literature as an important defining trait of tribes, resulted as a consequence of the experiences of exploitation and oppression they underwent. But now, the tribespersons have been driven to the wall, and have progressively taken the paths of protest movements and violence, as some articles in this volume show.

The entry of 'outsiders'–the government officials, surveyors, landlords, moneylenders, liquor vendors, etc–to tribal territories began a long time back with the advent of the British rule. The British policy in India was not one of non-interference with tribal existence, as was the case with pre-British rulers (Fürer-Haimendorf 1967). The British were keen to survey the tribal area to know about its material wealth, which could eventually be siphoned off to build industries back home (Majumdar 1944 [1973]). The British were also interested in studying tribal peoples and their institutions, not only for making an academic contribution to the understanding of the 'other', but also, for administering these societies better, so that peace could prevail in them and they remain subservient to the colonial rule. The role of anthropology in tribal administration is well known (Kroeber, ed. 1953). The colonial interests, which, to use Dube's (1977) word, were 'diabolical', were couched in the idiom of 'civilizing people'. Tribesmen were described to be in a state of barbarism and wildness and should be phenomenally changed (and 'domesticated') so that they could become like rest in the 'mainstream', which actually meant the 'mass of British subjects'. Tribes started losing their customary rights over land, forests, and water with the coming of British rule, with their resources being alienated to non-tribes, the exploiters who had thronged tribal territories in search of newer mines of wealth. The process that the colonial rule started of 'civilizing' people by forcing them–or, 'forcibly persuading' them–to accept the packages the state offered them, has continued uninterruptedly with the development programmes of Independent India.

Estimates of the number of people displaced (or uprooted) from their traditional habitats (or 'ancestral homes') because of development programmes vary a lot. Fernandes (1993, 1994) puts it over sixteen million, of which about 40 per cent happen to belong to tribal societies. The Ministry of Tribal Affairs (2004) has, however, placed the number of tribals at 85.4 lakhs till 1990, and they constitute 55 per cent of the total displaced people. The area under forest cover has also abysmally declined; what used to be 40 per cent of the country's territory in 1854 was in the 1980s, just 10 per cent. As a large number of tribal people are forest dwellers, they have suffered the most. With the British forest policy came the state control over forest resources and the rights and privileges of tribes over forests were curtailed. Although the forest policy of Independent India has enlarged the rights and privileges the forest-based tribal communities enjoy, and the local communities in many parts of India are actively involved in the programmes of Joint Forest Management, there is no doubt, as a number of tribal studies and articles in this volume point out, that the condition of people in 'forest villages' has not shown any qualitative improvement. On the contrary, it has worsened, and the exploitation of people, particularly women, by forest officials has increased several folds. Pathy (1984) has found parallels between the life of the dwellers of forest villagers and that of the 'labour camps'. This issue as well as that of the land rights of other communities are under close scrutiny for remedying through a comprehensive forest rights legislation, now on the anvil.

Not only have development programmes displaced people from their traditional habitats, but also, a large number of 'outsiders', of different social strata, from moneylenders to government officials, have entered into tribal territories. Because of their links and networks, among themselves and with bureaucracy, which they use to their advantage, they have been able to control trade and commerce, siphoning off the local resources, in the same way as the British did before India's independence. As many observers have time and again reported, the outsiders have also made fun and ridiculed tribal practices and customs, thereby making people suspicious of their institutions with which they have been living for time immemorial (Alam 1993; Sarkar and Chakraborty, eds. 2003). Tribal culture, in some cases, has become a liability and embarrassment to its bearers, because of the sort of treatment it has received from outsiders. And here props up a much larger question rooted in the Constitution itself – social realities and the scheduling of tribes. In certain situations, the inapposite scheduling, often politically manipulated, brings misery to tribals through declaring 'outsiders' as 'insiders' eligible for all the benefits intended for tribes. Fürer-Haimendorf (1982: 196-7) comments on one such case–the scheduling of the Banjaras (who were immigrants in Andhra Pradesh) and how the Gond and Kolam lost their land after it:

> ...that year (1977) the Banjaras, also known as Lambaras, were notified as a scheduled tribe, and this notification invested them with all the privileges hitherto enjoyed only by the truly aboriginal tribes of Andhra Pradesh. The reason for this move on the part of the government was basically political, for Banjara leaders had been pressing for some time for their inclusion in the list of scheduled tribes, and as some 600,000 votes were at stake, the political party in power finally yielded to this pressure.

In its wake, industrialization brought in urban influence. Tribal areas, rich for their mineral and forest resources, as was noted earlier, were chosen for setting up industries, and around them emerged towns. Contrary to what was thought at one time about the positive and integrative effects of industrialization and urbanization, these processes have added to the woes of tribes. Besides the despoliation of their habitats, the gains of development have not dispersed to them. Neither have schools nor hospitals reached all of them; and a large number of their villages have yet to receive the benefits of electrification or irrigation. Many papers in this volume have noted that development has been lop-sided for tribal communities, and the rich 'outsiders' have monopolized its gains that in fact should have reached tribal areas. Development has created a class of what sociologists call 'surplus labour' (or 'underclass') from among the tribal people, who are largely unskilled, and have no option but to migrate to towns and cities in search of jobs, for basic survival, which they do not get easily. This has often set the stage for these 'underclass' tribesmen to take up crime as a way of life, and be stigmatized forever (Bhowmick 1978). Against this background, some anthropologists think that tribal communities constitute the 'fourth world', the most undeveloped of the undeveloped and underdeveloped world (Xaxa 2003).

The empirical studies contained in this volume amply point out that the condition of tribes differs widely from one geographical region to the other, and also, there are differences between the same geographical region. This abundantly supports the idea that anthropologists have time and again submitted that what is needed is 'context-specific' and 'ethno-local' model of development. At this point, it is relevant to remember Anthony Cohen's (1996: 28) observation:

> Our own experience surely leaves us in no doubt that the ubiquitous failure of development projects, of urban plans, indeed, of strategic planning of all kinds, often results from the planners' neglect of, or disdain for, the vital differences among people which their generalizing models obscure.

People's viewpoint can be understood and fully appreciated when they are involved in every development and welfare project right from its inception. Pingle and Fürer-Haimendorf wrote in 1998:

After fifty years of Independence and many government failures, the realization that the only way left for government to succeed in its efforts to reduce poverty in rural areas is to include the wide participation of the bottom third of the poor in their own development.

The message that this volume gives is that people will be empowered when they not only determine the course of development, but also develop their own measures and technology to evaluate its respective impacts on different components of society–i.e., people of different gender and age categories and strata. In addition, as K.S. Singh states in his article in this volume, the state should guarantee the 'rights of tribal people over their resources' and 'ensure their share in the power structure so that they exercise control over their resources for their own benefits'. Perhaps, this idea can be best expressed in the following maxim: 'The state should help people to help themselves.'

But, has the state been adequately helpful? Or, poor governance in tribal areas has gathered smouldering unrest, culminating in widespread and violent unrest, like the Naxalite hold over such areas. After its onset among the tribes of Srikakulam in Andhra Pradesh in the 1960s, the Naxalite struggle for 'liberation' is present today in nine states and largely involves the tribal belts–the Scheduled Areas. In fact, a distinctive pattern of administration for compact areas inhabited by tribal people has its historical background of a chain of rebellions and violent movements dating back to the 1770s as an aftermath of the extension of British rule to their areas. As early as 1948, in his comprehensive report on the socio-economic condition of aboriginal tribes in the Agency Areas of Madras (now, the Scheduled Areas of Coastal Andhra Pradesh), the veteran anthropologist, A. Aiyappan, had clearly linked the 'half-hearted' development approach of the colonial administration to tribal unrest. But, the later studies and reports of anthropologists did not factorize this vital element in their developmental and administrative planning. The growing discontent in tribal areas that had received some academic attention in the surveys of tribal movements is not reflected in the reports that the high-power committees of the government prepared from the 1960s to 1970s. When Srikakulam had become a burning problem from 1967 onwards, the Expert Committee that S.C. Dube headed in 1972 made no mention of the tribal situation as it was unfolding.

An important statement issued last year (2004) in the month of February was the Draft of thc National Policy on Tribals, which was reproduced in *The Eastern Anthropologist* (57: 3-4, July-December 2004: 421-9). It was the first time in the history of tribal India that the government formulated a National Policy on Scheduled Tribes, for there existed none during the colonial times. What existed at that time were the 'approaches' that aimed to provide a solution to the 'tribal problem'. These 'approaches' were generally grouped into three categories– viz., isolation, assimilation, and integration–but they were also classified into other heads. For instance, while Dube (1968: 108-12) spoke of four approaches, respectively titled 'social service', 'political', 'religious', and 'anthropological', Vidyarthi (1968: 121-5) thought in terms of the three, i.e., anthropologists' approach, social workers' approach, and missionaries' approach. The term 'policy', whenever used, was used rather loosely; for instance, Verrier Elwin's suggestion for temporarily isolating tribes that had been subjected to a lot of exploitation was sometimes termed 'National Park policy' (Vidyarthi 1968: 127).

A 'national policy' on tribes is definitely a further reinforcement of the idea that notwithstanding a myriad of measures that the government has taken after independence, the quality of life of many tribes, especially the Primitive Tribes, which number seventy-five, has not shown any improvement. On the contrary, as stated earlier, the development programmes, which were undertaken to facilitate the process of integrating tribes with the mainstream of Indian society, have destroyed the life-support systems of many of these communities, weakened their social and cultural fabric, and made people seek 'refuge' in their own land. The entry of non-tribal outsiders in tribal areas has continued unabated, bringing in its wake a grave exploitation of tribespersons, their illegal and forceful ousting from their own land, and their perpetual existence in a state of penury, fear, misery, and destitute. Against this background, it is imperative that a National Policy on Tribals comes into existence albeit the fact that the Scheduled Tribes are well covered under the Constitution of India. Such a Policy will guide all thoughts and actions (of the governments and the NGOs, as well as of independent social activists and advocates) that are held and carried out in collaboration with people for amelioration of their condition.

The guidelines in the Draft of the National Policy as of now cover the following areas: formal education, health, displacement and resettlement, forest villages, land alienation, conservation of traditional wisdom and intellectual property rights, tribal languages, and the administration of their areas. It, however, appears to be more an exercise in homilies and repetitions than any charter for better governance and peoples' empowerment. The Draft of the National Policy will be revised and rewritten. Incidentally, the editors of *The Eastern Anthropologists* have invited comments and suggestions from its readers on this Draft, for its improvement and bringing out the best in it, to be eventually conveyed to the Ministry of Tribal Affairs, Government of India. The Draft, in its present form, appears to be hurriedly written, raising an obvious question about why the issuance of this Policy was really hastened. In fact, in a discussion on the Draft that the Indian Anthropological Association organized on 26 March 2004, almost all the speakers noted with dismay its poor quality. Some of them even suspected that perhaps those unaware of the contemporary state of Indian tribes had drafted the Policy. It once again brought to the fore the question about the rush to have this Policy, for one would have expected a document of national importance to be thought-provoking and all-encompassing, in addition to be of exemplary quality.

The aim of the Policy is defined at the outset: 'to bring [the] Scheduled Tribes into the mainstream of society through a multi-pronged approach for their all-round development without disturbing their distinct culture.' By this, one instantly understands that the approach the Policy puts forth is to 'integrate' tribes with rest of the society. Here, it is extremely important that the Policy discusses in clear and comprehensive terms what it means by the concept of 'mainstream', for it is well known that what north Indians understand by 'mainstream' is different from the meaning that south Indians attribute to it. Similarly, the 'mainstream' for the Nagas is different from the Assamese plains dwellers.

Like many other concepts in social anthropology and sociology, 'mainstream' is also a plural-concept, in the sense that it has many meanings. The meaning of the concepts of 'mainstream' and 'integration' the Policy intends to put forward must be clarified, because, for reasons not given, its Draft ends with the subtitle of 'Assimilation', which, as is well known, in the context of tribal studies, referred to the approach of social workers, according to which the problems of tribal societies were because of their continued isolation, and it was believed that the more they would come in contact with the outside world, the better it would be for their uplift. The solution to tribal problems, according to the 'assimilationists', lay in 'assimilating' tribes with the outsiders, largely Hindu, and imposing upon them the values they deemed proper (such as, prohibition of liquor, dressing up like caste Hindus). As critics have said, assimilation is utopian, undemocratic, unethical and unjust. Moreover, it is ethnocentric, nothing but imposingness, for, as Mehra (1987: 40) writes, tribes 'may or may not agree to what appears to those encouraging ...assimilation as a logical and more effective way of doing things, and they may prefer their own old ways.' Assimilation is the contrapuntal ideal type of integration. If assimilation symbolizes the 'melting' of tribal cultures in the culture of outsiders, integration stands for the 'respect' that tribes and their cultures receive from outsiders. If assimilation favours homogenization of cultures, integration subscribes to the Chinese maxim: 'Let the hundred flowers blossom, let the hundred schools of thought flourish.' Integration is a celebration of the principle of diversity and a denunciation of any variety of cultural imperialism.

This volume unflinchingly subscribes to the principle of national integration, the principle of unity in diversity, but attributes priority to the speeding up of the programmes of poverty-alleviation and economic development among tribal communities. Irrespective of its variability,

> the contemporary international and interdisciplinary discourse on development submits that all human beings, notwithstanding their cultural differences, want 'good life', a life free from hunger and illness, torture and oppression. All want their children to study, be gainfully employed, and move up in the system of social ranking. All long for peace and self-respect, and the feeling of fraternity among different communities (Srivastava 2005b: iv).

The glimpses of what 'good life' means to tribes are sensitively scattered through out this volume. The authors argue that the juxtaposition of different field sites will illuminate local dynamics, which is grossly missed out in a global analysis. The strength of anthropology lies in offering micro-level analyses, which have larger implications, of cultures that are no more bounded, but are constantly interacting with each other. These interactions have yielded a unity of opposites, in the sense that different systems now resemble one another more than what they did in the past. At the same time, each system is conscientiously aware of its identity, its separateness, which may sometimes be invented and celebrated. 'Objective culture' (i.e., 'culture in itself') has now become 'subjective culture' (i.e., 'culture for itself'). The ceaseless interaction between the processes of unification and segregation needs to be analyzed at the local field site, which the authors of this volume attempt.

ACKNOWLEDGEMENT

Except for the two articles (by D.R. Sahu and Nilika Mehrotra) that appeared in *The Eastern Anthropologist* (57: 1, January-March 2004) and another by Nadeem Hasnain and Aseem Hasnain, rest of the articles comprising this book were published as a Special Number of *The Eastern Anthropologist* (56: 2-4, April-December 2003) under the auspices of the D.N. Majumdar Centenary Year: 2003-2004. We are thankful to the Ethnographic and Folk Culture Society, Lucknow, for all help in preparing this volume.

REFERENCES

Aiyappan, A. (1948), *Report on the Socio-economic Conditions of the Tribes of Madras Presidency*. Madras: Government Press.

Alam, Javeed. (1993), Fragmented Culture and Strangulated Existence: Jharkhand's Cultural Encounter with the Modern. In Mrinal Miri (ed.), *Continuity and Change in Tribal Society*. Shimla: Indian Institute of Advanced Study (pp. 11-22).

Bhowmick, P.K. (1978), *Some Aspects of Indian Anthropology*. Calcutta: Institute of Social Research and Applied Anthropology.

Chaudhury, Sukant K. (2004), *Tribal Identity, Continuity and Change among the Kondhs of Orissa*. Jaipur and New Delhi: Rawat Publications.

Cohen, Anthony P. (1996), Against the Motion (1): Social Anthropology is a Generalizing Science or It is Nothing. In Tim Ingold (ed.), *Key Debates in Anthropology*. London and New York: Routledge (pp. 26-30).

Cohn, Bernard S. (1971), *India: The Social Anthropology of a Civilization*. Engelwood Cliffs, New Jersey: Prentice-Hall, Inc.

Cohn, Bernard S. and McKim Marriott. (1958), Networks and Centres in the Integration of Indian Civilization. *Journal of Social Research*, 1: 1-9.

Dube, S.C. (1968), Approaches to the Tribal Problem in India. In L.P. Vidyarthi (ed.), *Applied Anthropology in India (Principles, Problems and Case Studies)*. Allahabad: Kitab Mahal (pp. 107-12).

——. (1977), Introduction. In S.C. Dube (ed.), *Tribal Heritage of India, Volume 1: Ethnicity, Identity and Interaction*. New Delhi: Vikas Publishing House Pvt. Ltd. (pp. 1-7).

Fernandes, Walter. (1993), The Price of Development. *Seminar*, 412: 19-24.

——. (1994), *Development-induced Displacement in the Tribal Areas of Eastern India*. New Delhi: Indian Social Institute.

Fürer-Haimendorf, Christoph von. (1967), The Position of the Tribal Population in Modern India. In Philip Mason (ed.), *India and Ceylon: Unity and Diversity; A Symposium*. London: Oxford University Press (pp. 182-222).

——. (1982), *Tribes of India, the Struggle for Survival*. New Delhi: Oxford University Press.

Geertz, Clifford. (1983), *Local Knowledge, Further Essays in Interpretive Anthropology*. New York: Basic Books, Inc., Publishers.

Gumperz, John J. (1958), *Dialect Difference and Social Stratification in a North Indian Village*. American Anthropologist, 60: 668-82.

Hasnain, Nadeem. (1982), *Bonded for Ever*. Delhi: Harnam Publications.

Joshi, Vidyut. (1998), Genesis of Tribal Problems. In Vidyut Joshi (ed.), *Tribal Situation in India, Issues in Development (with Special Reference to Western India)*. Ahmedabad: Sardar Patel Institute of Economic and Social Research, and Jaipur and New Delhi: Rawat Publications (pp. 13-27).

Kroeber, A.L. (1953), *Anthropology Today, An Encyclopedic Inventory*. Chicago: University of Chicago Press.

Lewis, I.M. (1976), *Social Anthropology in Perspective, The Relevance of Social Anthropology*. Penguin Books.

Macfarlane, Alan. (1991), An Interview. *Indian Anthropologist*, 21 (1): 57-75.

Majumdar, D.N. (1944), [1973]. *Races and Cultures of India*. Bombay: Asia Publishing House.

Mandal, Hrisikesh, Sumit Mukherjee, and Archana Datta. (2002), *India, An Illustrated Atlas of Tribal World*. Kolkata: Anthropological Survey of India.

Mandelbaum, David G. (1970), *Society in India*. Bombay: Popular Prakashan.

Mehra, J.D. (1987), Tribal India: Continuity and Change. In *India, Specially Published for the Festival of India in the U.S.S.R.* New Delhi: Brijbasi Printers Pvt. Ltd. (pp. 35-41).

Mishra, Ujjwal. (2002), The Jarawa: Contact and Conflict. In K. Mukhopadhyay, R.K. Bhattacharya, and B.N. Sarkar (eds.), *Jarawa Contact, Ours with Them, Theirs with Us*. Kolkata: Anthropological Survey of India (pp. 13-9).

Moffatt, Michael. (1979), *An Untouchable Community in South India, Structure and Consensus*. Princeton: Princeton University Press.

Moore, Henrietta L. (1988), *Feminism and Anthropology*. Cambridge: Polity Press.

Nanda, Bikram Narayan. (1994), *Contours of Change, The Story of the Bonda Highlanders*. Sage Publications.

Ortner, Sherry B. (1996), *Making Gender, The Politics and Erotics of Culture*. Boston: Beacon Press.

Parkin, David. (1987), Comparison as the Search for Continuity. In Ladislav Holy (ed.), *Comparative Anthropology*. Oxford: Blackwell (pp. 52-69).

Pathy, Jaganath. (1984), *Tribal Peasantry, Dynamics of Development*. New Delhi: Inter-India Publications.

Pingle, Urmila and Christoph von Fürer-Haimendorf. (1998), *Tribal Cohesion in the Godavari Valley*. Hyderabad: Booklinks Corporation.

Quigley, Declan. (1993), *The Interpretation of Caste*. Oxford: Clarendon Press.

Roy Burman, B.K. (1982), Transfer and Alienation of Tribal Land. In Buddhadeb Chaudhuri (ed.), *Tribal Development in India, Problems and Prospects*. Delhi: Inter-India Publications (pp. 69-82).

Sah, D.C. (2004), Partnership Ethics and Environmental Politics: Evidences from Southwestern Tribal Belt of Madhya Pradesh. In D.C. Sah and Yatindra Singh Sisodia (eds.), *Tribal Issues in India*. Jaipur and New Delhi: Rawat Publications (pp. 307-40).

Saksena, H.S. and Chandra Sen. (1999), *Putting People Last – Tribal Displacement and Rehabilitation*. Delhi: Inter-India.

Sarkar, Jayanta and Jyotirmoy Chakraborty (eds). (2003), *Transition, Change and Transformation, Impacting the Tribes in India*. Kolkata: Anthropological Survey of India.

Srinivas, M.N. and André Béteille. (1964), Networks in Indian Civilization. *Man*, 64: 165-8.

Srivastava, V.K. (2005a), On the Concept of Nature. In Nadia Tazi (ed.), *Keywords, Nature*. New Delhi: Vistaar Publications, and New York: Other Press (pp. 141-85).

——. (2005b), Foreword. Pragya Sharma, *Tribal Society in a Flux (An Anthropo-Sociological Study of Raika)*. Jaipur: Panchsheel Prakashan (pp. i-iv).

Vidyarthi, L.P. (1968), Anthropology, Authority and Tribal Welfare in India. In L.P. Vidyarthi (ed.), *Applied Anthropology in India (Principles, Problems and Case Studies)*. Allahabad: Kitab Mahal (pp. 120-36).

Vidyarthi, L.P. and B.K. Rai. (1976), [1985]. *The Tribal Culture of India*. New Delhi: Concept Publishing House.

Xaxa, Virginius. (2003), Tribes in India. In Veena Das (ed.), *The Oxford India Companion to Sociology and Social Anthropology*. Delhi: Oxford University Press (pp. 373-407).

List of Contributors

Archana Singh, Faculty of Sociology, School of Social Sciences, Indira Gandhi National Open University, New Delhi.

H.S. Saksena, Ethnographic and Folk Culture Society, Lucknow.

Vinay Kumar Srivastava, Professor of Anthropology, Delhi University, Delhi.

B.K. Roy Burman, Centre for the Study of Developing Societies, Delhi.

Manu Bhaskar, Professor, Department of Sociology, University of Kerala, Thiruvananthapuram.

K.S. Singh, Former Director General, Anthropological Survey of India.

Amrit Srinivasan and **Akhilesh Ranjan,** Department of Humanities & Social Sciences, IIT, Delhi.

Bhupinder Singh is presently a Member of the Second Scheduled Areas and Scheduled Tribes Commission, New Delhi.

Urmila Pingle, Medical Anthropologist associated with the National Institute of Nutrition, Hyderabad.

Sachchidananda, former Professor of Anthropology and Vice-Chancellor, Ranchi University, Ranchi.

Roxanne Hakim, Social Anthropologist, World Bank, Washington D.C., U.S.A.

Lancy Lobo, Director, Centre for Culture and Development, Vadodara, Gujarat.

Sukant K. Chaudhury, Reader, Department of Sociology, Lucknow University, Lucknow.

K. Gopal Iyer, retired Professor of Sociology, Punjab University, Chandigarh.

P.K. Misra, former Professor of Anthropology, North-East Hill University, Shillong.

Paramita Majumdar, Urban Studies Department, Institute of Social Sciences, New Delhi.

Indu Sahai, Professor and Head and **Sameera Maiti,** Lecturer in the Department of Anthropology, University of Lucknow.

Shalina Mehta, Professor, Department of Anthropology, Punjab University, Chandigarh.

B.B. Mohanty, Reader, Gokhale Institute of Politics and Economics (Deemed University), Pune.

Naresh Kumar Vaid, Adviser and former President, Experiments in Rural Advancement (ERA), AG 317, Shalimar Bagh, Delhi.

R. Shankar, Professor and Head, and **M. Thamilarasan,** ICSSR Doctoral Fellow, Department of Sociology, Bharathidasan University, Tiruchirapalli.

Samata and **Mines,** *Minerals and People,* Hyderabad and New Delhi.

D.R. Sahu, Reader, Department of Sociology, Lucknow University, Lucknow.

Nilika Mehrotra, Assistant Professor, Centre for the Study of Social Systems, School of Social Sciences, Jawaharlal Nehru University, New Delhi.

Nadeem Hasnain, Professor, Department of Anthropology, University of Lucknow.

Aseem Hasnain, Samavesh Institute of Governance and Development, Bhopal, M.P.

1

An Overview of D.N. Majumdar's Contribution to Tribal Studies

Archana Singh

The contributions of a scholar to the field of knowledge is part and parcel of the history and development of that field. Whether it is beneficial or not, it marks a stage in the progress of a science which when viewed later, forms that rung of the intellectual and academic ladder on which others climb to higher echleon D.N. Majumdar's contributions to social anthropology must be therefore, viewed in this perspective.

If one looks at history to trace the origin and development of anthropology in India, the colonial impact on, not only anthropology, but areas of higher education in India, seems to have been immense. The colonial influence and demand for trained Indians for subordinate posts in administration and judiciary, especially in practical sciences, such as, engineering, medicine, etc., was a major factor leading to the distinctive moulding of higher learning in India. Anthropology, like English language, is said to be the gift of the British imperialism.

It is without doubt that the colonial roots of anthropology rendered it suspect to the Indian nationalists. It smelt of 'British ethnocentrism' and as Wissler has pointed out, its point of view was that of "European observing the rest of mankind" (cited in Majumdar 1947: l.) Due to this connotation of the discipline of anthropology, the academic climate was not wholly propitious for it after Independence, unlike the discipline of sociology. Sociology as a discipline has, from the beginning "enjoyed greater esteem because of its proximity to philosophy and Indology–two disciplines highly rated in the country" (Dube 1975: 30).

Talking of anthropology in general terms, Edmund Leach (1962) graphically describes the nature of anthropology at the time of its origin. He says that:

> part of the original appeal of this new arrogant and ethnocentric science was that it fitted perfectly with the ethos of the era of European colonial expansion.

This fact definitely holds true for India where the first ethnographic treatises in the latter half of the 19th century were attempted by scholars such as Sir Herbert Risley, William Crooke, J.H. Hutton and several others. The first census in 1901 will always be remembered in the history of Indian anthropology (Sarana 1961: 105-121).

In India, anthropological studies can be said to have their beginning in the investigations by Indologists like Sir William Jones (1746-94), a judge, linguistic genius and Indologist. He founded the Asiatic Society of Bengal in 1774. He stated in his inaugural lecture that the society should undertake inquiries concerned with "man" and "nature" in India in order to reveal the past of India through the study of Sanskritic texts. He also stressed the importance of collecting of ethnographic and ethnological data (Madan and Sarana 1962).

Anthropology as a scholarly discipline was formally recognized in 1920 when the University of Calcutta included it as a subject in its curricula. Among the earliest persons to receive their Master's degree in anthropology from this University was D.N. Majumdar. At that time anthropology was general, which meant that all university trained anthropologists did work in all fields of anthropology, such as, social anthropology, physical anthropology, prehistoric archaeology, etc.

This orientation is clearly evident from Majumdars' works. All his books deal not only with social factors, economic factors and kinship organizations, and so on; but also with details regarding race, anthropometric variations and serological maps of various tribes and castes. His *Races and Cultures of India* (1944), best illustrates the kind of anthropology practised during his time.

As a descendent of the anthropologists belonging to the epoch of Bengal Renaissance, such as N.K. Bose, T.C. Das, S.C Roy, and K.P. Chattopadhyaya, who had the 'Civilisational Perspective', Majumdar had inherited the concern for "reform" and "progress" in Indian society (Jain 1980).

Trained as a general anthropologist, Majumdar found increasing emphasis upon specialization characteristic of contemporary research in social anthropology as crippling, although he realized its inevitability. For him, therefore, an ideal anthropologist was Kroeber. He also pleaded for the application of the findings of social sciences to the task of national reconstruction. Perhaps it was this conviction in the utility of applied sociological research which made him undertake in 1954 a survey of the industrial city of Kanpur. In another book, *Himalayan Polyandry* (1962), too, he has discussed this aspect.

Amongst the vast body of work produced by Majumdar during his life-time, I am focusing here mainly on his works in the area of tribal studies. Most of his books and monographs deal with the tribes of Uttar Pradesh and Bihar. He has also discussed the criminal tribes and other tribes of Gujarat, Orissa, etc. It is in these studies that

Majumdar has introduced the element of theory. This was a turning point in anthropology of his time when the main aim of anthropology was considered to be the observation and collection of data from the field. A person who introduced theory in his anthropological writings was considered to be an 'arm chair' anthropologist. This was supposed to be the worst kind of fate to befall an anthropologist belonging to the 'empiricist tradition'.

Anthropology began in many ways as the 'study of the other cultures', and these other cultures being the primitive societies. Those who studied these primitive societies, the founding fathers of anthropology, belonged to the so-called advanced European society. It began as a search for the origins of human society and the theory of evolution discovered by Darwin. Herbert Spencer endeavoured to apply the theory of evolution to societies. It was the Victorian notion of progress that the institutions of the non-European societies represented stages through which it was speculated that even European societies must have passed long ago. Thus, the study of tribes began as an exercise to discover those elements of a culture which could be considered to be the most primitive, simple and undisturbed forms of early human existence.

In India too, the early anthropologists, both European and Indian, academically trained and self-trained, began with collection of ethnographic data on tribes. Copious details of single tribes written in monographic forms emerged at this time. These works had very little to do with theory and were based upon intensive fieldwork. This was the empiricist positive tradition where all kinds of speculation of evolutionary or diffusionist kind were avoided. However, the prevalent influences of both these schools were present, but the dominant school of thought, when Majumdar came to this field, was of Malinowski's functionalism and Ruth Benedict's patterns of culture theses.

In keeping with the tradition of the early anthropologists, Majumdar, like his teacher and guide S.C. Roy, considered to be the 'father of Indian anthropology', began with the study of tribes of Chota Nagpur, Bihar. It was Roy who had first published the first full length monograph *Munda and Their Country* (1912). Majumdar studied the Ho of Singhbhum (Bihar). The data collected from his fieldwork amongst the Ho constituted his Ph.D. thesis which he did under T.C. Hodson in Cambridge University. This thesis was published in the form of a monograph, *A Tribe in Transition: A Study in Culture Pattern* (1937). In this monograph, Majumdar, like most of his predecessors, begins with describing the environment and the ecological setting of the Ho of Kolhan which was a government estate in the district of Singhbhum. However, Majumdar revised, expanded and updated this same monograph and developed further the root ideas of culture dynamics and social change amongst the Ho, and published this revised edition under the title, *The Affairs of a Tribe: A Study in Tribal Dynamics* (1950). In this book, the influence of Malinowski is considerable since Majumdar has treated Ho culture as an 'integrated whole' with an elaborate concept of culture development and advanced the thesis of acculturation which he had already established in his earlier works (Majumdar 1939; 1947).

In his former works, such as his article on 'Race and Adaptability' (1929), he says that tribes in India are rapidly disappearing due to increased contact with the higher cultures. If this disappearance of the primitive tribes will lead the unfettered tribals to a life of so-called ordered existence and degraded serfdom which have been more or less responsible for a complete change in their mental outlook, he says that:

> it is all the more essential that the factors of this civilisation should be analysed and some sort of protection should be provided for in order to enable

> them to hold their own against the onslaught of foreign ideas. (1929)

In this paper he has also discussed the various factors which are responsible for maladptation of the primitive stock and has shown how far groups can progress through a process of acculturation provided the impact of foreign cultures is not too violent.

In *Tribal Cultures and Acculturation,* which was his Presidential Address at the 26th Indian Science Congress, 1939 at Lahore, he says that there is one inherent defect in the monographic delineation of cultures. This defect becomes increasingly vital as one proceeds to describe cultures which have been penetrated by other cultures. Thus, he argues that:

> the monographic method in amateur hands has invariably failed to separate the 'native warp from the foreign woof,' and had failed also to evaluate the importance of the role of diffusion in culture progress. In India most of the tribal groups have come in contact with higher social groups and rites and customs introduced from highly organised societies have blended with those of a primitive or infantile character.... How far social life has deflected from tribal norms under pressure of alien cultures needs to be estimated before the picture of a culture may be complete... Analysis has shown how significant are the effects of such contacts, how social groups are adapting themselves to changed socio-economic condition, also how maladaptations are leading to tribal extinction or absorption into more dynamic and vital cultures. (1939)

In these works, as Madan says, there is an explicit acknowledgement of gradation of cultures (as has been stated before). He comments that Majumdar never subscribed to the notion of 'culture relativism' which was made popular by certain American anthropologists like Herskovits. According to this notion, truth, goodness and beauty have as many expressions as there are cultures. Majumdar, however, argued for an approach to the tribal problem which was based on a concept of creative or generative adaptation. For him Elwin's 'national park policy', i.e. to leave the tribals alone, and Ghurye's campaign for considering the tribals as backward Hindus amounted to Rousseauwean romanticism on the one hand and a political posture on the other, rather than the results of a scientific inquiry (Madan, 1982: 9).

In his *The Matrix of Indian Culture* (1947), Majumdar enumerates the processes 'through which tribal cultures are usually transformed or modified'. These processes are:

1. Simple adoption or taking over.
2. Acculturation which involves (a) acceptance and (b) adaptation.
3. Assimilation (a) social commensalism (b) plural association.

Majumdar defines acculturation as:

> the process of change due to contacts with other people, for example, contacts with civilisation have been found to affect the various sections of tribal people in India in different ways (1947: 165).

He says that the process of acculturation may be acceptance or adaptation. While the Munda tribes have accepted some of the traits from their neighbours, the Rajbanshis have shown an adaptation to Hindu culture, one that has given them a Hindu status, but also has brought certain disabilities.

When a tribe has to adopt traits of a culture, the adoption must be selective and the growth or decay of a tribe results from such selections. According to Majumdar, a well-knit social group where each individual shares the dominant traits of a culture with one another manifests inordinate solidarity in its cultural life, when confronted with a group in which the development of personality in its members has brought about some disunity and disintegration; as for example, where individual initiative has undermined social cohesion, the impact may not be conducive to the survival of the integrated group.

Therefore, as Majumdar says, acculturation is selective and often is an extremely important process in cultural contacts as the fate of tribal groups depends upon the manner in which alien traits are accommodated or adapted by them. But acculturation is only a means to an end. It is determined by the same urge, according to Majumdar, as the one which made man to invent tools and techniques, to aid him in his struggle against his environment and therefore, for survival. Thus, it is a tool of adaptation. But an efficient tool or weapon if put in the hands of negligent and careless person (or persons) can prove to be a source of embarrassment. The same goes for acculturation, which is a tool of adaptation and if put in the wrong hands or misdirected can lead a tribe or social group into trouble.

According to Madan (1982: 167), Majumdar clearly prefers the process of acculturation but at the same time he acknowledges the risk of reaction or 'contra-acculturation', the evidences of which he has recorded in some of the tribes he had studied. Majumdar holds the opinion that:

> what is needed is mutual respect and understanding, and where the dominant or ruling group has shown... respect and understanding, culture adjustment has been smooth and easy. It is, I think, possible for the tribes today to feel more secure and take greater share in the cultural progress of the country provided the attitude forced on the caste people by the numerical preponderance

> of the tribes and backward groups is not merely used for political expediency but as a sincere gesture towards a broad cultural movement seeking to absorb and assimilate the bulk of the primitive and backward substratum of population. If the political leaders of the country fail to recognise the trends of political thought and aspirations surging in the minds of the newly conscious tribal groups and exterior castes, a possibility which however cannot be ruled out as the indication goes, the future of Indian culture must be viewed with misgivings (1947: 174-185).

These words which have a contemporary ring about them were written in the year of India's independence.

Two years later, Majumdar restated his position on the problems of acculturation and the notion of development of culture in his book, *The Affairs of a Tribe* (1950) written in the old style of a monograph, as mentioned earlier. He says in this book that:

> the Hos are overwhelmed by the superiority of their neighbours..., when they adopt or initiate alien habits or ways of life, they find themselves cut off from their own tribesmen, but are not considered equal to those whom they imitate.

Thus, this inequality and non-acceptance of the tribals amongst the wider fold has led to inferiority complex amongst some and some have even reverted to their own belief systems and values. This revivalism finds an outlet in a new identity and tribal solidarity as well as greater political consciousness which manifests itself in the *adibasi* movement, a sub-nationalism, which Majumdar says is the result of contra-acculturation.

Earlier it was believed, especially in case of African cultural contact, that it was due to the impact of western civilisation and the reaction thereto of the indigenous culture. Malinowski too held this opinion. Majumdar, however, does not agree with him. He says that this view seems to ignore a vital strand, the strand on which we lay great emphasis from the point of view of theory and practice, viz., the contingency of inter-tribal influences of one African culture on another, or the elasticity of a culture with regard to the basic factors of the environment, such as, resources, area and the degree of cooperation within the society. For Majumdar, a more comprehensive and scientific approach consists in the study of such dynamic changes, in both intra and inter-tribal settings, apart from the influence of contacts with alien cultures.

According to Majumdar, the relation between needs and responses, the organism and imperatives, which produce institutions, cannot be isolated from the terrestrial factors since these supply the basic postulates of a culture or cultures. These terrestrial factors are made up of several elements which themselves are variable. The area is terrestrial, resources are made up of animals and plants, soil, minerals, technology; man is the organism with basic needs and cooperation is producing 'derived needs' which is human culture. Here cooperation includes conflict as well. Thus, Man (M), Area (A), Resources (R), and Cooperation (C) is an inter-dependent functional unit which provides the base of a culture, MARC. It is necessarily an elastic concept to a certain extent for any change in one of the factors leads to a corresponding change as determined by the direction of the resultant. The base of a culture is a function of MARC or B (base)=K=f where K is the resultant.

Majumdar says that the attitudes that determine achievement or define the limits of a culture in the context of MARC result from what may be called the 'density' of culture. When the density is low, ideas and attitudes do not find ready acceptance, so they are not important, but when the density of a culture increases through the interpretation of ideas within the culture due to the increase of cooperation between members of the group and the borrowings that occur due to personality reactions, the attitudes take shape rapidly till all the possible ones are forced to make the configuration asymptomatic with regard to the attitude. At this time we reach the concept of *Gestalt* or configuration. Therefore, it follows that MARC is the base on which culture is built up in its final form. Thus culture is limited by attitudes and the various parts of the culture become linked and inter-linked as the density of a culture rises to a saturation point. In this sense, Majumdar maintains that no culture is superorganic, no culture is mere organic, but inter-penetrative and linked but limited by the base or MARC. But the base cannot be equated with a region for it is the resultant of factors and neither is it determined by the sum total of the factors, M, A, R, C. Therefore, when a culture reaches saturation density with regard to traits, indigenous and borrowed and the base still remains narrow, it may show signs of intolerance, become isolative, or the base may show cracks or fissures, resulting in a cultural malaise. In these cases, detribalisation, disintegration of beliefs and practices and economic maladjustment lead to the destruction of the base of its culture and makes it inoperative. He cites the examples of tribes like the Toda of Nilgiri, the Korwa of Mirzapur, etc., where such a situation has arisen.

Majumdar writes that the Ho culture today has become 'dense' fully integrated with regard to its base, and with the indigenous traits as well as those which it has borrowed from others, it has developed a pattern. But this pattern is not what Benedict has described with regard to the three cultures she analysed. The Ho have acculturated to Hindu culture represented by the lower castes in their neighbourhood and have reacted to it, but as Majumdar says, this reaction is informed rather than hostile. Thus, in his opinion, every culture is to be studied in the context of change or cultural dynamics, whether the cultures have been affected by Euro-American civilization or its technological complements. The roots of culture change are to be traced in the factors or forces that create the base (or K) of a culture. (1950: *xviii*).

Madan (1982), commenting on this work, writes that in it, Majumdar has made one of his most clear statements of the notion of development of culture in his concluding words:

> The past must be understood in the context of the present, and the present will stabilise the future if it can find its fulfilment in the moorings of the past. There was no golden age, there can be none in the future. Life is a process of adjustment and in its unfolding, it has thrown out individuals who are misfits and the latter have both helped and hindered cultural progress, the misfits and misfits in the context of a dynamic setting, and if only the misfits could be fitted into the structure of life, the process that is life will continue to unfold itself, adjust and march on to man's destiny through an integration and synthesis that constitute the core of the dynamics of culture change and culture crisis. (1950: 324).

According to Madan's interpretation, the unfolding mentioned by Majumdar refers to the unfolding of the potentialities of a culture, its spontaneous development, and synthesis. It is interesting, no doubt, but he says, it will be rather far fetched to read into them any deep ideological (Hegelian or Marxian) significance or interest in a macro theory of social development. In his view, Majumdar was essentially a field worker, interested in attending to concrete problems like 'a clinician' (Madan 1982: 12).

In keeping with the primary concerns of the anthropologists of his time, Majumdar wrote a lot about the social composition of Indian population and its correlation with the tribes and castes of India in his books (1944; 1947), and also in his *The Fortunes of Primitive Tribes*

(1944). In this book, he wrote about social stratification in India, saying that:

> the most outstanding feature of the Indian population structure is a system of social gradation or a hierarchy with the primitive and aboriginal tribes at the bottom of the ladder, and a few higher castes at the top, the intermediate rungs being composed of a number of clean and unclean castes at various levels of purity and pollution. Although birth determines the social status of a person, the various groups constituting the intermediate rungs of the social ladder claim a higher status than to which they belong, supporting such claim by conformity to the tradition and customary patterns of behaviour, beliefs and practices of the culturally superior groups. These claims have been conceded in some cases, reducing thereby the social distance between them and those whose status they covet, though such social transition may have taken decades or even centuries. Such a population structure has remained largely unaltered by conversion into religions that claim to be casteless. (1944)

In these words, Majumdar reveals his deep knowledge of Indian social structure and social mobility. He has recorded that the aspect of caste system in India which was at that time believed to be more or less a rigid system of hierarchy—its dynamic, flexible nature which was decades later developed into the concept of 'sanskritization' by Srinivas whose words are quite similar to those written by Majumdar, when he says:

> The caste system is far from a rigid system in which the position of each component caste is fixed for all time. Movement has always been possible, and especially so in the middle region of the hierarchy. A low caste was able, in a generation or two, to rise to a higher position in the hierarchy by adopting vegetarianism and teetotalism, and by Sanskritising its ritual and pantheon (Srinivas, 1978: 32).

In the book mentioned above, Majumdar (1944) has discussed how the impact of dominant culture and changed environment has led to the gradual extinction of some tribes like the Korwa while other tribes like the Tharu have shown greater vitality and adaptability and thus maintained their strength and pattern of culture. This book, like his other one (1937), examines the change in the mental outlook of primitives who find themselves threatened by outside forces. Thus while the Korwa represent the most primitive element in the population of U.P. and a culture that is facing disorganisation and disintegration, the Tharu exhibit a vitality that has helped them to tide over various crises and to adapt themselves to changed and a changing economic environment. The Korwa have withdrawn themselves from contacts, the Tharu have thrown their lot deliberately with the people that surround them. The fear of strangers and the horror of the magic of their neighbours have transformed the Korwa into an inbreeding endogamous group. But the knowledge of magic, sorcery and witchcraft have made the Tharu dreadful people and yet they have constantly revitalised their blood by exogenous marriages, which today, as it was in earlier days, is the most popular means of securing wives among them. In this book, Majumdar has also dealt with the Khasa of Himalayan region and the criminal tribes which are spread out in most parts of U.P.

Another of Majumdar's major study written in the form of a monograph is *Himalayan Polyandry: Structure, Functioning and Culture Change- A Field Study of Jaunsar Bawar* (1960). It is about the polyandrous tribes of Khasas who consider themselves Rajputs, inhabiting the foothills of Himalayan region. This study, however, was published posthumously. In this book, besides discussing history, i.e., origin, caste hierarchy and social stratification, kinship structure and social organisation, economy, education and religion, Majumdar has also traced out the impact of community development programmes (CDP) which had been newly introduced by the government after Independence and the change of cultural pattern amongst the Khasa. He has also given a general appraisal of CDP. Here one can clearly see Majumdar's concern for national reconstruction and his firm faith in the utility of social anthropology.

Majumdar's contribution to the anthropology of tribes is of such a fundamental nature that no student of anthropology, no scholar who wants to understand tribal India, and even politicians and economists, can ignore his works. His book, *Races and Cultures of India* (1944), is indeed a Bible for them, besides his other works, for the understanding of the composition of Indian social and racial structure. His book, *A Tribe in Transition* (1937), has been applauded by anthropologists, sociologists and psychologists all over the world. In fact, *British Journal of Psychology* (1944) has the following to say about this book:

> This work can be heartily commended to the attention of any social psychologist who is interested in the effect of the contact of differently organised social groups, and who is prepared to make his study of their effects a matter of serious concern.

The science magazine, *Nature*, said that this book is an important contribution to Indian ethnography, particularly in its estimate of the impact of Hinduism on the culture of the Ho, and marks a rather new departure in Indian ethnographical literature.

Majumdar's description and analysis of the Dussehra festival which is an institution of an advanced culture, celebrated by the ruling family of Bastar, Chhattisgarh, illustrates the intimate link that was present in Bastar society between the highest, most prestigious tip of the social hierarchy, i.e. the king and the lower castes, to the lowest rung of the tribes. He says that:

> the peculiarity of this celebration is that it has brought together the various cultural groups in Bastar as sharers of a common heritage for even the lowest caste has not been denied its share in the communal worship (1939).

This observation and analysis of a cultural item made by Majumdar is of great significance in the field of cultural anthropology. It is this aspect of cultural continuity in Indian social structure which has been later elaborated and theorised by many anthropologists, both Indian and American. Morris Opler, McKim Marriott and Robert Redfield have done considerable study of this aspect. In fact, Redfield's theory of the continuum of Great Tradition and Little Tradition and McKim Marriott's concept of universalization and parochialisation have acquired international acclaim. The description of the celebration of Dussehra festival amongst the people of Bastar well illustrates the relationship of the Great Tradition with the Little Tradition.

As has been said about anthropological studies in India, Jain maintains that Majumdar's work neatly illustrates the process of graduation from tribal studies to those of caste and goes to even urban communities. Jain says that "the shock of discovering the 'other' in tribal cultures of India or the urge to relate the cultures in a meaningful way to Hindu civilisation, was in Majumdar's case subsumed by an exploration of their racial difference." (Jain 1980: 4-5).

Concluding remarks

Majumdar had taken up the study of the forms of a dissolving structure. His deep interest in 'cultures' in contact, of primitive cultures with dominant cultures, even his choice of the study of primitive tribes, is not without a conscious selection and shaping of ideas. Like the anthropologists of his time, he too was a 'general' anthropologist and was trained as such. Physical anthropology which included anthropometric surveys, serology, etc., was an unshakable part of 'general' anthropology.

From the beginning, Majumdar combined anthropometric surveys with ethnographic investigations. It was later, in 1953, in London that he acquired an improved technique of serology under Morant and Gates. He added to his other qualifications and interests—demography, growth, study of culture change, village studies and urban surveys. He also kept his interest in prehistoric archaeology alive. Although he did not engage in any investigations, except for heading two expeditions to the 18,000 ft. high Rupkund lake in 1956, to investigate the large litter of human bones and skulls discovered there. He kept abreast of the major developments in the field and had occasionally lectured on subjects like 'Stone Age Cultures of Europe', a lecture given at Lucknow during the summer of 1950.

Majumdar's abiding interest was, however in culture change. In this field, as well as others, his works were influenced by the ideas developed by Malinowski and Benedict. Functional method has influenced his interpretation of primitive cultures to the extent that he spent many days staying with the Ho where he was first initiated to field work by Roy. Amongst the Khasa too, he spent many years and participant observation had been his major technique of study. His holistic approach and the treatment of cultures as an 'integrated whole' is illustrative of the impact of Malinowskian notion of culture. His monographs deal less with theory and more with ethnology which reminds one of Malinowski's *Argonants of the Western Pacific*.

He has also adopted another interpretation of culture, i.e. patterns of culture (or configurations of culture) as formulated by Benedict. She has pointed out that a culture, like an individual, is more or less a consistent pattern of thought and action and that within each culture there are characteristic purposes which stabilise behaviour and consolidate experience. Thus, in his first book, *A Tribe in Transition,* he clearly states that his approach to the field study of the culture pattern in the Chhotanagpur plateau is a synthesis of Malinowskian and Benedict's approach to the study of culture. Benedict's influence is prominent in his study of the tribes of United Provinces too. In this study, he has explored the nature of varying reaction of different tribes to the impact of dominant alien cultures.

A tribe like the Korwa of Mirzapur, when confronted by forces which were of a debilitating kind, starts shrinking into itself. It stops having any kind of relations with other tribes or other peoples, instead starts inter-breeding and in due course of time, it would become extinct. Another tribe, the Tharu, reacts in a totally different manner. They spread out and do not hesitate to bring in women from other tribes through marriage. Magic is their weapon and they use it to survive and they guard their traditional beliefs and practices. They have not become pessimistic like the Korwa who do not care for anything, not even death. Instead, the Tharu are happy, optimistic people whose population is not dwindling like the Korwa.

The pattern of culture, personality, attitude and behaviour pattern of these tribes of U.P has been well documented and illustrated by Majumdar. He also retains in his study on ethnology, in his all-comprehensive ethnography, the influence of his guide and teacher, Roy, who was one of the first self-trained anthropologists of India. He too had worked amongst the tribes of Chhotanagpur. It was he who had introduced Majumdar to the art of fieldwork.

In all his ethnographic works Majumdar included a discussion of 'cultural dynamics'. Like Malinowski, he too believed that, although changes are occurring forever in a culture, yet it retains its character of being an integrated whole. He himself maintains that in all the psychological approaches there is a tacit recognition of cultural unity or integration and that both functional and configurational approaches whether they observe 'a culture' or 'cultures' look at cultures as 'whole' in their totality; but they raise the question of structure or form and a base is the most important part of a structure. Base here implies the base of a culture which is a function of four variables–MARC.

Thus, Majumdar discovered that due to the impact of a dominant culture, the weaker culture experiences cultural stress and strain. If this impact is of a fundamental kind, the weaker culture changes to reach an equilibrium of a different nature. But if this impact is not of a dynamic nature, the weaker culture tends to absorb the shock and it reverts back to its original form. This, in essence, is what Majumdar had studied amongst the Ho, who were experiencing the stresses and strains of dominant alien cultures, like Christianity, Hinduism and the impact of industrialisation. Thus, most of his analyses of 'culture' dynamics deals with the process of adaptation, assimilation and acculturation of alien cultural items. Majumdar, according to his friends and colleagues, was an inveterate optimist and a man of action. He seldom waited for responses and characteristically he initiated several studies of the problems and processes of planned development.

Majumdar's contribution to the field of cultural or social anthropology lies not so much in theoretical construction, as in the immensity of his ethnographic literature. His ethnology and the description of various tribes, their culture and social structures, etc., his village studies and finally urban study is an end in itself. The very minuteness of details recorded by him is a considerable achievement in the life-time of a scholar. His theory might be unsophisticated, but what he has contributed to the field of anthropology is ground material, on the basis of which coming generations of anthropologists and sociologists can base their theoretical models. His description of tribe-caste interrelations, his description of the nature of caste system, the relation amongst tribe, the rural community, and urban community, an intermixture of values, etc., is epic in content. The seeds of sophisticated concepts developed by later anthropologists can be perceived in his works. He would have developed a 'theory' but his untimely death prevented him from doing so. Yet, he achieved a lot.

Majumdar was a product of his time, the restrictions of which or the guidance of which has shaped his work. He was optimistic about the future when India attained freedom, unlike his other colleagues like Radhakamal Mukerjee or D.P. Mukerji. Madan (1982; 1994) writes that:

> it is noteworthy that he (Mujumdar) had no use for Radhakamal Mukerjee's idealist speculations nor for D.P. Mukerji's socialist aspirations for or fears about the future. As an anthropologist, he had always concerned himself with the 'here-and-now' of the peoples he had studied. Thus, it was precisely for this reason that he took up the study of Community Development Programmes, social surveys of Kanpur city, its problems of adjusting migrant labour, housing, education, etc. His study of unemployment of university educated is also guided by this philanthropic bend, his desire for and firm faith in the utility aspect of his anthropology.

I will, therefore, conclude with his own words which depict in a simple artistic way his entire attitude as a social scientist. He writes:

> We can build for the future if we know what to avoid and what to lay our hands on. That is what the social scientists are expected to do. They have to answer what they can do and what they must do, and how they can do it and how they should do it.... Ideas have wings, and knowledge is power. The

mistakes of the past are lighthouses for steering new courses; the achievements of the past in the realm of thought are the beacons that keep our paths alight. Social scientist must seize the opportunity with both hands and prepare them for service. (1961: 45)

REFERENCES

Benedict, Ruth.

1953 *Patterns of Culture.* A Mentor Book, New American Library.

Beattie, John.

1964 *Other Cultures: Aims, Methods and Achievements in Social Anthropology.* London: Routledge and Kegan Paul.

Bose, N.K.

1972 *Anthropology and Some Indian Problems.* Calcutta: Institute of Social Research and Applied Anthropology.

Dube, S.C.

1973 *Social Sciences in Changing Society.* D.N. Majumdar Lectures, 1972. Lucknow: Ethnographic and Folk Culture Society.

(ed). 1977 *Tribal Heritage of India, Vol.I: Ethnicity, Identity and Interaction.* New Delhi: Vikas Publishing House.

Fürer-Haimendorf, C. von

1960 'Dhirendra Nath Majumdar, 1903-1960', *Man,* 272.

Gross, L.P. (ed).

1967 *Sociological Theory: Inquiries and Paradigms.* New York: Harpar and Row.

Herskovits, M.J.

1974 *Cultural Anthropology.* New Delhi: Oxford and IBH.

Jain, R.K.

1980 *Social Anthropology of India: Theory and Method.* New Delhi: ICSSR.

Jha, M.

1983 *An Introduction to Anthropological Thought.* New Delhi: Vikas Publishing House.

Kroeber, A.L. (ed.)

1953 *Anthropology Today.* Chicago.

Leach, E.

1982 *Social Anthropology.* New York: Oxford University Press.

Madan, T.N.

1961 'Dhirendra Nath Majumdar 1903-1960', *American Anthropologist,* 63, 2, Part I: 369-374.

1968 "Dhirendra Nath Majumdar 1903-1960', *International Encyclopaedia of Social Sciences,* Vol.9: 540-541, New York.

1982 *Builders of Indian Anthropology: Dhirendra Nath Majumdar.* Varanasi: N.K. Bose Memorial Foundation.

1982 *Culture and Development,* Fifth D.N. Majumdar Memorial Lectures, under the auspices of Ethnographic and Folk Culture Society, Lucknow. Delhi: Oxford University Press.

1994 *Pathways: Approaches to the Study of Society in India.* Delhi: Oxford University Press, Delhi.

Madan, T.N. and G. Sarana (eds.)

1962 *Indian Anthropology: Essays in Memory of D.N. Majumdar.* Bombay: Asia Publishing House.

Majumdar, D.N.

1923 'The custom of burning human effigies', *Man in India,* 3: 97-103.

1923 'Notes on Kali-nauch in the District of Dacca', *Man in India,* 3: 202-216.

1923 'Customs and taboos observed by an East Bengal woman from pregnancy to child birth', *Man in India,* 3: 232-242.

1929 'Race and adaptability', *The Journal of Royal Asiatic Society of Bengal* (NS), 25, 1.

1937 *A Tribe in Transition: A Study in Culture Pattern.* Calcutta and London: Longmans Green & Co.

1939 *Tribal Cultures and Acculturation*, Presidential Address, Section of Anthropology and Archaeology Procedings from the 26th Indian Science Congress, Lahore.

1944 *Fortunes of Primitive Tribes.* Lucknow: Universal Publishers Ltd.

1944 *Races and Cultures of India.* Bombay: Asia Publishing House.

1947 *The Matrix of Indian Culture.* Lucknow: The Universal Publishers Ltd.

1950 *The Affairs of a Tribe: A Study in Tribal Dynamics.* Lucknow: The Universal Publishers Ltd.

1940 'Bongaism'. In J.P. Mills, D.N. Majumdar *et al.* (eds.) *Essays in Anthropology. Presented to Rai Bahadur Sarat Chandra Roy:* 60-70. Lucknow: Maxwell Co.

1955 'Rural analysis: Problems and prospects'. In K.S. Mathur (ed) *Tribe, Caste and Peasantry.* 285-295. Lucknow: The Ethnographic and Folk Culture Society.

1956 'Role of the sociologist'. In *Sociology, Social Research and Social Problems.* Bombay: Asia Publishing House.

1962 *Himalayan Polyandry: Structure, Functioning and Culture Change, A Field Study of Jaunsar Bawar.* Bombay: Asia Publishing House.

Majumdar, D.N. and Madan, T.N.

1958 *An Introduction to Social Anthropology.* Bombay: Asia Publishing House.

Mukherjee, Ramakrishna.

1979 *Sociology of Indian Sociology.* Calcutta: Allied Publishers (P.) Ltd..

Penniman, T.K.

1935 *A Hundred Years of Anthropology.* London: Gerald Duckworth.

Redfield, R.

1955 *The Little Community.* Chicago: Chicago University Press.

Roy, S.C.

1970 *Mundas and Their Country.* Bombay: Asia Publishing House.

Sarana, G.

1961 'Dhirendra Nath Majumdar 1903-1960'. *The Eastern Anthropologist:* 105-121.

Vidyarthi, L.P.

1978 *Rise of Anthropology in India. Vol.I, The Tribal Dimension.* Delhi: Concept Publishing Co.

2

Situating *Chhor Ka Ek Gaon* in the Writings of D.N. Majumdar and Indian Village Studies

H.S. Saksena

I

In this paper I propose to focus on Professor Majumdar's least known, in fact almost unknown, work *Chhor* which is a village study in the then Mirzapur (now Sonbhadra) district of Southern UP. This work does not feature in any of the synoptic reviews of Majumdar's works such as Madan (1983), Archana Singh's comments on Majumdar's contributions to Indian social anthropology and Vandana Madan (2002) on village in India. The reasons for this fate befalling the book appear to be that it was in Hindi, and then, it was published posthumously. Since original works and that too of *Chhor's* status are even now never published in Hindi, it has escaped the attention of the social sciences academics. It is gratifying that recently it was included in the recommended readings for the post-graduate anthropology students in the Lucknow University.

Chhor is a full-fledged village study which was carried out in village Chitaura near Dudhi—a tehsil town of Sonbhadra district—in the years 1955-57. This area, almost the entire district of Sonbhadra, has been very aptly referred to as a 'fringe' (*chhor*). It is inhabited by a number of tribes along with Hindu castes. Geographically, it is the farthest district of UP and shares its borders with Palamu district of Jharkhand and Sarguja of Chhatisgarh. Moreover, till independence it was a Partially-Excluded Area under the Government of India Act, 1935, which meant it was under a special kind of administration. The area was a 'government Zamindari. In 1950, though, the tribes in this area, thirteen in number, were scheduled as scheduled castes and not scheduled tribes. These communities were included in the list of scheduled tribes in January, 2003. Thus, the area is on the fringe in almost every sense of the term. Majumdar had worked in this area and studied mainly the small Korwa tribe and came forward with the conclusion that: Among the Korwas a lack of interest in life and all that it connotes has engendered a social solidarity and passivity which are both ill adapted to the present day conditions and it is no wonder that they have developed a sense of despair and frustration (1944: 64).

The subsequent village study in this very area was broadly speaking ethnographic as well as an evaluation of the impact of community development programme undertaken in the Dudhi block in early 1950s. Thus it was both a study of the village life in all its aspects as well as a study of the tribes in the area, the tribe-caste relations, acculturation, symbiotic living and the social dynamics of village life as also the changes brought about by planned development programmes. The study developed 'fringe' village as a concept and goes on to explicate its various dimensions.

He found that tribe caste relations in their multiple aspects here presented a unique situation which could be regarded as of great importance in the context of village life in India. The significant features of a fringe village (1960: *Jha-Ta*), roughly rendered in English, could be:

1. The presence of a number of castes as well as tribes creates a situation where there are

no permanent relationships among them—as if there was no equilibrium—the different castes assuming importance at different times. Therefore, no caste can achieve dominance because combinations of other castes frustrate such attempts. Majumdar has used the picturesque expression, 'Andalucian blue', to describe this configuration.

2. The living standards of different castes and tribes did not have much differences.

3. In a fringe village a continuous and not easily perceptible kind of a trans-culturation is facilitated. Not only the tribal communities adopt cultural traits from their advanced caste neighbours, the vice-versa also happens.

4. While in other villages, which are not fringe villages, wealth, social status, etc., greatly contribute to village politics, here the government's patronage has an upper hand and its controls are far more effective.

5. In the villages, migrations bring about a new value system because the migrants have to orient themselves to the value system and aspirations of the original inhabitants (the tribals), and this makes the caste norms elastic, leading to a symbiotic pattern of living.

6. A significant feature of tribe caste relations in fringe villages is that the migrant caste population initially gives a lot of respect and precedence to the leading tribal families and leaders but in the course of time the migrant caste groups set about exploiting the tribals, grab their lands and erode their status and influence.

7. Here, comparatively, more of tolerance is seen in the social behaviour, rituals, religious beliefs, etc. This awareness and tolerance brings about intensity and width of participation on social occasions.

8. Even though tribals adopt some of the customs and rituals of the migrant caste population, this acculturation does not lead to a loss of tribal identity. The tribals are able to retain their cultural configuration because there are no dominant castes to impose their own caste norms on the tribals. The continuance of tribal structures, tribal practices, rituals and kinship terminology, etc., in the fringe villages is indicative of this situation.

In the light of these specific features relating to the fringe villages, Majumdar expresses the view that the presence of a dominant caste in the Indian village and its role in the village life and politics has been overemphasized. He goes on to say that the concept of dominant caste could not have a universal validity because it is rooted in the feudal history and backdrop which many of the villages studied by the anthropologists and sociologist shared—and the fringe villages did not have (1960: *Ta*). He also argues that the emergence of a new leadership and a more fertile base for developmental changes in the village life at the fringe was possible due to the interplay of the elements of village life as spelt out is the concept of a fringe village.

II

Madan (1983) outlines Majumdar's contribution to Indian anthropology through three different phases, broadly. Starting with a study of culture traits and not giving so much prominence to a concern for culture as a whole, Majumdar outlined the process of social change particularly, in a situation of culture contact. Subsequently, with the help of Malinowski's functionalism and his own theoretical model of MARC (the base of a culture being the function of four variables—Man, Area, Resources and Co-operation), he analysed cultures as wholes. Subsequently, he thought that culture could be graded and through contacts some cultures grew or evolved while some cultures stagnated and died. Majumdar was of the view that tribal contacts with caste Hindus resulted in tension and conflict and brought about what he called, 'the decline of the primitive tribes of India.' He referred to or labelled cultures as dominant and decadent without hesitation and emphasized that decadent cultures could hardly hope to survive except by 'surrendering their values and even identifying completely with the dominant culture' (1983: 12). Majumdar had also earlier delineated the processes through which tribal cultures are usually transformed or modified—through simple adoption, acculturation which involves acceptance and adaptation, and social communalism or plural association. He regarded cultures as open to synthesis and indicated a clear preference for acculturation. But he was also aware of the risk of a reaction or contra-acculturation which he had seen among the Ho. And, therefore, in *Matrix* (1947) he wrote:

> What is needed is mutual respect and understanding, and where the dominant or ruling group is shown as having respect and understanding, acculturation and adjustment has been smooth and easy.

To my mind it appears that the situation he observed in the Dudhi area and its fringe village enabled him to further spell out this very approach as it was lived, and then developed it into the concept of 'fringe culture'. Had he not discerned in the village life at the fringe a strategy for a vitally functioning tribe-caste co-existence, not just a continuum, and could not fringe cultural configurations seem to be a pointer or a blueprint? A blueprint not only for a evolving cultural scenario but also for a far more receptive climate for planned social change? Who knows Majumdar would have developed this strategy as a part of his 'tribal re-habilitation' through more of empirical data, as he was 'essentially a field worker' (Madan 1983: 15). And in D.P. Mukerji's words,

> He was veering round theory———. It was, however, too late in the day ———. He should not have died so young! (1962: 9-10)

III

Around mid 20th century the village came to be an important area of intellectual concern for anthropologists, whose earlier forte were tribal or primitive communities and they started taking up in-depth village studies. The studies were detailed and informed directly on various aspects of life or culture in the studied villages. The idea of extension of the village into wider society became central to many village studies in the 1940s and 1950s. McKim Marriott spoke of how the ties that related the village to the outside world also brought in the wider society to the village. Caste relations, kinship and social relations and the changes in policy through the democratic process after independence gave a fillip to the extension of the village links beyond village boundaries. In the second half of the 20th century the village studies assumed further dimensions with the evaluations of the impact of planned developmental programmes on village life. Subsequently the complexion of the village studies underwent a change from monographic ones to those with thematic foci To quote Vandana Madan (2002: 12):

> The 90s were marked by the village becoming a Mecca for the activist and policy maker, with an occasional monographic study or a re-study of the village.

Beteille has stressed the importance of the village and village studies as a continuing source for the deeper and wider understanding of the society, economy and polity in contemporary India (Vandana Madan 2002:12).

If we trace the holistic village studies on a map of India it emerges that most of the studies were made in Uttar Pradesh, Karnataka, Tamilnadu, Andhra, Kerala, West Bengal and Central India. The villages were chosen on the basis of their being multi-caste villages except for Bailey's studies in Orissa. The village studies hardly included any full fledged tribe-caste configurations. During that period Majumdar undertook two village studies and a study of tribal polyandry in Jaunsar for which three villages formed the sample. Thus, Majumdar appears to be the single scholar who undertook studies of a caste village, tribal villages and a tribe-caste village, the latter being *Chhor*. Thus *Chhor* emerges as a very important dimension of village studies of the mid 20th century, taken up by the anthropologists.

IV

We may now turn to examine some of the specificities of documentation regarding village Chitaura studied in *Chhor*. To begin with, the study gives basic geographical and topographical details of the area and lay-out of the habitations therein. Detailing the inhabitants in general the main Hindu castes and tribes in the area have been described and a socio-gram of the status of various castes and tribes shows that the hierarchy is topped by the Brahmin and Thakur while the untouchable caste Chamar and a tribal community Bhuiya come at the bottom. Significantly, the upper castes, especially Brahmin and Baniya are migrants from Bihar and

> These castes came here for business and trade and indigent Brahmin families started practising *jajmani* by providing (ritual) services to the tribal and semi-tribal communities in their indigenous festivals and other occasions (1960: 2).

Brief ethnographic details of the tribes document the process of acculturation of the tribal communities. For instance, Majhi have achieved a level equivalent in status to agricultural castes in the Dudhi area but people of the same tribe living near Sarguja are nomadic. Kharwar have started wearing the sacred thread and claim Chhattriya origins. Cheros who were tribal priests and *ojha* for the tribal groups have started providing ritual services at the Hindu festivals and they have assumed an important role in the rituals connected with agriculture now practised by both the castes and the tribes. The Chero have also adopted the worship of several Hindu deities specially Kali. In this context Majumdar specifically mentions the Korwa as the most primitive of the tribes, a frustrated group moving back towards Sarguja. A minor tribe is that of Pathari who are bards of the Gond.

Describing the village, he stresses on the history of its settlement tracing it to the late 18th century. The tribal communities of Majhi, Panika and Pathari were its earliest inhabitants. The social and economic contours of the village, its cycle of agriculture and other details of economics have been described. It is seen that apart from agriculture, animal husbandry and economic sustenance from some forest products and groves in the area supplement agriculture. People following traditional occupations are the Hindu artisan castes and Aghariya are primitive ironsmith forging agricultural tools. Details regarding material culture highlight how tribal artifacts find place along with more urban items in the caste Hindu houses. The pattern of land ownership has been traced to earlier times and a continuing process of alienation of tribal land by land-grabbing moneylenders has been highlighted. Significantly, tribal indebtedness receives focal treatment as a problem faced by the tribal people. It also shows how Baniya traders have cheated the tribals in barter trading of agricultural produce with household items like salt, tobacco, *bidi,* kerosene oil, and cloth, etc. and forest produce such as lac.

Leadership pattern has been discussed in the context of traditional caste/panchayats for a group of villages and the newly set up statutory gaon sabha and adalati panchayat. Their functioning has been described through factual cases illustrating the kind of disputes and crimes that each one deals with; and how the caste panchayats often act in a partisan manner.

In the context of leadership, the village politics and the role of factions has been documented in great detail. Taking the history of settlement back to the time when Britishers established their administration and brought this tribal area under a government zamindari with *Superdars* for managing the village, Majumdar divides its history into five periods—four of the different *Superdars* and the fifth starting after abolition of zamindari. This discussion highlights a situation where it is seen that most of the poorer tribal communities do not have any significant village level leadership, the exception being Baigas (Chero) and Panikas. Larger communities, even tribal, have factional leaders. However, a pan-village leadership or a leadership which can be said to have a sway over some adjoining villages as well is found to be lacking except in one leader. It has been noted that women have no place in village leadership. Mentionable among the villages leadership is also a Brahmin teacher posted in the village in the first decade of the 20th century who resigned from his job and settled here. The study traces the rise of factions in the village to land disputes and for power (to become a *Superdar*) in the earlier phases. Subsequently, it has been accentuated by the weakening of joint family and growing prosperity of a few families due to the changing economic and political situation.

Inter-caste relations have been documented through various situational observations such as the presence of Brahmin pandit at rituals, acceptance of food and water, salutations and other behaviours of members of one caste/

tribe towards other caste/tribe members and participation in festivals. A few socio-grams help in tracing the recent changes in the pattern of intercaste relations. In brief, it emerges that there are certain factors which contribute to reducing inter-caste/tribe differences and bringing about a more egalitarian pattern. There are significant differences in the beliefs relating to different types of food which make the system of food and water acceptance more equitable or less discriminatory—for instance *roti* is accepted by nearly all the castes/tribes from each other because it is regarded as *pucca* food and many tribal and Hindu castes who are deemed to be clean here are not so in non-fringe areas. Chero as a tribe occupies a unique position because the Baiga come from that community and the Baiga 'lords over the land and ceremonial customs and rituals'. Ethnographic data relating to kinship and marriage and life cycle rituals have been documented separately for different castes and tribes. Tribal rituals and beliefs have been clearly described and, then, their reflection in similar practices seen among castes has also been detailed. These practices and some other religious and magical customs and practices go on to show the continuity between 'little' and 'great' traditions, as it has emerged in the fringe area.

The study originated in the evaluation of the impact of community development programme which was introduced in the Dudhi block in 1953. Construction of village roads and *panchayat ghar* through *shramdan* and a large number of economic activities including setting up of a co-operative society have been evaluated. Further, certain social education programmes such as adult education, youth clubs, conducted educational tours for villagers to some selected cities and institutions, etc., have been commented upon. A general evaluation of the programme in a totality brings out its strong points as also the weakness in the content of the programmes as well as its implementation process. The significant issues are:

1. The people living in this fringe area were seen to be discriminating enough to welcome and to participate in good activities and indifferent to activities which were not felt to be so useful.

2. They appreciated good extension workers and criticized corrupt and ineffective government functionaries.

3. The people could also see what beneficial activities of the programme could not be pursued because of a wrong approach on the part of extension workers.

4. The people from the lowest castes and backward tribes (included among the scheduled castes though) felt neglected and, furthermore, the programme did not try to tackle some very undesirable practices such as drinking, while some very desirable activities like Gram Lakshmi Kendras (which benefited the women) were given up abruptly.

The general evaluation ends with a positive note that the community development programme had brought an awakening and an urge among the people to inprove their lot.

V

Chhor Ka Ek Gaon carries forward Majumdar's approach to the study of Indian society in a number of directions. It brings out how cultures adopted traits from each other and how tribal cultures fare in this process. The Korwa who were living in the fringe of this otherwise fringe area have not been able to gain through the contact situation but other tribes like Cheros and Manjhis have benefited and have developed what Majumdar calls a *modus vivendi*, and gained strength through acculturation. The documentation here effectively exemplifies what Majumdar had said much earlier (1939: 41).

> The contacts between social groups have led to miscegenation of cultures. A group which has not lost its interest in life and possesses vitality must adopt traits from other groups. This adoption of alien traits is usually selective and it is on the nature of this selection that the future of the group depends. The process of selective adoption may be called acculturation. When several cultural groups coming from different geographical areas meet and settle down in the same place, they react and adjust themselves to one another and may develop the closest co-operation between them. What Dr. Nadel calls a symbiotic relation is connoted by the process of acculturation and we have seen how reciprocity and mutuality of obligations between the various social groups of a culture area have led to acculturation which has linked section with section and produced an interesting culture complex.

This study also takes up an examination of two concepts advanced by M.N. Srinivas. 'Sanskritization' in Srinivas' studies comes out as a process where certain traits peculiar to the higher castes are adopted by the lower castes in their endeavour to improve their status. *Chhor*, however, shows that the process of acculturation is a two-way traffic and there is both 'Sanskritization', and 'de-Sanskritization'—Brahmin and Thakur accepting certain tribal rituals performed by a Baiga for instance. This gives rise to a pattern of community living in the fringe area with significant cultural implications. 'Dominant caste' is another concept which has been advanced by Srinivas and subsequently used in many village studies. Majumdar in *Chhor* is critical of this concept at two levels: Firstly, the presence of a dominant caste in a villages or in an group of villages or in an area is traceable to the feudal days and thus it has no validity in areas like Dudhi where zamindari was of a different pattern; and secondly, over-emphasis on this concept may also derail our strategy in 'village re-habilitation' and under value the emerging new leadership scenario in the villages. Optimistically, Majumdar feels that this new emergent leadership among tribals would lead to a better acceptance of planned development (1960: *Tha*). As Madan (1983: 22) comments on Majumdar's optimism:

> He was a representative social scientist of his generation, and then there are many social scientists today who hold the same views as Majumdar did on development and the role of social sciences——.

D.P. Mukerji has also called him an 'incorrigible optimist' (1962: 9-10)

VI

Majumdar had developed *Chhor* (fringe) as a concept for analyzing the 'integrated way of living, thinking, feeling or as a constellation of parts, such as material culture, occupation ——' (1958: 325). As he himself states;

> A concept, if it is to be a useful one, must be clear, precise and logically consistent, A tool is expected to be a refined instrument, and should be as adequate as possible to meet its requirements (*ibid*: 331).

Further, one can add that a concept should, apart from its applicability to study and research, also have an applied and diagnostic use for the purposes of social engineering to '——build for the future——That is what the social scientists are expected to do.——.' as Majumdar had advised them (1956: 142-43). This amplification as spelt out in *Chhor* has assumed a greater contemporary relevance from these angles. The last quarter of the 20th century has seen tribal transformations on a far more quantitative and qualitative scale, mainly through the intensified planned efforts under the tribal sub-plan, processes of democratization and decentralization ushered in with the creation of tribal states and the grass-root empowerment through panchayti raj and its special central law for the tribal areas. On the other hand, heavy displacements of the tribal people by development projects, mining, etc., and the march of globalisation and privatization is also contributing much to the change, often for the worse. All this is creating many more focal areas of tribe-caste conglomerates, acculturation and symbiotic living through peasantisation. The process is far from smooth and peaceful, in fact often leading to loss of resources, tensions, confrontations and identity crisis—tribes hitherto assuming caste identity later re-forming and re-asserting their tribalness. Recent studies by Surajit Sinha, David Hardiman and many more are cases in example. *Chhor* with its analytical/theoretical content can command a contextual importance providing extremely handy conceptual and discursive models.

In a modest way this author can state that some of the dimensions or components of the concept came as ready tools while he was studying the widespread problem of displacement, social movements and resultant change in the later decades in this very area. For instance, the situation that the people here suffered repeated displacements, four or five in 20-25 years, without any organised protest or movement and a large section of the tribals so affected moved away to Sarguja or Palamau rather than resettling themselves here itself. This situation was indicative of the absence of a dominant local leadership or say the diffusion of village leadership in this fringe area leading to some extremely negative consequences as well. Saksena and Sen (1999: 100-102) found that in this area the vital problem of people's land rights vis-a-vis later declaration of reserved forests and re-habilitation of villagers displaced as a result of various power/irrigation projects (NTPC, NCL, UPSEB and Rihand) which were set up between 1950s did not for at least two decades lead to any organized movement for their rights on the part of the peoples so seriously affected. Saksena (1998: 131) has also pointed out that even with extreme deprivation suffered by inhabitants only some sporadic incidence of the peoples' agitation could be found. In fact the absence of any effective indigenous leadership resulted into a situation where a Sarvodaya worker who came to the area for Bhoodan work later led them and created a powerful Bhumi Haqdari Morcha for claims to land ownership, and another strong agitation of the people affected by projects. Both the movements came about much after the actual displacements or denial of land rights. The agitations eventually achieved some positive gains for the affected tribals and other people as a result of interventions by the Supreme Court.

REFERENCES

Madan, T.N.

1983 *Culture and Development.* New Delhi: Oxford University Press.

Madan, Vandana (ed.)

2002 *The Village in India.* New Delhi: Oxford University Press.

Majumdar, D.N.

1939 *Tribal Cultures and Acculturation.* Calcutta: Indian Science Congress Association.

1944 *The Fortunes of Primitive Tribes.* Lucknow: Universal Publishers Ltd.

1947 *The Matrix of Indian Culture.* Lucknow: Universal Publishers Ltd.

1956 'What the sociologists can do, what they must do, how they can do, and how they should do it', *The Eastern Anthropologist,* 10:2:130-43.

1960 *Chhor ka Ek Gaon* (in Hindi). Bombay: Asia Publishing House.

Mukerji, D.P.

1962 'Majumdar: Friend and Scholar'. In T.N. Madan & Gopala Sarana (eds.) *Indian Anthropology.* Bombay: Asia Publishing House.

Saksena, H.S.

1998 'Tribal movements in Uttar Pradesh'. In K.S. Singh (ed.) *Tribal Movements in India,* Vol. IV *Antiquity to Modernity in Tribal India*. New Delhi: Inter-India Publications.

Saksena, H.S. and Chandra Sen

1999 *Putting People Last—Tribal Displacement and Rehabilitation*. New Delhi: Inter-India Publications.

Singh, Archana

2002 'Historicity of anthropological studies in India—An overview of D.N. Majumdar's contribution to tribal studies' (unpublished paper).

—

3

A Note on the Tribal Situation in India

Vinay Kumar Srivastava

'Give us back our forests or we have no alternative but beggary left to us. The coming of the NALCO factory in Damanjodi has not helped us in any way. The promise of jobs has not been kept. The houses at Indiravasi colony are in no condition to be lived in. We have lost our lands, our forests, and our whole life-support system and have to work in such demeaning jobs as being prostitutes for the workers who have migrated all the way from Kerala to this area. Our men migrate in search of better opportunities. Few come back to their families, leaving them in the hands of destiny. The wives keep waiting.'

—— Excerpts from an interview with a tribal woman delegate from the district of Koraput (Mishra and Roy Choudhury 1993: 50).

With a five-hour working day, plenty of food, friends all around and enviable health, it is not surprising that they [the Jarawas] want to stay the way they are, far from the madding crowd of the so-called civilized world.... They only take as much as they need for the day from their forests and never disturb nature's regeneration process... "Many of the Jarawas have visited Port Blair many times and are no more shocked by what they see. But they never want to stay for more than a few days. They prefer to return to their life in the forest."

——— Excerpts from *Sunday Hindustan Times*, New Delhi, 4 April 2004 (p. 8).

Consensus does not exist on the number of communities in India that could actually be classified as 'tribal'. Because of the changes that have occurred (and are occurring) among them, one line of argument is that Indian tribes do not subscribe to their textbook definitions. When anthropologists speak of tribes, they mean communities of people who have remained outside of the state and civilization, whether out of choice or necessity; that was the reason of calling them 'non-civilized', but not uncivilized. In India, 'they all stood more or less outside of Hindu civilization' (Béteille 1992: 76).

This was the reason why tribes were designated as the 'followers of animism' as opposed to Hinduism. As time rolled by, they became incorporated into the state and the fabric of civilization. The consequence of this process has been that anthropologically speaking, tribes do not exist in the contemporary world of linkages and networks created by the migration of people across different physical spaces, as they existed some centuries ago when they led, relatively speaking, an existence of autonomy, self-sufficiency, self-determination, and geographical and cultural isolation. The present world is one where migration of people over different landscapes goes hand in hand with information technology that endeavours to unify it. Today, tribes are far away from their traditional conceptions, though anthropologists and others who study them might like to see them conforming to their image of 'primitives'. A cartoon titled 'Hey, Anthropologists are coming!' captures this contradiction very well: Adorned with headgears, decked with leaf-skirts, the spear-wielding tribesmen are hiding their television sets on seeing the arrival of the anthropologists! The underlying message is that anthropologists look for the 'primitives', and also, the latter want to adhere to this image. However, it is no more the reality.

Against the background of change, these communities may be called 'tribes in transition', or, perhaps, the appellation 'tribe' may be dropped altogether for them (see Srivastava 1994). They may simply be called 'communities', with this word suffixed after their name (for instance, 'Santal community', 'Birhor community', 'Seharia community'). The word 'community' may also be used for caste people or urban neighbourhoods. I have also heard anthropologists say that in contemporary times, the term 'tribe' has become as pejorative as were the terms like 'primitive', 'savage', 'rude', 'non-civilized', and several others of the same type, in the mid-twentieth century and subsequently, they went out of currency. Today, when these terms are used, they are always put in inverted commas, for they are value-loaded, indicating a special meaning that was once attributed to them and the meaning for which the contemporary scholars hold no sympathy.

Therefore, there are debates on whether one should continue to use the word 'tribe', or should one think in terms of alternatives to this term. But, little disagreement exists with respect to the meaning of the Scheduled Tribes, which is a Constitutional term and there exists an all-India list of these communities that are entitled to a set of privileges under the policy of compensatory discrimination. In its well-known People of India Project, the Anthropological Survey of India counted 4,635 communities in India, of which 461 were tribal (Singh 1992: 14; 1993: 12). However, different sources give different numbers of communities classified as Scheduled Tribes. In a revised version of Nirmal Kumar Bose's *Tribal Life in India*, published in 2002, the list given is of 300 communities, while the Draft of the National Policy on Tribals, issued in February 2004, records 698 Scheduled Tribes. Today, when anthropologists use the word 'tribe', they mean:

1. the communities included in the list of the Scheduled Tribes;

2. the communities that were isolated at one time and later had their integration with the outside world, but have continued to call them tribe because of their vested interests; and

3. the communities that still dwell in remotely situated forests and hills and are backward in terms of the indices of development, although they may not have yet found a place in the list of the Scheduled Tribes.

Contemporary tribal societies differ so widely in their habitats, social organizations, modes of production, and cultural practices, that to venture a definition of tribe may turn out to be disappointing.

II

Tribal societies in India have undergone an array of remarkable and long-lasting changes particularly during the last fifty years, although changes had started settling among them from the latter half of the nineteenth century when they came in contact with the British administration. At that time, perhaps, the inter-tribal inequality was not so pronounced as it is now. For instance, have a look at the pictures of tribespersons in various monographs published in the late nineteenth and the first half of the twentieth century. Strikingly, they all seem to have several similarities in their lifestyles, notwithstanding the geographical area from which they hail. In other words, they closely subscribed to the 'image' and the 'construct' of tribes as both tribesmen and non-tribal people happened to carry in their heads.

A comparative study of the ethnographic monographs on tribal communities reveals that the cultural difference between 'us' (the ethnographer, who was always an outsider, from a non-tribal community) and 'them' (the subjects of anthropology) was so much (in fact, excessive) that it appeared almost unbridgeable. Virtually, all tribal societies were pre-literate, scantily dressed, relatively cut-off from other societies of the wider world, had few personal effects, lived in similar types of habitations and worked with a technology that could easily be learnt, and the values of accumulation, investment, gain, profit, and surplus were largely alien to them. Irrespective of the differences between tribal societies, or between different sections of the same society, one could easily speak of the tribal world as 'homogeneous' in juxtaposition to the heterogeneous universe of non-tribal people. And, that was the reason why anthropologists, administrators, and policy makers did not hesitate in formulating a definition of tribe.

Although it was never said, for it would have been contrary to the basic anthropological premise that every society has its own dynamism, the impression the ethnographies intended to give was that 'primitive' societies would continue to remain the same over time and attempts to change them exogenously would destroy their social fabric rather than contributing positively. Rarely did an anthropologist of those days think that there would be a time when the erstwhile 'primitives' would read what the others had written on them and judge the merit and value of these writings, and would direct their energy to create a tradition of parallel scholarship under the respectable rubric of 'native anthropology' (Narayan 1998). I remember some years ago I asked a boy from the community of Maring Nagas why he had joined an honours course in anthropology. Much to my surprise at that time, he said that as a schoolboy, he had read the writings of anthropologists on Nagas and particularly on his community, which he thought had several inaccuracies and were not able to answer many questions. His sole aim of doing anthropology was to research into his own culture and traditions, and later produce an authentic (insider's) account of his people.

In those days, in a true sense, the tribal world was the 'other'. An anthropologist's mastery over the skills of his trade lay in depicting it as correctly (and as faithfully) as possible in words, sketches, and pictures. The anthropologist's world and that of the people were phenomenally different. There were no cultural similarities between them. The relation the anthropologist had with the people of his study was of 'humanity' – they were all human – and not of 'culture', i.e. sharing the same way of living. Obviously, at that time, the world had not become one; there was no 'global culture', no 'world society'. For understanding, the anthropologist was expected to learn the cultural grammar of the people, because the 'internalization of the other' was the key to know the alternative ways of life. Tribal lifestyles were shown as alternatives to those of the west; or the western way of life was an alternative to that of the tribal. Put either way, though each has different political implications, anthropologists were keen to learn the enormous diversity of human living and the attempts people have concertedly made to defy the imposition of lifestyles of dominant groups on them.

III

At the beginning of the last century, the tribal world conformed to its image and stereotype. But, a look at the tribal situation during its second half dismantles the image and picture of tribespersons that students of anthropology tend to nurse in their books and monographs. A vast gulf exists between what they learn from their books and what the field view actually teaches them. Shadows of confusion lengthen when one starts approximating the real tribesmen to their characterizations as 'relatively isolated and semi-isolated' communities, which are self-sufficient and holistic, and may be studied without referring to the outside world. I am instantly reminded of my first fieldwork of November-December 1971 with the Oraons of the village of Kamre in Ranchi. Contrary to the isolation and closed nature of tribal communities, the Oraons interacted with the other people, of other castes and communities, in their village and outside. The influence of a Hindu cult founded by an outside ascetic, popularly known as Kamre Baba, on Oraons and other people was tremendous. It was difficult to distinguish 'tribal' people from non-tribal unless one conducted a direct enquiry. An unbroken continuity existed between tribal and non-tribal communities; the distinction between them was a matter of 'book-view' and not 'field view'. Books freeze concepts; fieldwork questions them and shows their dynamism.

That was 1971. Since then the pace of change has accelerated. Today, tribal societies are on the road to modernity and development. In certain parts of India, their members are 'global actors', not an inch inferior or lower to their non-tribal counterparts. A couple of decades ago, they were taking up the jobs of physical training instructors, schoolteachers, pharmacists, and fourth-class employees in governmental and non-governmental departments. In modern India, they are bureaucrats, politicians, professionals, university professors, and are often said to score over others because of their 'tribal instinct for survival'.

There may not be a better example of the hiatus between theory and reality than what one finds in the definition of tribe and its existential order. Today, tribe is no more a mode of social formation or a fossilized community (the 'noble savage'), unwilling to change and unwilling to participate in the life of the wider world, which scared it to the marrow. The example of the Jarawas, cited in the epigram previously, is an exception, and there are reasons for this. It is rather a 'cultural artifact' in a multicultural world to negotiate with the state (and other grant-giving and developing agencies) one's interests and the strategies to fulfill them. Tribe exists in a world that has several other cultural artifacts, such as caste, gender, race, region, religion, language, etc, which also serve the same purpose. Cultural artifacts are constituted of one or the other primordial category, but are effectively used as instruments in the contemporary world where each group is expected to safeguard its interests. Against the background of an acute shortage of resources and positions of privilege and power, the instrumentality of cultural artifacts scores over its primordial contents. Whether the Oraons speak Kurukh, or whether they repose faith in Tana Bhagats, is immaterial, till the time they stand up as one against all other communities, and struggle for achieving their interests and coveted positions in the political and other decision-making bodies.

IV

No more is tribal world inhabited by equals, as was the case a century ago. For instance, a comparative study of the lists released for the last some years of the successful candidates under the reserved category for the Civil Services Examinations will reveal that over years the posts for the Scheduled Tribes go to a handful of their communities, because the latter have done exceptionally well under the policy of positive discrimination and other development programmes meant for tribes. They have come to know the value of the premier services in India and prepare themselves adequately. The level of modernization and education is very high among tribal communities of the northeastern part of India. Each year, the number of boys and girls from these communities traveling to the other parts of India for study is steadily increasing. Some of them stay in metropolitan universities for research degrees as well. Although J.H. Hutton's typist was an Angami (1921), he could not have imagined a time when Angamis would write doctoral dissertations on their communities.

The Minas of Rajasthan, whose one group at one time guarded the trove of the princes, have also set an example of a developed community. Tribespersons who embraced Christianity in central India have also made several strides of progress. And, expectedly, communities located close to cities – the centers of civilization – are far more developed in comparison to those in far-flung and relatively inaccessible areas.

If one pole of the continuum comprises those tribes (or their sections) whose stories of success reinforce one's confidence in development programmes, on the other are those whose starvation deaths often make headlines of national dailies. Within the same region, there are tribal communities known for their achievement, and those, which have lagged behind. In Rajasthan, for example, Minas have done extremely well but Van Bawari, Girasia, or Seharia, are caught in a dismal state of poverty.

Anthropological literature of the last two decades has sensitively documented the stories of the victims of development, who either did not understand its meaning or thought of it as Aladdin's lamp, or Midas' touch, which would transform their penury into affluence and their hitherto subservience into a system of dominance and forwardness.

But, alas, their hopes were belied when development programmes, instead of ameliorating their condition, displaced them to barren lands, jeopardizing their life-support systems, and making them perpetually dependent upon the state for doles. In some cases, on their lands, from which they were evicted under the name of a development project, stand multistoried housing complexes for middle and upper classes. During the second half of the twentieth century, poverty among tribal people has multiplied several folds and their oppression has continued unabated.

Unsurprisingly, as a consequence of this state, some tribal families succumbed to begging, some to illegal activities. Some moved to towns and cities for employment. Singh (1993: 15) wrote: '...tribals displaced by a dam have turned to rickshaw pulling in the towns of Madhya Pradesh.' Fürer-Haimendorf (1982) noted the 'proletarization' of displaced tribes, who received ridiculously low compensations, and little was done to rehabilitate them and train them for work in the new industries and institutions. He (1982: 321) wrote: '...in the streets of Ranchi one can still see Munda and Oraon riksha pullers who not long ago were independent cultivators tilling their own land.' A common practice in middle and upper class houses in Delhi is to employ full or part-time servants and maids for domestic work. If a survey is conducted in these households on the social background of servants and maids, one is likely to find that a large number of them hail from tribal areas of Jharkhanda and Orissa, where survival has become so precarious that they have no option but to move out in search of jobs. The penurious existence of tribes in some parts of India has given place to condemnable activities – such as human trafficking. But looking from their perspective, perhaps, they were constrained to resort to them for ensuring their survival for some time.

V

With respect to the outside world, tribal communities have responded broadly in the following ways:

1. They have changed qualitatively – their health profiles show tremendous improvement; they have fared well economically; the level of education among them (both men and women) has substantially increased; they have been able to enter into new occupations and professions not only in their homelands but also in other parts of India; they are upwardly mobile in systems of class ranking; and know well the benefits that accrue from the policy of preferential treatment. The examples of these tribal communities, though few in number, are the Naga tribes (particularly, Ao, Angami, Tangkhul), Mizo, Khasi, Mina, and those sections of tribal communities in central India which have embraced Christianity. In a nutshell, these communities have reacted positively to the changes being introduced from outside.

2. This group includes those tribespersons for whom development measures have been a curse. They have been displaced from their traditional habitats. Measures to rehabilitate them have been grossly inadequate. Adequate and sustainable programmes of development have not been introduced among them, and those introduced, have made no impact. A vast section of tribal communities can be placed under this category.

Both these groups try their level best to maintain their identity, technically conveyed by using the concepts of 'tribalism' and 'ethnicity'; the first does it to ensure that benefits keep on reaching it, and status quo is maintained, while the second reinforces its unity for a better deal with the government.

As said above, a majority of tribes fall in the second category. They concern policy makers and administrators more because of their state of existence. Some of them have been silent sufferers of these changes, but many of them have reacted sharply and vehemently. For a crystallization of their responses, many non-governmental organizations and independent leaders have played significant roles. They have provided the necessary resources, leadership potentials, and ideological wealth for the struggle of tribes. However, it may also be remembered that some self-appointed leaders and social workers in tribal areas have also misguided them. One may refer here to the example of Dara Singh, who was recently sentenced to death in the murder case of Australian missionary Graham Staines and his two minor sons.

VI

Whichever be the response, tribal identity has emerged stronger and clearer, rather than getting diluted, effaced, and marginalized, as was thought at one time.

Today, tribes are not being transformed into castes, as was happening till the mid-twentieth century, a process which was quite closely connected with state formation among them (Sinha 1962; Xaxa 1999). Both 'casteization' of tribes and the emergence of state created stratification among them (Sinha 1981). Kshatriya tribesmen and 'chakravarti' tribal kings (*rājā*) received the services of Brahmin priests, and also of the other 'pure' occupational castes, had their respective clan Hindu goddesses, and tried to forge their matrimonial alliances with Rajput families in multi-caste villages (Bose 1975). The processes of upward mobility at that time were of Hinduization ('adoption of the Hindu way of life') and Sanskritization ('emulation of the ritual idiom of upper, twice-born castes') (Mandelbaum 1970).

Now, tribes know full well that their control over and ownership of resources depends upon the political power. In certain parts of India, they know they constitute an important repository of votes. If its prospective strength is used for exerting pressure on political parties, tribes could hope for their economic and social uplift. At the core of the political bargaining is a 'show of strength', an 'exhibition of oneness'. Obviously, tribes should remain tribes; they should not become castes. Rather than remaining a 'group *in* itself', they should become a 'group *for* itself'. Rather than existing as an 'objective' reality, which the observers find out after conducting a study among them, tribes should emerge as a 'subjective' entity, conscious of their identity. 'Tribe *in* itself' should become 'tribe *for* itself'.

Tribes have learnt that vigorous attempts should be carried out to reinforce one's identity as 'pure' as possible. All terms conjoined with the tribal name must be dropped immediately. Thus, those Bhumij, who at one time called themselves Bhumij-Kshatriya, discarded the term 'Kshatriya' from their name, because this was quintessential for building their tribal identity

(Mandelbaum 1970: 603-4). In a field study in Sadri (Rajasthan), I enquired from a group of two men about the identity of the hamlet to which they belonged. One of them, a middle-aged man, said they were Minas, to which I asked who the Minas were. 'Adivasi *jāti*,' came the instant reply from that man. Immediately, the other man, who happened to be a schoolteacher as I learnt later, corrected his co-tribesman's reply: 'We are Adivasi, not *jāti*. *Jāti* is found among Hindus, but we are tribal.' Ethnographers will provide many examples of this type where explicit accretions of caste are cauterized to uphold one's 'true', 'pure', and 'unadulterated' tribal identity.

At this juncture, one is faced with the following question: Is there a concomitant revival of the primordial (and pristine) characteristics of a community? Or, is the strengthening of tribal identity independent of cultural revitalization, or does it depend upon a revival of tribal characteristics that in any case would have weakened with the passage of time? Undoubtedly, de-tribalization has been going on right from the time the tribal people came in contact with non-tribal communities. However, its pace accelerated during the period of colonialism because of the British policy of opening up of the country and 'civilizing' the communities. Much of de-tribalization is irreversible – tribes cannot return to the 'golden age of savagery', if there was any. Hence, a rejuvenation of traditional institutions and practices in contexts where not only are they out of place but also, in many cases, portray the community in a bad light, would be a waste of energy. I have not heard of a community that wants to revive its practice of infanticide, headhunting, polyandry, etc. However, tribes have made attempts to revive those characteristics of theirs that are useful, congruent with contemporary times, do not paint them as rustic, bumpkin, backward, or inferior, and also, aid their political unity. The Rabaris of Rajasthan and Gujarat want their men and women to come to various social gatherings and council (*panchāyat*) meetings in their traditional dresses, however on other occasions, they are free to wear what they want. Their councils have also put restriction on the number of feasts that are given at the time of marriage and death. In other words, the Rabaris are changing all those aspects that need to be changed, but are retaining those that give them identity, without painting them in derogatory terms.

VII

It is wrong to assume that tribes are conservative and want to revive and glorify their past. One is likely to get this impression from cases where tribespersons crave for returning to their traditional methods of cultivation, especially slash-and-burn. Ask a Baiga. He would trace the prime cause of his poverty and long periods of hunger to prohibition on shifting cultivation. When he was practicing it, he would tell you, he was 'able to grow bumper crops of twelve types of grains'. His misery began when he started plowing the land, which amounted to 'tearing the breasts of mother earth' (Srivastava 2003: 159). Similarly, the Kondhs of Orissa attribute their miserable state to the fact that they have not been performing 'human sacrifice' since the time the British banned it (Chaudhury 2004: 183-4).

Such statements, couched in ideological terms, should not mislead anthropologists, for they abundantly tell the story of the non-adaptation of a community to the changes. Baigas have been forced to give up shifting cultivation without being given proper economic alternatives acceptable to them. Neither were they trained in the technology of plough cultivation nor were they apprised of the fact that shifting cultivation would not be able to support their growing population. The deleterious effects of shifting cultivation on forests, which have also been gradually decimating over time, were not explained to them. And, none of the action researchers and planners started a dialogue with them on the contextual relevance of their belief that forbade them to adopt plough cultivation. If proper alternatives are offered, and people understand them, realizing their efficacy, there will be no reason for them to cling to an anachronistic ideology.

Tribespersons, who have come in contact with the outside world, want to be affluent, educated, healthy, employed, and lead a life full of amenities, quite like middle and upper classes of this country. Certainly, they hate to remain in an appalling state in which they find themselves because of historical accidents. The processes of modernization, now globalization, have brought to their doorsteps the images of riches, fulfillment, and 'good life'. Like all others, tribes also desire to capture these images in reality. However, the route to 'good life' is political. It expects their unconditional solidarity, built from 'sharing the same vision of future' rather than the 'old, broken bricks of traditions'. Because of their migration to different areas, making use of locally available opportunities, tribespersons have become internally differentiated. They have picked up cultural traits of local populations. In this process, they have also lost many of their traditional customs and practices. Thus, tradition does not bind them; what really binds them is the 'vision of good life'.

But, locally, it is likely that tribesmen may attempt to revive some elements of their tradition, with an explicit aim to remain as one, but, as said previously, those traditions that are antithetical to their interests and image are certainly not revived. To give an example: The Rebari council, as said earlier, expects its members to attend its meetings in their traditional dress, and anyone who dares to come in any other types of clothes is fined. But it also expects its members to send their children to the school, look for jobs in the government sector, take their sick to the dispensary rather than the local healer, not to sell the females of their herds, observe the norms of physical cleanliness, etc. The Rebaris want to progress; they are far from being conservative. They have been able to strike a balance between their tradition and aspirations (the 'vision of a good life').

As noted earlier, tribes are now internally differentiated, passing through different stages of acculturation and transculturation. Therefore, it would be difficult to define them purely in cultural terms. Today, tribe is a cultural artifact to negotiate with the state its 'vision of good life'.

VIII

At one time, tribes submitted to the will of outsiders. They embraced the ethos and religion that the missionaries and zealots were enthusiastic about spreading. They bore the brunt of ridicules and castigations to which their value systems and lifestyles were subjected. The practice of seeking a 'bride by force' was interpreted as 'kidnapping'; consumption of liquor on social and ritual occasions was 'alcoholism'; pre-marital sex was 'prostitution'. Tribal gods and goddesses were dismissed as 'inferior', 'punitive', and as 'perpetrators of evil', by contrast to those of the outsiders, who were 'superior', 'transcendental', 'epitomes of kindness and mercy', and 'boon-fulfilling'. When their women were sexually exploited and children made to work as slaves, the tribes quietly underwent humiliation and pain, leaving everything to their fate to decide. The outsiders were 'big people'; they controlled all institutions; and the chief good of tribespersons lay in submitting to the will of their 'masters'. Tribal ethnographies provide many example of this: for instance, Majumdar (1949: 43) wrote: 'The Hos are overwhelmed by the superiority of their neighbours.'

A colleague of mine told me the following story that amply shows how tribes were subjected to cultural impositions the outsiders designed for them. In the early 1950s, Prime Minister Jawaharlal Nehru was scheduled to visit Bastar. The local administration decided that since Bastar was a tribal area, it would be better if tribal people, gathering in large numbers, welcomed the Prime Minister. But, it was also thought that as local tribes were scantily dressed, the Prime Minister might find the sight embarrassing. For according a decent welcome, the local tribal people must be 'clothed' – so, men were made to wear white *dhotī* and *kurtā*, and women, white blouse and *sāri*, and were queued up to receive the Prime Minister. When the Prime Minister came, he was surprised to see thousands of men and women clothed white, 'as if it was a gathering of Congress workers.' When he learnt that they were tribal and were dressed up in a particular way to greet him, he was extremely unhappy with the local administration and severely criticized it for interfering with the lives of people. He said he would have loved to meet people in the way they lived. Nehru was a staunch critic of cultural impositions. It is well known that in his Foreword (dated 16 February 1957) to the Second Edition of Verrier Elwin's *A Philosophy for NEFA* (1957), the first principle he enunciated was: 'People should develop along the lines of their own genius and we should avoid imposing anything on them.'

In contemporary age, things are different from what they used to be in the past. Surely, even today, there are examples of tribal communities that unequivocally submit themselves to the will of their neighbours and outsiders. But, several others do not accept a case of highhandedness or maltreatment lying down. They confront their exploiters and those who initiate certain changes among them that they resist with full might. The opposition may begin with a consideration of a minor practice; however, it is symbolic of a larger protest. For example, in some areas of central India, tribal people have opposed the reformers because they are forcing their women to wear brassiere, but it is in fact a reflection of their opposition to outsiders, for the latter symbolize the dismal state of their existence. In another context, the Oraons rejected the use of bicycle, which at one time they had found very useful, because it represented their exploitation at the hands of the British (Roy 1928).

Protest movements in tribal India have taken diverse forms. Underlying all of them rests a strong feeling and conviction that their abysmal state of life has its genesis in myriad oppressive and exploitative contacts with outsiders. Now, tribes also know that their cultures and photographs are marketed; they know their medicines fetch money, so do books written on them. Far from being considered as 'sympathizers', tribes see particularly 'outsider' anthropologists (in opposition to 'insider' or 'native' anthropologists) as another kind of 'soft-spoken, humble and bent, sophisticated, and compassion-seeking' exploiters, who eventually trade in their culture and its products. That is the reason why tribesmen often ask the anthropologists working in their areas about what they would receive in return for the information they painstakingly provide, and how their life would be affected after books and articles on them are published.

IX

The most important concern of the state and all the other agencies dealing with tribal societies must be their economic welfare. Alleviation of their poverty needs to be their first priority, as it was for all times since the tribal areas were opened up. In 1949, when perhaps the condition of tribes was not as bad as it is now, Dube (p. 34) had written: 'Economic rehabilitation...must have precedence over empty sermonizing.' And, Majumdar (1949: 42) had noted in the same volume of *The Eastern Anthropologist*, which was titled the 'Tribal Number': 'In some cases, prior to education and employment of tribal teachers, *the problem of bread must be solved*' (emphasis added). Economic development of tribal communities is essential for their integration with the other sections of Indian society. One of the main reasons of ethno-political movements among tribes is their state of acute poverty. Against this background, the development programmes, especially designed for tribes keeping in mind their specific characteristics, require the foremost attention of the state. And, the state has to ensure that funds earmarked for tribes reach them. For planning development for communities, the following aspects need to be considered, for they are basic to what has come to be known as 'endogeneous', 'culturally-rooted', 'holistic', and 'people-oriented development.'

1. People should decide about the type and nature of technological and institutional changes they want.

2. Sometimes, people may need intellectual help from outside, from those associated cross-culturally with development projects, for clarification of concepts and a proper comparative understanding of changes they desire.

3. Sometimes, people wish to discuss the proposed changes with others for their sustainability and suitability. Sometimes, the assistance of outsiders is sought for organizing and regulating meetings and group discussions, especially in faction-ridden situations.

4. One may not envisage a situation where no outsider (technically qualified or one dealing with the management of human resources) is involved in a programme of directed and planned change.

5. However, the outsiders are expected to refrain from imposing their ideas on people. They should not coerce people with their ethical and value judgements.

6. Although people are true planners of their future, it is likely that they may like to retain some of the cultural practices and revive certain customs that might have fallen into oblivion or might have been legally prohibited. In such contexts, the development expert should start a dialogue with people, questioning as humbly as possible their decision to revive traditions.

7. Once the development programme has been finalized, for the task of its execution, people's involvement is essential, for they should internalize at every level that the project is theirs, and its success depends upon their commitment and engagement.

8. All strata of people must be equally involved. Development programmes should not create stratification and cleavages in society.

9. The programmes must be periodically evaluated, using a proper methodology of impact-assessment, for their efficacy and viability, and appropriate changes must be introduced as and when required. One should begin with the premise that each programme is tentative, likely to change over time, depending upon the responses of people.

10. Both people and development experts learn from the processes of planning and executing development programmes. These experiences are extremely valuable for planning development programmes in other contexts.

At each stage, the development experts should interact with people to learn from their reactions and experiences. At the center of development are the people, the future beneficiaries and the builders of their community.

REFERENCES CITED

Béteille, André.

1992 *Society and Politics in India: Essays in a Comparative Perspective*. Delhi: Oxford University Press.

Bose, Nirmal Kumar

1971 (revised edition 2002). *Tribal Life in India*. New Delhi: National Book Trust. Revised by C.B. Tripathi.

1975 *The Structure of Hindu Society*. Delhi: Orient Longman.

Chaudhury, Sukant K.

2004 *Tribal Identity, Continuity and Change among Kondhs of Orissa*. Jaipur and New Delhi: Rawat Publications.

Dube, S.C.

1949 'Some aspects of the tribal problem'. *The Eastern Anthropologist*, 3 (1): 28-35.

Fürer-Haimendorf, Christoph von.

1982 *Tribes of India, the struggle for survival*. Delhi: Oxford University Press.

Hutton, J.H.

1921 *The Angami Nagas*. Oxford: Clarendon Press.

Majumdar, D.N.

1949 'The changing canvas of tribal life'. *The Eastern Anthropologist*, 3 (1): 40-7.

Mandelbaum, David G.

1970 *Society in India*. Bombay: Popular Prakashan.

Mishra, Nita and Arundhuti Roy Choudhury

1993 'Voices of the indigenous peoples. *Seminar*, 412: 48-50.

Narayan, Kirin

1998 'How native is a 'native' anthropologist?' In Meenakshi Thapan (ed). *Anthropological*

Journeys, Reflections on Fieldwork. New Delhi: Orient Longman (pp. 163-87).

Roy, S.C.

1928 *Oraon Religion and Customs*. Ranchi: Man in India Office.

Singh, K.S.

1992 *People of India: An Introduction*. Calcutta: Anthropological Survey of India.

1993 'The problem'. (Statement to the Volume on Marginalized Tribals). *Seminar*, 412: 12-8.

Sinha, Surajit

1962 'State formation and Rajput myth in tribal central India'. *Man in India*, 42 (1): 33-80.

1981 'Tribes and Indian civilization: transformation processes in modern India'. *Man in India*, 61 (2): 106-42.

Srivastava, V.K.

1994 Indian Tribals, An Overview. *The Toppers' India*, 1 (1): 25-30, and 1 (2): 30-2.

2003 'Some responses of communities to social tensions in India'. *Anthropos*, 98: 157-65.

Xaxa, Virginius

1999 'Transformation of tribes in India, terms of discourse'. *Economic and Political Weekly*, 34 (24): 1519-24.

4

Tribal Identity, Globalisation and Planned Development

B.K. Roy Burman

Tribal identity connotes two different cognitive realms. In a fundamental sense it implies the attributes by which a social entity may be categorised as a tribe. But in a more general sense it implies a community of persons with all or some of the historico-culturally valued attributes of a tribe in the fundamental sense and having mechanism of reproducing itself, though not always without conscious or unconscious inclusive/exclusive/coalescence process as an adaptive mechanism to new needs and/or challenges.

Fusion of geographical space and social space

In the fundamental sense, at the level of ethos, though not always empirically, the tribal social entities represent values of conviviality, reciprocity, sharing and caring and extension of the self to surroundings—animate or inanimate. It is the last attribute which imparts to the tribal people a sense of custodial responsibility towards the endowments of nature in the geographical space, which through diverse procedures are also considered as social space for the different tribes. Such fusion of geographical space and social space with mystic affective splash of varying intensity and sense of custodial responsibility, irrespective of the status of the geographical space in law, frequently provides the material base for defining the identity of a tribe. In recent years this construct of tribal identity has been highlighted by various forums of UN and its ancillaries. The UN Human Rights Committee in its 1314 meeting held in April 1994 adopted a resolution which while inter alia dealing with cultural right enshrined in the UN Covenant on Cultural Social and Economic Rights stated that:

> culture manifests itself in many forms including a particular way of life associated with the use of land resources, specifically in the case of indigenous peoples.

With this situational appraisal along with others as the backdrop, the Committee resolved that indigenous peoples have the right to control their lands, territories and natural resources and to maintain their traditional way of life. This perception has been further spelled out in 1997 in the American Declaration on the rights of indigenous peoples:

> in many indigenous cultures, traditional collective system for the control and use of land, territory and resources, including bodies of water and coastal areas, are a necessary condition for their survival, social organisation, development and their individual and collective well-being and that the form of such control and ownership is varied and distinctive and does not necessarily coincide with the systems protected by the domestic laws of the states in which they live.

This statement is also an endorsement of the indigenous and tribal peoples' right to self-determination as incorporated in ILO Convention 169 of 1989.

Emergence of tribe as a unified social category

It has been stated earlier that the identity boundaries of tribal peoples are not always rightly fixed. Sometimes consciously or unconsciously identity boundaries adjust to new needs and challenges. Even a casual glance of the ethnographics and demographic data in respect of tribal peoples in India or in any part of the world shows considerable differences among them with reference to differential rate of spread of education, urbanisation, intensity of outside contact, access to productive resources, life style and so on. But as the outcome of the common experience of dispossession from age old rights of access to and control and management of resources, marginalisation in significant spheres of decision making in the state process, intended or unintended assault on deeper structures of their cultures and history, the tribal peoples are emerging as a unified social category. In India, for sometime emulation of dominant culture through sanskritization and so-called westernization swayed the tribal peoples, but these hardly improved their social status or material conditons of life. Through the processes of reinterpretation, syncretism, revivalism, revitalization of the core, innovative focus on humanist essence of respective cultures, most of them have retrieved the lost ground. As a cumulative effect of these, while historically they were many, existentially they are tending to be one in the contemporary world (Roy Burman 1995:5). One should not however ignore that there are many twists and turns in human situation. One should not be surprised if there are also atavistic reversals under many covers or many pretexts. At the same time it is important to note that a global network of tribal peoples and peoples analogous to tribal social category has come into existence, as a not inconsequential force in the emerging world order.

Normative one-ness of 'tribe' and 'indigenous' and contradictions among global hegemons

In various international forums including those sponsored by UN, the word 'tribe' is being replaced by the word 'indigenous'. But the word indigenous is used in two senses. First, in the sense of autochthons of the land, and second in the normative sense, which combines two features, namely inherent egalitarian convivial world-view and also non-dominance and marginalisation in the context of state system. In the international documents one finds code switching from one meaning of the term to the other, thus creating considerable confusion. In the first sense it is difficult to say that all the tribes of India are autochthons of the country or that there are not others who are not inhabitants of the country since much before many of the tribes arrived here. The same situation prevails in most of the countries of Asia. In the second sense—in other words in the normative sense—the indigenous peoples of the Americas and Oceania and also those of the Scandinavian countries, the pastoralists of the mountains of Balkan Alpines and the Basques of South France and North Spain are also analogous to the tribes of India, in contrast to the organs of UN, ILO in its Convention 169 of 1989 relating to Indigenous and Tribal Peoples shows a more realistic approach. It defines indigenous in a way which is a synthesis of two meanings of the term, and defines tribes more or less in the same manner as presented here, by adding to it the normative aspect of the concept of indigenous. But ILO approach also is not free from a snag. ILO has uniformly described tribes as 'people' but has described the pre-invasion inhabitants of the Americas as 'population' ignoring the fact that before the European invasion there were Maya, Aztcch and Inca empires in Central and South America, indicating that the inhabitants thereof were politically organised peoples.

The dichotomous use of the terms peoples and population by ILO should not be brushed aside as semantic aberration. If the pre-invasion inhabitants of the Americas are recognised as 'peoples', the white settlers there will have to negotiate for every single inch of land under their current occupation which was not covered by any formal treaty during the 15th to late 19th centuries. Even for lands covered by breach of treaties, the position under international law would require re-examination particularly in USA and Australia. The UN approach suits the interest of the white masters of the Americas fairly well; on the other hand the ILO approach would fully protect European interest, while conveying an ambiguous warning signal to the Americas (Roy Burman 1995).

Prelude to the examination of the impact of globalisation—Uninformed rhapsody and its obverse in respect of right to self-determination

Article 1(2) of the Charter of United Nations stated that to develop friendly relations among nations based on respect for the principle of equal rights and self-determination of peoples, and to take other appropriate measures to strengthen universal peace is one of the core purposes of the Organisation. Paradoxically, association of the "rights to self-determination" with 'peoples' has affected two categories of persons at opposite polar ends to one another in an identical manner. It is because of misreading of the connotation of term 'self-determination' (Hannum 1996: 873-78). On 4 December 1960, the UN General Assembly adopted Resolution 1514 (XV) entitled "The Declaration on granting of independence to colonial countries and peoples". As Hannum observes, the thrust of the Declaration is clear: all colonial territories have the right of independence. However a closer reading reveals uncertainties arising from varying uses of the terms 'peoples', 'territories' and 'countries'. Although the title of the Declaration refers only to 'colonial countries' and peoples, the operative paragraph refers expansively to the right of 'all peoples to self-determination'. But the same resolution has also laid down a fundamental limiting principle to the effect that:

> any attempt aimed at the partial or total disruption of the national unity and the territorial integrity of a country is incompatible with the purposes and principles of the charter of the United Nations.

The position has been further clarified in UN Resolution 2625 (XXV) of October 29, 1970 which states that:

> Nothing shall be construed as authorising or encouraging an action which would dismember or impair, totally or in part, the territorial integrity or political unity of sovereign and independent states conducting themselves in compliance with the principle of equal rights and self-determination of peoples as described above and thus possessed of a government representing the whole people belonging to the territory without distinction as to race, creed or colour.

This position was confirmed by the Secretary General of UN in 1970 and by three expert committees, the latest one being in 1994 (Roy Burman 2002). In spite of these authoritative statements, both secessionists and diehard bureaucrats go on creating a misunderstanding in public mind that right to self-determination automatically means right to secession. There is reason to believe that this provided a pretext to India at least, for not ratifying ILO Convention 169. Perhaps several other countries also have gone by this miasmic vision. This is unfortunate. Had India and many more countries ratified ILO Convention 169, some of the negative effects of hegemonic globalisation could have been neutralised.

Indigenous and tribal peoples as repositories of diverse political economies

Till late medieval period homage and/or tribute paying sharing and/or custodial mode prevailed in most areas of concentration of indigenous and tribal peoples, almost all over the world. In the late medieval period a tendency to convert tributes to rent became perceptible. The tendencies during colonial and postcolonial period will be briefly mentioned with particular reference to India. During the colonial period rent receiving system either directly or through intermediaries gained momentum, particularly in the central tribal belt. In many areas recipients of tribute or rent collectors were recognised as land owners, but even then due to inadequacy of communication and administrative infra-structure the relations on the ground did not change much. The tribal peoples by and large retained their communal rights of access to and control and management of the endowments of nature. Subsumed within community rights, individual rights also certainly did exist. Frequently however the systems operated under the shadow of non-feudal or nascent feudal patriarchy (even in matrilineal and/or matrilocal or uxorilocal societies as in North-East India). While in the ancient and medieval kingdoms, the kings enjoyed political jurisdictional rights even in the frontiers generally inhabited by the indigenous and tribal peoples, by and large their economic rights or ownership rights on lands and forests were confined to the areas and aspects which the concerned peoples conceded to them on various considerations. The system was obverse of the systems of *res nullius* and *terra nullius;* it was guided by the principle of *lex loci rei sitae* (rules by which the people defined their life support systems). In the post-colonial period, with the extension of communication and administrative infra-structure, many of the colonial provenances which existed only on paper, were put into operation. Thus rather than rectification of colonial aberrations, these were legitimised and reified. In the process, community rights and within the orbit of that, individual rights which existed in different forms were either eroded or previous non-existing rights of such individuals as played the role of compradors and delinked from the regulating system of the community were promoted. In the process, post-colonial ghost-colonialism was whipped up to life in many tribal areas, particularly of west and south India where cash crop and agro-forestry based capitalist economy made considerable inroad. This obviously suited the interests of bureaucracy-capitalist-farmer nexus—more than in other parts of the country, accentuating the phenomenon of land alienation of the tribal peoples to a considerable extent.

Indigenous and tribal peoples in the focus of world geopolitics in the 21st century

In India except for small gaps there is almost a contiguous habitat of tribal peoples from Thane district of Maharashtra to Tengnupal district of Manipur. Some of the scheduled tribe peoples in the borders have their counterparts in China including Tibet, Pakistan, Bhutan, Myanmar and Bangladesh. These transborder peoples in their turn have agnates in Thailand, Laos, Campuchea. Thus there is a contiguous belt of differentiated but analogous social entities from Arabian Sea to the Pacific Ocean. In this mega socio-physical space of Asia, the tribal peoples of India constitute around 70 per cent of the population of the same category, if in China only the analogous social formations, and not the rashly located 'indigenous' by forums close to the UN are taken into consideration. In a world system perspective, the contiguity can be extended further. Skirting the Himalaya, peoples analogous to the tribals in normative sense including the pastorialists are found in Central and West Asia and beyond, with dated discontinuity in space reaching upto the Pyrenees, the abode of the Basque, who are considered by some scholars to contain Dravidian elements in their speech. And then there are the Sami in the Nordic countries, and the Inuit in Greenland. Crossing the Atlantic, where the East and the West fuse and also the Pacific where similar fusion is more marked there are peoples analogous to the tribal peoples of Asia and Africa. Recognition of this fact has led to global networking under the label 'indigenous'. Even while the label is debatable, the global linkage of tribal and analogous peoples, irrespective of the label by which they are denoted, is a reality today. Not only the tribal and indigenous elites but large number of tribal commoners are conscious of this emerging global scenario and are influenced by the same. Presence of such peoples with consciousness of belonging to the same globally marginalised socio-political category, cutting across state boundaries, has considerable implication for the geopolitics of the 21st century.

It is estimated that the tribal and indigenous peoples constitute around four percent of the population of the world. But many of the endowments of nature like oil, minerals, silvicultural and other biotic objects, which constitute and will continue to constitute important factors of production in the 21st century, are having much higher concentration in the territories traditionally inhabited or claimed by the tribal and indigenous peoples. While this makes the tribal and indigenous territories targets of the greed of the global hegemons and their compradors in the different countries, the resistance of the concerned peoples is also hardening up.

Life history of globalisation and death of humanism

Globalisation is essentially a contested concept. On the one hand it has been identified as a complex set of distinct but related processes economic, cultural, social but also political and military through which social relations have come to be understood in a common world framework. On the other hand, it has been described as a process through which peoples from one part of the globe move to all corners of the globe taking with them their ideological, technical and cultural achievements which resulted in the changes in the parts of the world so reached (Basu 2002).

While agreeing that definition of globalisation remains vague, D' Monte (2000) observes that in its most common usage globalisation refers to the fact that in recent years a quickly rising share of economic activities in the world seems to be taking place between peoples who live in different countries rather than in the same country. However Barry Coates of World Development Forum points out that as barriers to movement of capital fall, barriers to the movement of people are erected; there are fewer opportunities for migrant workers to work in richer countries and remit funds to their relatives (ibid). As against this illiberal facet of so-called 'globalisation and liberalisation', as pointed out by Amin (1997:28) a programme of authentic liberalisation on a world scale was put forth by the Group of 77 (third world countries) and the Non-Aligned Movement in 1975 under the name New International Economic Order (NIEO) which included the following points: (a) Opening Northern markets to Southern industrial exports, (b) improving the terms of trade for tropical agricultural products and mining products, (c) providing better access to international financing, and (d) creating more normal conditions for technology transfers.

The NIEO project was more or less unanimously rejected by the North. Instead the latter manipulated a system of hegemonic globalisation consisting of five monopolies, namely: (a) technological monopoly, (b) financial control of worldwide financial markets, (c) monopolistic access to the planet's natural resources, (d) media and communication monopolies, and (e) monopolies over weapons of mass destruction (ibid: 4-5). This has resulted in economic crises for most of the world giving birth to burning economic, social, political and even military conflicts during the last quarter of the 20th century. The GDP ratio between the richest and the poorest countries was 3:1 in 1820, 11:1 in 1931, 35:1 in 1950, 44:1 in 1973 and 72:1 in 1992 (Mayur 2000).

Globalisation in unequally structured global economy reflects imperialist impulse of capitalism involving social coercion of labour and restructuring state machinery to serve large corporations. Unacceptable and unaffordable degradation of the environment which may endanger the continuation of life, particularly of the homonids on the planet should be added to the list.

Theo Ben Guirab, President of 54th session of UN General Assembly, in his opening remarks observed that globalisation and unrelenting powers of transnational corporations were overwhelming governments, especially in the developing world (Guirab 1999). Camdessuss (2000) the chief of IMF in his last address before laying down the office admitted that whereas globalisation was expected to improve the human condition throughout the world it had 'operated at the whim of more or less autonomous financial and technical forces'. The International Peoples' Tribunal of G7 in its Tokyo verdict in 1993, has identified the consequences of Structural Adjustment Programme (SAP) initiated during Reagan regime as follows:

> sharp increase in unemployment, fall in remuneration of work, increase in food dependency, grave deterioration in environment, health care system, fall in admission to educational institutions, decline in productive capacity of many nations, sabotage of democratic systems, and continued growth of external debt (Amin 1997: 12-23).

Further, globalisation has led to the erosion of autocentric nation state (ibid:3). An illustration of this has been provided by Idemyor (1999), who focuses on the fact of how Nigeria had to take to military action to protect the interests of transnational corporate oil enterprise. Even UN is now seen to be coming under the shadow of big business. In February 2000, Kofi Annan, Secretary General of UN and the International Chamber of Commerce issued a joint statement affirming their commitment to 'partnership' for world development.

Glimpse of a paradigm shift for planned development

It is to be examined whether current concepts of development and planning are adequate to meet the challenges facing the human kind today. Hegemonic globalisation is not only a process of domination, dispossession and oppression of the majority of human individuals and collectives by a small minority, but is symbolic of deprivation of human values—deviation from the basic nature of human nature. The first issue of development is humanist retrieval and in this the tribal and indigenous peoples in a more fundamental sense of the terms as stated at the outset of this paper have an important role to play. It means power-centric worldview must be replaced by conviviality or companionate value oriented world-view, rooted in empathy and expansion of the meaning of the 'self'. But this cannot be done simply by wishing or preaching. For this, right to self-determination of the indigenous and tribal peoples is an indispensable condition. But then there is the grey area of articulation of the institution managing self-determination of the indigenous and tribal peoples and the institutions drawing their legitimacy and functional efficacy from the state system. Here it is also to be noted that though state system is undergoing a process of erosion, rolling back of the state does not automatically augment the roles of the institutions reflecting values of conviviality. More frequently the gaps erected by retreat of state are filled up by transnational corporate enterprises. To counter this process a system of synthesis of state sovereignty and peoples' sovereignty cutting across state boundaries but without changing them are to be thought of. In an incipient and not much effective form one can see this in the institution of Sami Council with jurisdictional rights on some agreed matters over the traditional activities of the Sami living in Norway, Sweden and Finland and also to some extent in Kola Peninsula of Russia. The expanding jurisdiction of Sikh Gurudwara Prabandhak Committee is also a proto-type though not much visible. Even the non-territorial functional role of the Vatican is not without some significance, even though neither Sikh Gurudwara Prabandhak Committee nor the Vatican reflects people's sovereignty. They draw upon Supreme Supernatural sovereignty without compromising state sovereignty.

While deeper thought is to be given and many experiments will have to be made as to how to bring about synthesis of peoples' sovereignty and state sovereignty, the issues that currently affect the lives of the peoples, in the present case particularly the indigenous and tribal peoples, require urgent attention. Among them the most important is the recognition of indigenous peoples' rights in respect of land and resources. In March 1996 a seminar of UN Experts on Indigenous Land Rights and Land Claims *inter-alia* recommended that governments should renounce discriminatory legal doctrines and policies particularly around the: (a) doctrines of *terra nullius*, (b) doctrine that indigenous communities do not have the capacity to own land in their collective capacity, (c) doctrine that indigenous land, title or ownership may be taken or impaired by the state or third parties without due process of law and adequate and appropriate compensation, (d) doctrine or policies that indigenous lands must be held in trust regardless of the will of the indigenous peoples concerned, (e) doctrine and policies imposing an extinguishment of indigenous land rights, title or ownership, and (f) policies which exclude some indigenous people from the land claims process established by the state. It further recommended that: (*i*) ILO Committee of Experts should clarify the interpretation of Article 14 paragraph 1 of ILO Convention 169, (*ii*) military and occupation practices carried out by governments, individually or collectively, which have an impact on the ways of life of indigenous peoples, should be open to international consideration in accordance with international human rights standard and the impact on lands and the ways of the life of the indigenous peoples should be subject to appropriate environmental review in conjunction with the indigenous peoples, (*iii*) the implementation of sustainable development should take fully into account the indigenous peoples' values, knowledge and technologies, in order to ensure resources for the future generation, (*iv*) United Nations, its specialized agencies and other inter-governmental organsiations should assure that indigenous peoples' cultural diversity, traditional values and ways of life are protected and institutional arrangements are made for follow up action, and (v) governments should welcome, encourage and open up trade among indigenous peoples and other parties from different countries and facilitate such trade. In respect of the last item a system of double veto should operate. No resources from indigenous territories should be extracted, exchanged or processed without consent of the concerned indigenous peoples and the government, both.

A special note should be taken of the United Nations Declaration on Human Genome. For the purpose of scientific study human genome surveys are being conducted among the indigenous peoples on a priority basis. But it has been reported that on the basis of such a survey the genetic composition of a tribe in Indonesia has been patented by the US Government. Thus the most basic unit of the physical built, not only of the present generation, but even of the coming generations of that tribe has become a property of US government. There cannot be greater disregard and abuse of human dignity and human rights. Though under the regime of hegemonic globalisation this is not unexpected, the academic community has the responsibility of raising its voice against commodisation of human body in such a depraved manner.

It must be recognised that the launching platform of any planned development cannot but be the struggle to retrieve human dignity and human endeavor to respond to the sonic invitation of the cosmos in all its forms.

REFERENCES

Amin, Samir

1997 *Capitalism in the Age of Globalisation.* Delhi: Madhyam Books.

Basu, Gautam Kumar

2003 'Globalisation, democracy and the third world,' *Bharatiya Samajik Chintan,* Vol. 4, January.

Camdessus, M.

2000 'Message to US Trade Talk', *Indian Express* 14 February.

D'Monte, Darryl

2000 'Dissenting globalisation', *Frontline,* 15, 21, October 14-27.

Guirab, Theo Ben

1999 'Opening Remarks: UN General Assembly', *UN Newsletter,* 54-37, New Delhi.

Hannum, Hurst

1996 'Rethinking self-determination'. In H.G. Steiner and P. Alston (eds.) *International Human Rights in Context.* Oxford: Clarendon Press.

Idemyor, Vincent

1999 'The role of multinational oil companies in Nigerian Federation', *IWGIA*, April-June.

Mayur, Rashmi

2000 'Challenges of New Millenium', *The Hindu,* January.

Roy Burman, B.K.

1995 *Indigenous and Tribal Peoples and the UN and International Agencies,* New Delhi: Rajiv Gandhi Institute For Contemporary Studies: 4-5.

2002 'On self-determination of peoples in the present scenario', *The Mainstream,* December 14, XL, 52.

5

Globalisation and Empowerment of Capital and Disempowerment of Tribals

Manu Bhaskar

> *While both humanization and dehumanization are real alternatives only the first is man's vocation. This vocation is constantly negated. It is thwarted by injustice, exploitation, oppression and the violence of the oppressors, it is affirmed by the yearning of the oppressed for freedom and justice and by the struggle to recover their lost humanity*—Paul Freire.

The term globalisation refers to the growing integration of the world economy. In an era of open economy and globalisation, the issues of the survival of the poor are based on politico-economic actions by national governments, General Agreement on Tariffs and Trade (GATT), Convention on Biological Diversity (CBD) and international agencies including the World Bank, International Monetary Fund (IMF) and more recently by World Trade Organisation (WTO). In a knowledge-based economy Intellectual Property Rights (IPRS) are key to the international competitiveness of both national and multinational firms.

CBD, TRIPS and the tribals

The tribals have become arenas of the global 'free' market economy and there is a gradual process of monopolization of resources by the dominant economic forces. This effort has been symbolised by the CBD signed during the 1992 United Nations Conference on Environment and Development at Rio de Janeiro, and by the GATT agreement. The WTO agreement on Trade related Intellectual Property Rights (TRIPS) which deal with patents and effective *sui generis,* legislation on property rights, plants and animal varieties and genetically modified organisms is an effort to control the traditional knowledge system. Apart from granting patents to pharmaceuticals and agro-chemicals, India's concerns are related to patenting micro-organisms or life-forms and patenting of products on bio-diversity and traditional knowledge in other parts of the world and establishing an effective *sui generis* system for protection of new plant varieties. Further, the reversal of 'burden of proof' under TRIPS would force the tribals each time to prove that they are not guilty of violating the patent laws. Other provisions of the TRIPS causing concern to the tribals in India relate to change from product patent to process patent. In a regime of process patent, even if changes were brought about in a process the tribals would have to continue to pay royalty on the earlier patented product.

The developed countries are naturally to gain because of their superiority in the field of technology. Hence it is difficult for bio-rich countries and techno-rich countries to be equal partners. Developing countries thus face two kinds of disadvantages. One, these countries lack the scientific capability to plant new materials and are not even in a position to fully catalogue the natural resources of biomaterials they currently possess. Two, there is a group concentration of transnational corporations (TNC) in biotech industries, notably in the seed sector. This concentration enables these industries to extract monopoly rents from farmers worldwide. Dependence on TNCs for critical inputs like seed and medicinal plants is feared to bring a chain of developments, which may undermine the very survival of the tribals. The creation of monopolies in seed supplies through IPRs in seed and plant varieties is an example of 'biopiracy' (Shiva 1995). The genetic resources and knowledge used by multinational corporations for claimed patents is the product of centuries of innovation and selection by the tribals. Owing to the IPRs and patents imposed on plants, farmers will no longer be able to save their seed for sowing in the next year.

Tropical Botanical Garden Research Institute (TBGRI) has commercially utilized 'aryogapacha', an herb used by a tribal group in Kerala; and has agreed to share a part of revenue with the tribal group. This is ironical since most plant diversity originates from the tribals but the seeds and plant material are under the control of TNCs and further it is sold back as patented material. As a result, the companies will reap monopoly profits, while the genius of the tribals will go un-rewarded and they will be banned from using their own seeds with payment of royalties. The Patents Second Amendment Bill 1999 allows compliance with TRIPS. It addresses the question of biopiracy by imposing the disclosure of the source and geographical origin of biological materials in a patent invention.

The World Bank by funding mega projects of dams is able to exercise control not only over rivers and water sources but also over energy, agriculture, land and people especially of the third world. Evidence from around the world shows that large dams lead to wholesale destruction of agricultural land, forests, the ecology of riverine systems and economy and culture of native people. Recent floods that hit areas never previously affected have been attributed to deforestation caused by illegal logging and over cultivation of fragile mountainsides by the poor. (Kothari and Bakshi 1989). However, much of the global deforestation is caused by the corporate giants such as Mitsubishi, Maxus and Georgia Pacific, who are tearing apart millions of acres of tropical rainforest to supply timber for Japan, North America and Europe (Bandarage 1997). According to some estimates, around 50 per cent of the medicines sold in the market are pirated from tribal communities, analysed and patented by pharmaceutical companies.

Impact of Bio-Diversity Act on the tribes in India

Our Bio-Diversity Act 2002 is in response to the CBD signed at the Earth Summit of Rio de Janeiro in 1992. The Act together with the adverse policy changes and legal measures by the government will have serious impact on the livelihood of the tribals. According to the Land Acquisition Act, 1894 land can be acquired for private companies by the government not only for work which would be in the nature of public purpose but also for engaging in productive activities that is likely to prove useful. However, there is no clause to recognize resettlement and rehabilitation as a basic right of the displaced people. The risk of displacement is further exacerbated as instead of land-to-land resettlement the law offers cash and hence renders them more vulnerable. Besides, there are attempts by the eco-development projects to integrate the buffer zones of sanctuaries and national parks with the larger markets to create an ecological damper between market forces and the forest. The move of the central government to set a paramilitary force for wild life protection has to be seen in the context of increasing pressure of commercialisation and industrialisation of natural resources. The hegemony of privatization has supplanted the dominance of the state in order to deprive people of their rightful control over natural resources (Ekka 2001).

India is one of the twelve major biodiversity resources of the world. Within India, the Northeast is among the richest. The tribals are found in almost all the states and union territories. In terms of geographical distribution, about 55 per cent live in Central India, 28 per cent in Western India, 12 per cent in North East India, 4 per cent in South India and one per cent elsewhere (Roy Burman 1994). A common feature shared by the tribal inhabitants is that of remoteness and marginal quality of their resources. Earlier exploitation of such poor regions was found both difficult and uneconomic. But in recent decades of technology advancement and the unraveled economic and political strength of world capitalism we witness a creation of favourable conditions for invasion on natural resources from the ecologically fragile regions inhabited by the tribal people. Accordingly, the gigantic development projects like dams, mines, agro-business, national security aspects and so on have been distressingly routine and ever increasing phenomenon threatening the integrity of the tribes. After all, the tribals constituting 8 per cent of the population, occupy nearly 20 per cent of the geographical area, which contains 70 per cent of the minerals and the bulk of forests and water resources. (Pathy 1999). The powerlessness of the inhabitants provides easy access for the TNCs and their agents. The new corporate forces will soon lead to the loss of food entitlements and the cultural degeneration of the tribal peoples. The resultant loss of survival complexes has led to a number of massive struggles of the tribal peoples. In post-colonial periods their land and forests have been taken away not only by the non-tribal rich manipulators but also by the government in the name of public interest through the Land Acquisition Act. Thus political movements continue as fiercely as before. The case of Kerala tribes can be taken as an illustration.

Empowerment of capital vs. disempowerment of tribals: Kerala scenario

In Kerala the total population of the scheduled tribals (S.T.) according to the 1991 census is 3.2 lakhs. This is 1.02 per cent of the state's total population and constitutes only 0.2 per cent of the total S.T. population of India. The conditions of the tribals in Kerala like their counterparts in other parts of India are one of poverty, malnutrition, illiteracy, socio-economic exploitation by the settlers, and sexual exploitation by the non-tribals. Today, the increasing starvation deaths and unwed mothers who are victims of non-tribal men are issues of wider concern.

The tribal economy of Kerala was forest-based until the infiltration of plainsmen into those regions. Subsequently, the unique characteristics of the tribals gradually began to be destroyed. Historical evidence shows that immigration of the non-tribals was during different periods in different regions of Kerala. While in the Malabar region in the north it was before the formation of Kerala State, in the Travancore and Cochin regions, it took place much later. As the forest policies in the princely state of Travancore and Cochin were more favourable to the tribals, land alienation was prevented to a great extent in the princely regions rather than in the Malabar region. Moreover, in the Malabar region the immigrants entered the forest while the tribals were still leading a migratory life, whereas in the Travancore-Cochin region it was after they had taken to permanent settled life. Consequently, there are regional differences with regard to land holding, income and literacy levels. Prominent among the basic reasons for the pauperization and proletarinisation of the tribals in Kerala is land alienation. In Kerala unlike other states of India, the tribal lands were passed on mainly to non-tribal settlers who migrated from the former Travancore and Cochin states to Malabar. The Kerala Land Reforms Act, 1963 which brought an end to the feudal landlordism went against the tribals. During the early part of the 20th century non-tribal agriculturists not only leased tribal land but also usurped the land from the tribals through encroachment. When the land reforms were implemented the tribals were considered landlords while the wealthy and politically powerful were considered landless *pattakkar* (tenants) and consequently the rights of land was passed on to the non-tribals. The tribals legally failed to regain their land for want of proper ownership documents (Kunhaman 1989; Dilip 1994). Sreekumar's study (2002) brings out very clearly that development induced development has mostly adversely affected the tribals and fishermen of Kerala. Murickan *et al.* (2000) estimate the land acquired for devlopment projects in the state during 1951-95 as 1,47,767,90 hectares, which is about 3.8 per cent of the total geographical area. Table 1 indicates that land acquired for development projects was mainly forestland.

Another way through which the tribals have been dispossessed of their land is large-scale hydro-electrical projects (Kerala 1964). The creation of protected areas too leads to the dispossession of land thereby the tribals lose the rights of managing their resources. They are also burdened with the indirect costs such as crop damage and loss of life caused by protecting wild animals. Thus there always arise conflicts of interests between conservation and maintenance of livelihood of local communities. Similar situations and issues exist in the Periyar Tiger Reserve of the Idukki district where tribal communities who had traditionally lived deep inside the forests and enjoyed the rights and use of forest resources were uprooted and pushed to the fringes for establishing the wild life sanctuary (Arun *et al.* 2001). The entire Reserve is divided into three zones: core areas (350 sq. km) buffer zone (370 sq. km) and tourism zone (50 sq. km). The area of the sanctuary was declared a national park in 1982. Through the eco-development projects the buffer zone of sanctuaries and national parks are integrated with the larger markets.

The Kerala Scheduled Tribes (Restriction on Transfer of Lands and Restoration of Alienated Lands) Act provided legislative clauses for the restoration of all lands alienated from Kerala's tribal households from January 1, 1960. This act if implemented would have been in favour of the tribals as most of the land was alienated before 1960. Nothing was done to implement the provisions of the law until 1986. As a result, the formulation of the regulatory framework did not result in any positive action. It was only after the intervention of the judiciary in 1993 that the state government was directed to implement the law. However, it was only in 1996 that the state government introduced the Kerala Scheduled Tribes (Restriction on Transfer of Land and Restoration of Alienated Lands) Amendment Bill. The bill turned out to be an attempt to protect the interests of the land grabbers by giving legal validity to transactions of tribal land between 1960 and January 1986. Simultaneously, the tribals started voicing their protest over land and livelihood issues and started forcibly occupying and taking control of vested forestlands, which in turn led to police action. Although this continued in several tribal pockets it culminated in an agitation in front of the state secretariat, which lasted for forty eight days under the leadership of C.K. Janu, a women tribal activist. The issue was resolved on October 16, 2001 with the agreement between the government and the Adivasi Dalit Council. The features of the settlement were:

1. The government wherever possible will provide five acres (two hectares) to each landless family.

2. A five-year livelihood programme will be implemented on the land until it becomes fully productive for *adivasis* to sustain themselves.

3. The state will enact a law to ensure that the land provided to *adivasis* is not alienated as had happened in the past.

4. The state government will pass a resolution asking the central government to declare the *adivasi* areas as scheduled areas administered under the fifth schedule of the Constitution.

5. The government also gave commitment that it will abide by whatever decision the Supreme Court takes on its appeal against the Kerala High Court Order quashing Restoration of Lands to Scheduled Tribes Bill passed in 1999.

6. The maximum possible land, at least 10,000 acres, will be found and distributed in Wyanad district where there is the largest concentration of landless *adivasis*.

7. The government will also implement a master plan for tribal development with active participation of the *adivasis*.

One wonders how the agreement signed by the Kerala government can be fulfilled when the government has not yet identified the required land needed for distribution to the tribal families. Moreover, the third and the fcurth clauses in the agreement are to be made effective by the central government. But the central government itself is reportedly considering an amendment to the Para (2) of the V Schedule in order to remove the 'prohibition and restrictions on the transfer of land by the tribal to non-tribals, for non-agricultural operations including prospecting and mining', which will in one stroke open the flood gates to unfettered alienation of tribal land, water, and resources. Needless to say, that the V Schedule is a major constitutional provision safeguarding the resources of the tribals. The move by the central government to amend it will only lead to the disempowerment of the tribals and serve the commercial interests of the TNCs. Thus the future of tribals is going to be a battle between them, central and state governments and the judiciary.

The report of the M.S Swaminanthan Commission on W.T.O. concerns constituted by the government of Kerala (2003) becomes relevant in this context. The growing polarization of social and economic power in the hands of a few in the process of globalisation would leave the majority dispossessed and disinherited. This would lead to the destruction of their livelihood, food and ecological securities. The Commission has mooted the 'livelihood, security box' as an alternative negotiating principle and strategy to empower developing nations to face the challenge of providing livelihood to its people. The developing countries, however, have always been asking for trade opportunities rather than aid. Therefore, it would be pertinent to examine whether the creation of the 'livelihood security box' would be in the direction of trade or aid.

Table 1

Land acquisition for development projects

Purpose	Private	Common	Forest	Total	Forestland%
Water resources	27995.98	349.80	2122626.65	49573.43	42.82
Transport	5112.41	NA	NA	4637.13*	NA
Industries	9262.10	131.19	386.29	9778.58	3.95
Others**	15401.33	409.36	863.32***	16674.01	5.18
Total	59118.29	1222.29	40673.2	14776790	27.53

* This is a figure based on extrapolation of data.

** Land taken for urban development, building educational institutions, non-hydel power, tourism, etc. are clubbed in here

*** This figure does not include 231554 hectares of land taken for sanctuaries and parks.

Source: Calculated from Table 1 of Murickan *et.al* (2000) adapted from Sreekumar (2000).

Empowerment of capital thus leads to the disempowerment of the tribals. Hence there is need a to strike a balance between the survival needs of the tribals and the interest of capital.

REFERENCES

Arun, L.K., *et.al,*

2001 *Bio-Diversity Conservation and Livelihood Issues of Tribesfolk: A Case study of Periyar Tiger Reserve,* Discussion paper. 37. Thiruvananthapuram: KRPLLD,

Bandaranage, Asoka

1997 *Women Population and Global Crises.* London: Zed Books.

Bhaskar, B.R.P. (ed.)

2001 *Human Rights.* Bangalore: Vigil India Movement.

Dilip, K.G.

1990 *Beliefs and Myths in Tribal Societies.* (Unpublished Thesis).

Ekka, Alex

2001 'Adivasi rights: Empowerment and deprivation'. In B.R.P. Bhaskar (ed.) *Human Rights.*

Kothari, Smitu & Rajni Bakshi

1989 'On laws and protests', Editorial, *Lokayan Bulletin,* 7:1.

Kerala

1964 *Report of the K.K. Viswanathan Committee.* Trivandrum: Government of Kerala.

2003 *Report of the Commission on W.T.O. Concerns in Agriculture.* Thiruvananthapuram: Government of Kerala.

Kunhaman, M.

1989 *Development of Tribal Economy.* New Delhi: Classical Publishing House.

Murickan, J.M. *et. al.*

2000 *Development Induced Displacement in Kerala—Summary Report of a Study.* Thiruvananthapuram: Loyola College of Social Sciences.

Pathy, Jaganath

1999 'Tribe, region and nation in the context of the Indian nation', *Sociological Bulletin,* 48:1-2.

Roy Burman, B.K.

1994 *Tribes in Perspective.* New Delhi: Mittal Publications.

Shiva, Vandana

1995 *Women, Ecology and Economic Globalisation.* New Delhi: IAWS.

Sreekumar, T.T

2002 'Democracy, development and new forms of social movements'. *The Indian Journal of Labour Economics,* 45:2.

6

Concept of Tribe: A Note

K.S. Singh

The term tribe has evolved from a Latin root, the *tribuz,* an English term which meant three divisions into which the Romans were grouped. The Concise Oxford Dictionary defines tribe:

> As a group of (esp. primitive) families or communities, linked by social, economic, religious, or blood ties, and usually having a common culture and dialect, and a recognised leader or any similar natural or political division.

Every society has its own terms for such divisions. We had terms like *jati* and *jana, kulam, samudaya, nyata, biradari,* etc., for endogamous groups and a number of terms in *bhasas* for exogamous divisions.

The forest dwellers

There is no term for tribe in ancient literature. There are words for forest dwellers in both Sanskrit and *bhasa* literatures. The forest dwellers are variously described as volatile, hospitable and powerful in Sanskrit literature. The Persian accounts repeat at places the other sanskritic perceptions of tribals being savage, barbarous, etc. The tribe is an Anglo-Saxon word, a colonial concept. A tribe officially notified as a scheduled tribe today lives in deserts, riverbelts, the plains, the islands, in relatively isolated habitats but mostly in forests. The tribes of today and the forest dwellers of yesterday are almost similar. We have today a profile of 3000 communities including tribes which share a good many features such as endogamy, commensality, hierarchy, exclusion, etc. There are differences between communities and between regions. The tribal communities spread all over the country are marked by relative isolation and distance cohesiveness, egalitarianism, incipient forms of hierarchy, rapport with environment, subsistence economy and simple tools of production.

From the forest dwellers to tribes

The colonial period witnessed the transformation of forest dwellers into tribes and the processes of transformation of tribes into castes. Ethnographers earlier described all communities as tribes. The distinction between tribe and caste did not fully emerge until the census of 1901. Though D. Ibbetson in Punjab was aware of all pervasiveness of caste structures and caste values, he tried to make a distinction between caste and tribe. Occupation was the primary basis of castes, reinforced by status and caste rules. A tribe was bound by the notions of "common origin, common habitat, common customs and modes of thought". A tribe, particularly a clan was strongly linked with territory. Ibbetson applied the structure or category of caste to identify the social organisation among the Brahman, Hindu non-agricultural, mercantile castes of the Khatri, Arora and Bania, who were held together by rules of endogamy, notion of purity and pollution, etc. The concept of tribe was applied by Ibbetson to agricultural castes based on the notion of common descent and Muslim communities such as Baloch and Pathan and to pastoral and other groups on the periphery. However Ibbetson also describes tribal divisions within the priestly and mercantile castes, among artisans and 'menial' castes and among women. It is obvious that the situation was fluid. Today there are few who share his view, though they agree with Ibbetson's view on the dynamism of the caste and of the social situation and the change noted by him in meanings of such groups such as Jats, Rajputs not only historically but also ethnically. The ethnographic profile of India that emerges under the People of India Project which is closer to the ethnography of Ibbetson has community rather than tribe and caste as its focus which shares a lot of traits, to larger or lesser extent, and the tribe is a community relatively isolated, distant and backward.

The tribes variously or successively were described in the censuses and ethnographic literature as hill tribes, forest tribes, primitive tribes and backward tribes. It was under the Government of India Act of 1935 and the Constitution of India that the nomenclature of the scheduled tribes fully emerged. The Constitution of India however gives no definition of tribe. The notion of the scheduled tribe has two aspects. First, it is administratively determined by the criteria of backwardness and remoteness and it is a political decision. The second is that all tribes are not scheduled, the presumption being that there are still some communities similar to the tribes which are outside the ambit of the schedule. This understanding gains support from the fact that the listing of communities notified as the tribes under Article 342 of the Constitution is an ongoing process.

As we look back at the attempts since 1901 to define a tribe and the elements constituting the definition, the present position appears to be different. A tribe today does have an occupation or a set of occupations. There is much less of blood feud now. The tribes speak many languages. They are very mobile and some of them have moved across a large part of the country. They are endogamous. They have a set of commensal norms. They have all types of marriages, such as marriage by intrusion, marriage by elopement, marriage by service, but marriage by negotiation is the most prominent now. Though the most primitive groups of the country are tribals, all tribals are not as primitive. Sections of the tribes are as advanced today as sections of non-tribal middle classes anywhere. Isolation is coming to an end. Most of the tribes are no longer nomadic, or have nomadic habits. They cannot be distinguished only by 'a love of drinks and dance'. They have cultural systems, which has sustained them, in spite of their exposure to all manner of alien cultural influences.

Soon after independence, the tribes were somewhat differently defined for administrative reasons. It should be noted that primitiveness and backwardness were the tests applied in preparing the lists of scheduled tribes in 1950 and 1956. In revising the list in 1965, other criteria looked for were "more indications of primitive traits, distinctive culture, geographical isolation, shyness of contact with the community at large and backwardness". In the late 1960s the 'anthropological' definition of the tribes emerged. A Committee set up by the central government in 1965 looked into the question of the definition of the tribes. According to the Committee, primitiveness and backwardness were the criteria applied in framing the 1950 and 1956 lists of the scheduled tribes. In considering the revision of the lists of scheduled tribes, the Committee looked for indications of primitive traits, distinctive culture, geographical isolation, shyness of contact with communities at large and backwardness. It further opined that tribes whose members have by and large mixed with the general population were not eligible to be in the schedule of tribes. In the post-independence period the tribe caste question seems to have become non-issue. In different language areas the tribals started defining themselves locally and nationally as *kaliparaj, adimjati, adivasi, janajati, vanyajati,* etc.

Tribes into *Dalit*

From the very beginning the social historians have tried to explore the process of the assimilation of the lower order as *sudras* into the *varna* order. Until the colonial period, the tribes unlike the *dalit* were absorbed in the *varna jati* order both as *sudras* and *kshatriyas*. During the colonial period and afterwards the communities described as tribes were generally accepted as the people who stood outside the *varna jati* order. No notion of pollution and no stigma of untouchability attached to them. These communities remained in possession of the resources in land and forest. They enjoyed a fair measure of cultural autonomy and political control over resources. Unlike tribes the *dalits* were part of the Hindu social order and hardly had any resources like land of their own. Since the 1980s the concept of *dalit* has replaced the word *harijan* and is not sought to include the tribal as part of political mobilisation of 30 per cent of the population of India in pursuit of power and share of opportunities for development called diversity in the Bhopal Declaration. In the process the legitimate differentiation among the two components necessary for forging the right strategy is being ignored.

Globalization, Indigenous People and *Adivasi*

A new dimension has been added to the concept of the tribe with the onset of globalization since the 1980's. The forest dwellers with their rich resources are becoming global players. While the question whether the tribes of India are an indigenous people is widely debated, the scheduled tribes of India were recognised as indigenous people by the World Bank in 1991, and the Indian Council of Indigenous and Tribal People treats *adivasis* as indigenous people. The government of India has however disagreed. The question is not yet resolved academically and is charged with emotion. The anthropologists believe that the *homo sapiens* who emerged more than hundred thousand years ago are indigenous to eastern Africa and the rest of all of us are migrants. The morphological types came up about 70000 years ago, and the word languages surfaced around 30,000 years ago. These landmarks are established. Our tribes are certainly the oldest settlers in the hills and forests but so are non-tribals in other ecological niches as peasants, pastoralists, fisherfolk, etc. It is for the DNA based studies on people of India to indicate the pattern of settlement and come to a conclusion about who came first or who came later. This by no means dilutes the importance of the tribes but puts matters in a perspective.

Identity, tribal and ethnic

The international agenda for indigenous people deals with the rights related to land and natural resources, culture, education and language, development, self-determination, autonomy and self-government and health. These are important issues which deserve to be discussed, while making a note of the fact that the Indian situation is historically different.

The processes of the enfranchisement of tribal communities like other communities have been faster and more complete in India than elsewhere in the world. Tribal communities along with others were granted limited franchise under the Government of India Acts of 1919 and 1935. The complete enfranchisement took place under the Constitution of India. Not only were tribals enfranchised, they were also given a complete set of political rights like other sections of the Indian people. These fundamental rights include the right to equality, freedom, religion and culture and educational rights. Article 29 states that any section of citizens having a distinct language, script and culture of its own, shall have a right to conserve the same. Similarly, Article 46, under the Directive Principle of State Policy, provides for the promotion of educational and economic rights of scheduled tribes. Part VI of the Constitution stipulates special political rights for scheduled tribes and for special political dispensations under the Fifth and the Sixth Schedules.

While there has been considerable debate about the indigenous people, there is no ambiguity about the notion of a tribe. Even though this term has not been defined in the Constitution, there is abundant literature on how the term evolved and acquired its present definition over the last hundred years. The application of the term indigenous to the Indian situation has aroused fears because there are communities which claim to be as indigenous as the tribes.

National self-determination was a concept that developed during the struggle against the colonial regimes in the Third World. The present-day notion of self-determination is being increasingly interpreted to imply the rights to self-management of resources, and to acquire a share in political power. It excludes the right to secession.

There are issues relating to the interface between tribal and non-tribal people particularly in a country like India where tribes and non-tribes are derived from the same ethnic stock, the same language families, and the same civilisational and cultural streams and where they have interacted a great deal. However, the tribes have maintained their identity, speak their own languages, live in relative isolation and are undeveloped.

India has witnessed the formation of seven tribal states. It is currently engaged in the debate on various modes of empowerment of tribal people. Various suggestions about devolution of power and transfer of funds are under discussion.

There have been no explicit, categorical judicial pronouncements on the tribals' collective rights over resources, in India as in Australia and elsewhere. There is, of course, recognition of customary laws and rights of the tribal communities in the areas under the Sixth Schedule. One reason for this is that tribes in India were not sovereign nations, like in the New World, where they entered into treaty relationship with the colonial powers.

The state in India was sovereign. The ruler was *bhupati*. The right to reclaim land and extend conservation in forest areas was recognised by rulers from ancient to colonial times. So the rights of the tribal people, as recalled in their myths and folklores were never recognised by ancient or medieval states and even less so by the colonial state. The ideas of private property deeply penetrated tribal society at many levels. Therefore, there is need to reconstruct tribal notions of right and document them.

The political rights of the tribes have to be redefined and reaffirmed in response to the challenges the tribals are likely to face as pressure mounts on their resources such as land, minerals, forests and water. Many tribal groups are engaged in a struggle for acquiring a share in profits accruing from exploration of their resources. Royalty has been paid in one case for the use of tribal resources such as medical herbs. This process is likely to encompass more areas.

Globalisation paradoxically has highlighted identity of all groups particularly tribes and galvanised their resistance and consolidation. The basic problem today is to guarantee the rights of tribal people over their resources and to create an apparatus that will ensure their share in the power structure so that they exercise control over their resources for their own benefit.

REFERENCES

Singh, K.S.

1993 'The problem: Marginalised', *Seminar* 412, December.

1995 'Reflections on the current debate concerning the indigenous peoples'. In Amar Kumar Singh, M.K. Jabbi, (eds.) *Tribals in India, Development, Deprivation, Discontent*. New Delhi: Council for Social Development and Har-Anand Publication.

1995 'The Scheduled Tribes in India: A profile', *Consultants*: Asian Development Research Institute, July.

1997 'Tribe into caste: A colonial paradigm (?)'. In Dev Nathan (ed.) *From Tribe to Caste,* Shimla. Indian Institute of Advanced Study.

1998 'Political rights, devolution of powers, autonomy and participation: A preliminary statement' In B.K. Roy Burman and B.B. Verghese (eds.) *Aspiring to be Tribal/Indigenous Condition*. New Delhi: The Commonwealth Human Rights Initiative and Konark Publishers Pvt. Ltd.

2001 'Re-thinking forest history', Panel Dissussion on 'Tribes, Forests and Social Formation in Indian History', Indian History Congress, Bhopal, December 28-30.

7

Frontier Identity in the Terai: The Tharu

Amrit Srinivasan and Akhilesh Ranjan

In this paper, the particularly thorny issue of tribal relations with the mainstream will be examined in some detail for the Tharu of West Champaran in Bihar. The differential claims to political identity made by the Tharus over the last sixty years or so, it will be argued, reflect in a very interesting way, the co-existence of both isolationist and integrationist tendencies amongst them. The paper thus seeks to go beyond the literature which has so far been overly preoccupied with tribal *integration* into Hindu society. Instead it argues for Tharu identity as a 'frontier' identity, in dynamic exchange with Hindu and Buddhist 'civilisational' influences over time. These socio-cultural features of frontier history are further linked to Tharu ecology. As indigenous inhabitants of the Terai—a border region lying between the foothills of the Himalayas and the Indo-Gangetic plain—the Tharu are to be found in the area stretching from Nainital district of Uttranchal to West Champaran district of Bihar and adjoining parts of Nepal. Any anthropological discussion of Tharu identity consequently must focus on its spatial spread and go beyond territorial divisions between (1) the two sovereign nations of India and Nepal, and (2) the two independent constituencies of Bihar and Uttar Pradesh (now Uttranchal), within India. For purposes of this paper, the 'community' identity of the Tharu can be presumed upon its ecological moorings, which even traditionally entailed a complex and fluid internal reality. Geo-political separation of the terai into three distinct units has highlighted the paradox of simultaneous processes of unification and diversification going on amongst the Tharu today.

A large volume of anthropological work, even prior to independence, remained focused on tribes and their "integration" with Hindu society (Bose 1941; Elwin, 1944; Ghurye 1959; Roy Burman, 1972; Vidyarthi 1977). This preoccupation was evident in the different classifications of tribes provided by eminent anthropologists. Roy Burman even while cautioning against making facile assumptions about tribes inevitably 'becoming' castes, himself distinguished tribes as those (*i*) incorporated in the Hindu social order, (*ii*) positively oriented towards the Hindu social order, (*iii*) negatively oriented towards the Hindu social order, and (*iv*) indifferent towards the Hindu social order (1972). Vidyarthi (1977) talked about tribes as (*i*) living in forest, (*ii*) living in rural areas, (*iii*) semi acculturated, (*iv*) acculturated, and assimilated. Elwin (1944) classified them as (*i*) purest of pure tribal groups, (*ii*) in contact with the plains but still retaining tribal mode of living, (*iii*) forming lower rungs of Hindu society, and (*iv*) fully adapted to Hindu faith and living in modern style. In a sense all these classifications accepted the ultimate transformation of tribe into caste society.

Rejecting these assimilationist assumptions, the paper argues for the frontier identity of tribal society as a distinct socio-cultural spatial formation in dynamic exchange with its neighbours. Historically, tribals as residents of the forest were by definition opposed to village-based (read 'caste') society. Indeed, any uncultivated space, whether desert or wooded (*aranya, vana*) with an absence of bounded habitation, was seen as naturally external to the village social system in India (*gramya*). Even so, ancient Hindu texts indicate that the forest way of life was not totally separate from the settled way of life Rather it existed neither totally opposed to it nor entirely subsumed by it. Caste polity sought in various ways, through the renunciatory ideals of *vanaprastha* for instance or the forest prescriptions of the *aranyakas,* to incorporate the wilderness into the *gramyaaranya, grihasta-sannyasin* orientation of Hinduism, based on the proper performance of sacrifice (Malamoud 1998). In this context, Hutton's observation (1946) that tribals have not reached the stage of accepting Brahmins as priests or of attaching any sanctity to the cow (domestic village animal) or of worshipping Hindu temples in their areas, seems to confirm tribals as forest dwellers living in dynamic polarity with the world of caste.

The particularly thorny issue of tribal relations with the mainstream will be examined now in some detail for the Tharu of West Champaran district in Bihar concentrated in "Tharuhat", an area constituted of four Community Development Blocks of Northwest Champaran-Sidhaw, Gaunaha, Mainatar and Ramnagar. Fieldwork was conducted in the Devaria, Lakshmipur, Barawakala and Bairiya settlements of the Tharu in two sessions covering the period 1999-2001. The differential claims to political identity made by the Tharu over the last sixty years or so, it will be argued, reflect in a very interesting way, the coexistence of both isolationist and integrationist tendencies amongst them. These frontier features will be further related to the Tharus' physical location in the terai, a border region lying between the foothills of the Himalayas and the Indo-Gangetic plain. All discussions of identity and exchange between the Tharu and their neighbours, will consequently be firmly rooted in the geo-political relations of the region, whether within or between India and the adjacent sovereign country of Nepal.

Historically, the Tharu were simply the inhabitants of the terai. The terai denotes the "transitional", sub-Himalayan geographic region stretching west to east. It lies across the border of Nepal and Bhutan, from Garhwal district of Uttar Pradesh (now Uttranchal) to Darrang district of Assam. The region is located between the lowerpart of the Himalayas to the north and the Gangetic plains to the south (Tucker 1998). The Tharu are found in India, in the area stretching from Nainital district of Uttaranchal to West Champaran district in Bihar and in the adjoining parts of Nepal. They are not to be found in Bengal or Assam. West Champaran has the second highest population of the community in India after Nainital district of Uttaranchal. The district of West Champaran occupies the north and west part of the state. It extends from 26º35¢ to 27º37¢ east north latitude and 83º5¢ to 84º55¢ east longitude (Singh 1985).

The terai of West Champaran is located between the foothills of Sumeshwar and Dun of Himalayas on the North and Gangetic plains in the south. The north west part of the terai in the district is known as Tharuhat or land-of-the-Tharu. The Tharuhat is an isolated area constituted of some hills but mostly forested and swampy plains, extending nearly 60 kilometers in length and 10-20 kilometers in width. The geopolitical division of the terai divided this community into three territorial units that of India and Nepal and within India, Bihar and Uttar Pradesh. Political separation has lent a divisive aspect to what was traditionally a complex, plural and fluid situation within a unified community identity. The Tharu of Champaran now have to negotiate with the labels forced upon them by the state.

First categorized as an aboriginal tribe under colonial rule, the Tharu themselves claimed a high Kshatriya status in the 1940s itself, in keeping with their common ancestry and community links with Nepal's Rana Tharu (Diwakar 1959; Kroskopff 1998). In 1951 however the independent state of India identified them as a Backward Class based on various official criteria of socio-economic deprivation.

The first Backward Classes Commission 1953 identified the groups falling under these categories excluding the scheduled castes and scheduled tribes (SCs and STs). In real terms however, anthropologists have argued, the Backward Classes are merely an administrative label for Backward Castes or Sudras falling between scheduled communities and the forward or high castes (Galanter 1984; Roy-Burman 1992; Béteille 1992).

Included with other Sudras, the Tharu agitated against their new identity, which attempted to assimilate them into the lower rungs of the local caste hierarchy. In 1972, marking the culmination of a contra-sanskritic movement amongst them, they demanded to be classified afresh as a scheduled tribe. The demand was not accepted. Instead, they were categorized as OBC (Other Backward Caste) in 1990 with the implementation of the recommendations of the second Backward Class Commission set up in 1978.

Interestingly, the different labels applied to the Tharu of Champaran, whether recognized by them or not, have remained spatially distinct and isolated from other sections of the community spread over the terai. Thus the Tharu of Uttar Pradesh are scheduled as a S.T. since 1967 (Bist 1994). The Tharu of Nepal continue as a segment of the high-caste Ranas or Kshatriya (Diwakar 1959), while the Tharu of Bihar have moved from being officially categorized as a Backward Class (within the broad framework of Hindu Sudra identity) to OBC despite their own demand for a scheduled tribe status.

Under colonial period

Under the British, isolated areas where tribals are usually to be found were specified and constituted as

Scheduled Tracts (Act of 1874) to exclude them from operation under ordinary rules (Verma 1995). The terai was one such area known as Terai Pargana. The reason for scheduling the tract, as is well documented, was to prevent tribal revolts known to have occurred in other parts of Bihar, viz. the Kol mutiny (1831) and the Santhal revolt (1855) even prior to the 1857 mutiny or the first war of Indian independence (Fürer-Haimendorf 1985; Sarkar 1995; Verma 1995; Chandra *et al.* 1998). Another reason was the growing awareness of the commercial value of the forest and its produce—teak, indigo, sugarcane—which had influenced British policy since early 19th century (McLeish 1921). The British administration recognized the people of the Scheduled Areas under different names—aboriginals, forest tribes, primitives, animists and tribal people, etc. and used these labels to denote them in the official literature such as censuses and government reports till 1941. Shifting official policy was reflected in the different labels that were adopted over time (Prasad 1998).

In 1872, the British administration started its first Census in India. In this Census the role of religion was seen as crucial and the people of India were classified into five crude categories on its basis—Aboriginal Tribes, Semi-Hindu Aboriginal, Hindus, Persons of Hindu origin not recognizing caste and Mohammedans. Under this original system the Tharu were classified as an aboriginal tribe (Nesfield 1885; Risley 1891). The Census of 1891 added occupational features to this classification. Bains, the Commissioner of Census recognized castes in India according to their traditional occupation (1891). Under the Agricultural and Pastoral Caste category the "aboriginal tribes" of the 1872 census now became "forest tribes".

In the Census of 1901, Risley classified tribal people as "animist". It was the first religion-based classification of the tribes after the initiation of secular and liberal rule under the Crown government. The same pattern was followed in the next Census of 1911. Gait, the Commissioner of Census now recognized the Tharu as "tribal-animist or people following tribal religion". Indian scholars and some selected British administrators did not accept the religion-based division and expressed disagreement over such classification of tribal people. As Tallents, the Superintendent of Census for Bihar and Orissa observed:

> the difficulty of distinguishing the religion of such persons from lower types of Hinduism has always been experienced at every census (Ghurye 1959: 2-3).

J.T. Marten, the Commissioner of Census 1921, considered the above disagreements and changed the previous criteria of classification. The Census now recorded the Tharu as "hill and forest tribe". J.H. Hutton, Commissioner of the Census 1931, retained the heading "Tribal Religion" in the report and used the term "Tribal" in distinction to Hindu, Muslim, Christian, etc., describing the communities as "primitive tribes" (Roy Burman 1994). Hutton agreed with the opinions expressed above and argued that to draw a distinguishing line between tribal religion and Hinduism was very difficult. Wherever hill or forest tribes lived in permanent and daily contact with Hindus, their religion rapidly assimilated itself to that of their neighbours. However, Hutton (1946) also accepted the differences between them and the wider society.

W.G. Lacy, the Superintendent of Census 1931 for Bihar and Orissa, described the situation thus:

> an aboriginal will adopt certain Hindu customs, he will join certain Hindu processions, he may even make certain offerings to Hindu deities and at the same time he may adhere to his old tribal beliefs and practices. It is often quite impossible to say when he has crossed the line to Hinduism. Again he will often call himself a Hindu for no better

> reason than that he believes he will thereby improve his social status. (Quoted in Ghurye 1959:4).

The Government of India Act, 1935 gave up religion based distinctions and specified the isolated people living in forests, hills and mountains as 'backward tribes'. In the census of 1941, they were simply classified as 'tribe'. The assimilationist understandings of nationalist scholars like Ghurye (1959) came to the fore after independence. In contrast to the reservations expressed by some British scholars, Ghurye had a totally integrationist view for the tribal people. According to him the inclusion of tribals into Hindu fold had always been easy:

> ... the so called Aboriginals who form the bulk of the scheduled tribes and have been designated in the censuses as "Animists" are best described as "Backward Hindus" (1959:20).

Even Sinha (1958) viewed tribe as a dimension of the little tradition that can not be understood unless it is seen in relation to the great tradition of Hinduism. Historian Nihar Ranjan Ray (1972) spoke about the coexistence of two groups of people *jana* (tribe) and *jati* (caste) in India from times immemorial with eventual incorporation of the tribes into the caste system. Some sought a way out of the dilemma by seeing the tribes as groups 'in transition' (Majumdar 1937). But for N.K. Bose (1941) the symbiosis between tribes and wider society was very clearly the 'Hindu method of tribal absorption'.

Rejecting these views, this paper agrees with Béteille (1991) that Indian ethnography cannot reduce the definition of a tribe to the problem of its changing religious and cultural identity vis-a-vis the mainstream. Way back in 1960 itself Bailey had argued for an independent political and cultural identity for the Kondh of Baderi in Orissa vis-a-vis caste society. The presence of both isolationist and integrationist tendencies amongst the Tharu is not a matter particular to them but a feature of tribal society in general which throughout history acted as an ecological and cultural 'bridge and buffer' zone via-a-vis mainstream neighbours (Roy Burman 1972). The geographic location of tribes along state borders ideally suited them for the task. In the context of the powerful Buddhist influence in the region of the Tharuhat, it would be inappropriate to use the concept of Hinduisation or Sanskritisation alone to examine the relations between the Tharu of Champaran and their neighbours. Better would be to see their 'betwixt and between' role vis-a-vis the two great religions as the structural expression of their frontier identity.

The replacement of 'frontiers' by 'borders/ boundaries' in nearly emergent nation-states has been commented upon by Embree (1977) and Giddens (1990). In India, the process we can see has rigidified very quicky in those regions where the threat to sovereignty is perceived more immediately. Thus since 1947 itself, to make an understatement, India has had a tense border situation obtaining with West Pakistan in comparison with East Pakistan. The strictest attention is paid on India's North-Western borders to all Line of Control infringements. By contrast, the boundary line demarcated on the Bangladesh side is so ambiguously drawn that it has left pockets of citizens marooned in 'enclaves' on alien territory. The political consequences of this and of 'porous' borders in general are being reflected on with some seriousness only now (Van Schendel 1998; Bagchi and Dasgupta 2002).

As against both the above, the Indo-Nepal border continued in all this period to retain its fluid, froniter aspect more or less intact. Indeed, the open border treaty in operation between India and Nepal since 1951 has come under threat only recently in the face of incidents of cross border infiltration from Pakistan via Nepal. The integrationist focus of Indian anthropology/sociology, a knee jerk reaction to the violent creation of Pakistan, an Islamic state, from within civil society itself, has tended to ignore palpable evidence of reciprocity and exchange between Hinduism and other religions. From the Nepal side, a fair number of studies testify to the cultural, particularly the Buddhist-Hindu, contours of this frontier situation in some detail (Fürer-Haimendorf 1966; 1975; Allen 1973; Bechert and Gombrich 1984). From the Indian side on the other hand, there has been a significant dearth of such work. It is to filling this lack that the paper hopes to contribute through examining the case of the Tharu of Champaran.

As inhabitants of the terai, the Tharu are neither of the hill nor the plains. Ecologically, these are relative terms. In Nepal, the terai counts as the 'plains', with the higher status communities living in the Valley and the lower hills as distinct from the remote heights occupied by the Sherpa. In India, the terai is the forested, swampy land between the Himalayan range and the Indo-Gangetic plains. The more isolated hill Bhutiyas of the Tibet region display Buddhist features more clearly just as the plains people display features that are Hindu. However like the Newari of Nepal who display both Hindu and Buddhist features, the Tharu can be said to act as a frontier between these two religious faiths. Sharing a boundary with Nepal with its continuing Hindu-Buddhist exchanges, they have been influenced by the latter as much as by Hinduism (McLeish 1983; Gellner 1993).

It is the border attributes and exchanges of the Tharu of Champaran that help us correct our conventional anthropological understandings. Community interaction and interrelation with Hindu society over a long time has not eventually resulted in the Tharu becoming Hinduised. The Tharu, it is important to note have not 'become' a caste in the local Hindu society. They have of course adopted some components of the Hindu way of life, just as local society has adopted some of theirs. Equally, they have adopted some components of the Buddhist way of life and vice-versa.

Similar kinds of frontier exchanges in the region, between Hinduism and Buddhism, have been very well brought out for the Newar of Nepal by Rosser (1966) and Gellner (1993), and for the Chetris and the Thakali of the same region by Fürer-Haimendorf (1966). McLeish, writing in 1921 gives historical evidence of this eco-cultural situation. The Hinduism introduced into the region by the Gurkha invasion of 1769, he argues, was so greatly affected by Buddhism that by the twentieth century the majority of the population of Nepal was Buddhist:

> If Brahmanism prevailed prior to the coming of Buddhism, when India cast out Buddhism, Nepal retained it. When Islam overran India it did not reach the fastnesses (sic) of Nepal. The result has been a compromise, so that a kind of Brahma-Buddhism is the state religion today (1983:122).

The Thruhat is 'betwixt and between' not just geographically but culturally. However, in the literature, it is the constant orientation towards Hindu society as an integrational order for the tribal, which presents itself in the writings on the Tharu. As early as 1891, Risley (1891) saw the religion of the Tharu as a compound of animism, nature worship and some popular elements borrowed from Hinduism. He mentioned Rikheshwar as a principal deity for worship. Today this deity is unknown throughout the Tharuhat, but the Tharu do worship Shiva, Hanuman, Satyanarayan, Kali, Durga, Brahma, and other deities of Hindu traditions. They also observe Hindu festivals-Chhat, Diwali, Holi but this catholicity is not unknown even for the Buddhists of the region such as the Newar. In Nepal, according to Gellner (1993:60) Newari Buddhism (Vajrayana) is in a sense 'assimilated' to Hinduism. Vajrayana's acceptance of the householding life as permissible to the monk (*sakya*), gives a 'caste-like mould' to its ascetic vision. Allen (1973) supports this argument. For their own part, the Tharu claim descent from the Sakya, the Buddha's lineage—a claim supported by historical fact (Fuhrer 1972). They have no indigenous Brahmins, and Kshatriyas are the elite whether as guru, priest or ruler. They pray to Buddha's wife, have *tantrik* affiliations and observe no rules of purity-pollution vis-a-vis one another. Their villages display their egalitarian pattern of co-existence, where rich and poor, high and low, live together in nucleated settlements, along common streets surrounded by kitchen gardens and agricultural lands. This is quite in contrast with caste-based village settlements.

While explaining their culture the Tharu themselves say they are positively oriented towards the Hindu social order but do not accept that they are Hindus like everyone else. In fact they make a sharp distinction between themselves and non-Tharus (*bazi*). At the level of language, the Tharu have adopted many elements of Hindi, Bhojpuri and some Nepali words. However they have their own dialect (*Tharuai*). They earn their livelihood from a variety of occupations—both agricultural and non-agricultural. But they have not become a 'caste' with any definite standing in the caste hierarchy.

The Tharu and their neighbours

Historically, the Tharu never lived in complete isolation. The movement of people from neighbouring areas into the terai started long back even before the colonial period. Whether imposed or desired, contact and interaction of the Tharu with the wider society has been a historical fact in the terai. There are clear evidences to show that the region was in contact with many other parts of India. Monolithic pillars of Mauryan dynasty have been found in the terai of Champaran. These pillars are near Bhikhna-Thoree pass and other passes along the river Gandak in the terai and give a clear evidence of interaction with the outside world. The region was also annexed by Harsha and on his death in 648 A.D., Arjuna, one of his ministers usurped the throne. Meanwhile the Chinese emperor had sent his embassy under Wang-Hieun-Tse and with the help of the Tibetans and Nepalese defeated Arjuna. Nepal, which had been integrated with Harsha's empire, regained its independence thereafter with Arjuna taking shelter in Nepal.

The terai of Champaran was used as a pilgrim and trade route between Indian centres of Buddhist pilgrimage such as Bodh Gaya and Vaishali with those in China and Nepal. Later, as the meeting point of two dominant languages and cultural regions, Nepalese and Bhojpuri, hills and plains, the densely forested and swamp-ridden terai acted as a buffer zone between the Mughal and the hill people. In 1764, the Mughal emperor had passed on Champaran with Bengal and Bihar to the East India Company (Roy Choudhary 1961). By 1767, the Champaran Tharus lay sandwiched between two major polities: the expanding Gorkhali state in Nepal and British controlled Bihar. In 1811, the Gurkha governor of Rauthat, Nepal crossed the border and acquired some part of the East India Company's domain. By 1814 however the British troops attacked and Gurkhas had to evacuate the terai. On 28 November 1815 a treaty was signed between the East India Company and the Nepalese at Sugauli in Champaran. By this treaty, the East India Company acquired the terai. The Nepalese left and the terai existed as a buffer zone. Yet, as late as the sixties, lower hill people of Nepal were migrating to the terai on account of agricultural opportunities opened up there (Krauskopff 1998).

All through the period the Tharu maintained their independent identity between these two different political and cultural zones of the hills and the plains. The distinct regions were locally controlled first by the Buddhist Newar of Nepal and the Hindu zamindars under Mughal and later by the Hindu Gurkhas of Nepal and the Hindu zamindars under the British. The kingdoms of the plains had little motivation to keep the terai region directly under their subjugaton because of the swampy terrain and low commodity value of the forest products in the existing market conditions. Even the British at first declined to exercise actual authority over the terai. Later, they realized that unless the terai was brought under their effective control, the security of the bordering areas, of Bihar and Uttar Pradesh could be endangered. Also, British planters' wanting to make their fortunes in indigo and sugar shifted to this region from Bengal in the nineteenth century after a peasant revolt there pushed them out. The region of Champaran had attracted them, because it was a productive indigo area where the planters could carry on .their business undisturbed by the politics of Calcutta climaxed by the events of 1859-62 (Mittal 1978).

Dominant Hindu zamindars had already occupied the region long back in the fifteenth century, during the Mughal period. Now under colonial rule, British planters and local zamindars acting together encouraged immigration from other parts of the district as well as from other districts of Bihar to the terai to 'settle' the area and to grow commercial crops. In early nineteenth century, forest clearing *pattas* (documents giving ownership rights) had already been giver to the Tharu, who were known to be immune to malaria and kalazar, endemic to this region (Amin 1984:29; Tucker 1998:463-4). But the Tharu lacked expertise in agriculture work leading to the forceful infiltration into Tharuhat of outsiders such as the Hindu plains people and the Oraon tribal from south Bihar.

The vast tract of the terai of Champaran was in those days thinly populated and was controlled by two zamindari estates, Bettiah Raj and Ram Nagar Raj. The indigenous, forest-dweller Tharu had very little interest in settled agriculture. It was primarily for indigo and sugarcane cultivation that outsiders were brought in. A similar process of push factors induced hundreds of

'Hindustanis' from U.P. and Bihar to go as indentured labour to the plantation economies of Trinidad, Guyana, Fiji, Mauritius, etc., in the late nineteenth century. Later, in the aftermath of the Partition, Burmese and Bangladeshi refugees were rehabilitated here just as Punjabis in the western terai of U.P. This process certainly forced the Tharu out of their relative isolation into close interaction with the wider society, just like the Munda, Oraon and Santhal in other parts of Bihar. However it also put them in a subordinate position locally. As Bose (1941) has argued, the caste based economy and its division of labour enabled it to support populations of larger size and density than the tribal economy whose material base was low. When this became precarious due to expansion of population, a tribe sought economic security through closer attachment to the wider society. This attachment was generally granted by the wider society on the condition that the newly attached group took the lowest position in it. Thus the tribal community could aspire to establishing a relationship with Hindu society but only at the lower levels.

The Tharu as Kshatriya

Bose's model can be questioned on many grounds. It is true that 'integration' of tribals with the wider society was mainly based on economic activities. However as the Tharu experience shows, bulk of the tribals became settlers, cultivators or land-less labourers in a system imposed on them from outside. The caste system hardly provided any protection against the plantation capitalist economy under zamindari. It only increased competition in these peripheral occupations. Gandhi's Satyagraha against the Tinkathiya system in Champaran provides ample evidence of this exploitation and destruction of agricultural bonds or the rural economy under capitalist agriculture. However having been pulled into the mainstream economy, many tribals did opt for dominant models of upward mobility like Sanskritization rather than opting out[1]. As mentioned earlier, the Tharu, even in the 1940's stressed their Kshatriya status before local caste Hindus. It was their identification with the high Kshatriya of Nepal, which lay behind these attempts to be accepted by caste society in independent India. As a device for mainstream acceptance this demand had gained momentum in the colonial period itself. Krauskopff (1998) gives evidence of this 'Kshatrisation' among the Rana Tharus who adopted the ethnonym of 'Rana' in the British period. In 1951 consequently the Tharu agitated against the government's decision to include them in the new state based list of underprivileged, primarily Sudra groups, collectively referred to as the Backward Classes. The Tharu opposed the first census of independent India in the same year, in which they were recognized as such. But their economic deprivation worked against them and they could not achieve their goal.

Perhaps interaction and interrelation with the settled way of life of caste Hindus, initially attracted the Tharu because it provided a decisive socio-economic framework for work and social transformation. The Tharu had already experienced a process of exploitative interaction under zamindari and so the demand for recognition of their separate identity after independence was not that strange. The associated attempt to be recognised for their royal/ Kshatriya ancestry was born out of status rather than religious motivations. Theoretically, it is possible to be Buddhist or embrace a non-Hindu form of faith and practice without being totally rejected by the Hindu society. But as the Tharu case shows Hindu society only makes room at the bottom for aspiring outsiders.

In 1950 the Tharu's demand to be classified in the census as Kshatriya stated their origin to be from the Rana of Rajasthan and Buddhist Sakya-Kshatriya of Nepal, both royal lineages. Their reference point was their relatives in U.P. and Nepal who continued as Kshatriya. The elderly talked of the Tharu's link with Rajasthan. It was during Muslim rule (13-15 century AD) under Allaudin Khilji of

Delhi Sultanate and Akbar of Mughal, according to them that they were forced to leave the Thar region of Rajasthan and migrate to the terai. Of course the British official literature does not support this at all and stresses that the terai has always been the original habitat of the Tharu (Risley 1891; Nesfield 1885). What is interesting in these statements however is the historical link made between Hindu and Buddhist Kshatriya tradition. The Sakya were lineage members of Buddha, who refuted Brahminism, but not the *jati* order. Under Buddhism it was Kshatriyas who both as rulers and monks controlled the social order (Gellner 1993).

To demonstrate their superior status, the Tharu insisted on wearing the sacred thread like other high caste Hindus. Some influential amongst them, also started taking services of Brahmins at their marriages along with the community services of the *Gajua* and *Gajuin*—sister and brother-in-law of the groom or his father's sister and brother-in-law-acting as priests (Pandey 1979). These Brahmins however remained immigrants in the terai and were never indigenous to it. The Hindu way of life was variously integrated by the Tharu without losing their own traditional customs, some of which had existed even prior to their claim to Kshatriya status. The claim furthermore was a modern claim made for the whole community as a political unit under democracy and not for any segment.[2] Largely rejected, the claim to Kshatriya identity nevertheless helped the upper strata of the Tharu community get accepted by Hindu society. At the same time they continued to remain outside caste society proper. Their forest association kept them distinct from village society (*gaon*). At the same time it did not prove adequate even for special privileges under the Constitution.

The Constitution (Scheduled Tribes) Order of 1950 included tribals in the Schedule for the first time in independent India. The Tharu were not one of them. The high concentration of tribal population in south Bihar (now Jharkhand), and the non-scheduled status of the Tharus in the neighbouring state of Uttar Pradesh[3] made Bihar state authority hesitate to include the Tharu in the schedule of tribes[4]. Bihar state had the third largest tribal population, after Madhya Pradesh and Orissa. The position continued till the creation of a new state, Jharkhand carved out from south Bihar in 2000.

Tribal population of undivided Bihar was 7.66 per cent (Census of 1991) of the total population of India. Retrospectively speaking, the Tharu of Champaran lost their bargaining power vis-a-vis the state on two counts: (*i*) They were 'tribals' but isolated in the wrong part of the state—north west, whereas it is the south which has today won full statehood for themselves, on the basis of an autonomous tribal identity, and (*ii*) They were BC but in a state where it was eventually the Backwards such as the Yadav, Koeri and Kurmi, commercially wealthier and better integrated with the upper caste society, who would gain power. Neither their head start as BC nor their later classification as OBC in the state would prove advantageous in a similar way.

The Tharu as Backward Class

The government of Bihar in free India conclusively deemed the Tharu a Backward Class—a newly created category covering many Sudra or service castes. That this was influenced by the geo-political situation in Bihar is clear from the fact that their community members in Uttar Pradesh were permitted to retain their Kshatriya dentity for fifteen years and eventually scheduled as a tribe in 1967 (Srivastava 1958; Khanna 1992). Their numerical weakness compared to the vast tribal population of Bihar certainly worked in their favour. As we have seen, the Bihar government was loath to include one more group as 'tribal' under the reserved category, given their vast concentration in the South. The appellation of Backward Class was also motivated by real politick. It linguistically avoided low caste association for the Tharu at the same time that it denied them independent community aspirations as high Kshatriya, whether Rana, Sakya or Khettri.

The first Census of independent India in 1951 did not recognize the Tharu as a scheduled tribe. Instead the state government of Bihar classified them as Backward Class (BC) in Annexure-1, despite their demand to be recognized as Kshatriya. Bihar government composed two lists of Backward Classes comprising both Hindu and Muslim caste groups, who were neither scheduled castes, nor scheduled tribes (*Adivasi*). The list of BC included mainly Sudras, last of the four-tiered Hindu *Varna* system. These groups were considered economically, educationally and socially backward in need of special governmental assistance, particularly by way of educational help. The two lists came to be known as Annexure-1 and Annexure-2. The Annexure-1 could be thought of as More Backward Classes meaning lower Shudra and Annexure-2 as Less Backward or Upper Shudra (but still in need of help) groups. Annexure-1 included 78 Hindu and Muslim castes, in which the Tharu were also included. By this classification the Tharu were categorized under lower Shudra. The Annexure-2 included only 30 castes (Blair 1980). The Tharu felt that their identification as Backward Class provided them an entry only into the lower rungs of caste society. They agitated against their new classification.

The above list of backward communities was also supported by the recommendations of the first Backward Classes Commission[5] constituted at all India level in 1953 under Kaka Kalelkar. In an effort to fulfill their responsibility towards the backward classes as laid down in the Constitution the Commission had submitted its report in 1955. It identified 2399 castes of which 837 were Most Backward Classes (Roy Burman 1992:20). In Bihar,

127 castes (again both Hindu and Muslim) were listed in the report. The Commission had recommended 28 communities of Bihar in the Schedule of Tribes. Significantly the Tharu were in that recommended list of 28 communities but the state or central government did not implement the recommendation (Prasad 1998).

In 1964, on a move by a high caste person, the Patna High court declared the state list of Backward Classes (both the Annexures) of 1951 to be unconstitutional, as it was prepared on the basis of caste rather than actual educational and social backwardness. The government of Bihar responded to this legal rejection by appointing a new Commission under Mungeri Lal in December 1971. This new Commission submitted its final report in February 1976, settling on a new list of 128 castes/communities as 'Backward', essentially the old version including an additional Christian group. In this list, 94 and 34 communities were classified as 'Most Backward Classes' (MBC) and 'Other Backward Classes' (OBC)[7] respectively (Blair 1980).

In 1978, Karpoori Thakur, the first Chief Minister from the backward communities. a barber (Nai) by caste, recommended job reservation for Backward Classes in government jobs on the basis of the recommendation of the Mungeri Lal Report. The reserved seats in government services were now twelve per cent for MBC, eight per cent for OBC with an additional 3 per cent for women of any caste and three per cent for economically backward groups, generally interpreted as the poor of the high castes (ibid). This is popularly known as the Karpoori Thakur formula (Roy Burman 1992). The class division—Forward and Backward—in Bihar never actually linked with educational and economic criteria and was exclusively based on caste division. In Bihar it was exclusively high caste or twice born Hindus—the Brahmin, Bhumihar, Rajput and Kayastha—who were socially, politically and economically powerful in the state. These high castes or 'Forwards' of the state had been far ahead of the remaining communities even during colonial period. All the zamindars were from the high castes and so were the chief Ministers (CM) till 1978, when Karpoori Thakur became CM that changes in authority forced change in the social structure of feudal Bihar. The new political class now displaced the Forwards as a dominant force in Bihar politics, right from village to Assembly.

Communities like the Tharu however remained marginalised in all these political realignments including the positive discrimination policies of the local government of Bihar as also the centre. In 1952, the Community Development Programme started by the central government, tried to achieve rural development through popular initiatives and participation of the rural population but under this scheme, the target groups remained SC and ST. Legally, in independent India, the two scheduled groups got special protection from atrocities and exploitations. They also got assistance to fight in their own interest against anyone in a court of law but the BCs were in this matter not specially provided for.

The other setback for the Tharu was the implementation of panchayati raj. In 1962, the state government introduced the concept of democratic decentralization and established the system of local self-government through village panchayats. The rules in distributing the benefits were as followed in Community Development Programme. Again, the Tharu could not properly participate in local self-government the way the scheduled communities were doing. Even the tribal Oraon who had migrated from south Bihar to work as labourers and the low castes in Champaran in the late nineteenth century were specially considered in every village panchayat but not the Tharu. In recognition of their political failure over the years, the Tharu in 1973 put out a consolidated effort to fight for ST status. The educated youth wanted this for jobs, the uneducated for financial support from the state agency and the rich Tharus for more legal/financial benefits based on state assistance.

Demand for scheduled tribe status

Anthropologically, 'tribe' identifies a social group/ cateogry, the members of which live in a common territory, have a common dialect, uniform social organization and cultural homogeneity with a common ancestor, political organization and religious pattern. It would be very difficult however to find many tribal groups in India who possess all these characteristics (Chaudhary 1992). To add to the complexity, there are historical instances when some tribal communities identified themselves with caste society in a particular period and later re-asserted their tribal identity. Today this has become a big political issue in India, where many caste groups want to be classified as scheduled tribes and not as scheduled castes because the latter is lower down in status. The "oscillation" in Tharu identity consequently, is part of a larger trend in India, which is sociologically very interesting because of the differential rate of success achieved by the groups concerned.

In the 1980s, rapid changes in the sociio-political arena around the Tharu, made them increasingly aware of their exploited identity and demands for tribal privileges intensified. The demand for ST status is in any case not uncommon in India. Today, according to tribal activist B.D. Sharma (personal communication), hundreds of claims exist with the Government of India for inclusion in the Schedule of tribes. Indeed there are many groups whether tribal or not, who have through political pressure managed to get scheduled in some states and availed educational, political, economic privileges. This has often led to local conflicts between the tribes and aspiring outsiders (Virginius Xaxa, personal communication).

In a democracy the question of absolute numbers within a state also matters. In UP we have already seen, the low overall tribal population in the state worked in favour of the Tharu. In Rajasthan on the other hand, where tribals are many, the numerical prepondencrance of the Bhil and the Meena, constituting 44.50% and 49.47% of the tribal population respectively, worked to their comparative advantage against others. Neither of these advantages was available to the Tharu community because of their political location on a frontier which scattered them as a minority in the three areas of Bihar and Uttar Pradesh in India and Nepal outside. Consequently they are identified differently as a ST in Uttar Pradesh and Uttaranchal, OBC in Bihar and high caste Hindu/Buddhist (*Savarn*) in Nepal. Other factors too have affected Tharus' decision to push for ST status. In 1971, the assembly constituency of Bagaha, which represents the Tharuhat in Champaran, was reserved for scheduled caste representation under Article 332 of the Constitution. In this constituency, the Tharu are more populous. Consequently, the state's move to reserve the constituency for the SC was provocative and led the educated and rich Tharus to push their demand. It was too much for them to accept the fact that a member from low caste Harijan group would represent their constituency. The Tharu had also been losing land to high caste as well as low caste outsiders (*Bazi*). Both these factors became an instant ground for organising and demanding to be included in the schedule of tribes.

It was only as late as 1996 that the state government, through the Governor of the State, sent the community's request for inclusion in the S.T. list to the Union Government. According to the district officials the Tharu have given strong arguments in their request to support their claim for tribal status: (*i*) that they had been recognized as a tribe during British India, (*ii*) that the first Backward Class Commission (1955) had also recognized them as a tribe and recommended their inclusion in the schedule, and (*iii*) the Tharu of Uttar Pradesh have already been included in the schedule of tribes.

The first list of scheduled tribes—the Constitution (Scheduled Tribes) Order, 1950 was based on the Census of 1931. The particular criteria considered then were: primitiveness, geographical isolation, distinctiveness of culture, shyness of contact with community at large, backwardness—socio-economic and educational, simple technological development and specific tribal language (Pathy 1992). It was the decision of the Registrar General of India not to include the Tharu in the Schedule (Roy Burman 2002).

It is interesting to see that the constitutional criteria for recognition of a tribe are more politico-legal than ecological or cultural. The Constitution itself gives no provision on the matter and allows polity to decide who is or is not to be scheduled as a tribe. Significantly, tribes in whole or in part may be scheduled as scheduled caste (Art. 341) but not vice-versa. This too reflects the assimilationist preoccupations of the Constitution.

As the constitutional notification of a scheduled caste or tribe is an instrument of polity, left open to the historical and subjective decision of the union government in consultation with individual states whether they recognize a group/community as a tribe or not. The first Backward Commission (1953) itself was quite vague, stating that the scheduled tribes lead a separate exclusive existence and were not fully assimilated in the main body of the people. It also stated that they may belong to any religion and if they were to be listed as scheduled tribes, it would be because of the kind of life led by them. This definition may also be criticized as dependent on subjective attitude of persons in authority. If structural distance from the main body of the people of the country is an inherent principle in operation, then those drawing up lists of Indian tribes may have their own in-built biases.

Time is another factor leading to vagueness. The verification of a community or group in respect of a set of criteria and eventual notification takes years to complete. The process follows lengthy procedures. The state/Governor sends the request of an aspiring group to the Union government for scheduling only after due consideration. The concerned ministry then gives the request or demand to the Registrar General of India (Census) and to the National Commission for Scheduled Castes, Scheduled Tribes. These two bodies examine the claim on the basis of a set of criteria and their recommendation is considered by the union cabinet which if it agrees decides to move a bill in this regard in the Parliament. The Parliament may constitute a select committee to evaluate the bill or directly pass it on the floor.

The Tharus as Other Backward Class and after

In the year 1990, when the Union government implemented the second Backward Classes Commission Report (Mandal Commission) the Tharu were freshly recognized as OBC in the state despite their on-going demand to be scheduled as a tribe. This provided an opportunity to the non-SC and non-ST sections of the Backwards to enter into the central services with 27 per cent reservation. In Bihar, the new scheme of reservation added only one percent as an additional quota to the 26 per cent already existing for the Backward Classes.

The concept of caste association and the benefits accruing to its membership now became more significant. A new class of beneficiaries surfaced to get benefits from the government. They consolidated and got power at the state as well as at the centre level through their own caste men in politics. However the Tharu in Champaran could not get benefits from the new political alignments because of their isolation and a low rate of education among them. They could not enter the jobs through competition with better qualified groups. They were also at a disadvantage vis-a-vis the Kurmi and Yadav and other Sudra groups like them, who had a longstanding service association with upper caste households and had over time imbibed the latter's educational and cultural values and modern, middle-class aspirations.

The Tharu have once again been marginalised as members of the OBC. The demand for ST status has consequently become the sole focus of the consolidated aspirations of the unfortunate Tharus today. Their continuing backwardness as also the terms of the constitutional provisions themselves have in a sense further isolated them by sealing the fluid boundaries that earlier existed between Tharus and non-Tharus. By giving a specific legal identity to the status of tribe, which it lacked in the past, modern polity has brought the Tharu's regional tribal consciousness to the fore at the cost of all others. Until recently a tribe did not feel part of a regional system and tribes from different regions had little to do with each other. The tribes had lived their separate lives without a sense of their common identity. The new legal and political order has changed this to some extent.

Priorities have now been reversed. The lure of the new constitutional category and its privileges, so manifestly being enjoyed by others to the west and south of them in UP and Bihar itself, forces the Tharu to maintain distinct tribal identity. And yet at the same time (unlike other regional Indian groups who have gone separatist in the North East and in Andhra) to pursue their political goals through mainstream legal procedures and precedents.

Beginning from the seventies, the Tharu have organised themselves around their demands. The educated and the rich amongst them have formed many organizations. Later only one organization, the Akhil Bhartiya Tharu Kalyan Mahasangh, which was initially registered in March 1971 as a welfare organization survived and the rest have all merged with it. The name of this oganization appears to be national, but its range of activity is limited to the Tharuhat of Champaran. Through its agency, several issues related to the community have been raised, most frequently the demand to be scheduled as a tribe.

Despite these efforts, most Tharus remain poor, working as labourers. They work either on the farms of the non-Tharus (*Bazi*) or on the land of rich Tharus. Lack of communication and their dense forest habitat continues to comparatively isolate them in the terai. The recent changes in their life have come from changing attitudes towards education and realisation of their political failure over the years to get maximum benefits from the state. Large sections of the Tharu have now started getting education. NGOs have begun many initiatives in this direction. Forces of new technological change too have entered the terai. The Tharu have availed of the new transportation facilities to get connected with the district and state headquarters. This has opened a new way for them to see the outside world. Comparing themselves with the Tharu of Uttar Pradesh, they have realized their overall deprivation. Their failure to benefit and cash in on the advantages whether of forward or backward politics in Bihar has come to them. It is surely paradoxical, one can conclude, that despite their high ancestry as Kshatriya and their state granted privileges as BC/OBC, the Tharu of Champaran are left today craving for a tribal identity—an identity they themselves had initially rejected in independent India[6].

NOTES

1. Srinivas' observation (1996) that communities lower down the rung tend to emulate the lifestyle of dominant castes of

the region, conforms to all India varna rather than local jati models. By 1960s, Sanskritization as a process had lost its momentum, but according to Roy Burman (1992) many tribals are still adopting the Hindu way of life in this way.

2. The community is divided among different *Kuris*, e.g. Rana, Routar, Bantar, Dhangaura, Kochila, Gadhwali, etc. Generally the *Kuri* is named after occupation or the group's place of origin. Earlier inter-*Kuri* marriages were not allowed, now they are well accepted.

3. In U.P., the Tharu were not scheduled as a tribe earlier for different reasons. It was the state policy under G.B. Pant, first Chief Minister of Uttar Pradesh (1951), not to recognize any tribe in the state. He wanted to avoid the politics of tribalism. Their later request to be classified as a scheduled tribe was however granted in 1967 because their small numbers did not affect state politics in any significant way. The privileges flowing from ST status as also the economic opportunities opened up by the aggressive cultivation of the western terai under the post 1947 refugee resettlement programs (Montgomery 1991), helped U.P. Tharus achieve a much more 'developed' status than their Bihar brethren. For that very reason however, they have become assimilated in the mainstream and lost their singular identity.

4. Scheduling of a community as a tribe is decided upon by the centre after consultation with the state (Art. 342).

5. Article 340 of the Indian Constitution writes about appointment of a Commission to investigate the conditions of socially and educationally backward classes.

6. The Tharu have been included in the list of scheduled tribes for Bihar vide notification in the Gazette of India, January 8, 2003, pp. 4-5.

REFERENCES

Allen, N.R.

1973 'Buddhism without monks: The Vajrayana religion of the Newars of the Kathmandu Valley', *South Asia*, 2.

Amin, S.

1984 *Sugarcane and Sugar in Gorakhpur: An Inquiry into Peasant Production for Capitalist Enterprise in Colonial India.* Delhi: Oxford University Press.

Bagchi, J., and S. Dasgupta

2002 'Porous borders divided selves', *Seminar,* 510.

Bailey, F.G.

1960 *Tribe, Caste and Nation: A Study of Political Activity and Political Change in Highland Orissa.* Manchester: Manchester University Press.

Bains J. A.

1891 *The Census of India Report.*

Bechert, H. and R.F. Gombrich (eds.)

1984 *The World of Buddhism: Buddhist Monks and Nuns in Society and Culture.* London: Thames and Hudson.

Béteille, A.

1991 *Society and Politics in India: Essays in a Comparative Perspective.* London: The Athlone Press.

1992 *The Backward Classes in Contemporary India.* Delhi: Oxford University Press.

Bist, B.S.

1994 *Tribes of India, Nepal, Tibet Borderland: A Study of Cultural Transformation.* New Delhi: Gyan Publishing House.

Blair, H.W.

1980 'Rising *kulaks* and Backward Classes in Bihar: Social change in the late 1970s', *Economic and Political Weekly,* XV:2.

Bose, N.K.

1975 *The Structure of Hindu Society* (1st edition 1941). Translated from Bengali by A. Béteille. Delhi: Orient Longman.

Chandra B. *et. al.*,

1998 *India's Struggle for Independence*. New Delhi: Penguin Book.

Chaudhary, B.

1992 *Tribal Transformation in India,* Volume III: *Ethno-Politics and Identity Crisis*. Delhi: Inter India Publication.

Das, A.N.

1984 'Class in itself, caste for itself: Social articulation in Bihar'. *Economic and Political Weekly,* Vol. XIV, No. 37.

1992 *The Republic of Bihar.* New Delhi: Penguin books.

Diwakar, R.R.

1959 *Bihar Through the Ages*. Bombay: Orient Longman.

Elwin, V.

1944 *The Aboriginals*. Bombay: Oxford University Press.

Embee, A.T.

1977 'Frontiers into boundaries: From traditional to the modern state'. In Richard G. Fox (ed.), *Realm and Region in Traditional India*. New Delhi: Vikas.

Fuhrer, A.

1972 *Antiquities of the Buddha's Birth Place in the Nepal Terai*. Delhi: Indological Book House.

Fürer-Haimendorf, C. von

1966 *Caste and Kin in Nepal, India and Ceylon: Anthropological Studies in Hindu-Buddhist Contact Zones*. Bombay: Asia Publishing House.

1975 *Anthropology of Nepal*. Warminister: Aris and Phillips.

1985 *Tribes of India: The Struggle for Survival.* Delhi: Oxford University Press.

Galanter, M.

1984 *Competing Equalities: Law and the Backward Classes in India,* Delhi: Oxford University Press.

Gellner, David N.

1993 *Monk, Householder and Tantric Priest: Newar Buddhism and its Hierarchy of Ritual.* Cambridge: Cambridge University Press.

Ghurye, G.S.

1963 *The Scheduled Tribes* (1st edition 1959:) Bombay: Popular Prakashan.

Giddens, A.

1990 *The Consequences of Modernity.* Palo Alto, Ca: Standford University Press.

Government of India

1951 *Census of India.* Delhi: Publications Division.

1961 *Census of India.* Delhi: Publications Division.

1981 *Census of India.* Delhi: Publications Division.

1991 *Census of India,* (as on 1st September 1991). New Delhi: Ministry of Law and Justice.

Hutton, J.H.

1946 *Caste in India,* Cambridge: Cambridge University Press.

Khanna, D.P.S. (ed.)

1992 *Glimpses of Indian Tribal Life.* New Delhi: Sarita Book House.

Kraskopff, G.

1998 *The Anthropology of the Tharus: An Annotated Bibliography,* http://www.macalstr.edu.

Majumdar, D.N.

1937 *Tribe in Transition: A Study in Culture Patterns*. London: Longman Green & Co.

Malamoud, C.

1998 'Village and forest in the ideology of Brahmanic India', In C. Malamoud (ed.) *Cooking the World: Ritual and Thought in Ancient India*. Translated by David White. Delhi: Oxford University Press.

McLeish, A.

1983 *The Frontier People of India* (First edition 1921). Delhi: Mittal Publication.

Mittal, S.K.

1978 *Peasant Uprising and Mahatma Gandhi in North Bihar*. Meerut: Anu Prakashan.

Montgomery, R.H.

1991 'From cattle to cane: The economic and social transformation of a tarai village. North India'. Unpublished Ph.D. thesis. Cambridge University, Cambridge.

Nesfield, J.

1885 'Tribes and Castes in India', *Calcutta Review*, January, referred in *Gazetteer* of *Champaran*.

Pandey, T.N.

1979 'The anthropologist-informant relationship: The Navajo and Zuni in America and the Tharu in India.' In M.N. Srinivas, A.M. Shah and E.A. Ramaswamy (eds.), *The Fieldworker and the Field*. Delhi: Oxford University Press.

Pathy, J.

1992 'The idea of tribe and the Indian scene.' In B. Chaudhary (ed.) *Tribal Transformation in India*, Volume III: *Ethno-Politics and Identity Crisis*. Delhi: Inter India Publications.

Prasad, D.

1998 *Smarika: Tharus Mahotsava Bagaha.* Motihari: Kamla Press.

Ray, N.R.

1972 'Introductory address'. In K.S. Singh (ed.) *Tribal Situation in India.* Shimla: Indian Institute of Advanced Studies.

Risley, H.

1891 *Tribes and Castes in Bengal,* Vol. 2. Calcutta: Firma, K.L. Mukhopadhay.

1901 *Census of India Report.*

Rosser, C.

1966 'Social mobility in the Newar caste system'. In C. von Fürer-Haimendorf (ed.) *Caste and Kin in Nepal India and Ceylon: Anthropological Studies in Hindu-Buddhist Contact Zones.* Bombay: Asia Publishing House.

Roy Burman, B.K.

1972 'Tribal demography: A preliminary appraisal'. In K.S. Singh (ed.) *Tribal Situation in India.* Shimla: Indian Institute of Advanced Studies.

1992 *Beyond Mandal and After: Backward Classes in Perspective.* New Delhi: Mittal Publications.

Roy Choudhary, P.C.

1961 *Bihar District Gazetteer: Champaran.* Patna: Government of Bihar.

Schwartzberg, J.E. *et.al.*

1978 *A Historical Atlas of South Asia.* Chicago: The University of Chicago Press.

Sherrings, M.A.

1974 *Hindu Tribes and Castes* Volume-I. Cosmo Publication. Delhi.

Shukla, P.K.

1994 'The Tharus of Bihar: A historical and anthropological study', *Proceedings of Indian History Congress*, Aligarh.

Singh, K.S.

1985 'A Tribe in Transition with Special Reference to the Tharus of West Champaran'. Unpublished Ph.D. thesis, Gorakhpur University, Gorakhpur.

Sinha, S.C.

1958 'Tribal culture of India as a dimension of little tradition in the study of Indian civilization: A preliminary statement,' *Journal of American Folklore*, 71.

Srinivas, M.N.

1966 *Social Change in Modern India*, Bombay: Allied Publishers.

Srivastava, S.K.

1958 *The Tharus: A Study in Cultural Dynamics*, Agra: Agra University Press.

Tucker, R.

1998 'Non-timber forest product policy in the Western Himalayas in the British rule', In R.H. Grove, V. Damodaran & S. Sangwan (eds.) *Nature and the Orient*. Delhi: Oxford University Press.

Van Schendel, W.

1998 'Where smuggling is illegal, *Calcutta Online, 12:354. www.netguruindia.com/news/apr98%5cn040498.html.*

Verma R.C.

1995 *Indian Tribes Through the Ages*. New Delhi: Publications Division (GOI).

Vidyarthi, L.P. and B.K. Rai

1977 *The Tribal Culture of India.* Delhi: Concept Publishing Co.

8

The New Panchayats in Tribal Areas, Potential and Prospects

Bhupinder Singh

There are accounts which describe the existence and functioning of panchayats in India in the olden days. Metcalfe called them 'little republics', the way they conducted the affairs of local, mainly village communities. According to him, the existence of these village communities, each one forming a separate little state in itself, has contributed more than any other cause to the preservation of the people of India and these have lasted where nothing else lasts. In the context of limited out-reach of numerous feudatory states dotting the land all over, as also the limited sanction of any hegemonic central authority, the local bodies held sway. It is possible at this distance of time to glorify and idealise them as models. The bright side of the system was that the door-step administration could not avoid being diaphanous, attracting approbation or opprobrium. But its flip side, to an extent reflecting the characater of the extant society is said to have been generally, its feudal-casteist proclivities which determined its conduct. We may recall the trenchant observation in the Constituent Assembly of B.R. Ambedkar who said that the old panchayats were "a sink of localism, a,den of ignorance, narrow mindedness and communalism".

He was glad that the draft constitution had discarded the village as a unit.

Our purpose here is neither to extol the good work done by these time-honoured pervasive institutions nor to denigrate them for the ills besetting them. We need to look at them straight, untrammeled by the prisms of pride and prejudice and to evaluate their newly constitutionally mandated role. The objectivity acquires salience when we consider the bodies managing the village and local affairs in tribal areas. The reason is simple. Broadly speaking, tribal societies, relatively isolated from the plains peoples, have been much less stratified and, almost free from the shackles of caste system. It would not be erroneous to maintain that an enviable feature of these societies has been their more or less egalitarian character. Consequently, the bodies which have discharged local responsibilities in tribal areas have hardly suffered from the afore-mentioned ills, though they might have been prone to other human frailties telling upon the principles of good governance and justice. But let it not be imagined that there was lack of organization and administration in tribal areas, considered so backward and so poorly connected with the outside world. The fact is that the tribal societies devised their own systems of management extending to social, economic, political, cultural, religious, etc., spheres through a comity of office-bearers (virtually specialists in their own way) and a small hierarchy of institutions. Mention may be made of village councils and regional councils of which we have evidence among a number of tribal societies like the Muria, Munda, Santal, Saora. Studies of governance have also revealed rough distribution of responsibilities and assignment of accountability. The assessment should be made in the context of tribal milieu and adequacy or inadequacy should be adjudged by the yardstick of each community's ethos and requirements. It may fall short of expectations, as can happen elsewhere, but may still represent the art of the possible. What is germane in our present context, is that, the attempts at pitch-forking in the tribal areas of the new panchayat institutions of the 73rd and 74th Constitutional amendments need to be appreciated in this background.

The PESA Act 1996

Recognising the distinctiveness of the socio-cultural milieu of areas in the country predominantly inhabited by tribal people, Article 243 in Part IX of the Constitution, inserted consequent on passage of the 73rd amendment relating to panchayats incorporated clause M (4) (b) to the effect that Parliament may, by law, extend its provisions to the Scheduled Areas and tribal areas, subject to such exceptions and modifications as may be specified in such law. The Scheduled Areas are underdeveloped, backward, compact tracts inhabited predominantly by scheduled tribe people and notified as such by the President of India, as per Para 6 of the Fifth Schedule of the Constitution. Scheduled Areas have been notified in the states of Andhra Pradesh, Chhattisgarh, Gujarat, Himachal Pradesh, Jharkhand, Madhya Pradesh, Orissa, Rajasthan and Maharashtra. The use of the phrase, 'tribal areas' in the aforesaid clause is also specific. It refers to some preponderantly tribal districts in the north-east, viz., the North Cachar Hills and Karbi Anglong districts in Assam; Khasi, Jaintia and Garo districts in Meghalaya; Chakma, Mara and Lai distsricts in Mizoram and Tripura Tribal Areas district in Tripura. These districts are Sixth Schedule districts.

In consequence of the provisions of clause M (4) (b) of Article 243, in 1994 the Government of India appointed a committee of Members of Parliament and experts headed by D.S. Bhuria to make recommendations on extension of the provisions of the 73rd and 74th Constitutional Amendments to the Scheduled Areas. The Bhuria

Committee submitted its report in 1995. The present writer had the privilege of playing a major role in drafting the report. Broadly endorsing its recommendations, the Parliament passed The Provisions of the Panchayats (Extension to the Scheduled Areas) Act 1996 (PESA). Containing guidelines, this act calls upon the state legislatures to ensure that in Scheduled Areas, the panchayats at the appropriate level and gram sabhas are endowed, inter alia, specifically with

(i) the power to enforce prohibition or to regulate or restrict the sale and consumption of any intoxicant.

(ii) ownership of minor forest produce (MFP).

(iii) the power to prevent alienation of land in Scheduled Areas and to restore unlawfully alienated tribal land.

(iv) the power to manage village markets.

(v) the power to exercise control over money-lending to scheduled tribes.

(vi) the power to exercise control over institutions and functionaries in all social sectors.

(vii) the power of control over local plans and resources for such plans including the tribal sub-plan and certification of utilization of such funds.

To cap it all, PESA calls for state legislations endowing:

> Panchayats with powers and authority as may be necessary to enable them to function as institutions of self-government and containing safeguards to ensure that Panchayats at the higher level do not assume the powers and authority of any Panchayat at the lower level or of the *Gram Sabha*.

One may venture to describe the total design as a *magna carta* of democratic empowerment of the lower rungs of federal representative hierarchy.

The role that PESA Act cuts out for gram sabhas deserves some attention. Article 243 defines 'Gram Sabha' as a body consisting of persons registered in the electoral rolls relating to a village within the area of panchayat at the village level. Article 243A lays down that a gram sabha may exercise such powers and perform such functions at the village level as the legislature of a state may, by law, provide. For Scheduled Areas, that generally have a relatively lower density of population living in small scattered hamlets, the PESA clarified that a village shall ordinarily consist of a habitation or a group of habitations or a hamlet or a group of hamlets comprising a community, and managing its affairs in accordance with traditions and customs. Further, that, every village shall have a gram sabha consisting of persons whose names are included in the electoral rolls for the panchayat at the village level. This means that there could be more than one gram sabha in a village panchayat. We may juxtapose this inference with the powers and functions that PESA would have state legislatures conferred on a gram sabha, viz.

(i) safeguarding and preservation of the traditions and customs of the people, their cultural identity, community resources and customary mode of dispute resolution.

(ii) approval of plans, programmes and projects for social and economic development before such plans, programmes and projects are taken up for implementation by the panchayat at the village level.

(iii) responsibility for identification or selection of beneficiaries under poverty alleviation and other programmes.

(iv) certification of utilization of funds by village panchayat for plans, programmes and projects referred to in (ii) above.

(v) prior consultation with it, before land acquisition and before resettlement or rehabilitation of oustees.

(vi) planning and management of minor water bodies.

(vii) its prior recommendation for grant of prospecting license or mining lease for minor minerals.

(viii) its prior recommendations for grant of concession for exploitation of minor minerals by auction.

Thus, the gram sabha occupies the pride of place in the panchayat schema. All taken together, the idea of tribal empowerment inheres through the district panchayat, intermediate panchayat, gram panchayat down to the very grass-root, viz., the gram sabha. It is, indeed, a revolutionary instrument. Instances of the exercise of the new powers by some gram sabhas reveal the transformation they are likely to bring about. In Andhra Pradesh, some gram sabhas successfully thwarted plans for illegally converting forest into agricultural land. In the Bastar district of Chhattisgarh, some gram sabhas stood up and opposed establishment of a steel plant since it involved take-over of their land, which is their mainstay, and were not sure of alternative livelihood. If gram sabhas assert their powers, they would emerge as a major force to reckon with.

However, the 73rd and 74th Constitutional amendments and PESA Act 1996 cannot, *ipso facto,* confer empowerment. In the first instance, the realization that the modern panchayat bodies have not been, in recent times, the result of gradual and conscious evolution from below but have been the creatures of national legislation, should enable us to appreciate that exogenous structural changes rather than conceptual and attitudinal internalization have placed them in position. We witness no prolonged labour pains. Secondly, in the play of political games, those entrenched in the power echelons, for example the state legislators, generally balk at enroachment by the panchayats on their power, patronage and position, simultaneously posing on stage as champions of people's empowerment. The two trends have been manifest in the delay and character of enactments of the state legislatures. The degree of genuine autonomy vested is the issue. Mere administrative decentralization can mean only extension of central authority to lower levels. Devoid of political and financial content, it might amount not merely to withholding of lower level empowerment but even to accretion in centralization, whereas the real issue is non-centralization.

Some factors and impediments

There are some impediments to the functioning of the panchayats in the Scheduled Areas. The crux, however, is that the PESA embodies guidelines and it calls upon the state legislatures to 'endow Panchayats with powers and authority' and build in:

> safeguards to ensure that Panchayats at the higher level do not assume the powers and authority of any Panchayat at the lower level or of the Gram Sabha [section 4(n)].

In fact, it enjoins that the legislature of a state shall not make any law under Part IX of the Constitution which is inconsistent with the features it describes in clauses (a) to (d). Thus, the responsibility of creating assonance of state legal enactments with the PESA lies with the state legislatures. When we examine some of them, we find that they do not echo the PESA in letter and spirit. This is evident from comparisons made in Table 1 between the PESA and the relevant laws of Orissa, Gujarat and Madhya Pradesh:

Taking the Madhya Pradesh law, there were high expectations from it. On scrutinizing it, a number of deviations from the central law may be discerned. The provisions in the central law, that prior consultation with the gram sabha and panchayat at the appropriate level is required before acquisition of the land and resettlement of project affected persons [section 4(i)], that prior recommendation of the gram sabha is mandatory before grant of prospecting license or mining lease for minor minerals and for exploitation of minor minerals [section 4(k) and (1)], that ownership of MFP vests in the gram sabha and the panchayat at the appropriate level [section 4 (m) (ii)], that the state legislature should endeavour to follow the pattern of the Sixth Schedule while designing administrative arrangements in the panchayats at the district level in the Scheduled Areas [section 4(n)], that inconsistencies between the central act and other state laws relating to panchayats should be removed within one year [section 5] do not find place in the Madhya Pradesh law, and there are important deviations.

In the Orissa law, it is clear that its focus is on the zilla panchayat, called zilla parishad, while the PESA focuses on gram sabha.

The Gujarat Act defaults, among other items, on the question of ownership of minor forest produce.

The Andhra Pradesh Panchayat Raj Act 1994 amended in 1998 with a view to bringing it in tune with the provisions of central law in application to the Schedules Areas, has some deviations. In the first instance, while section 4(d) of PESA confers competence on a gram sabha to safeguard and preserve the traditions and customs of the people, their cultural identity, community resources and the customary mode of dispute resolution, the Andhra Pradesh law qualifies it to apply "without detriment to any law for time being in force". Secondly, in section 4(j), PESA entrusts planning and management of minor water bodies in the Scheduled Areas to panchayats at the appropriate level; the Andhra act qualifies this planning and management "in such manner, as may be prescribed". Thirdly, the Andhra law omits conferment of powers like ownership of MFP, as mentioned in section 4(m) of PESA.

West Bengal has no Scheduled Area, but the West Bengal Gram Panchayat Act 1973, as amended from time to time, the latest amendment being of July 2003, is elaborate. It is interesting to note that each of the three-tier panchayat consists of executive bodies, viz., Gram Panchayat, Panchayat Samiti and Zilla Parishad, as well as corresponding deliberative body called Gram Sansad, Block Sansad and Zilla Sansad respectively. The local MPs, MLAs and MLCs are members of Panchayat Samitis as well as Zilla Parishads. The number of members at each tier of the panchayat system is large. The powers, duties and functions of the different panchayat tiers are wide ranging. Generally, a block and a panchayat are conceived to be development-oriented bodies, but the West Bengal law goes further and empowers them under section 133 even to levy tolls, taxes and fees, etc.

For the state laws to be operative, the requirement of a set of rules under the state act voted by the legislature is a *sine qua non*. This condition remains to be fulfilled in many cases. For instance, the states of Jharkhand, Andhra Pradesh and Himachal Pradesh have yet to frame rules and regulations to operationalise the state laws. Till that is done, PESA remains inoperative.

Further, only the actual operation on the ground of the law and rules thereunder can be expected to exhibit the degree of congruence or daylight any gaps or differences or discrepancies between the prevalent traditional practices and the laws, the grey areas between the practical requirements and available provisions in the laws. For instance, grey areas may be said to exist even in PESA: Section 4(a) calls for state legislation that should be in tune with the traditional management practices of community resources. The questions arise: Which specific items are covered by the term community resources? Are the water bodies covered? Who (the state or the panchayat) commands ownership of the community resources? Is it not necessary for the local people, and specifically the tribal people, to continue to have a sense of ownership over the different common property and resource items like common land, village forest, drinking water sources, small irrigation sources, rather than push these items into the eminent domain with remote and indifferent maintenance regimes by unconcerned officials?

A fourth important factor is that incompatibilities between the provisions of PESA and other extant laws are manifest. In terms of section 4(i) of PESA, a gram sabha or the panchayats at the appropriate level has to be consulted before making acquisition of land and before resettlement or rehabilitation of displaced persons. Since no such provision exists in the Land Acquisition Act 1894, which is a colonial hang-over, its amendment becomes necessary. To give another instance, PESA confers ownership of minor forest produce on gram sabhas and panchayats under section 4(m)(ii), but the Indian Forest Act 1927 implicitly and, perhaps, even explicitly vests the entire range of forest produce, whether major or minor, in the state, meaning thereby the forest department. The revenue, excise, irrigation, markets, forest law and regulation regimes, antedating PESA thrusts, call for removal of inconsistencies. An argument advanced is that like the Indian Forest Act 1927 there are other special laws and, as per court rulings, the special laws over-ride general laws.

In this view of the matter, PESA is regarded as a general law to be subordinated to a special law. But this argument ignores the fact that since the PESA deals with specific matters confined to one segment of the population, viz., the scheduled tribes, it also has to be categorized as a special law. In any event, since the central law is imbued with certain well-defined conceptual nuances, the need for a broad congruence between it and state laws mus be recognized.

Article 243E prescribes a life of five years for a panchayat, the maximum period of a break on dissolution or otherwise being six months. In other words, an elected panchayat is a body in perpetuity. For the purpose of elections to the panchayats, a state election commission has been prescribed in Article 243K. But elections have not been held in some states, even after the coming into force of the 73rd Constitutional Amendment incorporating Article 243. For instance, in Jharkhand, elections have not been held so far; the last elections were held in Bihar in 1978. Even the constitutional provisions and PESA have failed to move the authorities to hold elections. The lack of a formal status in such circumstances is a big handicap in the ability of gram sabhas and panchayats to conduct themselves effectively, particularly in putting programmes through as well as in dealing with other organizations.

The phenomenon of growth and multiplicity of parallel committees, some of them having formal backing like *van suraksha samitis,* joint forest management committees, water users' groups, water-shed groups, ayacut committees, women's groups functioning independently may be noted. While some of these groups and committees have been acquitting themselves well and rendering useful service, the over-all effect of the existence of manifold 'parallel committees' in the panchayats context has to be assessed carefully. Their functioning independent of the panchayat structure may tend to negate a coordinated approach and integral perspective. They may not have a symbiotic relationship with panchayats, as has been the case so far with official agencies like Integrated Tribal Development Project/Integrated Tribal Development Authority. It is desirable to evolve rational and effective network, curtailing multiplicity.

A brief sketch of the West Bengal Panchayat Act has been given earlier. In general, the question of ensconcing MLAs and MPs in the tiered panchayat structure in the Scheduled Areas has been debatable. While their presence in these bodies may contribute, in some measure, to coordination with and upto state and national legislatures, it may be inhibiting and unnerving to the simple, inexperienced and, may be, unlettered *panchas,* particularly women, *dalit* and tribal. It may also accentuate the generally held perception of local self-government bodies being little subsidiaries of the mammoth state. The effort, on the contrary, should be to construct citadels of people's empowerment where the voice and sway of the common man, the woman, *dalit* and tribal, reverberate in the chambers of these institutions and corridors of history. To this end, a hierarchical ladder may be contemplated. That is to say nominated or elected members of a gram sabha as decided by the gram sabha, may constitute a gram panchayat. Sarpanches of gram panchayats may, among others, sit in the panchayat samiti at the intermediate tier. Chairpersons of panchayat samitis in a district should comprise the core of a zilla parishad. The representative relay-ladder makes for accountability and synergy, generating at each level impulses that should traverse through and up to the highest rung of the federal hierarchy on the one hand and absorb and assimilate ideas navigating downwards from the national and state levels, on the other. The osmosis is likely not only to harmonise the working of the representative federal institutions for socio-economic development but also to weld them in a socio-political frame for nation-building.

One flaw prevents rail-roading panchayats fully, seemingly on account of lack of appreciation. That is lack of a definitive inter-face between the panchayats i.e. the people's deliberative and decision-making bodies on the one hand and the delivery system i.e. the techno-administrative official executing agencies on the other. While, for good or bad, some relationships subsist among the legislature, political executive and bureaucratic executive at the state and central tiers, the need for putting in place an appropriate relationship to ensure a performing apparatus for panchayats has not attracted enough attention. Construction of a grand arch with the humble central key-stone missing cannot but be an exercise in futility. The Bhuria Committee had worked it out for the Scheduled Areas, as the annexures A to D to its report (1995) will show. Based thereon, PESA provided for control of the gram sabha and panchayats "over institutions and functionaries in all social sectors" [section 4(m)(vi)]. Undoubtedly, full-scale tie-ups have to be unfolded and binary (deliberative and delivery) systems secured in tandem with each other. But in doing so, it has to be ensured that no staff should be dumped on them as would even remotely be suspected to lack full loyalty to the panchayats, and more than that an empathy for the tribals. We have the experience of the Autonomous District Councils in Assam to which some state government staff has been seconded. The complaint of the Karbi Anglong Council has been that such staff tends more often to look beyond their shoulders towards the state headquarters.

The Westminister political system adopted in India has spelt multi-party system, in evidence both at the national and state levels. The model has already made inroads at the district and infra-district tiers in the non-tribal areas. Fortunately, in a few tribal areas the traditional village and regional organizations still play a role. In Nagaland, for instance, the village councils and village development boards have been recognized by the state government for their functions. In Meghalaya, the Nokmas, Dolois and Syiems hold sway still, though the traditional set-up has come in for attrition from the present-day political processes. In the considered opinion of not a few authorities of the north-east, the elective panchayat system may not be workable in some tribal regions. In other states of India also, some, traditional tribal organizations still minister to the tribal communities. The Munda-Manki system in Jharkhand is a well-known example. The hegemony of dominant sections in a village community perpetuating itself in some form or other is a negative factor to be wary of. However, it seems that particularly the younger elements of some tribal societies are being swept by the tidal wave of the elective panchayat system notwithstanding the evidence of traditional socio-political tribal organizations. It seems the merits and demerits of the modern elective system and the traditional consensual system have not been debated at length. More specifically, the tribal societies need to understand thoroughly the pros and cons of both. They should be given the option of casting the die. They might also consider blending such beneficial elements of the two as may be feasible. The aim, as I see it, should be to avoid the feudal trappings of the old modes and the corrosive divisions of the current political factionalism. As the Constitution Review Commission (2002) has recommended, positive democratic elements like gender justice and universal adult franchise should be built into these institutions to make them broader-based.

Finance

Having observed during the last nearly five decades the working of the panchayats as they have been, it appears that if, for a moment, we overlook other aspects, one which is among the prominent, is that they have been hamstrung by lack of finances in executing development works. Based on experience, the situation may be explained to have generally arisen on account of two causes. One, that the panchayats have not made enough exertions to collect revenues to which the laws and rules may entitle them to. Secondly, that they have not been recipient of adequate finances from the government. Inadequacy from both the sources has largely handicapped them. Article 243 mandates creation of state finance commissions for devolution of finances. The essential condition is that these commissions should not only exist and should operate effectively and equitably in consonance with the spirit of Part IX of the Constitution but funds should actually reach the panchayat bodies. The demand that the centre should fund the zilla panchayats directly instead of channeling finances through the state governments, as is currently being done for the District Rural Development Authorities has been growing. If and when conceded, it should be accompanied by a caveat that the zilla panchayat should concomitantly devolve the funds on the panchayat samitis and lower bodies on the basis of equitable formula or formulae within prescribed periods. Recently, the Prime Minister has assured that the government would introduce an amendment bill in the Parliament for giving financial powers to panchayats. Should that happen, along with concretization of other reformative measures in the political and administrative fields envisaged in the Eleventh Schedule and elsewhere, the bottom-up methodology should translate into reality.

The sixth schedule pattern

In their report, the Bhuria Committee made a significant observation when it said:

> The Sixth Schedule confers powers of legislation and administration of justice on the district councils apart from the executive, developmental and financial responsibilities. We note that the Panchayats and Municipalities of the 73rd and 74th Amendment Acts have been entrusted with such wide-ranging responsibilities. We are of the view

> that we should adopt for districts in Scheduled Areas and Tribal Areas, the Sixth Schedule format but expand it to include subjects that are indicated in the two Acts. Further, that the village community, that is at the level of Gram Sabha, should have the responsibility of safeguarding the rights of tribals in matters relating to land, water, forest, minor forest produce, etc. They should be vested with the power to regulate and use community land, forest (other than reserve forest), water, air and other natural resources, local schools, dispensaries, roads, ferries, markets, etc. Government servants serving in the respective Panchayats should be under their control. The right to mineral leases should be pre-empted in favour of the community. (1995)

Based broadly on the recommendations of the Bhuria Committee report, PESA laid down guidelines for formulation of laws to be passed by the concerned state legislatures. I have mentioned in an earlier part of the paper some salient features of the guidelines. One which I reserved for this part needs to be reproduced from its section 4:

> The State Legislature shall endeavour to follow the pattern of the Sixth Schedule to the Constitution while designing the administrative arrangements in the Panchayats at district level in the Scheduled Areas.

The reason why the Bhuria Committee found it necessary to advert to the Sixth Schedule district administrative pattern, that is that of autonomous district councils, and PESA incorporated the recommendation in it, is that the Sixth Schedule is more or less a charter of self-management. Its salient points may be summarized:

(a) It entrusts considerable legislative, administrative, financial and developmental power to a district-level elected body, i.e. the

autonomous district council (ADC) comprising largely elected ST members and a few nominated members.

(b) It enables retention of the traditional mode of justice at the lower tiers and modern legal system for heinous crimes at higher level.

(c) It allows the ADCs to regulate social customs, inheritance of property, marriage and divorce, appointment or succession of chiefs or headmen.

(d) Applicability in the concerned districts of certain acts of the state legislatures of Assam, Mizoram and Tripura has been qualified in respect of subjects falling within the legislative jurisdiction of ADCs. Similarly, even enactments of the Parliament have been made restrictive in certain circumstances.

(e) A separate fund called a district fund has been authorized for each of the Sixth Schedule districts in the north-east and, theoretically, the ADCs have autonomy in budgetary matters.

The Sixth Schedule has its strong points and its weaknesses. This is not the place for a critique thereof. One observation is relevant, however. A strong elected or nominated representative institutional infrastructure supporting the ADCs from below has not been embodied in it. Such traditional institutions as have been extant do uphold it but seemingly the support is not uniformly adequate. Nevertheless, on the whole, the Sixth Schedule represented an innovative constitutional device which could, with certain reforms and requisite representative underpinning infrastructure, become a vigorous vehicle of continuity and change in the nine districts of the north-east region, but which could also be thought of for extension to the tribal districts in central India with beneficial consequences.

Training of panchas

The PESA places political and administrative power in the hands of the people, that is tribals. The power extends to formulation of programmes and schemes and exercise of decision-making functions. In doing so, it implicitly takes cognizance of the capabilities and competence of the tribal people to manage their affairs. But it cannot be gain-said that the traditional environment in which their faculties developed and evolved were different from today's world. Their competence related to fields of specific contemporaneous tribal concerns in their own limited universe. We may note the physical isolation till lately of the tribal communities, leading to the exiguity of social, economic and political inter-face with the non-tribal systems. With the expansion of tribal-nontribal communications and inter-course, particularly after independence, the tribal communities have been led to embark on momentous but unfamiliar courses. The exposure and inter-action have obliged traversal of uncharted terrains and inculcation of new ideas, insights and skills. The halting quasi-assimilation exhibited by many tribal communities indicates on the one hand the odds confronting them and, on the other, the protracted nature of the process. While some communities have shown relatively higher degree of adaptability and acculturability, a number of these have not felt equal to grappling with external agencies, particularly the sprawling network of oppressive and exploitative bureaucracy. They have been under severe handicap in dealing with its members. The stresses under which they live is apparent in almost all the communities, but markedly so in smaller communities like the Birhor, Saora and scheduled tribes of Andaman and Nicobar groups. In accordance with the recommendations of the Bhuria Committee, PESA directs that a state legislature should ensure that in the Scheduled Areas the panchayats at the appropriate level and the gram sabhas are endowed specifically with the power to exercise control over institutions and functionaries in all social sectors. In coming to new terms with them, as embodied in the law, the office-bearers and members of the panchayats are apt to be ill-at-ease. Doubtlessly, in the long run, with experience they will acquire the requisite acumen and confidence. But they need to be enabled to equip themselves, braced up adequately in the short run through education and training.

The panchayats and character of change

A recurring motif in the thinking pattern of not quite a few social scientists during the past couple of centuries has been their concern over the character of change occurring among tribal communities consequent on progressively increasing culture-contact with the outside world. The museum piece theory has been and, if persisted in, may be rubbished. But it is vital to understand the change. Suffice it to say that it is desirable to postulate that the nature of change and its pace should be in harmony with the genius of a tribe and, for the purpose, should be ordered and regulated by the tribal community itself. The Constitution Review Commission had the important issue in mind when it observed.

> The process of protection of identity and the process of development and change are extremely sensitive. These twin processes need to be understood in the framework of a changing world and the role of all communities, small and large, in that world.

In fact, the question of preservation of identity amidst rapid change all around generally and among tribal communities particularly, is an emotive bristling issue at the heart of many impulses dubbed as irrational and, at times, even anti-national. Witness the Naga movement, for example, springing from a self-identity sentiment core. Conflicts may arise from the intensity of emotion on the one side and inadequate understanding on the other. Wherever and whenever they existed, the self-governing bodies of the traditional mould, as in the north-eastern region, gave expression to self-identity in various ways. In tribal Central India, the identity suffered considerable erosion under the impact of new-fangled ideas and forces during the colonial and post-colonial eras. Now that the legislation permits scope for modern and traditional tribal organizations to exist side by side, and to blend traditionality with modernity, while liberally streaking them with democratic infusions, the expression of the genius of a tribal community through these organizations in various aspects of life like life-styles, occupations, development, culture should receive fillip and become a reality. Through their institutions like panchayats the tribal communities should be able to define and evolve their concepts of development and change in unison with their concepts of identity and culture. A plural society like ours should not only accept this idea, but should also encourage it. Celebration of diversity through expressive democratic devices bonds the constituents together, in a way nothing else can. Hence, the panchayats as conceived here, can emerge as powerful devices not only for self-governance in tribal areas, but also for nation-building.

REFERENCE

India, Government of

1995 *Report of the Committee an Extension of Panchayati Raj to the Scheduled Areas* (Bhuria Committee Report). New Delhi: Ministry of Rural Development and Panchayati Raj.

Table 1

Comparative provisions of the PESA Act 1996 and the Panchayat laws in Orissa, Gujarat and Madhya Pradesh

S. No.	*PESA Act 1996 (Central)*	*State's Panchayat Act*
A.	**The Orissa Panchayat Act, 1997**	
1.	State legislations on Panchayats should be in consonance with state customary law, social and religious practices and traditional management practices of community resources [Section 4 (a)].	Not indicated.
2.	A village shall consist of a hābitation or a group of habitations or a hamlet or a group of hamlets comprising a community, managing affairs in accordance with traditions and customs [Section 4 (b)].	Same as in Central Act [Section 4, proviso]
3.	Constitution of a Gram Sabha [Section 4, (c)]	Same as in Central Act [Section 4 (2)]
4.	Every Gram Sabha shall be competent to safeguard and preserve the traditions and customs of the people, their cultural identity, community resources and customary mode of dispute resolution, etc [Section 4 (d)].	Departure in as much as after the words "dispute resolution", the words "consistent with relevant laws in force and in harmony with the basic tenets of the constitution and human rights" have been added. These words seem unneccessary, as the laws, tenets and rights have to be enforced even otherwise.

S. No.	PESA Act 1996 (Central)	State's Panchayat Act
5.	Powers of the Gram Sabha to approve the plans, programmes and projects for social and economic development prior to implementation by the Panchayat at the village level [Section 4 (e) (i)].	Same as in Central Act, except that "Gram Panchayat" has been substituted for by "the Panchayat at the village level" [Section 5 (3) (a)].
6.	Power of Gram Sabha to identify or select beneficiaries under poverty alleviation and other programmes. [Section 4 (e) (ii)].	Same as in Central Act [Section 5 (3) (b)].
7.	Every Panchayat at the village level shall be required to obtain from the Gram Sabha a certificate of utilization of funds by that Panchayat for the plans, programmes and projects referred to in SL. No 5 and 6 [Section 4 (f)].	Same as in Central Act [proviso to Section 5 (3) (a) and (b).

S. No.	*PESA Act 1996 (Central)*	*State's Panchayat Act*
8.	The reservation of seats in the Scheduled Areas at every Panchayat shall be in proportion to the population of the communities in that Panchayat for whom reservation is sought to be given under Part IX of the Constitution [Section 4 (g)]:	This provision has not been inserted.
	(i) Provided that the reservation for the STs shall not be less than a one-half of the total number of seats;	Same as in Central Act [Section 6 (i) proviso].
	(ii) Provided further that all seats of Chairpersons of Panchayats at all levels shall be reserved for the STs.	Same as in Central [Section 6 (ii) proviso] Whereas in the Central Act, all seats of chairpersons of Panchayats at all levels have been reserved for Scheduled Tribes, in the Orissa Act, the office of Sarpanches as Gram Sabha level has not been reserved.
9.	The State Government may nominate persons belonging to such Scheduled Tribes as have no representation in the Panchayat at intermediate level or the Panchayat at the district level. Provided that such nomination shall not exceed one-tenth of the total number of members to be elected in that Panchayat [Section 4 (h)].	This provision has been inserted in the Orissa Act for Panchayat Samiti and Zilla Parishad and not for the two other lower Panchayats.

S. No.	PESA Act 1996 (Central)	State's Panchayat Act
10.	Consultation with Gram Sabha or Panchayats before acquisition of land in the Scheduled Areas for development projects and before resettlement or rehabilitation of affected persons. The actual planning and implementation of the projects in the Scheduled Areas to be coordinated at State level [Section 4 (i)].	It is significant that neither the Palli Sabha (roughly corresponding to Gram Sabha), nor the Gram Panchayat, nor even the Panchayat Simiti have been allowed such consultation and only the Zilla Parishad is so empowered. Empowering any Panchayat below the Zilla Parishad was that relatively large areas of land need to be acquired and the matter should fall within competence of the Zilla Parishad. Since cases for acquisition of smaller land patches with which the Gram Sabha or Gram Panchayat or Panchayat Samiti may be locationally or jurisdictionally concerned consultation with these bodies should be deemed essential.
11.	The planning and management of minor waterbodies in Scheduled Areas shall be entrusted to Panchayats at the appropriate level [Section 4 (j)].	Neither the Gram Panchayat nor the Panchayat Samiti has been entrusted with such functions.
12.	Mining leases—the recommendation of the Gram Sabha or the Panchayat at the appropriate level is mandatory before grant of prospecting license or mining lease for minor minerals [Section 4 (k)].	The power has been conferred only on the Zilla Panchayat.
13.	Similarly, prior recommendation of Gram Sabha or the Panchayat at the appropriate level for exploitation of minor minerals by auction is mandatory [Section 4 (I)].	Ditto

S. No.	*PESA Act 1996 (Central)*	*State's Panchayat Act*
14.	While endowing Panchayats in the Scheduled Areas with such powers and authority as may be necessary to enable them to function as institutions of self-government, a state legislature shall ensure that the Panchayats at the appropriate level and the Gram Sabha are endowed specifically with	
14-A.	*(i)* the power to enforce prohibition or to regulate and restrict the sale and consumption of any intoxicant [Section 4 (m) (i)].	Such power has been vested in the Gram Panchayat subject to the control and supervision of the Gram Shashan.
14-B.	*(ii)* ownership of minor forest produce [Section 4 (m) (ii)].	Ditto
14-C.	*(iii)* the power to prevent alienation of land in the Scheduled Areas and to take appropriate action to restore any unlawfully alienated land of a Scheduled Tribe [Section 4 (m) (iii)].	Ditto
14-D.	*(iv)* the power to manage village markets. [Section 4 (m) (iv)].	Ditto
14-E.	*(v)* the power to exercise control over money-lending to the Scheduled Tribes [Section (m) (v)].	Ditto

S. No.	*PESA Act 1996 (Central)*	*State's Panchayat Act*
14-F.	*(vi)* the power to exercise control over institutions and functionaries functioning in all social sectors.	This power does not vest either in the Palli (Gram) Sabha or in the Gram Panchayat. The Panchayat Samitis have been empowered to exercise control and supervision, the nature and extent of which shall be such as may be prescribed over institutions and functionaries of various social sectors in relation to the programmes and measures, as the government may, by notification, specify. Thus the power has not been clarified, but circumscribed.
14-G.	*(vii)* the power of control over local plans and resources for such plans including TSP [Section 4 (m) (vii)].	No such power has been conferred either on the Palli Sabha or Gram Panchayat. It vests in the Panchayat Samiti. It is presumed that by extension it vests also in the Zilla Panchayat.
15.	The State Legislature may endow Panchayats with such power and authority as may be necessary to enable them to function as institutions of self-government and shall contain safeguards to ensure that Panchayats at the higher level do not assume the power and authority of any Panchayat at the lower level or at the Gram Sabha by Panchayats at higher level [Section 4 (n)].	This provision it totally absent.

S. No.	PESA Act 1996 (Central)	State's Panchayat Act
16.	The State Legislature shall endeavour to follow the pattern of the Sixth Schedule while designing the administrative arrangement in the Panchayats at district level in the Scheduled Areas [Section 4 (o)].	This provision is totally absent.
17.	Notwithstanding anything in Part IX of the Constitution, with exceptions and modifications made in this Act, any provision of any law relating to Panchayats in force in the Scheduled Areas, immediately before the date on which PESA received the assent of the President, which is inconsistent with the provisions of Part IX with such exceptions and modifications shall continue to be in force until amended or repealed by a competent legislature or other competent authority or until the expiration of one year from the date on which the PESA receives the assent of the President.	Not indicated.

B. The Gujarat Panchayat Act (as amended upto July 1998)

S. No.	*PESA Act 1996 (Central)*	*State's Panchayat Act*
1.	State legislations on Panchayats should be in consonance with state customary law, social and religious practices and traditional management practices of community resources. [Section iv (a)].	Not indicated.
2.	Village shall consist of a habitation or a group of habitation or hamlet comprising a community, managing affairs in accordance with traditions and customs. [Section IV (b)].	Same as in Central Act (Section 3)
3.	Constitution of a Gram Sabha [Section IV, (c)].	Same as in Central Act [Section 4 (2)].
4.	Gram Sabha shall be competent to safeguard and preserve the traditions and customs etc. [Section IV (d)].	Same as in Central Act, excepting the substitution of the word "competent" by "endeavour" [Section 3 (a)].
5.	Powers of the Gram Sabha to approve the plans, programmes and projects for social and economic development prior to implementation by the Panchayat at the village level. [Section 4 (e) (i)].	Section 3 (b) (i)
6.	Power of Gram Sabha to identify beneficiaries under poverty alleviation and other programmes. [Section 4 (e) (ii)].	Same as in Central Act, Section 3 (b) (ii).

S. No.	PESA Act 1996 (Central)	State's Panchayat Act
7.	Panchayat at the village level shall be required to obtain certificate of utilization of funds from the Gram Sabha [Section 4 (f)].	Same as in Central Act, Section 12 (1A).
8.	The reservation of seats in the Scheduled Areas at every Panchayat shall be in proportion to the population of the communities in that Panchayat for whom reservation is sought to be given under Part IX of the Constitution [Section 4 (g)]:	
	(i) Provided that the reservation for the STs shall not be less than a one-half of the total number of seats.	Same as in Central Act. Sec. 4 is for reservation in every village Panchayat Sec. 5 is for every Taluka Panchayat Sec 6 is for every District Panchayat respectively.
	(ii) All seats of Chairpersons of Panchayats at all levels shall be reserved for the STs.	Same as in Central Act in respect of Sarpanch of village Panchayat and President of Taluka Panchayat (Section 8 (i) and 9 (i) and reservation for President of District Panchayat provided under Section 10 (i).

S. No.	PESA Act 1996 (Central)	State's Panchayat Act
9.	State may nominate such Scheduled Tribes as have no representation in the Panchayat at intermediate level or the Panchayat at the district level. Section (h).	If for any reason an election does not result in the return of any member of ST in a taluka Panchayat or district Panchayat, then the State Govt. may nominate from amongst members belonging to STs who are qualified to be elected, such number of members as not to exceed one-tenth of the total members to be elected in that panchayat. *Comments* The two provisions are different. The contingency visualized in the State Act may occur rarely. The provision in the PESA Act needs to be followed.
10.	Consultation of Gram Sabha or Panchayats before acquisition of land in the Scheduled Areas for development projects and rehabilitation of affected persons. Section 4 (i).	Power given to Taluka Panchayat in respect of land acquisition and resettlement of persons displaced by development projects. Section 13. *Comments* It should be given to Gram Sabha also, depending on jurisdiction.
11.	Planning and management of minor waterbodies entrusted to Panchayats. Section 4 (j).	Planning and Management of waterbodies. Section 14 (2) (k-i).

S. No.	PESA Act 1996 (Central)	State's Panchayat Act
12.	Mining leases—the recommendation of the Gram Sabha or the Panchayat at the appropriate level is mandatory before prospecting of minerals lease of minerals. Section 4 (k).	Not indicated.
13.	Similarly, prior recommendation of Gram Sabha or the Panchayat at the appropriate level for exploitation of mining minor mineral by auction is also mandatory. Section 4 (1)	Ditto
14.	While endowing Panchayats in the Scheduled Areas with such powers and authority as may be necessary to enable them to function as institutions of self-government, a state legislature shall ensure that the Panchayats at the appropirate level and the Gram Sabha are endowed specifically with.	
	(i) the power to enforce prohibition to regulate and restrict the sale and consumption of any intoxicant. Section (4 (m) (i).	Same as in Central Act. Section (14) (I) (a).
	(ii) ownership of minor forest produce. Section 4 (m) (ii)	Section (11) (5) (a). There shall be vested in the village Panchayat minor forest-produce found (except found in the areas of national parks or sanctuaries) in such area of a forest as is situated in the jurisdiction of that village.

S. No.	PESA Act 1996 (Central)	State's Panchayat Act
15.	The power to prevent alienation of land in the Scheduled Areas and to take appropriate action to restore any unlawfully alienated land of a Scheduled Tribe. Section 4 (m) (iii).	Not indicated. *Comments* Conferment of this power on the Gram Sabha and Panchayat at the appropriate level essential.
16.	Power to manage village markets. Section 4 (m) (iv).	Not indicated.
17.	Power to exercise control over money-lending to the Scheduled Tribes. Section 4 (m) (v).	Same as in Central Act by amendment of the Bombay Money Lenders Act, 1946.
18.	Power to exercise control over institutions functioning in social sectors.	Section (14) (3) same as in Central Act.
19.	Power of control over local plans and resources for such plans including TSP. Section 4 (m) (vii).	Section 15 (e) same as in Central Act.
20.	Panchayats to function as institution of self-government and safeguards against erosion of authority of Panchayat and Gram Sabha by Panchayats at higher level. Section 4 (n).	Not indicated. *Comments* Should be included in the State Act.
21.	Replication of Sixth Schedule pattern while designing the administrative arrangements in the Panchayat Act at district level in the Scheduled Areas. Section 4 (o).	Not indicated.
22.	Continuance of existing laws and Panchayats, unless dissolved by a resolution passed by State Legislative Assembly.	Not indicated.

S. No.	PESA Act 1996 (Central)	State's Panchayat Act
C. The Madhya Pradesh Panchayati Raj Adhiniyam 1993		
1.	State legislations on Panchayats should be in consonance with state customary law, social and religious practices and traditional management practices of community resources [Section 4 (a)]	Section 129 C (i) of M.P. Panchayat Act 1997. Gram Sabha shall safegurad and preserve the traditions and customs of the people, their cultural identity and community resources and customary mode of dispute resolution.
2.	A village shall ordinarily consist of a habitation or a group of habitations or a hamlet or a group of hamlets comprising a community, managing affairs in accordance with traditions and customs. [Section 4 (b)].	Section 129 (A) (b). Village means village in the Scheduled Areas which shall ordinarily consist of habitation or a group of habitations or a hamlet or a group of hamlets comprising a community and managing its affairs in accordance with traditions and customs.
3.	Every village shall have a Gram Sabha consisting of persons whose names are included in the electoral rolls for the Panchayat at the Village level. [Section 4 (c)]	Section 129 (A) (a). "Gram Sabha" means a body consisting of persons whose names are included in the electoral rolls relating to the area of a Panchayat at the village level, or part thereof, for which it is constituted.
4.	Every Gram Sabha shall be competent to safeguard and preserve the traditions and customs of the people, their cultural identity, community resources and customary mode of dispute resolution, etc. [Section 4 (d)].	Please see reply to serial 1 above.

S. No.	PESA Act 1996 (Central)	State's Panchayat Act
5.	Powers of the Gram Sabha to approve the plans, programmes and projects for social and economic development prior to implementation by the Panchayat at the village level [Section 4 (e) (i)].	According to Section 129 C (v), Gram Sabha in Scheduled Areas shall also have the following powers and functions, namely: *(i)* To safeguard and preserve the traditions and customs of the people, their cultural identity and community resources and the customary mode of dispute resolution. *(ii)* To manage natural resources including land, water and forests within the area of the Village in accordance with its traditions and i*n harmony with the provisions of the Constitution and with due regard to the spirit of other relevant laws for the time being in force.* *(iii)* To manage village markets and Melas including cattle fair, by whatever name called *through the Gram Panchayat.* *(iv)* To control local plans, resources and expenditure for such plans including Tribal sub-Plans, and *Comments* The italicised words are additional to Central provision. *(v)* To exercise and perform such other powers and functions as the State Govt. may confer on or entrust under any law for the time being in force. Please see sl. 14 F&G.

S. No.	PESA Act 1996 (Central)	State's Panchayat Act
6.	Power of Gram Sabha to identify or select beneficiaries under poverty alleviation and other programmes. [Section 4 (e) (ii)].	No corresponding provision in M.P. Act.
7.	Every Panchayat at the village level shall be required to obtain from the Gram Sabha a certificate of utilization of funds by that Panchayat for the plans, programmes and projects referred to in Sl. No 5 and 6 [Section 4 (f)].	Ditto
8.	The reservation of seats in the Scheduled Areas at every Panchayat shall be in proportion to the population of the communities in that Panchayat for whom reservation is sought to be given under Part IX of the Constitution [Section 4 (g)]:	Same as in Central Act vide section 129 E of M.P. Act. 1997.
	(i) Provided that the reservation for the STs shall not be less than a one-half of the total number of seats;	Same provision as in the Central Act.
	(ii) Provided further that all seats of	Same provision as in the Central Act. Chairpersons of Panchayats at all levels shall be reserved for the STs.

S. No.	*PESA Act 1996 (Central)*	*State's Panchayat Act*
9.	The State Government may nominate persons belonging to such Scheduled Tribes as have no representation in the Panchayat at intermediate level or the Panchayat at the district level.	Same as in the Central Act, vide section 129 E (2) of M.P. Act of 1997.
	Provided that such nomination shall not exceed one-tenth of the total number of members to be elected in that Panchayat [Section 4 (h)].	Same as in Central Act.
10.	Consultation with Gram Sabha or Panchayats before acquisition of land in the Scheduled Areas for development projects and before resettlement or rehabilitation of affected persons. The actual planning and implementation of the projects in the Scheduled Areas to be coordinated at State level [Section 4 (i)]	Not indicated. *Comments* Such a provision should be made.
11.	The planning and management of minor water bodies in Scheduled Areas shall be entrusted to Panchayats at the appropriate level [Section 4 (j)]	Section 129 F. Without prejudice to the generality of powers conferred by this Act, the Janapad Panchayat or the Zila Panchayat, as the case may be in Scheduled Areas, shall also have the powers, namely to plan, own and manage minor water bodies up to a specified water area.

S. No.	*PESA Act 1996 (Central)*	*State's Panchayat Act*
		Comments The Gram Sabha and Gram Panchayat also should be empowered
12.	Mining leases. The recommendation of the or the Panchayat at the appropriate level is mandatory before grant of prospecting license or mining lease for minor minerals [Section 4 (k)]	There is no clear-cut provision in the Act. Gram Sabha *Comments* Gram Sabha and other Panchayats should be involved as about 80% mining is located in the vicinity of tribal habitations
13.	Similarly, prior recommendation of Gram Sabha or the Panchayat at the appropriate level for exploitation of mining minor mineral by auction is also mandatory. Section 4 (1)	Ditto
14.	While endowing Panchayats in the Scheduled Areas with such powers and authority as may be necessary to enable them to function as institutions of self-government, a state legislature shall ensure that the Panchayats at the appropriate level and the Gram Sabha are endowed specifically with.	Not indicated

S. No.	*PESA Act 1996 (Central)*	*State's Panchayat Act*
14-A.	*(i)* The power to enforce prohibition or to regulate and restrict the sale and consumption of any intoxicant [Section (4 (m) (i))].	M.P. Abkari (Sanshodhan) Adhiniyam 1997 permits preparation of home brewed liquor for domestic consumption and for social and religious functions.
14-B.	*(ii)* Ownership of minor forest produce [Section 4 (m) (ii)].	Gram Sabhas have been empowered in respct of ownership of MFP. *Comments* Gram Panchayats intermediate Panchayats and Zilla Panchayats, have not been brought into the picture.
14-C.	*(iii)* The power to prevent alienation of land in the Scheduled Areas and to take appropriate action to restore any unlawfully alienated land of a Scheduled Tribe [Section 4 (m) (iii)].	According to M.P. Land Revenue Code, only the Gram Sabha has been empowered in this behalf. *Comments* The Panchayat law should empower other Panchayats suitably.
14-D.	*(iv)* The power to manage village markets. [Section 4 (m) (iv)].	Section 129 C (v) confers power on Gram Sabha to manage village markets and Melas including cattle fair, by whatever name called through the Gram Panchayat. Section 129 D (ii) 2 confers power on the Gram Panchayat to manage village market and Melas including cattle fair, by whatever name called.

S. No.	PESA Act 1996 (Central)	State's Panchayat Act
		Comments Power does not seem to have been conferred on Janpad Panchayat and Zilla Panchayat.
14-E.	*(v)* The power to exercise control over money-lending to the Scheduled Tribes [Section 4 (m) (v)].	Nothing indicated in the Panchayat Act.
14-F.	*(vi)* the power to exercise control over institutions and functionaries functioning in all social sectors.	Provision in section 129 F (ii) same as in PESA Act, 96.
14-G.	*(vii)* the power of control over local plans and resources for such plans including TSP [Section (m) (vii)].	M.P. Panchayat Raj Act empowers control over local plans, resources and expenditure for such plans including Tribal sub-Plans on the Gram Sabha in section 129 (vi) the Gram Panchayat in Section 129 D (vii) the Janpad and Zilla Panchayats in section 129 F (iii).
15.	The State Legislature may endow Panchayats with such power and authority as may be necessary to enable them to function as institutions of self-government and shall contain safeguards to ensure that Panchayats at the higher level do not assume the power and authority of any Panchayat at the lower level or at the Gram Sabha by Panchayats at higher level [Section 4 (n)].	Not indicated

S. No.	*PESA Act 1996 (Central)*	*State's Panchayat Act*
16.	The State Legislature shall endeavour to follow the pattern of the Sixth Schedule while designing the administrative arrangements in the Panchayats at district level in the Scheduled Areas [Section 4 (o)].	Not indicated.
17.	Notwithstanding anything in Part IX of the Constitution, with exceptions and modifications made in this Act, any provision of any law relating to Panchayats in force in the Scheduled Areas, immediately before the date on which PESA received the assent of the President, which is inconsistent with the provisions of Part IX with such exceptions and modifications shall continue to be in force until amended or repealed by a competent legislature or other competent authority or until the expiration of one year from the date on which the PESA receives the assent of the President. [Section—5].	Not indicated.

S. No.	PESA Act 1996 (Central)	State's Panchayat Act
18.		**New provisions in the M.P. Act.** 1. Section 129E (3). In a Panchayat in Scheduled Areas such number of seats shall be reserved for persons belonging to other backward classes, which together with the seats already reserved for Scheduled Tribes and Scheduled Cates, if any, shall not exceed three-fourths of all the seats in that Panchayat.
19.		2. Section 27 of M.P Panchayat Raj (Sanshodhan) Adhiniyam, 2001. The provisions of the Madhya Pradesh Panchayat Raj Sanshodhan Adhiniyam, 2001 shall not apply to Scheduled Areas so far as they are inconsistent with the provisions of Chapter XIV A of the M.P. Panchayat Raj Act 1997 and "The provisions of the Panchayats (Extension to the Scheduled Areas) Act. 1996 (No. 40 of 1996).
20.		3. Section 129 F (iv). To exercise and perform such other powers and functions as the State Government may confer on or entrust under any law for the time being in force.

9

Empowerment of Tribal Institutions in Andhra Pradesh

Urmila Pingle

In spite of the establishment of Integrated Tribal Development Agencies in Andhra Pradesh in the fifth five year plan 1974-1979 very little development has trickled down to the poorest of the poor in areas having more than 50% tribal density. The social and economic indicators such as per capita income, infant mortality rate and functional literacy remain pitifully low as compared to those in the plains areas.

This paper will trace the historical development of tribal institutions in Adilabad district over more than four decades (Table 1). The main focus of the study will be to look into the evolution of tribal development and the recent paradigm shift towards genuine empowerment of tribal institutions especially women's self-help groups.

The study of Raj Gonds, the predominant ethnic group in Adilabad district from the early 1940s has been extensively documented by Fürer-Haimendorf in his classic monograph (*The Raj Gonds of Adilabad* 1948). The changing fortunes of the Raj Gonds over the four decades from the 1940s when they belonged to the Hyderabad State under the Nizam's government till after Independence of

India has been documented in Fürer-Haimendorf (1982). The State of Hyderabad was partitioned in 1956 and the Telengana districts merged with the Andhra districts to form the new state of Andhra Pradesh.

Empowerment of tribal panchayats

It was in the 1940s that Hyderabad State took an interest in the plight of the tribal people due to the reports submitted by Fürer-Haimendorf documenting the cases of exploitation and oppression of tribal communities. His reports, under the title of *Tribal Hyderabad* were published by the revenue department, headed by Sir Wilfred Grigson who held portifolios of revenue, police and forest, the departments most vitally concerned with tribal problems. The positive reaction of the government to these reports and the interest shown by Grigson helped in bringing in far reaching policy changes. The Tribal Areas Regulation Act of 1949 A.D was issued to invest and empower tribal panchayats with judicial functions to enforce the laws prohibiting transfer of tribal lands to non-tribals in the notified tribal area of Adilabad district as well as other tribal areas of Hyderabad State. This was backed by the social service department concerned with tribal welfare rather than the revenue department for more effective implementation. This regulation helped strenghten tribal panchayats to carry out monthly proceedings attended by members of several villages belonging to the respective panchayats. The records of decisions made during the proceeedings of the tribal panchayats were carefully maintained. The rules of this act helped provide a single window of governance for the tribal people instead of dealing with a multitude of officials and judgements of distant courts to solve their land alienation problems and exploitation by money-lenders. The adminstration of this notified tribal area was vested in the Collector (First Talukdar) and the Assistant Agent who belonged to the special social service and in a panchayat to be established by the Agent.

Weakening of tribal institutions with change of government

However, this empowerment of tribal panchayats was not to last long. In 1956 after the organisation of states and formation of the new state of Andhra Pradesh, the Tribal Areas Regulation was repealed in 1963 and replaced by the Andhra Pradesh Scheduled Areas Land Transfer Regulation, 1959. Though the new regulation protected the transfer of land of tribals to non-tribals, it did not provide for the maintenance of tribal panchayats. More importantly it stripped the social service officers of the authority and judicial powers. It was then left to the ordinary revenue officials who had no empathy for the welfare of the tribals and in many a case succumbed to the pressure of non-tribals. With the restoration of the authority of civil courts non-tribals could lodge an appeal when they were challenged by a revenue official for occupying tribal land. This led to large areas of tribal land being alienated in Adilabad district in the years 1970-1979.

Immigration into tribal areas and increased land alienation

In 1961, 90% of the population in Adilabad district was still tribal. However between 1965-1975 there was a peak in migration of non-tribals from neighbouring Maharashtra and tribal population fell to 65%. Land hunger and fertile blackcotton soils of Utnur taluka attracted farming communities from Maharastra state to come in large numbers, resulting in widespread illegal forest fellings and deforestation of most of the land along the road between Gudihatnur and Utnur. Gond villages along this road as well as the Utnur-Asifabad road to the east underwent a demographic change. Many of these villages were occupied by non-tribals and became commercial centres (Fürer-Haimendorf 1982).

Introduction of cash economy

The introduction of cotton in Utnur taluka in the 1950s totally transformed the cropping pattern of this area changing a food producing area into one of cotton production. By 1975 the Gonds were extensively cultivating cotton and their life style had completely changed. Flourishing market centres sprang up in Utnur, Jainur, Indervelli, Narnoor along the Utnur-Asifabad road. Merchants from states as distant as Gujarat moved in to establish these commercial centres. They were also the same shopkeepers who supplied the Gonds throughout the year with commodities. Their methods of trading deprived the tribals of the full profits from the changeover to cotton. They would delay payment in cash and promised to pay the Gonds after they had sold the crop in Adilabad. They would provide advances of food grains to some of the tribals. This method of inducing the Gonds to accept tied sales for their cotton deprived them of the full profits they would have otherwise got. The traders through a network of agents penetrated into remote tribal villages. The agents opened provision stores in these villages and encouraged barter transactions to procure cash crops. With heavy inputs necessary for cotton cultivation, Gonds became heavily indebted to the moneylenders and non-repayment of their loans resulted in loss of their assets both cattle and land.

Banjaras get tribal status in Andhra Pradesh

In 1945-49, 85% of Gonds had reasonable amount of land for cultivation and 160,000 acres of land was allotted to 11,198 tribal beneficiaries. Between 1965-75 Gond land was illegally occupied by Banjaras from Maharastra. In 1977 they politically manoeuvered to get their name included in scheduled tribe list. This helped them to corner the lion's share of all tribal welfare programmes. In 1978-1979 they were assigned 20,000 acres of land on *patta.* This is more than the entire allocation of land to tribals in the previous 25 years. Meanwhile, 31,943 acres of Gond land was alienated. The restoration of land back to the Gonds in spite of land transfer legislation was under mounting pressure by vested interests and political groups. Instructions from revenue secretariat in 1979 were issued to district officers that evictions of non-tribals should be carried out only if they had encroached on more than ten acres of dry land and more than five acres of irrigated land.

Establishment of Integrated Tribal Development Agencies (ITDAs)

In the same year (1977), the fifth five year plan set up an Integrated Tribal Development Agency in areas with more than 50% tribal concentration. High priority was given to develop agriculture and minor irrigation in tribal areas. GCC (Girijan co-operative society) was set up as a wing of ITDA for facilitating the tribals in marketing of minor forest produce and to supply the tribals many of their basic needs. This organisation has evolved over the decades to become a single line administration converging all line departments under the project officer. Though large amounts of government funds have been spent for tribal welfare it has not radically transformed the economy of tribals and has not tackled the fundamental problems that the tribals face today.

Innovative programmes and paradigm shift in tribal development

In the last decade the state government has made a paradigm shift towards decentralisation of development programmes. External funding from the World Bank, IFAD and DFID, etc., have designed their programmes to help towards empowerment of community institutions. Unfortunately, all of this policy has not been translated into action. The main reason is that the ownership of the programme is almost never handed over to the beneficiaries. Whether it is the tribal development department, forest, agriculture or irrigation departments there has been a reluctance to financially empower communities and instead the development works have been handed over to the contractors who have benefited more from poverty alleviation programmes than the poor themselves. This has resulted in works of poor quality and a corrupt nexus between the implementing line department and the contractors. Thus the policy of participatory development has not been genuinely grounded and the poor have remained poor. Sustainability of these programmes has been weak and community institutions that have been organised have remained non-functional. VTDAs, Women's Thrift groups, VSSs and water-shed committees have been largely programme driven.

Empowerment of tribal institutions in Utnur taluk

This is a case study of how a few enlightened officers of the tribal development department in Utnur have made a bold move to hand over the financial control of watershed works to women's groups or Auwal groups belonging to the poorest of the villages.

Objectives of the programme

The ITDA, Utnur extends over 646 villages with a tribal population of 3.6 lakhs (1991 Census). The tribal population is 18% of the total population of Adilabad district. The predominant indigenous tribals are the Raj Gonds, Kolams, Pardhans, Totis and Naikpods in the western part of this area and Koyas and Mannes in the eastern part of the district. The IFAD programme (International Fund for Agriculture Development) started in 1994-95 and was funded for a period of seven years. The aim of the project was to assist the tribal families engaged in shifting cultivation, to improve house-hold security, for development of rainfed agriculture and protection of envirnomentally fragile areas. The major new element introduced in the project is the stress on community based activities and development of self-reliant and sustainable village institutions.This strategy requires fundamental changes in attitudes of the implementing staff to effect a paradigm shift towards handing over the financial control and development works directly to the communities.

This programme became effective only in the last three years of the project's span when two of the top project staff had newly entered the programme. On evaluating the earlier works of IFAD they realised that the communities were not fully involved in planning the restoration of their own natural resources. The works were being only nominally executed by VTDAs but in reality the works were being subcontracted to contractors who were bringing in outside labour for implementing the works. Women's groups were kept out of this development. This defeated the goal of tribal participation and increase of credit activities and village based savings. The works were executed in piecemeal fashion, target oriented and did not converge the activities of other departments towards an integrated approach. The payments were being made in cash through withdrawals from joint accounts of officials and VTDA representatives. This encouraged the financial leakage of the funds encouraging the formation of a corrupt nexus between different players in the field.

Implementation strategies

Having evaluated the reasons for the failure of the programme, the officers in charge decided to empower the existing women's groups by handing over the contracts of the watershed works to them. This would enable the village communities to execute their own works in a manner they think fit, provide employment to their members and use the inbuilt profit margin incorporated in any government project for their group savings. These profits were previously going to the middlemen. The agriculture development co-ordinator (ADC) and community development co-ordinator (CDC) appointed for groups of villages would visit the villages and facilitate the tribal women and their men to do a PRA of their village needs as well as draw a map on the ground of the watershed works that they need to restore their ecology in a systematic way. Based on this the women would work out the quantity of work and stagger it according to their capacity to fullfill the works in lean periods. This would generate employment for their own members without the need to bring in outside labour. The total payment for the work done by the group was made by a crossed cheque into the group account. The cash would be withdrawn by the women after a village group resolution for making payments towards wage labour and the quantity of work would be recorded in a way that the people would understand. Earlier the muster roll system was a complicated and non-transparent method executed by the officials and the people would not know whether they had received all their wages.

A number of meetings were conducted by the executing staff in the villages over a period of a month before the works were actually executed. This helped group strenghtening and awareness building among the communities about the programme and the goals to be acheived. The government staff never got to handle cash and this helped in financial transparency .

Impact of the programme

This programme was initiated in 500 Auwal groups inhabiting 300 villages. The 300 villages are dispersed in all mandals of the ITDA covering approximately 50% of the total villages in Utnur ITDA (300/646 villages).These 300 IFAD villages belong to the poorest and most remote areas of the ITDA. Hence the success of this programme would benefit the poorest of the poor pulling them up from below the poverty level.

1. *Economic impact:* The total money spent on watershed works in 300 villages was Rs 15 crores and the SHGs saved Rs 3 crores (20%). This is besides the small savings that they continue to collect every month. The women use these savings to internally lend to the group members for various activities especially agriculture inputs. Repayment is excellent due to the peer group pressure. They are also taking loans from the rural banks. There is 100% repayment of the loans that SHGs take from the rural banks. The banks are very happy with the performance of these women's groups and are prepared to give more loans. The illiterate tribal women who previously very rarely went to a bank now visit the banks every month. They also find a change in attitude of the bank staff towards them and get good service. This increased capacity to lend internally has freed them in a short time from the exploitation of the local moneylenders. The savings of each member of an SHG group has contributed to a rise in income levels. A family benefiting from IFAD works has an annual income of Rs 26,000- Rs 30,000 (economic assessment of two IFAD villages) as compared to Rs 8000- Rs 21,000/ year/family in two non-IFAD villages. The savings of each female member from the watershed works has raised the family to above the poverty level. (Below $2/day is poverty as defined by World Bank). Food for work is a small part of this work component

and this has given every household food security for a whole year. With the savings the SHGs have also purchased assets such as autos and tractors which they hire out for rent. In some cases they have bought flour mills and broken the monopoly of the mill owner who used to charge a high rate for milling the food grains.

2. *Impact on ecology and agriculture productivity:* The total watershed area of a village was treated from ridge to valley to reduce soil run off and impound the water into small percolation tanks. All this helped to increase the water table and charge dried up wells. Non-timber forest produce saplings have been planted along trenches and diversion drains to consolidate the earthen works. Trees providing fodder, oil seeds and fruits have been grown in nurseries and distributed to surrounding villages. The crop productivity has doubled for most food crops due to more assured soil moisture. Area under cultivation has also increased.

3. *Social change:* The confidence that the programme has generated among the tribals as a whole and women in specific is very visible. The women feel that they have saved the money from their own work and that it is not a grant. This has generated among them a demand for works implemented in a similar way from other line departments. In fact in the village of Powerguda the women's group has stopped the use and entry of mechanical devices to do the works which would have reduced their profit margin and decreased their savings from these works. In

another village the women demanded that a contract of laying a road be given to them and they succeeded in obtaining it and doing a good job of it. Women's aspirations have increased and their interaction with government officials has built up their confidence. Before the programme the women in most villages tell you the same tale, the harrassment by the money-lender, forest guard, patwari and petty police official. All these people have moved away to the fringe and have no more power to evoke any fear in the women. The freedom from fear is the single most important indicator of genuine empowerment. The ITDA, bank, school teacher and PHC have moved closer into their lives and now they aspire for better quality of life. Their aspirations to send their children regularly to school is another sensitive indicator of the impact of this programme. Early indication shows a significant increase in female literacy as compared to villages where the programme has not been implemented.

4. *Spontaneous SHG clustering:* In the valley of Movad in Asifabad mandal the women's groups belonging to eleven villages have got together and decided to cluster so as to give them greater leverage to demand big development works such as minor irrigation tanks and roads. Another objective of clustering is to help economically weak SHGs to leverage works from different departments. They have been able to turn away insurgents from their villages because of their greater unity. This area was the most

remote area of Adilabad district and the hideout for Naxalites. The women fearlessly told the Naxalites that they would not be given food or shelter.

Formation of village clusters and *mandal* mahila federations

The SHGs strengthened under IFAD programme are dispersed in twenty *mandals* of Utnur. These SHGs belong to 50% of total villages in these *mandals*. The empowerment of a substantial number of SHGs helped seed the formation of village clusters or organisations (VOs). VO formation is going on rapidly in all these *mandals*. Velugu is a programme funded by the World Bank for the eradication of rural poverty. The programme is being implemented by the Society for Eradication of Rural Poverty (SERP), an autonomous institution backed by the state government. The Velugu programme being implemented in the tribal areas of Adilabad has recently converged under the ITDA and this has given impetus to instiutional building of women's groups belonging to the poorest of the poor including tribes, SCs, BCs and other minority groups. However, in the tribal areas of Adilabad the indigenous tribes such as Gonds and Kolams have been given special focus.

In contrast, the IFAD programme focussed exclusively on the poorest tribals especially those practicing shifting cultivation. The poverty alleviation programmes focussed on watershed restoration and increasing credit at the village level. Institutional building and microfinance on a larger organisational scale was not in the scope of this programme. Hence, with the completion of the IFAD programme and the initiation of Velugu this lacuna could now be addressed. However, the strengthening of SHGs in the villages was a necessary step for organising the apex bodies. Without the strong bricks to lay a good foundation the building of apex bodies would not be sustainable. It is therefore interesting that SHG empowerment was a necessary prerequisite for implementation of Velugu.

The formation of village clusters and direct convergence of funds called community investment money (CIF) into VOs for internal loaning to SHG members of the Cluster has given a further kickstart to institutional building. The CIF is the backbone of the programme and each VO given the fund is using it to do bulk purchases of agri-inputs and marketing of cash crops such as soyabean and redgram *dhal*. They were being cheated at different levels in the purchase and sale of these commodities. The history of the Gonds caught in a trap of cash economy has already been described. For the first time the larger community institutions can hope to break even in agri- buisnesses against the powerful network of traders who have been controlling the market forces. Alone they could never have hoped to get a good rate for their produce.

The apex bodies at the mandal level called *mandal mahila samakhya* (MMS) have been formed and will be registered as co-operative societies to be able to leverage loans from banks and other financial institutions. The MMS brings together all the VOs at the mandal level. The MMS is not a financial body and serves to help converge all services of the mandal to the different VO. The VOs themselves are evolving into autonomous bodies adopting innovative livelihood approaches specific to the nature of their area and problems. Since it is too early to say how these institutions will evolve, it is important that they be given flexibility to innovate. This can be achieved if they have their own financial independence. It appears that this is the direction that Velugu is taking to shape these apex bodies.

The proceedings of MMS meetings in two *mandals* give a clear understanding of how the process is devolving.

The women belonging to different ethnic groups but tied by the common thread of poverty are able to discuss, debate and finally come to a consensus on important issues. The perception they give is that they are learning on the job in adopting both marketing and other livelihood programmes and this will help them to understand the market forces and be able to beat the traders at their own game. However they do not underestimate these vested interests and proceed cautiously with marketing a commodity which is more risky. They have taken up the marketing of consumable food grains such a soyabean and redgram *dhal* but not cotton which has a more complex and distant market.

Challenges facing sustainabilty of these apex institutions

The sustainability of these organisations depends on good repayment and this issue is consistently focused upon and peer pressure on those SHGs not repaying back the loans is kept up. The challenges for this programme are the financial sustainability of these institutions and proper accounting procedures to be maintained. The programme is trying to train local educated people as book-keepers as the women are largely illiterate. This seems to be the weak link for dealing with larger amounts of money in the future.

The involvement of local panchayat raj institutions and their convergence is important for further strengthening of these organisations. Capacity building of members of the three tier panchayat raj institutions is an important component of Velugu programme and has been just initiated. Institutional building of SHGs, VOs and MMS is an ongoing process. Under this programme staff has been appointed for capacity building of the people's institutions as well as training of trainers. The effective functioning of book keepers appears to be the most important component of this programme which is based on micro-finance.

Conclusions

Poverty is a multidimensional problem and there are no simple strategies or solutions to tackling or eradicating poverty. As seen in the changing fortunes of the tribal people of Adilabad over five decades, eradication of poverty needs a will to devolve programmes to community institutions in a transparent manner and to empower the communities with long term legal rights over *jal, jameen* and *jangal* (water, land and forests). We are a long way from this kind of empowerment. But a beginning has been made in Adilabad district to converge different programmes directly to tribal institutions. The legal rights to forest protection committees (VSS) over the forest they are protecting with their lives needs to be addressed urgently. In principle, the forest department has agreed to converge their programme of community forest management (CFM) with other development programmes to the newly formed VOs in tribal areas. It remains to be seen how it will be translated from policy into action. Already large chunks of the forests in Adilabad have disappeared due to the shortsightedness of the forest department.

Another dimension of poverty that has been largely neglected is the development of human capital. There is a dearth of educated tribals. The comments of some of the tribals from Gujarat who visited villages in Adilabad is significant. To quote them:

> There is hardly any tribal development in these villages. There is not even a single graduate in the villages we visited. In Gujarat, the Bhils are highly educated. Not just in hundreds but in thousands and we range from professionals to IAS officers and tribal development officers.

Table 1
Historical timeline of tribal institutions in Adilabad district

1940	Gond villages dominated by headmen who had considerable authority.
1945-49	Tribal Areas Regulation Act issued in Hyderabad State under the Nizam's rule. Establishment of tribal panchayats with judicial powers to decide on land alienation cases in notified areas backed by the authority of Collector and social service department-85% of Gonds had adequate land with patta rights. Also allotment of 160,000 acres to 11,198 tribals (15 acres/family).
1954	Introduction of cotton resulting in commercial centres springing up along the main Utnur-Asifabad road.
1961	90% of population still tribal.
1963	Tribal panchayats weakened due to stripping of judicial functions to special social department.
	Hyderabad Tribal Areas Regulation, 1949 repealed to be replaced by Andhra Pradesh Scheduled Areas Land Transfer Act.
1965-75	Immigration of small farmers from Maharashtra into Utnur reached a peak. As a result tribal population fell from 90% to 66%.
	Extensive area brought under cotton and life style of the Gond changed due to cash economy.
1977	Illegal occupation of Gond's land by Banjaras from Maharashtra who were later included in the list of scheduled tribes in AP. Alienation of Gond's land reached a peak as a result.
	Establishment of Integrated Tribal Development Agency (ITDA) for an effective single line administration in areas of more than 50% tribal density.
	Gram panchayats based on large blocks of heterogeneous villages. Weak cohesion of gram panchayats unlike earlier traditional Gond panchayats. No authority to

sarpanchs and low budget to local bodies for executing village works.

1979 Increase in landlessness among Gonds due to further alienation of Gond lands (31,9430). Assignment of 20,000 acres of *patta* land to Banjaras.

1986-87 Traditional tribal councils of elders or Rai centres established by Gond elder of Gadiguda for revival of Gond unity and maintenance of Gond customs.

1990-1991 Government issued an order to district officials not to give co-operation to Rai centres since they would conflict with elected gram panchayat bodies.

1992 An NGO, Gondwana Sangarshana Samithi (GSS) consisting of committed and educated tribal professionals were actively involved in strengthening Rai centres and facilitating their people to protect their village forests. They helped form the first forest protection committee in the state (Behrunguda village, Jannaram division).

1993 Organisation of tribal women's thrift groups, called AUWAL committees. Enlightened officers of the ITDA and members of GSS and PARDHAN (NGOs) converged to pool their effort for this purpose. With government backing the two NGOs could help facilitate this process. VTDAs (village tribal development agencies) were created in each village for purposes of agricultural development. The innovative work of NGOs was adopted on a larger scale by the ITDA.

1994 Formation of VPCs (village protection committees) by forest department for joint forest management (JFM) funded by the World Bank (1994-1999).

2000-2003 VTDAs and Auwal groups further strengthened through financial control over their watershed works initiated by enlightened officers of the ITDA (funded by IFAD) Following on the footsteps of ITDA, clustering of Auwal groups and mahila samakhyas federated at *mandal* level by Velugu, an autonomous institution funded by World Bank. A government order helped converge Velugu with ITDA programmes to be more effective.

REFERENCES

Fürer-Haimendorf, C von

1979 *The Gonds of Andhra Pradesh.* New Delhi: Vikas Publishing Pvt. Ltd.

1982 *Tribes of India, The Struggle for Survival.* Delhi: Oxford University Press.

Pingle, Urmila and Christoph von Fürer-Haimendorf

1998 *Tribal Cohesion in the Godavari Valley.* Hyderabad: Booklinks Corporation.

Rao, Mohan K.

1999 *Tribal Development in Andhra Pradesh.* Hyderabad: Booklinks Corporation.

Poffenberger, Mark, Emmanuel D'Silva, N.H. Ravindranath, Urmila Pingle, Indu Murthy and Alex Tuttle.

2002 *Communities and Climate Change: A Case Study from Adilabad District, Andhra Pradesh, India.* Community Forestry International, California, U.S.A.

10

The Face of Change in Arunachal

Sachchidananda

Perched on the left shoulder of India, Arunachal is flanked by Bhutan on the west, China on the north and Burma on the east. Its strategic importance has been realised only after the Chinese incursion in 1962. It is the home of 110 tribes speaking 82 languages and dialects. Among them 26 are recognised as major tribes. In fact, the entire region is a veritable ethnographic museum. Its total population is over one million and the density of population is about 11 per sq. km.

The region has undergone fast changes both in material and ideational spheres. Though changes have been sweeping tribal areas in all parts of the country after independence, the pace and the direction of change differs from area to area. The difference is most marked between tribal majority areas and tribal minority areas. The tribal majority states in North Eastern India present a picture of very fast change. This is in striking contrast with change, occuring in the Fifth Schedule areas in middle and south India. The difference lies mainly in the self confidence displayed by tribals in the tribal majority states, particularly in their faith to be able to shape their own future and to protect themselves from the assault on their own culture or assert their right to prevent outsiders even though they may be tribals, to settle in their own areas. As in other states in the north east, Arunachal is protected by the Inner Line which is operative in this area from 1874. It prevents outsiders from settling in the area. They have gained from the opening up of new opportunities for business and trade. They have progressed in education and have experienced a steep rise in their life style. They have also tasted the value of student power and the use of political skills. They have not suffered from any exploitation. In fact they have used exploitation in the reverse, i.e., by exploiting non-tribal outsiders whom they use in their own business transactions. Arunachal has been chosen as an illustration of such a process of change.

During the last five decades tribal communities in Arunachal have experienced tremendous changes and have marched confidently to join the mainstream of the country in every sphere of life, political, economic and cultural. In this process, some traditional mores of tribal societies have either disappeared or undergone alterations. Stagnation over centuries due partly to the nature of difficult terrain and partly to the deliberate neglect on the part of Indian colonial government has been replaced by active interventions by the government in all fields. The strategic importance of the area has also made the present government pour funds both for defence and development. The fast progress of education has raised the level of political conciousness.

Administrative changes

After independence, the political and administrative status of the area now included in Arunachal Pradesh, has undergone many changes. The region was in charge of the Advisor to the Governor of Assam. In 1954, the North East Frontier Agency came into being. It provided an integrated administration for the entire region. Verrier Elwin, a well-known anthropologist, was appointed the Tribal Advisor for NEFA. He advocated a policy of gradual change so that the traditional tribal societies may not be swept off their feet. His five principles known as the 'Tribal Panchsheel' had the support of Nehru. The NEFA Administration worked to translate this policy into action. Its main ingredients were that the tribals should be allowed to develop according to their own genius, tribal rights in land and forests should be respected, tribal leadership should be encouraged, tribal areas should not be flooded with fast charges and that the results should be judged not by statistics alone but by the quality of life enjoyed by the people. For the first ten years upto 1964 when Elwin died, the NEFA Administration was fully inspired by this philosophy.

From the early sixties however, enlightened local leaders were impatient to accelerate the pace of progress. In 1964, a commission was appointed under the chairmanship of Daying Ering to explore the possibilities of the extension of self government in NEFA. As an outcome of the recommendation of this commission, the village councils were accorded the status of gram panchayats. The gram panchayats were grouped into anchal samitis which were linked to the respective zila parishads. The zila parishads in turn were linked to the Agency Council. In 1971 through a constitutional amendment NEFA became a Union Territory. The Agency council was replaced by the Pradesh Council. Adult franchise was introduced for the first time in 1972 and all the panchayat bodies were made elective. In 1975, the Pradesh Council was converted into a Provisional Legislature and the panel of five councilors appointed by the Chief Commissioner was constituted into a provisional Council of Ministers. The first election for the Arunachal assembly was held in February 1978. It was only in 1987 that Arunachal became a full fledged state.

The role of education

In Arunachal, education has been the prime mover of change. There has been tremendous expansion of educational facilities since independence. At that time there were only two primary schools in the area but by 1967, there were 455 educational institutions. This included one degree college at Pasighat, seven higher secondary schools, nine high schools, 28 middle schools and 410 primary schools. About 20,000 students were studying in these institutions. Ten students passed out from Pasighat college in 1968. These were the first graduates while 121 students were studying in schools, colleges, and universities outside Arunachal in 1966. Two students joined an engineering college in Assam. Two were studying medicine and two became law graduates. Four joined the Indian Frontier Administrative Service and were later absorbed in the Indian Administrative Service. By early 1970s the number of primary schools had gone up to 666 and middle schools to 75. The number of educational institutions has continued to rise. There is a very large number of inter-village schools and high and higher secondary schools. In 1994 there were more than 1200 primary schools, 277 middle schools and 140 higher secondary and secondary schools. The number of colleges has gone up to nine at present. The number of private schools has also increased. The Arunachal University came up in 1984. The medium of instruction is English. Earlier Christian missionary institutions were not allowed to function in Arunachal Pradesh and the Ram Krishna Mission was promoted by the government for opening educational institutions. Some tribesmen believed that their own religious practices could coexist with the Ram Krishna mission education. This accommodation between Christianity and their own ideology was not possible. However, later on this ban on Christian institutions was lifted and now a large number of such institutions have come up. The number of converts to Christianity has also gone up considerably. Christian influence is very much visible among the Nyishi. The percentage of literacy has risen from 11.29 in 1971 to 54.7 in 2001. The difference between male and female literacy is 20 percent. Both in towns and villages people are inclined in favour of education. However, they are not interested in going in for college education. College education is only popular in urban areas or in families which are very well off. A large number of tribal students are sent out for professional education outside the state by the government. As the number of such students is large they do not find employment on their return to the state. Most of them are not inclined to seek employment outside the state. The result is a growing resentment against the government and there is a demand for cent percent reservation for tribals in all posts.

Furer-Haimendorf (1982) has attributed the success of Apatani a small tribe in lower Subansiri district in the commercial field to the rapid spread of education which has led to the emergence of a class of businessmen capable of operating in an economy involving a measure of paperwork. Soon after 1950, when government schools were established in the valley they took advantage of sound education irrespective of parental means. Many Apatani who could afford, sent children to schools outside Arunachal Pradesh. As a result of all this, educational progress has been rapid and literacy is relatively high. By the beginning of 1980s, 45 Apatani had university degrees while many more were enrolled in the universities at Guwahati, Dibrugarh, Shillong and even Delhi. Some of them were taken on gazetted posts in the administration. Some qualified as doctors and engineers. One Apatani, was a fighter pilot in the Indian Airforce but later resigned to join public life.

The same pattern was followed by two other major tribal groups, the Nyishi and the Adi whose combined strength accounts for more than half of the tribal population in the state. The Adi, Nyishi and Apatani figure prominently in government service, politics and professional services in the state.

Changes in society and religion

Many tribal societies in Arunachal are stratified. In recent times, due to fast socio-economic forces at work along with spread of education, this stratification has been crumbling. Slavery was abolished in 1960. The distance between the patricians and commoners among the Monpa and Apatani has been reduced. Achievement motivation is slowly replacing the traditional ethos. The custom of marriage by capture is also disappearing. Among the urban educated folk bride price is losing importance. Polygyny is only confined among the affluent and among politicians. Women have entered the job market. They have gained economic independence. There is no struggle for survival among Arunachal tribals as in middle India. No absolute poverty is in evidence.

Arunachal tribals follow different religions. In West Kamang and Tawang districts the tribals profess Mahayana Buddhism. In the east two tribes, the Khamti and the Singpho profess Hinayana Buddhism. Tribals in other parts of Arunachal follow their own religion which is now known as Donyi Poloism. In recent times there have been conversions to Christianity. However, all groups cling to their traditional beliefs and practices and perform a large number of festivals spread through out their respective areas all over the year. The most important festivals are Mopin and Solung for the Adi, Dree for Apatani, Losar for the Monpa, Nyokum Yullo for the Nyishi. Now-a-days these festivals are celebrated on a community basis on a fixed date at a central place. These festivals are celebrated with great enthusiasm and geity. Some of them represent first fruit rituals, some are purely religious and some combine religious and agricultural elements. People of all walks of life participate in these festivals wearing traditional ornaments and dresses. All these are characterised by animal sacrifices, lavish food and drinks, songs and dances.

Change in land and forest management

Agriculture is the most important economic activity. The total cropped area is 2.20 lakh hectares out of which only 0.70 lakh hectare is under permanent cultivation. The bulk of the land is under shifting cultivation. Only 4% of the land is available for wet rice cultivation. On account of this, importance has been given to the cultivation of commercial cash crops such as oilseeds, potato, ginger, sugarcane, etc. Efforts have been made to introduce scientific shifting cultivation. Horticulture has been taken up in many areas. In the temperate zone, apple, plum, pear, walnut, etc. are grown abundantly. In West Kameng and Tawang apple and potato are the main crops. In the sub-tropical zone citrus, banana, lichi, papaya, etc are grown in large quantity. Pineapple, coconut, areca nut as well as cardamom is gaining popularity. Some land which was earlier under shifting cultivation has been converted into horticultural gardens. Apple and potato have added to the income of people in West Kamang area and this is reflected in their style of life. The same is the case with orange cultivation in Upper Subansiri and West Siang districts.

Forests occupy 62% of the total geographical area. The important forest products are timber. Such cash crops as tea, coffee, pepper, rubber, etc. are also grown. There are a large number of sawmills. There is great resentment against Supreme Court order on felling of trees. In Arunachal the tribals engage in rampant felling even in reserved forests. This is on account of the fact that traditionally the tribals do not make a distinction between personal property and government property.

Communication

Strenuous efforts have been made in the field of communication. Arunachal is characterised by hills and forests leading to isolation of many areas. The government, therefore, laid a great deal of emphasis on the construction of roads and airstrips. Now most of the districts and sub-divisional headquarters have been connected with the result that local produce is easily transported to markets for sale. Almost all the villages, even those on high hill slopes, have been electrified and arrangements for water supply have been made.

Trade and commerce

Another important source of income of Arunachal tribals is the money accruing from rent and commission from petty business. In Arunachal Pradesh no non-tribal can run any business or trade establishment. However, the need for such business is there. Permits are given to tribals for carrying out such business but it is actually done by outsiders. In return for this, the outsiders have to pay a monthly rent to the permit holder. Road construction has provided employment opportunity to large number of tribals over several decades.

Some of the educated tribals now go in for contracts in their own name or join this business as sub-contractors. A large number of students who fail to get their degrees join this profession and accumulate wealth. In many areas, educated and articulate tribals own shops and trade establishments. Many politicians and their sons own large business establishments such as restaurants, hotels, transport and car dealerships. In this they employ non-tribals also.

Politicization

In 1973 Dube made the following remarks on the politicization of tribals:

> After independence in the rapidly changing contexts of national life the tribals have been catapulted from their relative isolation into the vortex of competitive politics. An articulate and effective political elite have emerged in several tribal areas. It has not only acquired a taste for politics but is also vigrously contributing to the emergence of a new political idiom. It is not constrained by the conventional rules of the game; it makes its own rules as the play progresses.

These remarks are no where more true than in Arunachal. Politics has emerged as a principal avenue through which the tribal leaders are trying to find solutions to their problems. Many tribes particularly those in Arunachal Pradesh have experienced a revolution of rising aspirations. They are aware that in politics, competitive pressures determine one's place and share in the decision making process. There has been a shift in their political attitudes and strategies. They have moved over to the politics of pressure and protest. The politicization of the tribal scene is a natural and logical culmination of the democratic process.

When the elections to the newly formed assembly were held in February 1978 there were two political parties in the fray. These were the Janata Party and the People's Party of Arunachal. The Indian National Congress set up only one candidate. Since the Janata Party was in power in the Centre, Janata candidates won and the new council of ministers came into office in the middle of March 1978. This government was short lived and lasted less than two years. The then chief minister was obliged to go out of office due to defections. The new government was formed by the People's Party of Arunachal in September 1979. This ministry also collapsed and Gegong Apang of the Indian National Congress staked his claim to form the ministry. This was not allowed by the then Lieutenant Governor and there was a short spell of President's rule. Fresh elections were held in January 1980. The contest was between the Indian National Congress and the United People's Party of Arunachal. It was a keenly contested election. The Janata Party was nowhere. The Indian National Congress won the elections and the ministry was formed by Gegong Apang. He continued to be the chief minister for 19 years. In January 1999 there was a split in the party and one of his ministers Mukul Mithi formed the government. Unlike Apang, Mithi belonged to a small tribe and did not have a continued support of legislators. This government suffered huge defections in the last week of July 2003 and Gegong Apang returned as chief minister of Arunachal in the first week of August 2003 under the banner of United People's Front, which soon merged with the Bhartiya Janta Party. It may be observed that such changes in government reflected changes in government at the Centre. The general experience in the North-East is the absence of national parties and the ever changing affiliations of regional political parties.

Self esteem and Arunachal identity

One important impact of the new social and political order was the establishment of peace in the area. Formerly inter-tribal relations were marred by raids. There was a sense of insecurity all over. When this was gone, the path of development was made smooth. The improvement in communication by road reduced the distance between different tribal groups. Old tribal names such as Dafla and Abor familiar to anthropologists are now regarded as derogatory. These terms have been replaced by Nyishi and Adi respectively. The change in nomenclature reflects the anxiety of tribal groups to raise their social status and self esteem. Many of these tribal groups have their own youth organisations. The Apatani youth organisation was founded in 1973. The Nyishi youth organisation came into being in 1975. Such organisations advocated abolition of child marriage and bride price. While the Apatani favour inter-tribal marriage with the idea of developing a unified tribal consciouness, the Nyishi were much less concerned with building up a united tribal front. The same Nyishi youths who disparaged marriages with the Apatani expressed no objection to unions with Adi, Khasi or even Nepali. Now, however, there is no objection to inter-tribal marriages. Marriages also take place between Christian tribals and non Christian tribals.

Although elections and political party activities are centred round ethnic identity, one can find evidence of the evolution of an Arunachali identity. Arunachali tribesmen are patrilocal, patrilineal and patriarchal. Both nuclear and joint family systems are prevalent. Clan exogamy and tribal endogamy is the general norm. Monogamy is the most common form of marriage but polygyny is permitted and practised. Marriage by negotiation is most common. Bride price is paid both in cash and kind. In case of polygyny the first wife is regarded as the most important. Widow remarriage and divorce are permitted. The youth dormitory system is still prevalent among tribes like Adi, Nocte and Wancho. A wide variety of folk-songs are found among the Arunachali. They have their own musical instruments and different kinds of dances. They also produce different handicraft items. Both men and women excel in basket making with cane and bamboo, wood carving and making of masks. Carpet weaving of exquisite designs are also found in many communities. Arunachali tribal women weave beautiful designs on cloth produced on their loin looms. Arunachali identity is characterised by exceptional spirit of co-operation in working and living, self reliance, hospitality, courage in difficult conditions and a gay and cheerful disposition.

There has been a perceptible change in the mindset of the tribals in Arunachal. While they want to retain their distinctive identity, they are not averse to change in the fringe areas of their cultural ethos. There is a tremendous rise in the aspirations of people both in rural and urban areas. Everywhere people welcome education, both for boys and girls, as it opens new avenues for employment and supplements income. There are many cases of people rising from rags to riches. One politician started as an ordinary labourer. On account of his personality and ability to manage people, he became a labour leader and later entered politics. He now owns shopping complexes in Naharlagun and Itanagar and has been a minister for a long time. An Apatani who resigned from the air force to join public life is now a flourishing businessman. He was also the president of the state cooperative federation. Many tribal women are active in politics. Some of them have even been ministers in the state government as well as member of Parliament.

The debit side

There are some negative changes also on account of the large flow of development fund in the area from the central government. Corruption in public life looms large. Educated tribals do not like to work in the interior. At the lower level, people lack commitment to a healthy work culture and feel that they have been appointed just because the government wants to give employment to tribals. Such an attitude has proved detrimental in the field of education. Since tribal teachers are not willing to serve in interior areas, non-tribal teachers from Hindi speaking states have to go there. They are not able to create a rapport with tribal children. Such is the state of decline in work culture that even tribal officers prefer to have non-tribal assistants and orderlies.

Some decades back, Arunachal had almost a crime-free society and policing was not very much needed. Now thefts, robberies and murders occur everywhere and police work has become important. Earlier most of the cases were decided on the basis of the tribal customary law by village councils or *Kebang*. Their judgements were confirmed by executive courts. Now the Indian Penal Code is operative in the state. The judicial wing of the administration is being strengthened by starting 'fast track courts' in which lawyers are allowed. A bench of the Guwahati High Court has been opened in Naharlgun.

The face of change in Arunachal is a blend of the old and the new. The direction of change points to the mainstream Indian culture. Both the healthy and unhealthy features of mainstream Indian society are discernible in the wide spectrum of Arunachali life. The Arunachal panorama reflects a robust society looking to the future with hope and confidence in evolving a socio-economic order nearest to their heart's desire.

REFERENCES

Chaudhury, J.N.

1982 *Arunachal Panorma.* Itanagar: Directorate of Research, Government of Arunachal.

Duarah, D.K.

1995 *A Hand Book of Arunachal Pradesh.* Itanagar: Frontier Publications and Distributors.

Dube, S.C.

1973 *Tribal Situation in India.* Simla: I.I.A.S.

Fürer-Haimendorf, C. von

1982 *Tribes of India, The Struggle for Survival.* Delhi: Oxford University Press.

1982 *Highlanders of Arunachal Pradesh.* New Delhi: Vikas Publishing House.

Sachchidananda

1985 'Economic development, education and social change in Arunachal Pradesh', *Man in India.*

11

Changing Religion and Ritual in a Vasava Bhil Community Impacted by Involuntary Resettlement

Roxanne Hakim

The Vasava Bhils of Makhadkhada, an isolated village on the banks of the river Narmada in the Satpura Hills of Gujarat, western India, is one of several villages displaced by the controversial Sardar Sarovar (Narmada) Dam Project. Through long-term fieldwork (five years) both prior to and following displacement, my research aims to document and understand the impact that resettlement has had on the community's economy, religion and social relations.

Makhadkhada (Bharuch district) was submerged in the monsoons of 1994 and its six hamlets were resettled in four main sites in the plains, in Dabhoi taluka, Vadodara district in South Gujarat, a distance of about 90 km. from Makhadkhada, and significantly less isolated from mainstream India. Within just a year of resettlement, the Vasava appeared almost unrecognisable to outsiders. Not only had the house and village structure changed, but I observed that changes had come into almost every aspect of their lives. Women had almost given up wearing the dress they wore in the hills and now wore the *sari* with a short blouse as is found in most of India. They no longer wore the silver coin jewellery distinctive of hill Bhils. They avoided speaking their dialect in front of non-Vasavas, having picked up Gujarati - the state language, which in Makhadkhada only a few men could converse in. Their diet was fast changing as self-sufficiency became impossible with the loss of the forest. They had taken on some aspects of Hindu ritual such as the marriage ceremony. The importance of cattle stocks had been replaced by other indicators of wealth, such as steel utensils. And the sudden access to cash income through the sale of illegal wood, alcohol and available labour had encouraged a fondness for frequenting shops and buying clothes and jewellery.

This paper describes Vasava religion and ritual: its role within Vasava society and the transformation it is undergoing during these transitory years of resettlement. The analysis focuses on the role religion plays in the daily lives of Vasavas, and the way in which it is used to construct changing self-identity within the community, as well as Vasava identity as described by host communities (non-Vasavas).

Religion as a marker of self and 'other' identity

The impact of resettlement on the area of Vasava religion cannot be easily assessed during these transitory years during which the *adivasi*[1] hill Vasavas become exposed to the popular Hinduism of the plains. Changes in this sphere of life are not immediate, and may not always be tangibly visible; however the changes are likely to have a deep and permanent impact on the resettled community.

While the hill (*dungri*[2]) Vasavas' self-identity is articulated largely in terms of self-sufficiency in food production, plains (*deshi*) groups tend to define Vasava identity through criteria derived from religious and consumption practices (Hakim 1996, 2000 a;b;c). Where the *dungri* emphasises his distinction from the *deshi* in terms of the distinctiveness of (self-sufficient) production patterns, the *deshi* refers to consumption (food, dress) and religious behaviour when differentiating himself (most times stating his 'superiority') from *dungri* groups (Hakim 2000 a;b;c). However, the changes in production patterns following resettlement to the plains are eroding the self-sufficiency of the hill Vasavas. The philosophy of hill and plains agriculture is different: the former assumes land availability and emphasizes diversifying crops and planting techniques while the latter tackles the classic issue of maximizing yield on limited land (Hakim 2000 c). The skill/challenge in plains agriculture is not how to ensure household self-sufficiency, but to extract the best yield out of a household's agricultural land; this may require intensive agriculture of one high yielding crop, a mix of food and cash crops, irrigation and rain fed crops, a good knowledge of market prices and the ability to handle middle men. Moreover, hill grains do not give good yields in the plains, the community has to learn new agricultural techniques to adapt to flat lands and new cash crops. Kin labour obligatory networks are breaking down and the strong dependency on natural resources is no longer possible nor sustainable. As a result, the resettled community's newly emerging production patterns increasingly resemble that of other plains communities and hence can no longer serve as a strong distinctive marker of resettled Vasava identity.

The role of religion as a variable of group identity amongst resettled Vasavas has hence significantly increased: while it continues to be monitored by the host communities as an indicator of continuing but slowly 'shrinking' differences between the two groups, the Vasava themselves are now using their changing behaviour in religion and consumption practices to demonstrate their willingness to adapt to what they see as their new life.

As is described in the analysis below, the changes in the area of religious philosophy and ritual appears to be somewhat patchy: some individuals claim to begin to recognize some of the popular gods and goddess of the dominant Hindu pantheon, others focus on the fact that they are now attending *deshi* religious fairs and others highlight the changes in specific rituals like marriage and *holi* (spring festival) celebration. This approach underpins the resettled Vasavas' constant belief: that his self-identity continues to be strictly that of a hill Vasava. However, religious behaviour and ritual appears to be very important to gain the trust of host communities and the changes that have taken place are not seen as erosive to core identity creating aspects such as the community's origin myths, celebration of the four main annual rituals, and the justification of all ritual (old and new) through a strongly held notion that man must constantly negotiate and interact with the sphere of the Supernatural (rather than accept it which is the underlying norm in mainstream Hinduism). These somewhat superficial and patchy changes are serving their purpose at this stage; the host community clearly sees the 'backward' *dungris* as willing to change, and this has enabled the forging of good relationships (both economic and social) between the two groups. At the same time, the changes are not seen by the community as disruptive to their identity or resulting in a loss of group bond. However, this is no guarantee that as the years pass, the pattern of change will continue as now. With time, it will be interesting to see whether these changes become significant enough to warrant a threat to a common group bond and identity, and the way they play out on both individual and group 'self' and 'other' identity.

Religious behaviour as a 'way of life': Linking the supernatural to social morality

There is difficulty with defining which aspects of the hill Vasavas' life fall into the religious sphere, or are guided by what can be understood as a 'religious philosophy'. Vasava cosmology consists of a unique pantheon of gods, and appeasing them (and indirectly the forces of nature) takes place through rituals where the *badvo* (powerful shaman) cajoles the god into granting a wish or holding back her/his wrath. The community has no religious philosophy in the sense of a code of moral conduct decreed the 'right one' by myth, god/s or prophet as is the case of most major religions. In fact, moral conduct implicit in everyday action is derived from social rather than religious custom, and references to the Supernatural in most Vasavas' daily activities are minimal. The realm of the Supernatural is closely tied up with what are viewed as 'natural' activities. Weather, birth and death are regarded as completely within the control of the pantheon of gods and goddesses; other spheres such as crop yields and illness are regarded as being partly controlled by the Supernatural, and some human control over these areas is acknowledged. For instance, whilst Punja Vinya's poor *bhadi* (*panicum pilosun*) crop was partly attributed to the unusual rain pattern that year (he planted later than most others), lack of effort and his failure to summon enough kin labour for weeding were also seen as attributing to the poor yield. Most daily activities such as dietary habits, dress, social hierarchy, social relationships are not viewed as reflective of 'morality', and are regarded as outside the sphere of the Supernatural or any related philosophies and rituals.

Hinduism as viewed by plains host communities is not just a religion, but a way of life. In contrast to the hill Vasavas, where religion is rarely seen to impinge on daily behaviour, within the host communities, a large number of daily activities are imbibed with direct or indirect religious sanction. There is social pressure on the resettled community to adapt to the eating habits, dress code and rituals (such as marriage) of the host communities, all of which are loosely tied up within the structure of religion as indicators of social and moral hierarchy. Such attempts to *'Hinduise'* the hill Vasavas is often viewed by host groups as their 'duty' and often take on a moralistic tone of one 'improving the lot of the ignorant *dungri*'. Social hierarchy in the plains is linked to moral 'piety' and is influenced by variables such as food habits, the practice of marriage and other customs, religious practices and the behaviour of women. These daily activities which in the hills are devoid of moralistic undertones, and seen merely as social relationships, are given a deeper significance and moral 'value' amongst host communities (especially the higher caste groups) in the plains of South Gujarat.

As mentioned above, areas falling under the sphere of religion appear to be different in the host areas as compared to what I observed in Makhadkhada. Hence, while this paper is primarily about the impact of resettlement on religion, it discusses other areas of the community's life which they may not consider as having much religious significance (e.g. the fairs they attend), but which are seen as indicative of religious/moralistic behaviour in the wider definition ascribed to within the host groups. The paper focuses on the main Vasava rituals observed in the hills and new sites and attempts to analyse why and in what way certain aspects of ritual have been influenced by resettlement-related factors. The changing nature of festivals, ritual calendars and religious practitioners is also examined. Related to this is the increasing importance of allopathic medicine and the changing role of traditional *badvos* (shamans).

The 'potential' Hindu

The desecration of the Ayodhya mosque that sparked of Hindu-Muslim riots all over India in December 1992, had little impact on the sleepy villages in the Satpura hills. The rioting resulted in the declaration of curfew in many states in the country, as infrastructure services broke down. A few days into the riots, Govind Patel, the judicial head of the village dropped by my hut as he often did on the way to, or back from, the bus stop in Gadher:

> There is something up Ruksa, the bus has not come to Gadher for two days and the shop keeper says that there is no saying when it will come. They say that there is some government problem with *Miaas*[3], so there is no bus. I'm confused, so I thought maybe you know something.

A few others who returned from the bus stop, came back with similar stories. I had kept abreast of the situation through the radio, and tried as best I could to explain the nature of the problem to my friends in Makhadkahda.

But it was difficult. Most of them knew what a temple was. They dotted the banks of the Narmada, and the *parikramavasis*[4], locally referred to as *ghusayes*, stayed there during their pilgrimage. There was one in the nearby upstream village of Dhumna that most of them had seen but never been inside. A few had also seen the temple at the big Surpan fair across the river. But they never went inside. It was a *deshi* arena; one of the many differences in their two ways of life that they accepted. They also knew the *Miaas* whose community dominated the nearby plains villages of Haripura and Jetpur. I explained that a temple belonging to the *Miaa* community had been destroyed in a town beyond Delhi. It had been destroyed by a group called Hindus, who worshipped different gods from the *Miaas*.

This last sentence needed explanation on my part. Although the hill Vasavas' predominant grouping when dealing with outsiders is that of *dungri* and *deshi*, they are somewhat aware that *deshis* consist of different groups, often with distinctive customs. Just as the Guvars are also *dungris*, but eat, drink and marry separately from the Vasavas. There are Brahmins, Dheds, Miaas, Parsis,

Vanyas and many more *deshi* groups that they do not have contact with. To most Vasavas, each of the *deshi* sub-groups are as different from them as the other. Hence, in their minds, the *Miaas* do not stand apart from the Brahmins and Vanyas, as the latter two groups (both Hindus) are not viewed as sub-sects of a common larger group. Religion, as we understand it is not regarded as the dividing factor between *deshi* groups. It is simply custom and lifestyle: dress, eating habits, wealth and sometimes dialect.

The Vasavas of the Satpura hills like other relatively isolated *adivasi* groups, are often referred to, in documentation and common parlance, as 'backward Hindus' (Ghurye 1963) or 'potential Hindus' who need to be 'purified' (Padel 1992:2). As a villager in the lower village of Vaghrali once explained to me of the community in Makhadkhada:

> they are Hindus, but some of them do not know that. They have to learn how to behave properly, but the poor things are too isolated in the hills to pick up the correct behaviour from us.

However, the hill Vasavas never referred to themselves as Hindus. I had never heard them mention the word, and subtle reference on my part to common Hindu gods was invariably met with a quizzical look.

The night following Govind Patel's visit, I was sitting around a fire with a number of people from Nishat, Hamutade and Khalomaye hamlets when the discussion turned to the cause of the stoppage of the bus service from Gadher. Various opinions were expressed, each one hoping that what he/she had heard would help make things clearer. Hamji Kanji the young man emerging as a resettlement leader tried to make things clearer:

> The fight is between the *Miaas* and the other *deshis* who call themselves Hindus. We have all seen how

> the *Miaas* can get violent when angry. But we must not worry; if you are asked you must say you are Hindu. We must all remember that we are Hindus.

Chaman Segji, the elderly leader from Khalomaye arrived as Hamji was speaking:

> I returned from Kevadia on a truck and on foot. They say the fighting is bad in the area beyond Kevadia. Hamji is right; the *deshi* Hindus include us in their group. We are unaffected by the fighting in these hills. We have never had trouble with the *Miaas*; they collect our *timbru* (*diopyros melanoxylon*) and *asitra* (*bauhinia racemosa*) leaves, we have good relations with them. But if they involve us in the fighting when we are in town, then we will fight them.

The situation never flared up and was rarely ever mentioned again. I delayed going to Mumbai till it was established that the violence had died down. As Chaman correctly assured me:

> Ruksa, you are in the safest place in these hills. Most of our people don't even know that the rest of the country is in turmoil. There is no chance of it spreading into our lives.

There appears to be a contradiction in the hill Vasavas' inclusion into the Hindu grouping. Whilst most *deshis* are quick to stress the 'primitiveness' of the hill tribes and to emphasise that they are different from them in every way (including religious practices), they will simultaneously agree that the *adivasis* are in fact Hindus, and that the hill Vasavas should aspire to become 'proper' Hindus like themselves. In popular terms this usually means giving up meat and alcohol, stressing hygiene, worshipping in temples, hanging pictures of the Hindu pantheon in one's hut and being married by a Brahmin. The Vasavas do not label themselves as Hindus, nor do they worship (nor are familiar with) even the most popular of the Hindu pantheon such as Brahma, Indra, Shiva and Vishnu.

However, one can trace elements of Hindu ritual within Vasava culture. The use of coconuts and incense sticks in rituals, the *lingam* (symbol of Shiva) shaped stones that are symbols of the village pantheon of gods, and the strong belief in the history of regional deities such as *Dev*[5] Mogra which is shared by other hinduised plains groups are indicators of cultural exchange with Hindu groups. The extent to which these traits have been borrowed from outside or developed within the culture is difficult to determine.

Adivasi groups have always lived on the margins of dominant society; the fuzziness of the margins allowing them to simultaneously be a part of it and retain a strong distinctiveness. To try and determine whether hill Vasavas in Makhadkhada are really Hindus would be an irrelevant and futile excercise. The challenge lies in trying to understand the dynamics of the complexity of their link with the Supernatural, and the manner in which this manifests itself in their daily lives.

Influence of the pantheon on Vasava identity and the implications of resettlement

Accused of being stone worshippers and pagans by some *deshis*, the Vasavas of the Satpura hills cannot be regarded as such. All hill Vasavas have a strong belief in the existence of a *Bhagwan* or *Malik* who is considered the supreme power and who controls all the *devs*. Thus it would be wrong to refer to them as polytheistic. A *badvo* explained the relationship between *Bhagwan* and the *devs* as follows:

> *Bhagwan* is all powerful. He is the same for all people. The four winds, the stones, the *devs*, are in fact all part of the same thing, called by the name of *Bhagwan*. *Bhagwan* works through these different means, which we refer to as *devs*. Just as you have a name, I have a name, that boy has a name, in that way we have to refer to these *devs*—

> by different names such as *Gam no darvajo dev* (the god of the doors of the village), *Ba datnya* (the god of teeth), *Raja Phanta* (the god who controls the world of the living) and so on. They each have a different area that they function within. But in essence they are all *Bhagwan*. *Bhagwan* has come from stone. There are stones in the mountains and *Bhagwan* came from a stone. But that does not mean the stone created *Bhagwan*. It was a *mata* (mother goddess). She is called *Vadi ya* (Big mother). She created *Bhagwan* and all of us, and the trees, earth, *devs*....

The Vasavas' relation with the world is based on the assumption that *Bhagwan* and the *devs* control most phenomenon (natural and man made), and can be appealed to, to exercise power over their domain. Most of the communication with gods and goddesses is in the form of propitiation to ask for a favour, or make an offering in appreciation of a favour received. This is the institution of *manta* (sacrifice) and *poonja* (rituals), the former is performed on behalf of an individual, and the latter is aimed at the larger social unit. The village and household level *poonjas*, are performed on a yearly cycle, and are prescribed in their frequency, unlike the individual focused *mantas* which take place as and when the need arises (for example, when an individual falls sick).

The pantheon of *devs* can be roughly divided into three categories. Firstly, those *devs* who are physically represented and territorially inalienable. Secondly, those who are physically represented but not territorially linked. Thirdly, those who have no physical representation and no territorial link. These categories become very important with regard to the community's proposed resettlement, as it involves a total change of territory, and access to the submergence village is cut off. In contrast to the implications of religion and ritual on the economy, an issue to which the community had given considerable thought, the issue of religious change was not one I heard people talk about or discuss prior to relocation. During my stay in Makhadkahda, all rituals (*mantas* and *poonjas*) continued to be practised in the hills, as the community still regarded Makhadkhada as their 'home'.

The *devs* falling into the first category (i.e. those physically represented and territorially inalienable) are somewhat problematic in the context of resettlement. These include the mountains surrounding Makhadkhada, some of which will be submerged with the completion of the Sardar Sarovar Dam. Vasavas identify strongly with being 'mountain people' which gives them a different way of life from those living in the plains. The move from the hills to the plains is an important factor in restructuring Vasava identity, as both, they, and the plains peoples have always linked the community's identity to the hills. Vasava identity as hill people (*dungris*) is evident in the emphasis they place on self-sufficiency in production and consumption. It is the geographical location of the hills that both enables and necessitates this self-sufficiency.

The Vasavas' strong association with the hills is very evident in the respect and supernatural status that they attribute to them. Most of the more prominent mountains have a name and they are all referred to as *devs*. From one hamlet in Makhadkhada, a *bhua* (shaman) pointed out over 20 mountains that were regarded as *devs*. Much of this specific information on religion is restricted to the religious practitioners, some of whom claim to know the names of all the mountains in the whole range, stretching for several miles, and crossing three states. However, all Vasavas do show respect and great love for the mountains, and all of them are familiar with the most well known of them, such as the mountains of *Hirazu baba* (Father *Hirazu*), *Pavu* and *Phenai*. A story of the Supernatural powers of these mountains is often told to children, and is firmly believed by all. Makti Chima related the story to four of her children and me one night:

> My father used to tell me this story very often when I was a child. I'll tell it to you now. There was once a big flood. The *reva*[6] overflowed to such a degree that everything was destroyed. All the villages were submerged and all people were killed. Only one Dhed man and one Dhed woman survived. They were brother and sister. How did they survive? You know the big mountains of *Hirazu* and *Pavu*. Well, one of them climbed on *Hirazu* and the other on *Pavu*. And as the *reva* kept rising, the smaller mountains got submerged, and then the higher ones, but *Hirazu* and *Pavu* could not be conquered by the *reva*. As the waters grew and threatened to drown the peaks of *Hirazu* and *Pavu*, they would grow taller and thus the Dhed brother and sister climbed higher and higher and survived the flood. But mankind was all destroyed, so then what happened? The Dhed brother and sister then put their arms around each other, and held on for a while. They did not sleep together, just put their arms around one another.[7] And from there we were all born. The Vasavas, the Tadavis, the Dheds, the Guvars and all the other *jats*[8] that there are on this earth. So, in essence, we are all children of the Dheds, although we consider their *jat* to be lower than ours, and we observe food, drink and marriage taboos with them. We have all come from the Dheds.

Although the mountain *devs* have a fixed territory as their physical representation, their sphere of influence is not restricted to this territory and their help can be invoked anywhere, be it Makhadkhada, or Karnet new site. From Makhadkhada, of the three important mountains, only *Hirazu* is clearly visible. None of the hills is visible from Vadaj new site although some new sites have a view of *Paavu* and *Phenai*.

Vinya Lekji, the oldest *bhua* in Makhadkhada has a direct view of *Hirazu* from his house in Haamutaade hamlet. On mornings when I awoke very early, I often walked over to his house, to find him sitting outside, his gaze fixed across the shimmering Narmada, on *Hirazu* which was visible beyond. Vinya always emphasised the importance of these hills to his people, thus:

> These mountains have been around since the beginning, even before man came on this earth. You know how much we respect them and owe to them, they provide us with land to till, fodder for the cattle...moreover, they are our *devs* and we believe in their power. The *sarkar* (government) talks of this dam, and that it will submerge Makhadkhada, and yes some smaller mountains may be submerged. But I find it impossible to imagine that the *sarkar* can drown our *devs*. The taller peaks will remain un-submerged. Even part of the submerged part will resurface in the dry months. Most crucial to this is the fact that our *devs* are not purely physical. The *sarkar* may submerge a mountain with this dam of theirs, but that does not imply that the *dev* will no longer function. And besides, if it comes to that, the *devs* can surely live below the water. We will continue to respect them and believe in them as we do now. Of course we feel sad to move after being here all our lives but what can we do. We have no choice. I believe we will continue our ways in the new land. Our youngsters do copy *deshi* fashions and clothing and songs, we did that too, but essentially we are Vasavas, and we will continue to believe in our *devs*. That will not change.

Vinya's optimistic attitude was shared by the community, young and old alike, although the elders were more vocal about their optimism regarding the persistence of religious customs in the new site. The younger Vasavas, did not talk much about changes in the religious sphere. It was not an issue that was spoken about in their conversations about their new lands.

The term 'stone worshippers' used by outsiders and casual observers when referring to the hill Vasavas has arisen from the village pantheon of *devs* who are represented by *lingam*[9] shaped stones placed in a kind of sacred grove. The pantheon consists of the village god *Rojan dev*, and his *sakars* or helpers. Although the power of the village god is territorially linked to the boundaries of the village and to that extent is territorially inalienable, the stone representations are alienable/moveable to the extent that they are simply viewed as a 'representation' of the *dev*. Villagers say that the river Narmada had flooded its banks in the mid seventies:

> At that time the pantheon of village gods used to be in the valley below, where a rain-fed stream now runs. We used to farm that valley before. There were two big trees there and the big stones representing their *devs* was between the two trees. The 'big water' grew so powerful that everything in that valley was washed away. Even the largest stones were straining against its force. Some of the smaller ones were washed away, but an ancestor Kanji Ferangya saved the big one and placed it in its present place. The smaller stones were replaced by other ones.

The Vasavas responded to the issue of resettling the stone representations in what would appear to be an extremely logical manner. Since *Rojan* has his sphere of influence only in Makhadkhada, he will be of no use in the new land. They will no longer need to propitiate him, but instead take on the *dev* of the new village. That the host community has a very Hinduised pantheon of gods, and propitiates them in a different way did not seem to concern the Vasavas much. An important reason for this is that the Vasavas do not see themselves as following a different religion, with a different pantheon of gods. They believe in the universality of their religious beliefs, with only superficial changes such as different names of gods in different areas. They assume that the difference in religious practices of different communities are just variations along the same continuum. Hence, they do not expect to have difficulty adopting to *deshi* rituals and practices. Whilst they do acknowledge certain differences in practices amongst groups, they claim that these are minor. They are quite confident that with time, they will adopt the ways of the host, while retaining many traits of their traditional religious practices.

Since the village structure would be reorganised upon resettlement, I asked several people in Makhadkhada what the decision on the pantheon stones would be. I got various answers, each one assuming that someone else would take the decision when the time came. Hamji the young leader told me:

> we will probably let these stones be here and find new ones in the new sites...and anyway now we will have to ask for protection from the god of our new village whoever he may be.

The *Patel* replied to my query as:

> It is the *poonjaro* (village priest) who will take the pantheon with him to the site he goes to as only he can feed the village gods.

The *poonjaro* however told me:

> Who am I to take the decision on my own? I am the feeder of the gods, that is my duty; but these are village gods, and the older men will have a meeting and decide when the time comes. Why are you fretting from now? Perhaps they will decide to split the stones amongst the different new sites. Anyway, the stone is only the physical representation.

In fact what happened was that the stones still remain in Makhadkhada, but were moved to higher ground to prevent their submergence. The *poonjaro* like a few others continues to live in Makhadkhada, having rebuilt his house above the submergence zone. He is hoping for a change of new site and is undecided whether he will eventually move to his new site or continue to farm in the hills. Whilst he is there, the pantheon continues to be consecrated on the three festival days of *Divaho*, *Divali* and *Geem*.

In the first year following resettlement, all the sites waited for the pantheon to be consecrated in Makhadkhada. All the families contributed towards the sacrificial goat whose meat was distributed to them in their new sites, to be cooked and eaten in a ceremonial feast. The following year however, no meat from Makhadkhada was distributed in Vadaj, and most families in smaller sites such as Vadaj celebrated *Divaho* and *Divali* with the host village, i.e. on the appropriate day of the Hindu calendar recognised by the government as a public holiday. However, there was no ritual to mark the festival (as no pantheon has been erected in Vadaj new site), and the families simply cooked a meal of rice, lentil and in some cases meat. Other families in Vadaj new site who were from the submergence village of Gadher celebrated the festival with the new site of Sitpur where the bulk of their clansmen have been resettled. Larger resettlement sites of Makhadkhada such as Karnet, continued to time their celebration and ritual feast with the consecration of the pantheon in Makhadkhada which could take place even two months after the day appointed by the Hindu calendar. In the hills decisions such as sickness or crop failure in the village determine when a celebration can take place. The Hindu calendar plays no role.

An observation of how different submergence villages dealt with 'resettling' the village pantheon reveals that there was no thought out strategy regarding what should be done with the *dev* stones; there was no 'right' behaviour as dictated by what one may refer to as Vasava religious philosophy. Some submergence villages such as Danel and Sinduri across the river, left the *dev* stones behind and found new stones to erect in Somavale new site. Interestingly, although the inhabitants from these villages have all been resettled in a common new site, original village units and loyalties remain distinct. Thus each submergence village erected a separate new pantheon in the common new site. The celebration of village level festivals in Somavale new site takes place separately for each submergence village group, taking into account the needs and availability of old village unit members. Thus although Somavale is regarded as one new site, its inhabitants are identified with different 'village' pantheons. In contrast, the villagers of Gadher, downstream from Makhadkhada transported their stones in a truck to Sitpur new site.

The second category of *devs* are similar to the village pantheon in that they too have a physical representation. However, they are territorially alienable, and their powers are not restricted to a specific territorial area. Like the village god and his helpers, these *devs* are represented by stones, either *lingam* shaped or rectangular stone slabs, which are placed at various places within the hills.[10] The most important is *Vaghan dev* (tiger god). *Badvo* Butya Ferangya claimed to have actually seen *Vaghan dev* during his period of initiation into a *badvo*. He said:

> *Vaghan* is the son of *Pandore mata* and *Raja Phanta*. He is in all the villages. Wherever you may be staying in this world, there is *Vaghan dev* in your village. In *deshi* villages you do *Shiva poonja*. Regardless of whether you do this or not, *Vaghan* is there in your village. Your concept of *Shiva* is like *Vaghan dev*. People cannot see *devs*. Especially the sight of *Vaghan*. That is very difficult to see. His form is not like ours. It shines and shimmers all over. I saw it when I was crazy- when I spent 14 days in the jungle for my initiation I went mad. Then I saw him, but now even I cannot see him.

Thus *Vaghan dev* is believed to exist everywhere, and his powers of protection can be appealed to in any town, village or city, unlike Makhadkhada's village god, *Rojan dev* whose sphere of influence is territorially limited. Hence *devs* such as *Vaghan* and *Gam no darvajo* can be called upon and can function in the new sites too. However, it remained unclear as to what will be done with the existing stone representations of these *devs*. The community in Makhadkhada had not discussed the issue. The young headman claimed that they would simply find new stones from a nearby stream in the new site, and leave the old ones to be submerged in Makhadkhada. Others suggested that perhaps the stones would also go in the big trucks to the new sites with them, and they would be distributed amongst the various resettlement sites that the people of Makhadkhada will be dispersed in. The stones have remained in Makhadkhada and no new ones have been erected in Vadaj or Karnet new sites.

What is evident however, is that it is not the physical representation that is the main issue[11]. The *devs* are not perceived as contained within their visible shells. This is evident from the big flood incident of the mid 1970s (already described), as well as from the occasional abandoned stones one comes across when walking in the Satpura hills. There is one such stone of *Vaghan dev* in Hamutade *faliya* (hamlet) of Makhadkhada. Said Kalga Simji, whose *vaddo* the stone is on:

> It used to be given offerings many years ago, but now no one propitiates it any more. Yes, we still revere *Vaghan dev*. Its just that this particular stone has fallen out of use. There are many *Vaghan* stones all over these hills, in remote, hidden places. We still leave this stone here and just plough around it.

Thus one *dev* can have many stones representing him, and new ones can be introduced as well. Moreover, the *dev* can be invoked and communicated with in the absence of these physical representations.

Although the physical transportation and the submergence of some stones has become an issue in the context of resettlement, what is more significant is that the *devs* can be appealed to in the new sites (except the village god), and may even have new physical representations. *Devs* are not always associated with the same physical structure, and often may be conceived without form. Thus unlike other cults such as the Gwembe's 'cult of earth' in modern Zimbabwe, whose rituals and shrines were attached to inundated territories, and which hence did not survive resettlement - it was replaced by new ritual prophets - the hill Vasava's basic pantheon of gods continues to be appealed to from the new sites.

Mountain *devs* however, are more difficult to conceive of without form:

> The mountain *devs* are somewhat different from the others as their role is not as clear cut. We live amongst them, they give us our identity and our history. Our creation myths are embedded in them, living amongst them and seeing them everyday reminds us how closely our identity is tied up with these hills. But they no longer surround us once we move to live in the plains. Hence, they are less in our conscious mind, especially for the young ones. We will always respect them; the possibility of going on a pilgrimage up *Paavu* or *Phenai* will always be valued. But our relationship with these mountains and hills will change albeit in a subtler, inherently less visible way. Not being constantly amongst them, often not even seeing them, will, to some extent lessen their impact on our daily lives.

The third category of *devs* having neither a physical representation nor an obvious physical link with a particular territory, provide the least dilemma for resettlement. Thus like the Gwembe's 'cult of shades' which moves when people move, this component of the Vasava pantheon continues to function in the new sites. The bulk of the community's *devs* as well as their *bap dadas* (ancestors) fall into this category. The most frequently invoked *devs* are *Karhun mata* (to ensure a good grain stock), *Gaman mata* (for the prosperity of their livestock), *Kholo dev* (the god of the threshing ground who ensures a good harvest), and others such as *Raja Phanta*, *Gandu Thakur*, *Hukal Bukal*, *Eigda Vahan* and *Peigda Vahan*, all of whom play an important part in creation myths and legends about the supernatural world. Religious practitioners invoke these *devs* in the new site as and when their help is needed, just like in Makhadkahda.

Ancestors fall into this third category and are regarded as being somewhere between *devs* and living humans. Vasavas believe that some humans can achieve the status of *dev* upon dying. This is evident in their many myths, where the *devs* appear to have many human traits, and even deceive one another like humans. Thus the line dividing men and the supernatural is not an impenetrable one. Ancestors are remembered and offered a meal of *dangar* (unpolished rice) and *tuver dal* (split *Cajanus cajan*) with the sacrificial meat on the three days of *tyohar* following the consecration of the village pantheon on *Divaho, Divali* and *Geem*. On these occasions, the common Vasava deals directly with his ancestors. The food given to them is in lieu of respect for one's lineage, rather than as a propitiation to avoid harm and gain benevolence, as is the case with most *dev* offerings. To this extent, the Vasavas, like the Saora in Orissa believe that it is the "deceased who remain attached to the bereaved" rather than attributing agency to the bereaved to initiate contact with the deceased as in the Freudian model (Vitebsky 1993:103). Vasavas do not believe in rebirth in the Hindu sense of a cycle of life from which one must be freed, nor do they have a concept of *karma* that will determine whether and how one will be reborn. Occasionally if a child physically resembles a dead relative, he or she may be said to have come back, but the implication is rarely intended beyond the physical resemblance. Sometimes, people who have had sudden and violent deaths may be reported as having returned to their house at night as a *bhooth* (ghost/ spirit). People (more so young ones) do fear the dead if they hear strange sounds at night from burial or cremation sites.[12] Vasavas do not bury their dead except for small children and those who die from leprosy. Cremation is the norm, and this is done on the edge of the river or a stream. The actual site is rendered sacred only for three days, till the rites have been completed. After that, the area is not marked nor considered sacred anymore, although children may avoid it for some time out of fear of the dead person's spirit scaring them. Thus the issue of sacred burial sites, abundantly documented with regard to North American Indians does not arise here. In fact, it is closer to the Ghanaian situation where, it is believed that the physical and the supernatural worlds exist closely side by side and if a geographical move becomes necessary, it follows that the ancestral spirits must be called upon to make their move at the same time (Moxon 1969:163). The valley between the two *faliyas* of *Nishaat* and *Hamutade* where young children were buried, was left to be submerged. There was no attempt to unearth bodies or belongings that are buried alongside the dead.

Vasava religion has much of its symbolism in nature, on which they depend and are hence vulnerable to. Religion is considered to be important to maintaining their way of life, and their economic survival. Hence, what is important to their survival (e.g. the mountains, threshing ground, cattle) takes on a supernatural protector. To some extent, Vasava religion is need based. The concept of praying daily for general happiness, or simply as a preventive against disaster is far less evident in this society than in many of the devout, temple going Hindus of the plains.

Jatras and temples as sacred arenas

The annual Surpan festival (*jatra*) in early April, is a big event for hill communities and *deshis* alike. Days before the big event, youngsters in Makhadkahda talked about it. We set off a day early, to attend young Moosa Hamji's bride-price ceremony which was to take place at his future wife's home in Mewdi *faliya* in Gadher. The next day everyone rose early. The young girls spent hours bathing, trying on their clothes, some who had managed to borrow saris attempted to learn how to wear them; there was a strong feeling of excitement in the air. The evening meal was eaten at noon: a double intake of food to fortify them till the next day as they preferred to spend money on buying clothes and jewellery at the *jatra*. We set off towards the river at around 2 p.m. For the occasion, there were two dugouts to ferry people across. Ramka suddenly went tense. We had forgotten to get a dried coconut for the boatman as was the norm if one was menstruating. Now the boat would surely capsize. Persuasion on my part could not convince her otherwise. The walk back to the shop in Gadher was two hours each way. Eventually she agreed to come in the dugout, her slight body tense with the anticipation of drowning during the short journey across. On landing, I was in a dilemma. Had I made her question a belief she obviously had full faith in? We discussed the issue as we continued along the river, the flat sandy bank on the Maharashtra side was easier going than the steep paths we were used to on the Gujarat bank. "Perhaps we will have to pay the price when we cross back" she rationalised. We decided on a compromise. Tomorrow we would walk back home along the Maharashtra bank and swim across from Bamni to Makhadkhada, a section of the river we were confident to cross without the boat. That way we did not have to go by boat and could avoid its wrath.

The village of Manibeli was the first village scheduled to undergo submergence from the Sardar

Sarovar Dam. It served as the field base of the anti-dam campaign resulting in the till then unknown village making newspaper headlines as it became the venue for rallies, meetings and police-NGO clashes. The village is home to the Surpan/Shoolpaneshwar temple, an important stop for the *parikrama* pilgrimage along the banks of the Narmada. The *lingam* in the temple is said to be centuries old. The controversy of whether to move it or let it be submerged in the Narmada got much coverage in the press. The arguments for and against moving it were strong; both sides supported by scriptures, both sides had devout Brahmin priests who claimed to be authorities on the subject.[13] Manibeli was scheduled to be submerged in the monsoons of 1993. This year was therefore the last *jatra*, and the crowds it drew were immense.

We stopped to bathe in the river before we reached Manibeli. We approached the village just before sunset and saw crowds of people at the river bank. The city buses had arrived, the travellers eager to cleanse their sins by bathing in the sacred Narmada.

Jatras play an important role in the social life of the community. They provide an opportunity to meet other Vasavas as well as other communities who may attend the same festival. Although *jatras* (with the exception of the Surpan *jatra*) are located outside the submergence area of the project, the community's resettlement has implications on the role these festivals play in their lives. Since the festivals depend on the support of other communities who are not going to be affected by resettlement, the festivals themselves have remained the same. However the resettled Vasavas' participation in them has in some cases undergone change as relocation has made some locations too far to travel to, while encouraging participation in other festivals which were previously not attended by hill Vasavas.

A large number of festivals in the region are popular amongst *adivasi* groups such as Vasavas, Tadavis Ratthwas, Bhilalas as well as plains rural communities and high caste Hindus.[14] However, like with other *adivasi* groups such as Mundas (Chaudhuri 1980), the role these festivals play for the Vasavas and neighbouring tribes like the Bhilalas (Baviskar 1995 a, b), and these communities' interpretation of the festivals, is significantly different from that of *deshi* Hindu groups. This was clearly observable in the *Shoolpaneshwar jatra* which attracted a wide range of groups. Most *deshi* Hindu groups view the *jatra* as a 'religious' occasion: a holy site, housing both the sacred temple with its *Shiva lingam* as well as the holy Narmada river. A visit to the shrine, the singing of *bhajans* (devotional songs) and a cleansing dip in the Narmada are the highlights. My Vasava companions however, focused on a totally different aspect of the *jatra*. All night they roamed amongst the many stalls selling jewellery, clothes, and *deshi* food such as *gulfi* (Indian ice-cream), *dalya* (grams) and *jilbi* (a sweet). Interestingly, the vendors at these *jatras* are all *deshi* Hindus; Vanya who trade in jewellery and cloth that are particular to *adivasi* culture; designs that most *deshi* Hindus would not be attracted to. Bamti and Ramka sat with other villagers to watch the all night *palty* (theatre group) that entertained them with skits and songs.[15] Other youngsters disappeared into the crowd in groups of two or three. For many young Vasavas, the *jatra* provides a social arena in which they can get to know potential partners; the crowd, chaos and relative anonymity providing some private space. None of my companions visited the famous *Shoolpaneshwar* temple. For many devout Hindus, some of whom only arrive the following day, the main event in the *jatra* is the bathing of the holy *lingam* in the Narmada which takes place on the second day. By this time the shops are packing up and the Vasavas are on their way home.

Surpan *jatra* is one of the three main festivals attended by the Vasavas of Makhadkhada. The most important of them is the *jatra* of *Dev Mogra* or *Ya Mogi* (Mother *Mogi*) held at the village of the same name, seven hours journey from Makhadkhada. This festival is equally attended by plains Vasavas from Gujarat and Maharashtra, the strong belief in the goddess being the only obvious link between hill and plains Vasavas. Legend has it that *Ya Mogi,* the mother of *Vaghan dev* and wife of *Raja Phanta* roamed the whole world and eventually chose this village to settle in. Once a year, in the month of February, there is a huge gathering at the village to view the image of the goddess. She is believed to bring fertility, and many make *mantas* to her in the hope of begetting a child. Upon the wish being granted, they must return with the child, sometimes already several years old, and fulfill the promise. Thus crowds of people wait to view the goddess, and give her *mahuda* liquor, grain, cocks and goats. Chaman described the atmosphere:

> One year I waited over 11 hours before it was my turn to view her. There is nothing that can compare with *Dev Mogra*. There are so many people there, and the extent of their devotion has to be seen to be believed.

Some individuals go into trance and only the image of the goddess is said to calm them, therefore they are the only ones permitted to break what otherwise is an unusually disciplined queue by Indian standards. Many spend all five days there, enjoying the shows, stalls, and socialising with friends.

Unlike the new venue of the Surpan *jatra* which is far from many new sites and was not attended by any resettled Vasavas from Makhadkhada, the *Dev Mogra* festival is easily accessible by bus from the new sites and continues to be frequented by many. The festival is not popular with host communities around Vadaj[16]: most of its devotees come from the border area of Gujarat and Maharashtra, whose people historically share a closer cultural bond with hill Vasavas. Much of the region is affected by the *Devi* cult (Hardiman 1987). Thus villages resettled closer to this region (such as Somavale new site) experience less pressure from host groups to 'change' their ways.

The celebration of *Holi* in March is the most popular festival and all Vasavas participate in it. *Holi* is celebrated almost all over India, with the throwing of colours on people, the drinking of intoxicants like *bhang* and the lighting of a huge bonfire. All over Hindu India:

> ...*Holi* can undoubtedly be understood as a new year festival...at which the old year is symbolically destroyed in the fire to give way to a marginal period of reversal and chaos, before the normal order of things is restored (Fuller 1992:131).

Whilst the underlying rationale for the festival appears to be similar in the hills and the plains, *Holi* amongst hill Vasavas takes on a different picture. There is singing and dancing for five nights before the appointed day, which differs from the appointed day on the Hindu calendar. Men and boys dress up as *bawas*: some as part of a *manta* obligation, others do it only for fun and a little money they may collect. Some *bawas* tie *dohvis* (dried gourds) on their waists, and wear tall bamboo top hats (I could not help concluding that they must have picked up the idea from a colonial officer who ventured into the area years ago.) Others wear waist bells and peacock feather head-dresses, while the rest wear loin cloths, masks and carry bows and arrows. Some men dress up as women, donning their clothes and jewellery, and behaving in a way that is considered feminine. Troupes of *bawas*, accompanied by drummers travel through the Satpura hills, via various villages, to gather on an appointed evening at the village of Molgi in Maharashtra. Thousands of people meet there; an occasion where the larger bond of the entire tribe is visibly acknowledged. At around 4 a.m. a huge bamboo pole is set alight, and the *bawas* dance in a frenzy around its leaping flames, watched by thousands of Vasavas, scattered on the surrounding hillocks.

The following day Makhadkhada celebrates its own *Holi*, the *poonjaro* lighting the bamboo, around which *bawas* and other men, women and children dance to a frenzied rhythm. Those going into a trance have to be prevented from jumping into the fire. People often bring coconuts and chicks to be sacrificed at the fire, in fulfillment of a previous *manta* promise. Although *Holi* is celebrated at village level, it does not involve the consecration of the village pantheon, the element of ritual being overshadowed by the high level of excitement. As the Holi fire becomes smaller, the excitement of the last few days, fuelled by the consumption of large amounts of *mahuda*, invariably results in a few fights, some of which get violent, as old clan or family grudges re-surface. By midday, calm has returned as most people sleep off the excitement and exhaustion of the celebrations. By early evening, the *bawas* have started dancing again, everyone making the most of the last evening of the festival to enjoy themselves.

The trip to Molgi is no longer possible by foot from Vadaj as it was from Makhadkhada. The year following relocation, only Makti Chima went to Molgi, as her family from Bamni had been resettled in Somavale new site, and the festival provided an opportunity to visit them. Only two Vasavas in Vadaj new site dressed up as *bawas*, but there were not enough houses to go around dancing and getting money. A few host villagers gave some money but they did not join in the dancing as is the custom when a *bawa* visits one's home. The second year following relocation, no one went to Molgi and there were no *bawas*, although a group from a neighbouring new site did visit Vadaj. A few of the Vasavas joined in the dancing around the *Holi* fire lit by the Tadavis in Navi Nagri *faliya* at the edge of the new site. On the day appointed by the Hindu calendar, some children played with a bit of colour, but for the large part, there was nothing special to characterise the festival of *Holi* in Vadaj new site (except for the increased consumption of alcohol): there was none of the atmosphere that characterised the *Holi* celebrations I had participated in Makhadkhada.

It is the 'individuality' of the Vasava festivals that is beginning to fade with resettlement. Most of the Vasava festivals have some equivalent in the *desh*, and the community does not feel that resettlement will cause them to 'give up' any festival. However, observation shows that resettled groups are beginning to frequent a different range of *jatras* depending on the location of their new site and the influence of the host community amongst whom they are resettled.[17] Far more Vasavas from the new sites of Vadaj and Sitpur visited the *jatras* of *Bhadarva* and Chanod (which were never frequented from Makhadkahda) then went to even *Dev* Mogra. The main reason is the relative proximity of these festivals which implies minimum transport costs. These *jatras* are dominated by *deshi* Hindu groups, and lack the special location, music, stalls and goods that characterise festivals like Molgi. Although a few Vasavas did go into the temple at *Bhadarva*, none of them offered a *manta*, but watched with curiosity as other groups like the Tadavis danced with *manta* offerings of *jowar* (*sorghum bicolor)* seedlings carefully balanced on their heads in baskets. Being unfamiliar with much of the Hindu pantheon and associated symbolism, most Vasavas were more at ease roaming amongst the stalls below. The dispersement of the community due to resettlement means that Vasavas in different sites are being introduced to different *jatras*.

Thus the opportunity to meet other Vasavas is less, although the random allocation of sites has ensured that there is enough of a mix for *jatras* to continue playing an important role in the socialisation of young couples.

It is the 'sacredness' associated with most *deshi jatras*, their inclusion into the religious arena, that differentiates the hill Vasava's perception of these events from that of *deshi* Hindu groups. With the exception of the *Dev Mogra jatra*, Vasavas view *jatras* as outside the sphere of religion; their social and economic functions being the main ones: an opportunity for the young to meet others, a break from the routine of agricultural work and a chance to buy a range of goods in a relaxed and jovial atmosphere.

The exclusion of the hill Vasavas from the sacred arenas of *deshi* Hindu groups is not overt, nor is it entirely externally imposed. Host villagers in Vadaj often admonish resettled Vasavas for not visiting the many temples in the village, for not taking advantage of their new life and environment to 'uplift' themselves both spiritually and materially. At the same time, whenever I went past the large *Balaji* temple in Vadaj, it was either locked or there were a group of Patel women singing *bhajans* inside. None of the Vasavas had ever visited any of the nine temples scattered around Vadaj:

> We don't know what to do there, we don't feel comfortable there...occasionally we are told to go in, but the same voice implies that our dress is not respectful enough, that entering the arena of the temple warrants a change in our wider social behaviour, and that we are not ready to implement such changes.

Even prior to resettlement, the community did not regard the temples along the Narmada as sacred arenas. The priest in the Dhumna temple explained it as:

> the *dungris* do not regard this as a temple in the traditional sense of the word; it is not a sacred space to them. They fetch me water and some of them come in. But there is no reverence in the way they walk in here, in the way they regard the deity. It is curiosity rather than respect that characterises their behaviour.

Temples are an important component of the overall *deshi* image that is increasingly being viewed as the role model for the resettled community. Although a few Vasavas (especially men) are beginning to familiarise themselves with some of the Hindu pantheon, to some extent these remain outside what can be described as an active religious philosophy of the community. For *deshi* groups, religious philosophy strongly influences daily behaviour: what one eats, how one dresses, behaviour between the sexes, rituals like marriage - all of these are indicators of ones religiosity; and in turn, are influenced by the same. For the hill Vasavas however, the religious sphere is largely associated with the unknown, deeply entrenched in the natural world that they are vulnerable to, but need to exist within. To associate mundane ritual and social behaviour with religious intent would be to make the sacred profane. To bring religion into everyday behaviour and conscious thought would be diluting its strength. For most Vasavas, belief in the power of their pantheon and associated ritual is closely linked to the fact that much of the religious sphere cannot be touched or fully understood by common Vasavas. Keeping one's distance from these sacred aspects of the religious arena is the basis for a secure belief in its efficacy.

Feeders of the gods: Vasava religious practitioners

The pantheon of *devs* described above are never approached directly by any Vasava, nor are *Bhagwan* and the *devs* offered daily prayers. In fact, there is really no concept of daily prayer or any everyday ritual connected with appeasing or thanking the supernatural, as is common to most religious traditions. Vasavas communicate with their *devs* only when their help is needed, their protection sought, or when they have to be repaid for granting a request. At such times, the *devs* are approached by a 'religious practitioner'. There are three broad categories of such specialized people whose functions may overlap, depending on each individual's skill and knowledge.

Bhua is often used as a generic category to include all religious practitioners. *Bhuas* in Makhadkhada are not regarded solely as 'priests' as is understood by the term '*Brahmin*' or 'clergy'. They are also doctors, shamans and medicine men, these roles being closely linked to their ability to communicate with *Bhagwan* and ask him for favours and appease him through the institution of *manta* and *poonja*.

A *badvo* is simply a more powerful *bhua*. The distinction is one of degree, and no absolute line separates the two. *Badvos* are universally acknowledged to be *bhuas* as well, although some *bhuas* cannot become *badvos*, whilst others choose not to. The talent of being a *bhua* and/or *badvo* is not inherited. As *bhua* Vinya Lekji, rationalized:

> Not everyone can learn to communicate with *Bhagwan*. You have to be chosen by *Bhagwan*. I can teach my sons all I want, but if they don't have it in them to learn, then there is nothing anyone can do.

Butya Ferangya, the most powerful *badvo* in Makhadakhada added:

> To be a *badvo* one has to know every grass, tree, even the parents of every goat; it is very demanding, therefore *Bhagwan* reveals it only to few people". "I spent 14 days in the jungle during which I consumed no water or food. Not even *mahuda*. There I saw *Vaghan dev* and learnt the thousands of *dev* names that I talk to you about. The creation

> stories about our *devs* were revealed to me, and I learnt medicinal properties of various plants. I was half crazed for those days."

Bhua Vinya Lekji however, did not go through such a period. He partly learnt things from another *bhua*, and picked up a lot himself, as he had it in him to learn. Vinya is highly respected for his medicinal skills especially concerning child birth and he would spend hours talking about the cases of breech babies and other complications that he had handled successfully:

> Rima down in Bhumachiya *faliya* sent for me one night as they sensed something was wrong with her delivery. The baby was breech. First I cut my nails. Then I washed my hands and oiled them. I slipped my whole palm into the woman and I carefully turned the baby around. It came out without a problem. Then two nights ago I was up for six hours with Revli who had a hard labour. The placenta would not come out and that is dangerous as it can kill the mother...

Vinya claimed that he had consciously not developed his powers of witchcraft detection:

> I can detect if an illness is the result of witchcraft, and if I pushed myself I could detect the witch, but I don't, as it simply causes enmity. I do not want to develop my powers to become a *badvo*, as there is more risk involved in such powerful work.

The third category is that of the *poonjaro* who is the caretaker of the village pantheon and the only one who can consecrate or 'feed' it on the three occasions of *Divaho, Divali* and *Geem*. Unlike the other practitioners, the position of the *poonjaro* is hereditary and has always been held by the same family. During his life, the *poonjaro* trains one of his sons to take on his role. Says Partu Vanya, the son of the current *poonjaro* Vanya Pinya:

> I cannot feed the pantheon whilst my father lives. We cannot have two *poonjaros*. Only after he stops functioning as the *poonjaro*, will I take on that role.

In a way, the work of a *bhua* and *badvo* is seen as more demanding than that of the *poonjaro*, because it involves detecting witches, curing illnesses which may need strong *mantas* involving going into a trance. Thus the reliance on the magnetism of the individual is greater than that for the *poonjaro*, emphasising the necessity of being 'chosen' for the function. Although most *bhuas* and *badvos* are men, women can also be 'chosen' for this role. The *poonjaro* however, is always male.

I often came across *bhuas* performing *mantas* relating to illness when visiting houses or simply walking in the hills. *Bhagwan* is the one responsible for controlling illness and for an individual to get access to the cure, he must communicate with the supernatural. Hence, the *bhua* is needed, and a separate category of 'doctor' makes no sense. Whenever illness strikes, be it from an obvious, visible snake bite, an infection such as tuberculosis, or witchcraft, its origin must be determined, before treatment can proceed. Depending on the cause of the illness, an appropriate treatment is recommended, and on recovery the specified *manta* fulfilled.

For illnesses traced to natural causes, a treatment of herbs may be prescribed. If this is unsuccessful, or for illnesses of a more serious nature which are seen to have supernatural causes behind them, the herbal remedy is coupled with a *manta*. This dual nature of the treatment is according to the *bhuas* what keeps their hold over their profession. They claim that even if they revealed a medicinal plant to the layman, the latter would not know when to pick it, how to treat it or administer it to the patient. Moreover the layman would not be able to invoke and call upon the spirit of the Supernatural, which is imperative to the success of the *manta*. Only those 'chosen' by *Bhagwan* have these powers. The medicine without the *manta* is of no effect. While the former attacks the indicators of the illness (such as pain or a wound), it is the latter that is the antidote to the cause (such as witchcraft). One without the other is ineffective. Ratan Chima's parents had noticed some white spots on his back when he was two years of age and suspected leprosy. The *bhua* was sent for and a treatment of bark and leaves rubbed regularly on the spots was suggested. In addition, Ratan was put on a strict diet where he had to avoid strong foods such as chillies, garlic and spices. A year later the spots disappeared and a small *manta* involving the sacrifice of a chick and some *mahuda* was carried out.

In many cases of illness that I observed, the cause was detected as witchcraft which calls for stronger bhua powers if the witch is to be detected and the evil removed. One night Makti Chima awoke with terrible stomach pain. Her daughter and niece tried to soothe the pain by pressing wads of cloth heated by the fire on her stomach. When the pain showed no signs of subsiding, her young son Homyu was sent to summon *bhua* Vinya Lekji from the neighbouring hamlet. On arrival, Vinya asked Makti what her activities that day had been. She said it had been a normal day weeding in the fields. In the afternoon, she had weeded Jerma Veshta's fields along with others as he had summoned kin labour. Vinya asked for *urad* (*phaseolus mungo*) grains and put them on a *khakhra* (*butea monosperma)* leaf. I had seen *badvo* Butya Ferangya read the grains on several occasions; the sick or harmed individual (or cattle) is made to touch the grains, thus conveying information regarding their illness. The grains are then put on a *khakhra* leaf which is read by the practitioner. With his index finger he 'reads' the leaf like there was a script on it, moving his finger from left to right, working towards the bottom end of the leaf and then starting on top again like it was a new page.

> Ruksa, you read books which I cannot understand. Similarly I read *khakhra* leaves. So you see I am literate too. It is all written here, the picture is

> acted out before my eyes, just like a story. But one has to know how to read it.

As he reads, Butya describes what he sees, slowly building the situation from a few objects to a recognisable scene:

> I see two small houses...there is another house, no wait it is the house of bees. "Yes", interjects the client, we do have bees building a nest on the framework of an old cattle shed near our house.

Butya continues:

> there is a path leading off from the beehives, towards a *peepad* tree...it is early morning and I see someone walking up the path towards your house...

Helped by the client, the *badvo* attempts to create a picture of the scene to help identify the cause of the misfortune, in this case, the death of a cow and calf. Then he begins to describe the pain of ill luck that the individual is experiencing. The process can take from ten minutes to an hour depending on the seriousness of the case. If the need arises, the *badvo* may appeal to the supernatural to help him along; as enticement he may promise a chick or some *mahuda* which the client will have to provide. Only in very special cases does he reveal the name of a witch; in most cases he focuses on trying to find where the evil is buried and to counter-act it by letting the images lead him to the spot where the evil (a few stones) will be dug up and disposed off appropriately.[18] After the divination, some grain is tied in a cloth which is carried on the patient's person until she/he recovers and the promised *manta* is fulfilled.

Vinya is less elaborate in his reading. He quietly mutters to himself, then says that the stomach ache is related to jealousy:

> You Makti, are a hard worker and a quick weeder. This afternoon you weeded faster than the others and someone put evil on you at sunset. It is no use trying to find out who it is, but I will cure you by removing the evil.

Vinya first identifies the point of pain in the body. By depressing the point with his thumb, he traps the evil. He then blows some ash on the spot, and Makti simultaneously coughs out the evil. After ten minutes the pain abates but commences again. He now asks for *jowar* and *mahuda* to increase the potency of the offering and steps outside the house to offer it to the *devs*. He then asks me for a headache tablet and includes that in the offering, instructing Makti to swallow it. After an hour Makti falls asleep. The pain does not return and a few days later a *manta* involving some *mahuda* and *jowar* is carried out.

Vasavas do occasionally use the government and private dispensaries in town. Due to the time and money involved, visits to the town are reserved for more serious cases. Usually, a *bhua* or *badvo* is sent for. Most families have a preferred practitioner, often a close relative or someone living near by. In general people are quite flexible, and use whoever is available and near at hand at the time. Besides, different *bhuas* are well known for different things. For example, in Makhadkhada, the old *bhua* Vinya Lekji is highly respected for his skill in delivering babies, Partu Vanya the son of the current *poonjaro* (village priest) is said to be successful at curing leprosy, whilst *badvo* Butya Ferangya is approached with illness and ill luck of a more serious nature (such as the death of many cattle), which requires the identification of a *dhakan* (witch).

The Vasavas are not opposed to the use of modern medicine. In fact, it has been observed that their largest bulk expenditure is on police, crime cases and on modern medicine (Arch-Vahini data). They do not see it as a threat to their traditional medicine. The *badvo* explains the principle of his own medicine in terms of his experience with allopathic doctors:

> Just as sometimes the *davakhana* (dispensary) medicine works and sometimes not, in the same

> way, sometimes I can cure a patient and sometimes not. Ultimately it is all ordained by the supernatural world. But we have to try our best.

The *bhuas* frequent the town doctors, and so do not discourage others from going. Interestingly, I observed, that while many did visit town doctors, they often came back and went to the *bhua*, unsatisfied that the doctor did not give them the all powerful injection and only gave them some pills. Many go first to the *bhua* and only go to town when things become serious. Often hospitalisation is needed, which although free, incurs travel cost, and cost of housing and feeding the relative who accompanies the patient. Moreover, being unused to the city, many leave hospital before the treatment is complete, therefore not fully recovering. A *manta* is then invariably carried out.

Resettlement will decrease the use of the traditional medicinal practitioner due to several reasons. Firstly the hamlets of Vasavas will be broken up, so all new sites may not have a *bhua*. In many cases, access to government health centres will be easier than calling a *bhua*. This has already increased the community's use of government medical facilities in the new sites.

> Here in Makhadkhada the *bhua* is a few minutes away, while the town doctors are several hours and several rupees away. So we call the *bhua* and only go to town if his treatment does not seem to work. But when we go to the new site, the *sarkari* (government) doctor is right there in the host village, and we get free medicine, so we go there even for the slightest headache.

Secondly, the *bhua* will not have access to the medicinal plants that he finds in the hills. He does not appear to perceive this as a threat to his profession in the new sites:

> I have not as yet seen what is available in the new sites. But I am sure I will find what I need. The skill of a *badvo* is to be

> able to scour the countryside thoroughly, and find what he needs. If the exact thing is not there, there will be substitutes. And surely the hosts too must be using something. They have their *badvos* too.

The hosts do have traditional medicinal practitioners too, but in the *desh*, the distinction between the *Brahmin* or priest (albeit of a lower caste), and that of the doctor is strong. Whether the *bhua* will get absorbed into one of the two categories, or whether he will remain a unique combination of the two, has to be seen. Nonetheless, what he appears confident of, is that he will retain his special position within the community. The *bhua* is more likely to be influenced by the *bhagat* cults which are popular amongst Tadavis.

The *badvo, bhua* and *poonjaro* are rarely paid in cash for their services. A small token of Rs. 2 to 5 may be offered, but this is often declined, especially from kin. However, the practitioner does get much *mahuda* to drink and a meal of the grain and meat offering. It is not uncommon to see most of the *badvos* in a constant state of drunkenness. They often told me:

> If we do not drink we cannot remember the chants and *devs* names. Then we cannot communicate with the *devs* and get their blessings. Just as our gods need alcohol, we *bhuas* need it to, for our work demands much spiritual strength. I can go several days without food, if I have *mahuda*. I sometimes drink one whole *ras* (1000 c.c.) in one night.

Powerful *badvos* travel a lot, and in the course of this pick up much news and gossip. Hence they are the source of much entertainment in any hamlet where they rest during their travels. They are welcomed and freely offered food and shelter during their travels in the hills.

While the specialized skills of Vasava religious practitioners are respected within the community, *bhuas, badvos* and *poonjaros* do not form a separate clergy as is found in Hinduism and Christianity, nor are their individual identities dominated by their roles as communicators with the *devs.*[19] During a ritual the *bhua* appears similar to the Hindu *Brahmin* priest, in that it is him alone who communicates with the *Bhagwan* and makes him offerings. However, at all other times, the *bhua* is difficult to distinguish from any other Vasava and does not command the same degree of social superiority nor has separate rules of social interaction with other members of his community as does the Hindu *Brahmin*. An important reason for this is that the *bhua*, unlike a practicing *Brahmin,* is not limited in his activities to dealing with the supernatural. His role as a *bhua* is performed over and above his other role as a contributing member to the economy of the village. The more popular *bhuas* in their old age may spend a smaller proportion of their time farming, as demand for their religious and medicinal skills are high and a *bhua* cannot deny his skills to anyone. Other members of their family thus take over his share of agricultural labour. But such cases are rare, and most practitioners perform their rituals in the evenings and during months when agricultural work is less demanding. The only case I knew in Makhadkhada, is that of Butya Ferangya, whose powers as a *badvo* are said to be very strong, and who is in constant demand from villages far and wide. He has almost stopped doing other things to help around the house.

Within Vasava society, there is respect and awe resulting from fear (but in this community the latter is fairly invisible) that accompanies any relationship between the clergy and the common man in most societies. Thus although the *bhua* commands respect during his performance, there are no benefits for his family either economically or socially. Hence *Bhuas* interact with the rest of the society on an egalitarian basis, sharing the same experiences, and subject to the same economic hardships, unlike the *Brahmins* of *deshi* Hindu society who enjoy a superior economic and social position than lower caste groups.

The implications of resettlement on rites and rituals

The ritual of *Divaho* in August is performed for the green jungle, rain and cattle. It is one of the three occasions when the village pantheon is consecrated, the others being *Divali* in December and *Geem* in February (the latter corresponds to the *deshi* festival of *Maha Shivratri*). On these occasions, villagers collect around the *lingam* shaped stones which are otherwise carefully avoided, as the *devs* must not be disturbed unnecessarily. After the morning meal, men and children begin to assemble; women are not allowed in the sacred arena once menstruation has commenced. Only a few men and children attend the actual ritual, which is very low-key, compared to the singing and dancing that takes place for several nights prior to the day of the *Divaho* ritual. Once again, I straddle the line between being an insider and outsider. I am a woman, but Vanya Pinya, the *poonjaro* knew I was keen to attend.

> It's alright Ruksa, you already know more about our religious rites than most Vasava women. Let's just say you can come because you are not Vasava.

Like with most rituals the day had been chosen taking into account the workload of the community, and after ensuring that there were no serious illnesses or recent deaths in the village.

The *poonjaro* stands before the village pantheon, clad only in his traditional *kushti* (loin cloth). A group of five men, including his son Parta who will become the *poonjaro* after his father, sit around to assist in the proceedings. All the men have observed the cleansing process of not sleeping on a *khatla* (bed) and avoiding women for five days prior to the ritual. That morning they had bathed in the stream and washed their hair with sour milk, thus purified for their part in the ceremony. There is a pile of *jowar* tied in a *lugda* (piece of cloth), bottles of *mahuda*, some chickens and a goat: the standard offerings at large rituals like *Divaho*. Every household in the village contributes grain and *mahuda* flowers, and the cost of the sacrificial animals is shared equally amongst them (Rs. 5 per household). The *mahuda* is soaked and then distilled by men the day before the ritual. A special technique is used for *mahuda* which is to be offered to the *devs*: the distilled alcohol drips into a small container which flows out into bottles via a pipe, thus avoiding any human contamination.

Vanya chants, invoking the *devs* before the pantheon of *lingam* shaped stones. As he chants, he pours some grain from the large pile into small heaps before the stones. Small amounts of *mahuda* alcohol, are also placed in bottles before the *dev*. This goes on for some time, the chanting ranging from inaudible murmurings to the clear recitation of *dev* names: *Raja Phanta, Hukul Bukul, Gam no Darvajo*. Requests for a good monsoon and high crop yields are made and repeated; the large pile of grain steadily diminishes as it is added to the growing piles before the stones. It is now time for the animals to be sacrificed. The *poonjaro* stands with a hen, chants, and places some blessed grain (from the small piles) and *mahuda* on her head. If the animal shakes its head (a sign that the *dev* has entered it), it has been accepted as an offering and its head is severed and placed before the stones, on the grain pile. This is repeated with more hens and cocks and finally a goat.[20]

Two of the *poonjaro's* assistants hold the chosen goat by strings tied to its neck. Vanya puts some *jowar* and *mahuda* on its head, asking that it be accepted as a sacrifice. The goat however, refuses to shake its head. After several unsuccessful attempts the *poonjaro* becomes impatient, his voice rising as he attempts to reason and bargain with the *dev:*

> Why won't you accept this goat? It is a large one; we have all paid money towards it. What wrong has the village done you? We do *Divaho* ritual every year, we do *Divali* and *Geem* every year. You don't want it? Ok, that's up to you but I tell you it is a good goat. Why are you playing games with us? Have we not fed you well all these years?... do you wish that we desert you?.

Finally the goat shakes its head vigorously and one of the assistants raises his *kuvad* (axe) to bring it down heavily on the goat's neck. The animal bucks wildly, bleating loudly and manages to break loose from one string, half dragging the other assistant down the grassy hill slope. The *kuvad* comes down heavily again, but the handle breaks, the blade catching the goat on the neck causing it to bleat even more loudly. The *poonjaro's* voice rises:

> You are getting greedy now, why won't you take what we are offering you? No, Veshta (one of the assistants), don't bring another *kuvad*. We will kill it with this one, even if it is broken. Who says I am not *bhua* enough to make the *dev* accept our offering...he is just playing games, my powers can overcome such behaviour.

Finally, the head is severed and the *poonjaro* relaxes, his place in society once again secure, the villagers assured by his conviction and power.

The *Divaho* ritual is completed by men in turn coming up to the grain pile, pressing a *tini* (mark on forehead) of grain stuck with alcohol on their forehead, offering a token of few coins, and joining their hands in the Indian greeting of *namaste* as a sign of respect to the *dev*. Since an important purpose of *Divaho* is to ensure the well-being of cattle, the head of the Guvar family that looks after the villagers' cattle enacts his herding behaviour by lightly beating the men and children with a branch from the *bili* tree. As on other occasions (such as the death ceremony) such ritualistic behaviour re-enforces the strong inter-dependence of the Guvars and hill Vasavas. The remaining alcohol is drunk by all the men present and the blessed grain and heads are eaten by the important men. The body of the goat is distributed amongst all the families, which during my stay numbered 120 portions. Each of the three village rituals are followed by *tyohar* the following day. This involves a feast of *dangar* or rice and *tuver dal* with the sacrificial meat. The meal is cooked by each household, and is offered to the ancestors on *khakhra* leaves before the family consume it.

The mixture of supplication and bargaining described above can be observed in many Vasava rituals, and highlights an interesting aspect of the community's relationship with the supernatural. The dualistic nature of this relationship is the reason why Brahmin priests often refer to *dungri bhuas* as disrespectful towards *Bhagwan*. Communication with *devs* takes place through specific rituals conducted by the *bhuas* and is in the form of propitiation: to ask for a favour or to make an offering of thanks for a favour received. There is no direct link between the common Vasava and the pantheon of gods nor is there any concept of daily praying for general well-being. In fact, it is advised that the supernatural be left alone unless occasion arises to call upon a *dev*, and the village pantheon is never approached except on three occasions when it is consecrated. Initially I failed to understand the children's reluctance to accompany me to the site of the village pantheon which I wanted to photograph and sketch. When they did come, they fearfully stood some distance away. The mystery unravelled as I began to talk to people about it. I was told:

> *Bhagwan* is there always, he is always alert. But he has so much to do. *Bhagwan* can give both

> happiness and sorrow. Everything can be controlled by him. We believe that we must not disturb him unnecessarily. It must not be treated like a casual relationship. So we let him be unless we need his help. Why disturb him if things are fine with you? The children are wary of coming to the pantheon, in case they disturb *Bhagwan* without cause.[21]

The community thus communicates with the *dev* pantheon only through the performance of specific rituals. *Poonja* is accepted as a general term for any sort of religious ritual, but it is possible to further distinguish two kinds: *poonja* and *manta*. The term *poonja* has the equivalent of *puja* amongst *deshi* caste Hindus (Fuller 1992). Both refer to an offering made to the supernatural, usually by a priest in the case of (Vasava) *poonjas*, and always by a priest in case of (Hindu) *pujas*. However, they differ in some very essential ways. Firstly, *poonja* is not done in front of any deity, while Hindu *puja* usually has the presence of an idol (or a symbol) of the god being worshipped. Secondly, Vasava ritual invariably involves the sacrifice of an animal and the offering of alcohol whereas in the plains communities surrounding Makhadkhada, *puja* is vegetarian and devoid of alcohol. Thirdly, Hindu *puja* involves the chanting of *mantras* (chants/prayers) from the sacred Sanskrit texts, while Vasava rituals have no texts backing them, and communication between the *bhua* and *dev* is more like a dialogue around the specific purpose of the ritual at hand. Moreover, the *devs* and myths of the hill Vasavas are not known to the plains Hindus, and most Vasavas are unfamiliar with even the more popular gods of the Hindu trinity. Thus whilst the plains communities conform in general to Fuller's image of a *puja*, Vasava ritual appears to have greater similarity with what Fuller terms as sacrifice or *bali*. This similarity is restricted to the items offered and to an extent to the manner in which they are offered and killed.

The form taken by most *poonjas* and *mantas* is similar to the *Divaho poonja* described above. Besides the three village *poonjas* performed by the *poonjaro* on *Divaho, Divali* and *Geem*, there are household level *poonjas* conducted by *bhuas* and *badvos*. These village *poonjas* "ritually express village unity", which is important in Vasava villages where it is one's geographic unit i.e. hamlet, rather than village affiliation that is normally stressed (Fuller 1992:151). Some *poonjas* are prescribed in their frequency while others are performed as the need arises.

Whilst *poonjas* are normally prescribed in their frequency and performed for a group (e.g. village or household), *mantas* are performed for the individual (human and animal). In most cases *mantas* are aimed at counter-acting illness, or bad luck such as the death of several cattle. Thus they are not prescribed in their frequency and take place as the need arises. A *manta* is the promise or vow made to a particular *dev* or *mata*, or to *Bhagwan* at large, that he or she will be given a specified sacrifice consisting of grain, meat and alcohol, if the illness or bad luck is cured. The promise is not carried out if the ill luck persists. If an individual falls ill, a *bhua* is sent for. In most cases, along with giving medicine, exorcising a spirit or providing other treatment he will make a promise to the supernatural, that, in the event of healing, the patient will offer certain things to the *dev*. The same *bhua* that ordered the *manta* during the illness, must carry out the sacrificial ritual at the later stage. The *bhua* may give the individual some blessed grain tied in a cloth that must be worn around the neck or arm and only taken off after the completion of the promised *manta*. Sometimes, a sick person's hair may get matted, a sign that he is blessed, and this must not be combed or cut till the *manta* is completed. If, as the treatment progresses, there is no sign of improvement, the *bhua* may increase the value of the earlier *manta* assuming that the *devs* are not satisfied. *Mantas* thus offer scope for bargaining with *Bhagwan*, by increasing the amount of sacrificial offering promised. Hence these rituals can be costly. The Vasavas never forfeit the promised offering as there is a strong belief that if the *manta* is not fulfilled when the family can afford it, the person will fall ill again, or die, or the ill luck will multiply.

The ceremony that fulfils a large *manta* pertaining to an individual's health is called a *Paradi,* and can go on all night. The *badvo* invokes many gods, often going into a trance himself. Or sometimes, the *mata* (goddess) enters someone in the crowd, who leaps forward, shaking violently, throws himself or herself before the ritual pile of offerings, their head going around vigorously, and the goddess is believed to talk through them. A wooden structure or *babri* is planted at the site as proof that the individual and his family have fulfilled their obligation to the Supernatural.

The items offered to the supernatural are a significant component of any ritual as they are the objects through which dialogue and bargaining with the supernatural takes place. In Makhadkahda, *bunti (echinochloa crus)* is the most common grain used in *poonjas* and *mantas*, followed by *jowar* and occasionally *dangar*. This ritual grain hierarchy corresponds to the consumption value of the grain in Vasava society. Since *dangar* is relatively scarce and preferred over *jowar* for consumption, which in turn is preferred over *bunti*, often, a *badvo* or *bhua* may start a *manta* with *bunti*, but if it is not successful (for example, if the patient's stomach does not stop hurting), then he may go on to offer *jowar*. Similarly, chicks, hens, cocks, and goats have a hierarchy in terms of their potency to make a *manta* effective. Later the food is cooked and consumed by the *badvo* and other men of the extended family. Women are excluded from the consumption of 'pure' foods after the commencement of menstruation.[22] *Mahuda* alcohol accompanies every *poonja* and *manta* except that of the *kholo dev* who is a *suka dev* (dry god).

Resettlement is bound to create some change in ritual due to re-organisation of social groups (which formed the unit for *poonjas*), the unavailability of certain ritual items (such as *bili* leaves) and the *deshi* stigma attached to meat and alcohol, crucial elements in Vasava rituals, but considered 'vices' and 'impure' amongst many host groups. During the transition period, no rituals were carried out in the new sites and all *mantas* and *poonjas* continued to be done in Makhadkhada. However, upon relocation, the village was scattered, and as described earlier, each site has drifted into celebrating village *poonjas* separately or with host groups (i.e. on the day designated by the Hindu calendar). Since the *dev* stones remain in Makhadkhada, the new sites of Vadaj had no *Divaho* celebration. I went with some villagers to the nearby new site of Sitpur where families from Mewdi and Gadher *faliyas* of Gadher village had been resettled, to participate in their *Divaho* ritual.

The *poonjaro* from Mewdi had brought with him some of the *dev* stones from the hills and these had been placed at the corner of a field, amongst the big roots of a *peepad* tree. The ritual closely followed the one I had observed in Makhadkhada, although the part with the Guvar was omitted as there were no Guvars in Sitpur new site. The herder family who had been allocated land in Sitpur new site, had, like other Guvar families, given it for share-cropping, and returned to life in the Satpura hills, above the dam reservoir. Other *poonjas* and *mantas* that I observed in Vadaj, were performed as in the hills, any minor variations were traced to the performance habits of the *bhua* or *badvo* rather than to any prescriptive procedures.

For the large part, *poonjas* and *mantas* in the new sites remain a purely Vasava affair; host villagers are never invited, and the rituals take place in the privacy of the new site. Things are likely to change as resettled Vasavas make friends with host groups especially Tadavis, and are invited to attend their ceremonies. Besides, the unavailability of certain materials will mean that the rituals will invariably become Hinduised in many ways. *Bunti* is not grown in the new sites, nor is it available in the shops, as the demand for this coarse, mountain grain is negligible in the plains. The plains Hindus prefer rice as an offering in their ritual, along with *ghee* (clarified butter) and milk which are often poured into a sacred fire. I observed the use of *dangar* in rituals in Makhadkhada, although *bunti, jowar* and *urad* (the latter for tying a *manta*) were much more widely used.

During Chaggan Chaman's *Aathun poonja*, *bunti* was used with *dangar*, the latter not normally used in this ritual. His father, who was performing the ritual, later told me:

> Our *bunti* stocks have dwindled now. We no longer plough the hills so we have to start using what we have. We work with the assumption that it is the end which is important, not the means to the end. After all, the hosts live with the same uncertainties and problems we face here, and if they can satisfy the *devs* with *suka* (machine polished rice), that should work fine. We are not so dogmatic about that level of ritual detail.

Similar compromises were made at other rituals. *Bili* leaves were substituted with *peepad*, *mantas* that had promised a goat were changed by the *bhua* to two or three chickens, the sharp decrease in livestock making the large offerings I observed in the hills impossible for the resettled communities. In some cases *bhuas* who had made the original *manta* in the hills were resettled too far away or remained in the hills, hence the *manta* was fulfilled by another *bhua* from a neighbouring site, unless it was a very big and important one.

The issue becomes more problematic with reference to the use of *mahuda* alcohol in religious rites. Whilst jaggery alcohol can be substituted for *mahuda* in the context of social drinking, Vasavas stress that *mahuda* is *chowkhu* (pure), whereas jaggery alcohol is not considered as such, and hence cannot be offered to the *devs*. Whilst in Makhadkhada, most elders and religious practitioners were confident that religious rites in the new sites would demand *mahuda* alcohol and no substitute would do:

> The quantity needed only for the ritual is minimum, and we will use whatever *mahuda* we can get.

A few younger men suggested that with time, they might give up the practice of offering *mahuda* to the *devs* as the hosts did not use alcohol in religious rites.

My observation of *mantas* and *poonjas* in the new sites shows that *mahuda* is the preferred offering used, although jaggery alcohol was used in some small *mantas*. *Bhua* Mangji Chaman who relocated to Vadaj new site from Gadher, was often called upon by Vasavas from Makhadkhada to fulfill small *mantas* that another *bhua* may have initiated as the latter was now too far away. I watched him take some ash and rub it over Meki Hamji's back where she had been complaining of severe pain. He blew on it as he rubbed, in an attempt to get out the evil spirit that had been embedded within through witchcraft. Meki claimed relief after some time and a small *manta* was done with jaggery alcohol and some *jowar* grain. Mangji said that a similar *manta* may have taken on a different form in the hills.

> Here (in Vadaj new site) our situation is different. People don't have as many resources. Look around you...families that had 10 cattle, 15 goats and 7

> chickens now have just 3 cattle and 2 chickens. Where we had *burdyas* (large baskets) of *mahuda* in our *madas* now the *burdyas* are broken and lie empty. So us *bhuas* have to take this into account when we do the *mantas*. I may have prescribed a chicken and 2 bottles of *mahuda* for Hamsa's ritual in the hills. But here we fulfilled it with a *putli* (small bag) of jaggery alcohol and some *jowar*....I don't know, but we assume the *dev* will also adjust and will accept this instead. For larger *mantas* *mahuda* is still needed. Some of us get it from kin in the hills, some of us buy it from nearby markets or other sites where there are *mahuda* trees.

Rituals in the plains follow a different, more rigid calendar, compared to in the hills where each village set its day taking into account the particular problems and availability of its inhabitants. Vasava rituals such as *Divali, Divaho* and *Holi* have equivalent celebrations in the *desh*, but the form they take is often different. Although it is too early to identify specific changes that these rituals may take, it is likely that in time, certain aspects of the ceremony that are considered 'primitive' (such as the application of white ash and adornment of leaves, wearing of loin cloth by men after the *Divali* ritual) may get discarded (Chaudhuri 1980). Moreover Vasava songs, which are such an important part of village rituals in the hills, are changing as the young learn *deshi* songs from neighbouring Tadavi groups who often make fun of songs sung in the *dungri* dialect. The new songs are more inhibited in their expression, leaving less scope for creative additions, besides being in a different language. The community recognises that they will have to adapt:

> Of course we will miss singing our *Holi* songs on the hillock near the *poonjaro's* house. But it is submerged. We will still celebrate *Holi* with the hosts like they do. That is our new life and so we have to learn their ways.

Thus, although some rituals will be lost, many will simply take on a *deshi* adaptation, losing the very elements that distinguished them as *dungri* in the first place. Host religion and rituals invariably appear dominant, and resettled populations often adapt to these. For example, resettled Nubians expressed a greater interest in Islam, attended mosques and simplified lengthy, traditional rituals to resemble those of host Muslims (Fernea and Rouchdy 1991:192-194). This does not imply that the Vasavas will copy their hosts in every aspect. At the same time, those aspects of ritual retained by the Vasavas are likely to be those which are approved by the hosts. In time, these will be 're-clothed' and reinterpreted within the Hindu philosophy of the dominant groups in the plains.

Change as an aspect of Vasava philosophy and culture

Resettled Vasavas' desire to 'mix in' with the dominant host communities has meant that the resettled community is very cognizant of, and vocal about, the changes that are taking place in the spheres of religion and consumption: the two areas that in the past had played a pivotal role in emphasizing their distinctiveness from plains (now host) communities. This should not be taken to mean that resettled Vasavas are blindly copying their host communities. The changes I observed in these areas are much more selective: the desire to 'fit in' does not stem from an inherent feeling of inferiority amongst the Vasavas (as is the case with many minority communities), but from a desire to be seen as adaptive and willing to change. In fact, I observed that there is a deep rooted acceptance to adapting to change within the community's philosophy and culture. It is not limited to the younger generation; it goes beyond the traditional 'change/fashion receptive' areas of clothes, jewellery, and music; and it is primarily a result of a 'push' rather than 'pull' factor, i.e. the community makes the effort to adopt a new way rather than 'giving in' to something imposed by the dominant outside group. It was evident even while they were in the hills where outside contact and related 'push' factors were marginal.

This ease of acceptance of different behaviours across different aspects of life has been crucial in helping the hill Vasavas adapt to their involuntary resettlement. My research shows that although hill Vasavas are the most isolated group in Gujarat to be impacted by the Sardar Sarovar dam, their attitude towards their experience of resettlement has been relatively speaking, the most receptive and hopeful. This is not to deny or belittle the numerous issues that have been a tough battle in this process. This is not to imply that the process of resettlement has been smooth, or that it has not deeply impacted many aspects of this community's life and lifestyle. However, it is interesting that, compared to other groups who have always been more exposed to plains communities (such as the Tadavis and Ratthwas), and hence for whom the move can be assumed to have been less 'traumatic', the hill Vasava groups I worked with showed a much stronger mental acceptance of their situation. They tended to focus much less on the overall 'trauma' of the move itself – the discussions and debates were largely around the details: who had 'black' land and who had 'white' land, how would they learn the bus routes to visit relatives in the hills and in other new sites, who had successfully managed to find a honest middle man to sell cotton. This was unusual considering that the learning curve of new ways was steepest for this group compared to the more exposed Tadavi and Ratthwa resettlers.

The transformation of many aspects associated with religious life – individual rituals, attendance and behaviour at community fairs, performance of festivals, increasing familiarity with the common gods in the Hindu pantheon – are viewed by the hosts as good indicators of the resettled community's effort and willingness to adapt to the more 'developed' ways of the hosts. This attention to religion as a central indicator of the community's overall attitude to adopt *deshi* ways is traced to two reasons. Firstly, as mentioned earlier, religion (described by the institutions discussed in this paper) was/is one of the most visible ways that plains groups differentiate themselves from hill *adivasis*. Thus, plains communities/host groups see changes in this area as a sure sign that their hill friends are amending their 'primitive' ways. Secondly, the host groups 'credit' themselves as responsible for effecting these 'positive' changes in religion that will 'guide the hill *adivasis* onto the right path'. This gives them a sense of satisfaction and capitalize on every occasion to highlight their role in this process.

For the resettled community, the emerging changes in this area are not resisted strongly as they are viewed as "paying a good return". That is, they do not see them as very demanding or painful, they do not view them as being an imposition forced on them by the host groups, they see them simply as a consequence of the practical implications of moving (different availability of grains, distance from hill festivals, etc.); and they realize that the potential benefit in terms of acceptance of their community is substantial, due to the 'visibility' of the changes and the high attention the hosts give these aspects of their life.

At this relatively initial phase of resettlement, the Vasavas do not view these changes as a threat to their philosophy:

> What is most sacred to us is out philosophy, our stories of creation and our knowledge about our history and ancestors who have become *devs*. The *mantas, poonjas* and *jatras* are important but they are a human means to achieve something and hence there is less resistance to the details changing (e.g.

> using a different grain, celebrating a festival on a day defined by a Hindu calendar). Moving to the plains cannot force us to change our thoughts, to forget where we come from and our ties to our history and larger community. The *deshis* don't care about those areas that are most crucial to us. They are more concerned that *Divali* is celebrated when they consider it the right day, that we do worship what they see as a 'stone'...

At some level, it appears almost convenient, that the aspects of religion that get the largest 'pay offs' (i.e. positive recognition from hosts) from change, are the ones that the Vasavas are least resistant to changing. At this point, the changes in the religious sphere are not seen as a significant threat to their self-identity. The changes in production patterns following relocation, specifically the erosion of resettled Vasavas' self-sufficiency is perceived as the major threat to this identity and the focus of their current complaints and resources. As mentioned at the outset, Vasava self-identity is built around their self-sufficiency in production while living in the hills. However, their identity as constructed by *deshis* highlighted aspects of religion and consumption patterns (food, dress etc). This provides the underlying rationale for the observed 'willingness' of resettled Vasavas to change aspects of religious behaviour, and the high priority given to these changes by host/*deshi* groups.

It could be argued that this described 'willingness' to adapt to the dominant *deshi* ways amongst resettled Vasavas stems from a desire to rationalize the situation. Even if so, the fact remains that they choose to rationalize it rather than resist it. Their attitude may change with time. The next generation will grow up in the plains, away from the hills that serve as the setting for their historical memories. The new lifestyle will result in the resettled Vasavas having a different set of experiences as compared to their kin who remain in the hills. For example, they may no longer visit *jatras* like *Dev Mogra* which are important events that re-enforce their identity with other hill Vasavas, rituals such as *Divaho* that draw hill Vasavas from other villages will be replaced by more local Hindu festivals which are celebrated according to the Hindu calendar rather than other criteria as in the hills, the knowledge base present in the religious practitioners may fade and not be passed on to new recruits; if this becomes the trend then it is highly probable that their strong and conscious link to the physical and spiritual world of the hills that is acknowledged as the bond between different *dungri* Vasava clans, lineages and hamlets will fade.

However, this is not currently the case. As mentioned above, at this time, resettled Vasavas are not resistant to adapting many religious practices to the shape and form these take amongst the dominant Hindu host communities. In fact, this is the area where they are most open to adopting change and this is serving as an important factor in establishing host acceptance of this group.

NOTES

1. *Adivasi* literally translates as 'original inhabitant'. This word is used to differentiate certain tribal groups from caste society. Certain scheduled tribes or *adivasis* are entitled to positive discrimination designed for their improvement such as job quotas and educational grants. Baviskar (1995 b) makes a case for the use of this term over other ones such as 'tribals' and 'indigenous people'. Hakim (1996) has a discussion on these related terms in the context of the hill Vasava community.

2. Literally meaning one who lives in the hills but is commonly used with a negative connotation to imply 'backward' and 'isolated'.

3. A local term used to refer to the Bohra Muslim community who lived in plains villages below Makhadkhada.

4. Pilgrims who perform a pilgrimage walking along both banks of the River Narmada and which is said to take three years, three months and three days to complete.

5. A god who has a particular area of control and may have a physical symbol but who is viewed as being under the supreme God (*Bhagwan* or *Malik*).

6. *Reva* is a general term for river, but the Vasavas use it specifically to mean the Narmada river as it is the only river they are familiar with. Butya Ferangya, a *badvo*, informed me that although people referred to the river as *reva*, it is actually referred to as *hemal* in the creation stories.

7. The sexual taboo between individuals of the same clan is stressed here. Clan membership is determined patrilineally and therefore a brother and sister would necessarily belong to the same clan.

8. A term that is used for both clan and community and in this case it means community i.e. groups other than *dungri* Vasavas.

9. Phallic shaped. A *lingam* is the representation of Lord *Shiva* in Hindu mythology. However, the Vasavas never make this association with their stones. The stones used by them are naturally shaped by the river water and found in the river bed. Besides, they are grey in colour with pink streaks in them, unlike *Shiva lingams* which are of jet black stone.

10. Pallit and Mody (1992:40-58) have detailed documentation of similar Bhilala shrines. However, they do not analyse fully their role and meaning in everyday life.

11. Eluyemi (1994) provides an interesting account of Yoruba shrines and gods from the viewpoint of archaeological remains in terms of reconstruction of practices as well as the debate of moving sacred property.

12. One night, a young girl came running to my house, extremely scared because, while crossing the small

valley from one side of the hamlet to another, she had heard a young baby crying. The valley is the burial site for young children, and she was convinced that it was a dead child she had heard crying. However, after a few days, she forgot about the incident, and lost her fear of using that path at night.

13. The decision for each of the temples along the bank was ultimately left to the head priest. The *lingams* from Shoolpaneshwar and Hanfeshwar temples were relocated and new temple complexes built around them. The priest of the Dhumna temple near Makhadkahda left to go to another temple in Madhya Pradesh. The temple was submerged.

14. Within the larger category of Bhils, rituals and festivals often differ. Bhil groups in mixed villages have rituals which closely resemble *deshi* Hindu ones (Soni 1993:75-103).

15. This theatre group is composed of young plains Vasavas and performs comedy skits and plays. The language used is close to that spoken in Makhadkhada and so is understandable to even women and children, to a far greater extent than is the state language of Gujarati. The skits and songs are increasingly being based on Hindi cinema, and although the hill Vasavas are unfamiliar with Hindi cinema, the show put up by the *palty* is thoroughly enjoyed by them.

16. For the hosts, the equivalent of Molgi as the central hub of *Holi* celebrations, is Kavant. Here, the festival is greatly influenced by the Ratthwa culture, resulting in a very different atmosphere to that in Molgi. Kavant is too far away for Vasavas in Vadaj to visit, although those from submergence villages like Hanfeshwar and Ulva frequent the celebrations in Kavant.

17. Von Fürer-Haimendorf (1982:175-184) describes changing rituals and festivals of the Gonds of central India.

18. Hair is believed to be a potential source of invoking witchcraft, therefore people do not cut their hair near their house, preferring to do so near the river bank where the hair would be unidentifiable in the flowing water.

19. Stutley (1980) provides an interesting account of Indian magic and folklore as documented in the ancient Hindu texts.

20. Makhadkhada's *dev Rojan* is believed to eat a goat. Different gods are believed to prefer different food, thus *Ba Kome,* the *dev* of Chimalkhedi village downstream, eats buffalo which is sacrificed to him, and *Jalvat* the *dev* of Sinduri village across the river is fed a cow.

21. Bhagvat (1968) records a similar attitude to *Bhagvan* amongst the Gonds.

22. Taboos associated with menstruation are normally connected with edibles. Menstruating women refrain from going to the *kholo* (threshing ground) and *mada* (attic where grain is stored). Menstruating women must also give the boatman a coconut as offering if they take his dugout across the river as the chances of capsizing are substantially increased. Carsten (1989:124) and Firth (1966:105) have noted a similar belief amongst Malay fishing communities.

REFERENCES

Baviskar, A.

1995 a. 'Displacement and the Bhilala tribals of the Narmada Valley'. In J. Drèze, J., M. Samson, and S. Singh, (eds.) *Displacement and Resettlement in the Narmada Valley*. Delhi: Sage Publications.

1995 b. *In the Belly of the River: Tribal Conflicts over Development in the Narmada Valley*. New Delhi: Oxford University Press.

Bhagvat, D.

1968. *Tribal Gods and Festivals in India*. Bombay: D. Bhagvat.

Carsten, J.

1989. 'Cooking money: Gender and the symbolic transformation of means of exchange in a Malay fishing community'. In J. Parry and M. Bloch (eds.) *Money and the Morality of Exchange*. Cambridge: Cambridge University Press.

Chaudhuri, B.

1980. 'Changing religion and ethnic cycle of the Mundas'. In L.P.Vidyarthi, B.N. Sahay, and P.K. Dutta (eds.) *Aspects of Social Anthropology in India*. New Delhi: Classical Publications.

Eluyemi, O.

1994. 'Shrines and Yoruba gods'. In S.J. Shennan, (ed.) *Archaeological Approcahes to Cultural Identity*. One World Archaeology. Volume 10. London: Routledge.

Fernea, R.A. and Rouchdy, A.

1991. *Nubian Ethnographies*. Prospect Heights. Illinois: Waveland Press.

Firth, R.

1966. *Malay Fishermen: Their Peasant Economy*. London: Routledge and Kegan Paul.

Fuller, C.J.

1992. *The Camphor Flame: Popular Hinduism and Society in India*. Princeton: Princeton University Press.

von Fürer-Haimendorf, C.

1982. *Tribes of India: The Struggle for Survival*. Berkeley: University of California Press Ltd.

Ghurye, G.S.

1963. *The Scheduled Tribes*. Bombay: Popular Prakashan.

Hakim, R.

1996. 'Vasava identity in transition: Some theoretical issues', *Economic and Political Weekly,* XXX1:24, pp. 1492-1499, July 15.

1997. Resettlement and rehabilitation in the context of Vasava culture: Some Reflections. In J. Dreze, M. Samson, and S. Singh (ed.) *The Dam and the Nation: Displacement and Resettlement in the Narmada Valley*. New Delhi: Oxford University Press.

2000 a. 'From corn to cotton: Changing indicators of food security amongst resettled Vasavas.' In M. Cernea and C.McDowell (eds.). *Risks and Reconstruction: Experiences of Resettlers and Refugees and Resettlers' Experiences*. Washington: The World Bank.

2000 b. 'Identity, resettlement and perceptions of change: The Vasava Bhils of Gujarat, India'. *Goldsmiths Anthropology Research Papers 2000*, No 3., London: Goldsmiths College, University of London.

2000 c. "Agricultural land: The case of Hill Vasavas displaced by the Sardar Sarovar Dam, India". *The Eastern Anthropologist*. 53:1-2: 73-94.

Hardiman, D.

1987. *The Coming of the Devi: Adivasi Assertion in Western India*. Delhi: Oxford University Press.

Moxon, J.

1969. *Volta: Man's Greatest Lake*. London: Andre Deutsch Limited.

Padel, F.

1992. 'The position of tribal people in India'. Submission made to the independent review. Unpublished.

Pallit, C. & Mody, P.

1992. 'On the tribal path: A study of the SSP affected villages of Kakrana, Jhandana and

Anjanwada, Madhya Pradesh. Submission made to Independent Review, Unpublished.

Soni, L.N.

1993. *Bhil Sub-Groups in Caste Milieu*. Calcutta: Anthropological Survey of India.

Stutley, M.

1980. *Ancient Indian Magic and Folklore: An Introduction*. London: Routledge & Kegan Paul.

Vitebsky, P.

1993. 'Is death the same everywhere? Contexts of knowing and doubting'. In M. Hobart (ed.). *An Anthropological Critique of Development: The Growth of Ignorance*. London: Routledge.

12

Tribals and Christianity in Gujarat

Lancy Lobo

The word tribe is a British construct. Tribals are called by various names in Gujarat: *adivasis, raniparaj, kaliparaj,* 'backward Hindus' (Ghurye 1959) and Sangh Parivar has baptized them with a new name, *Vanvasis*. Like the British, the Sangh Parivar has given a specific identity to tribals with specific ideas and interests in mind and those interested in ushering inclusive change among tribals have to select an appropriate name and identity and we shall argue that the term 'adivasis' may be the better term. Adivasis (aboriginals) or Mulnivasis (indigenous) or better still the term autochthonous may also be considered. This identity will help the tribals to reclaim their lost natural resources or arrest the transfer of such resources which have been taking place before and after independence. The identity of tribals is in question.

One can usefully keep in mind the following indicators while assessing the change impacted by any intervening agency: Real development of the tribals will preserve their cultural autonomy, and mobilize them to participate in their own development. This in turn must be both equitable and sustainable, promoting a cultural autonomy, which will allow them to redefine their identity without in any way further compromising their dignity.

After giving a brief introduction of the tribals of Gujarat regarding their spread and movements for change, we shall dwell on Christian missionary interventions be it education, health, social work, development, social justice or faith formation. Missionaries developed their work among the tribals in three different phases: The first phase at the end of 19th century (1880-1950); the second phase from 1950 to 1980 and the third phase from the 1980s onwards. We give a few perceptions of the tribals on the impact of Christian missionary interventions collected through focus group discussions in 40 villages of six districts of south Gujarat, viz., Narmada, Bharuch, Surat, Dangs, Navsari and Valsad. It is argued that most missionaries have changed their approach to interventions from a relief mode to a service delivery mode to a rights mode. However, the state, particularly the ruling party, the Bhartiya Janata Party, has deliberately limited the missionary interventions to religious discourse alone. It is not religious conversion *per se* but the other interventions of missionaries that trigger off change, and subsequently protest, hostility and resistance. This paper also carries a critique on a section of missionaries. It is hoped that what is happening to Gujarat tribals may also be happening to tribals elsewhere in India to a great extent with reference to Christianity and change.

Gujarat tribals

The Bhil tribal belt ran from southern Rajasthan, eastern Gujarat, and Madhya Pradesh to Maharashtra about 100 years ago. This belt was largely dry hilly, forested. Today we have 28 named communities in the list of scheduled tribes (S.T.) in Gujarat. The major tribes are: Bhils (20 lakh), Dubla or Halpati (4.6 lakh), Dhodia (4 lakh), Rathwa (3 lakh), Gamit and Naikda (2.5 lakh each), Dhanka and Kokna (2 lakhs each), Warli, Patelia and Kanbi (one lakh each). There are five minor tribes recognized as primitive tribes because of their extremely poor economic existence and another 11 minor groups mainly in mainland and Saurashtra areas of Gujarat (Lal 1998).

Within the hilly and dry eastern belt one can distinguish three arbitrary divisions such as northern, central and southern. In the northern division one finds Rajput Garasia, Dungri Garasia, and Bhil Garasia. In the southern zone are Vasava, Tadavi, Dubla, Gamit, Kokna, Dhodia, Warli, Bhil, Naika and Choudhary. There are more than 32 talukas which have a population of more than fifty per cent tribals. Much of the economy was subsistence level depending on a good monsoon. Much of northern and central belt was drought prone.

The tribals of Gujarat had by and large interactions with non-tribals and were not totally isolated. Rajputs, Mugals, British rulers and the merchants, traders, Baniyas, Muslims, Parsees, Hindus, and then Christians had interactions with the tribals. And yet the tribals had their distinct linguistic, cultural, and demographic characteristics. The central Indian Bhil belt was parceled off after independence to Rajasthan, Gujarat, M.P. and Maharashtra and their languages were imposed on the tribals in the name of integrating them into the mainstream. Despite this effort substantial cultural and linguistic diversity exists among them even today. Tribes like Chaudhary and Dhodia have advanced economically due to education and irrigation.

The first phase (1880-1950) of missionary activity

Of the two major streams of Christianity it was the Protestant missionary who began their activities among the tribals of Gujarat. The Christianization process among the Bhil of Gujarat is only 120 years old. The Church Missionary Society (CMS), an Anglican body based in London, was the first to begin such work, starting in 1880 at Kherwara in Mewar. In the following years, mission stations were opened at Lusadia and Biladia in Idar state, and Kotra in Mewar. In 1887 it was Charles Stewart Thompson of the Church Missionary Society who pioneered the Christianization process in Sabarkantha district in Lusadia, Biladia, Ghoradar, Sarasu, Kotra and Baulia. Thompson provided medical services to Bhils, supervised schools and published a simple catechism and prayer book in Bhil dialect. The Chappania Famine (1899-1900) hit the Bhils very hard:

> The loss of life from starvation and disease was terrible, and was made worse by looting, for many were killed in defending their homes, and the survivors were left without food or the means wherewith to buy it.

The Commanding officer of the Bhil Corps wrote:

> Every palm tree has been cut down, pounded between stones, and eaten and now only the black rocks and sun-baked mud are left. All cattle are dead or eaten, and water is dried up in nearly all the wells.

Thompson who threw himself into relief works for the Bhils died of the Cholera that followed. The successors of Thompson continued the work and reaped fruits in the form of conversion of a number of Bhagats (Lobo 1991:43).

The Jungle Tribes Mission of the Irish Presbyterian (IP) Church began work in the eastern Panchmahals in 1892, and had its chief bases at Dahod, Jhalod and Sunth. The Church of the Brethren (CB), an American Mission, established its first base in South Gujarat at Valsad in 1895, and moved inland to the adivasi areas over the next decade, with bases at places such as Rajpipla, Jhagadia, Sagbara, Vuli and Umalla (Rajpipla state), Vyara (Baroda State), Dahanu and Veda (Thana district) and Ahwa (the Dangs) (Hardiman 2002:179).

The missionaries established networks of schools. There were secondary schools at their mission centres, often with boarding facilities for pupils who came from a distance. Primary schools were set up in villages which were staffed by Indian Christians from outside the area. For example by 1925 the CB Mission had organized 114 such schools in southern Gujarat and adjoining areas of Maharashtra. The schools provided a focal point for mission activities in an area, as described by a missionary writing in 1920 (ibid: 179).

The missionaries always carried medicine on their itineraries, and gave as much help as they could to the sick. In time, large numbers of adivasis began coming to the missionaries for treatment. For example, the CMS Mission hospital and dispensary at Lusadia treated nearly 13,000 patients in 1919. Missionaries on tour similarly attracted large crowds demanding treatment. As one account of such a tour stated:

> As soon as the news spread that we had come, we were simply besieged on all sides for medical help, and sicknesses of all kinds were brought to us.

The financial resources of people were extremely limited, so that whole areas of western allopathic medicine were beyond their reach. They could afford only the most basic drugs, and surgery was largely impossible without sterile and well-equipped operation theatres. They were particularly helpless in the face of serious epidemic disease, such as the great plague of 1896-98 and the influenza pandemic of 1918. There was little that they could do to help the people at such times (*ibid:* 180).

These early missionaries thought they had a civilizing mission to the primitive tribals. By Christianizing them the tribals would be changed and transformed.

1. Missionaries, mostly British, were moved by a belief that their own path to salvation through dedicated social work which would

pave the way for the saving of 'heathen' souls (Hardiman 2002:178). They did a lot of saving lives during drought and famine, from death and disease. They saved more lives than souls!

2. Did many tribals become Christians? Not really. It was mostly children from orphanages, destitute or the dying that accepted Christianity. These orphans eventually formed small Christian communities.

3. In this early phase the missionaries mostly did relief works and charities. In today's language they gave people fish to eat. They did not teach them to fish nor empowered them to fight for the fishing rights in a pond.

4. The first phase ended with independence. When most foreign missionaries died or left India, new ones did not replace them and their financial sources dried up.

The second phase (1950-1980) of missionary activity

The situation of the tribals after decades of independence had not improved, though tribes like Chaudhary and Dhodia had progressed educationally and some economic differentiation was taking place among them. In a study by SPIER (1984:219) one can see the poverty profile of the sub-regions of Gujarat. Percentage of the poor to the total poor is the highest in eastern hilly areas inhabited by the tribals. Of the hundred poor 31% were found therein and 15% in South Gujarat plains, 21% in middle Gujarat plains, 13% in dry areas of north Gujarat and 16% in Saurashtra peninsula. Though Gujarat was the second most developed state in India industrially and agriculturally the tribal areas were the most backward and poor. The tribals had to migrate seasonally to the plains and cities for wage labour.

The policies of the state actively transferred the resources like land, water, and forests to non-tribal areas and hands. Land was acquired by the state for industrial development at a cheap rate from the tribals. Forests were denuded in the name of giving employment to tribals through forest cooperatives. Hundreds of villages were submerged by a series of dams built in tribal areas. Nehru who spoke of Panchsheel policy with reference to the tribals laid the foundation stone of Sardar Sarovar Dam (SSP) on the Narmada. Implementation of relocation and rehabilitation package in the case of Sardar Sarovar project oustees was poor (Punalekar 1998:297). Ukai Dam on the Tapi river in the tribal areas displaced thousands of tribals with little or no compensation.

A number of agencies were also found working among the tribals such as Gandhian workers, modern Hindu religious sects, NGOs along with the state's developmental projects. There are about nine integrated tribal development project (ITDP) units in Gujarat under the tribal sub plan. Villages that have more than fifty percent tribal population are also grouped under tribal pockets under the tribal sub plan for developmental purposes.

Indicting the government, Lal (1998:75) writes:

> There has been almost a complete absence of programmes to generate countervailing forces of sufficient dimensions as to help the tribal community to become an equal partner in the process of growth.

Reviewing the tribal sub-plan he further comments that:

> a clear perspective about the long-term strategy for development of tribals of a specific region has not yet emerged (1998:74).

Another scholar Pathy (1998:276) notes that:

> development projects are handed down without any concern for the cultural-historical and ecological complexities prevailing in the tribal regions. Based upon anthropocentric premises of mutilating nature, customary institutions and values, imposition of individualism, statist ideology and reductionist worldview, the development practices have wrecked the physical, cultural and cognitive survival of the large masses of the country, specially tribals...Development has become a label for plunder and violence.

Against this backdrop we must discuss the entry of Catholic missionaries among the tribals.

The second phase (post-Independence) was largely a story of the activities of the Catholic missionaries among the tribals of Gujarat. Catholic Mission in Sabarkantha began working with Garasia Bhils. The period 1965-69 were years of scarcity and drought threatening Bhils with starvation and death. In Bhiloda, Meghraj, and Vijayanagar massive relief works were undertaken with the help of CRS, OXFAM, Misereor, USAID and Campania. Food for a work programme under USAID alone included construction of 2750 wells, 1896 houses, and 1384 bunding work of 279 miles for soil and water conservation. These have given periodic employment to 79,203 people and were a bulwark against famine in the years 1965-69 (Garriz 1984). In south Gujarat Jesuit priests, stationed at Bharuch to look after the religious needs of Christians were invited by Vasava tribals of the area to assist them. Soon an enthusiastic band of young Spanish missionaries began to work in Bharuch and Surat districts largely among the most numerous and poorest Vasava tribals in dry, forested, hilly areas. These tribals had been subjected to extortion and exploitation by money-lenders and traders.

The drought of 1965 again gave them an opening which brought in food for work projects from CRS,

OXFAM, Misereor and Caritas. Struck by people's misery, the missionaries plunged themselves into relief and developmental activities. They were glowing examples of missionaries who disregarded their own health for the sake of the tribals. Fr. Caricas could not be brought to look after his health when thousands of Vasavas were starving. He died a premature death on August 9, 1967 due to dysentry. Tribal missions also spread in other districts of South and Central Gujarat by different congregations of Catholic missionaries male as well as female. The main activities were limited to education, health and relief.

Different congregations of Sisters are also working among the tribals. Almost each mission station has a contingent of Sisters. Some congregations busy themselves with traditional activities such as dispensing medicine, education and religious instruction especially to women.

> The role of the Sisters in teaching the tribal women in the Christian faith and world view must be recognized. This is partly because women are culturally more accessible to women than to male missionaries. Some Congregations of Sisters have undertaken non-traditional activities such as developmental works, conscientization, bringing about social awareness and mobilization of women, and adult literacy for women, teaching tribal women alternative means of earning a livelihood and so on (Lobo 1991:47).

The Catholic missionaries today in eight districts of central and south Gujarat run the following activities and institutions: rural centres 40; city centers 15; with 400 personnel working in them. In the education sector: research and development centres 3; high schools 37; primary schools 15; ashram shalas 9; technical institutes 5; typing centres 2; tailoring centres 2; balwadis 224. In the health sector: hospitals 3; dispensaries 24; mobile clinics 6; social welfare hostels for girls 26; for boys 23; social welfare centres 19; milk cooperatives 4; homes for the aged 3; mahila mandals 337; legal aid centres 3 (*Directory* 2002).

The Catholic missionaries in 1980s began a series of primary and secondary high schools in tribal areas realizing the poor quality of education given to tribals. For instance, the Senior School Leaving Certificate examination results were around 15 per cent in schools in tribal areas but the missionary schools began securing fifty, seventy, ninety and even hundred per cent results. This had an indirect impact on non-missionary schools which raised their standards too. The high per cent of results secured by tribals enabled them to seek higher education in colleges and universities, thus making it possible for them to enter the mainstream professions like teachers, lawyers, doctors, nurses, etc. The Catholic nuns engaged themselves in starting *mahila mandals* (women's associations) basically for inculcating savings habit, but also for teaching preventive health care, awareness of women's rights, and so on.

The second phase is distinctly marked by a shift from charities and relief to transmitting skills to tribals for income generation. Missionaries began milk cooperatives in Vyara and Mandal in Surat district, Dediapada and Jhagadia in Bharuch district and also in Dang district. These helped significantly to raise income for the tribals. To carry forward the simile used in the first phase the missionaries continued giving fish to eat but also taught people how to catch fish by themselves. The emphasis was more on service delivery. Stress on education and health delivery marked this phase. From a relief mode the missionaries were making a shift to service mode, and a few even to the rights mode, viz., raising social awareness, fighting for justice-the liberation theology style.

Positive perceptions of tribals on missionary activity

Some tribal beneficiaries during my field work in the month of February 2003 reported that Christian tribals do not believe in witches but other tribals do. The buffalo scheme and milk cooperatives of missionaries have raised income in our villages. Watershed programmes have reduced migration considerably in our villages. Sisters come to our village and take care of our health needs. PHC medicines are not effective. There is a difference between government ashram schools and missionary schools. The trustees of the former eat up the money. They do not want our children to come up. The older missionaries mixed with us, they loved and served us. Because we studied in their boardings we are now economically better off. Sisters who run mahila mandals talk of women's rights and prepare us for struggle with the forest department. They also prepare us for income generating schemes.

Negative perceptions of tribals on missionary activity

The contrary viewpoints mentioned during the same field visits, *inter alia*, stated that the missionaries do not assist the Bhil who are the poorest in Dangs district through schools and other developmental interventions. They work more for the Kokna who are better off. No doubt the mission has sunk 25 wells in our village but most of them have no water. Watershed programme has given labour to our village but the social distribution of benefits has not been satisfactorily done. Two households have cornered 50 per cent of the benefits of watershed. Quarries do considerable damage to the health of children, women, and crops. For instance, silicosis, irregular monthly periods, still births, urinary tract infections have increased. But missionaries have not taken up the fight. So also about sanctuaries in Dangs, and in Bharuch districts. There are also the dam displaced persons of Ukai and SSP. The missionary tends to confine us to worshipping the Lord and not to indulge in dirty politics or fighting for one's rights. The younger missionaries do not easily mix, love and serve us like the older ones. There is a distance growing between younger missionaries and the tribals. Though the younger ones know our language better they show less intimacy. The missionaries have helped us and yet we are not self-reliant. Many missionaries operate on paternalistic lines when identifying the beneficiaries of their schemes. Sometimes they give more importance to running institutions than to the people for whom the institutions are meant.

What if the missionaries close their missions?

Some of the tribal responses to the above question were: If the missionaries closed the missions our children will suffer in their education. Our health will suffer. Our religion will suffer. Mission is in our hearts. We did not accept religion for material gains. We will manage on our own. But some said that if mission stops, religion will stop and the developmental activities will also go away. The missionaries provide us listening ears to our woes and empathise with us. This gives us dignity, which no one gives. Since others stated that by becoming Christians their vices like drinking and smoking are under control. With drinking gone their family life has improved and there is better economic wellbeing too. Their houses are clean, they dress clean, and their behaviour has improved. The lifestyle has changed for the better. There is peace in the house and less violence on women. If the mission stops then they might revert to an older lifestyle and habits. A few also said that in the past the missions gave education, housing, etc., free but it is no longer so. Therefore it does not matter if they close down.

Observations on the second phase

The Catholic missionaries were one of the many agencies working among tribals. The tribals had to negotiate with many competing agencies. Many Gandhian organizations and Hindu religious sects were instrumental in Hinduising the tribals. The Gandhians spread puritanism along with their service to the tribals. Most of the Hindu sects like Moksha Margis and Sat Kevals preached tee-totalism, taking daily morning purificatory bath, not eating meat but subscribing to vegetarianism and so on. The Hindu rightists were awakened after the missionaries worked for the tribals in inaccessible areas of jungles. Later the Hindu rightist organizations crept in gradually to nullify or counter the work of the missionaries and reconvert the tribals. They started dispensaries and ashram schools to win back the tribals. Hindutva organizations had begun giving service delivery to the tribals along with their agenda of Hinduising the tribals. Another significant aspect which emerges is that:

> the work of the missionaries among the exploited tribals was a pain in the eye for the non-tribal vested interests such as shopkeepers, moneylenders and landlords because the doormat (the tribals) from under their feet was pulled by the missionaries. The realization that the booty was slipping out of their hands dawned on them. They invented overt and covert ways of harassing the missionaries. The Hinduvta organizations further mobilized the police, the government bureaucracy and politicians against the missionaries (Lobo 1991:46).

It is fashionable not only for Hindutvavadis to discredit the missionaries but also for academicians and scholars. For instance, a noted scholar writing on the tribal situation in Gujarat, Lal (1999:80) hardly mentions the missionaries among the voluntary organizations stimulating and guiding social change among tribals. He mentions a whole list from Mahatma Gandhi, A.V. Thakkar, Jugat Ram Dave, Bhil Seva Mandal, Rani Paraj Seva Mandal, Arch Vahini, SEWA, Bhartiya Agro-Industries Federation, Sad Guru Seva Sangh, and Adivasi Seva Samiti.

The Catholic missionaries took a gradualist approach to religious conversion. On the contrary barring a few who were conversion oriented, most missionaries were development oriented. Conversions if any were a matter of a slow process after due reflection and deliberation from the tribal. Conversion was not tied to or linked to the development, relief or material interests. Developmental projects, education, health were open for all tribals. Certainly there were some conversions but one cannot speak of mass conversions.

The third phase (1980-) evangelical missions

A number of modern Pentecostal Protestant sects such as Alleluias, Pavitra Atmas, and Gospel Church Unionists have been sweeping the tribal areas with their brand of evangelism. Most of this new brand of missionaries was from South India. They did not believe in a gradualist approach of the Catholic missionaries but asked for a leap of faith, preaching that the poor could overcome their many problems through faith in Christ alone. They told the Adivasis that their old deities could no longer protect them, and that only prayer to Jesus could. Some of these missionaries claimed even to be able to cure the deaf, the dumb and the crippled through prayer alone, and they discouraged Adivasis from going to doctors. This struck a chord with many Adivasis, leading to a series of mass baptisms in the Dangs and surrounding areas.

Sects tap a crucial vein in the corpus of popular ideas, viz., those that relate to afflictions, sickness, misfortunes and calamities and a way to overcome them. Sectarianism supplies an oversimplified picture of a complex situation. For instance, it acknowledges that misfortune is brought about by a host of evil forces or agents who are employed by Satan and are to be conquered by the power of the Holy Spirit. The gift of healing involves the ability to diagnose the cause of affliction and to prescribe suitable remedies such as fasting, prayer, imbibing such substances as blessed oil, maintaining Bible as talisman, recitation of protective spells and so on. In their charismatic and prayer sessions, the Pentecostalists use the traditional tribal idiom of vibrating as if in a trance, and whipping up frenzy. Some of these sects forbid their followers to consult a physician or doctor and rely solely on healing by the Holy spirit.

Some sectarians who believe in a literal interpretation of the Bible have a strong tendency to dub any other religion or culture as idolatrous, pagan, evil and satanic. A group like the Adivasis that is going through a period of confusion, especially in the realm of their cognitive sphere, will accept a package that is simple, clear and absolute. Sectarianism appears perhaps to them as an answer to this confusion and anxiety as it reinforces fellowship, fellow-feeling and spontaneity in worship.

Sectarian evangelism affects Catholic missions in a significant way. On the one hand the former are gaining recruits and on the other they are pulling the rug from under the feet of the Catholic missionaries. The latter are not dramatic in their operations or liturgy but pay attention to the all-round development of the tribals, by introducing them to activities and modes of behaviour that are rational, with a liberal interpretation of the scriptures suited to the tribal context. Catholic missionaries show a healthy respect for the native culture. However, the evangelicals emphasize local participation and leadership unlike the Catholic missionaries. This may be one of the reasons why they spread faster than the Catholics. The activities of these evangelicals have attracted the attention of the government. But the government does not easily distinguish between the various types of missionaries. To them all missionaries are the same. So, Catholic missionaries also get smeared by the same brush (Lobo 1991:23-54).

Some observations on the third phase

The evangelical sects began to get a strong response from the tribals especially in Dangs district. In 1961 the Christian population of this district was 654, which was less than one percent of the population. In 1991 there were 7500 Christians—5 per cent of the whole. Estimates for the late 1990s put the figure at between 15000 to 20000 Christians.

This alarmed the Hindu nationalists who themselves were actively Hinduising the tribals. Conversions to Christianity went diametrically against the Hindu Rashtra ideology. They countered the missionaries by emulating the missionaries in education, medicine as well as disseminating Hindu culture by building temples, shrines, celebrating Hindu festivals, and reconverting the tribals. The success of the evangelical sects is largely because of the continuous marginalization of the tribals having little hope except in a religious package offered by these sects. The package could divert the attention of people from their miseries and real issues.

The success of these sects can be attributed to the failure of the state and other agencies to reach out to the tribals who were increasingly marginated year after year. The tribals who lived for centuries in the Dangs are made to feel that they are ill at ease in their own habitat. They are encroachers into the forest land. Their lands are taken away for wild life sanctuaries. They have to migrate for most of the year to the plains and cities for casual labour. In such miserable conditions evangelical sects come and preach a kind of short cut to miseries. 'Pray to Jesus, he will solve your problems.' These sects do not attend to key issues of tribals like land, forest (sanctuary, dams,) unemployment, but preach salvation. Before salvation we need livelihood.

Discussion

It is a bit difficult to identify the exclusive contribution of missionaries to change among the tribals as there are multiple agencies working among them. We need to work out in a more focused way the missionary impact in specific sectors like education, health, relief, development, social action, legal action, etc. Overall, despite the hard struggle of missionaries, early Protestants and then later Catholics, numerically few tribals have become Christians (0.42%). One cannot on this count say they have been successful. But on many other counts—education, health, development and social justice—they have been successful. It is after the 1980s under the modern evangelical Protestant sects that tribals in pockets like Dangs and its surrounding areas accepted this brand of Christianity in bigger numbers inviting the wrath of Hindu nationalists on a large scale.

When the missionaries run schools for urban middle classes no cry is heard against them but when missionaries start schools for rural tribals then the conversion bogey is raised. The urban middle classes want to appropriate and limit the excellent services of the missionaries to themselves. Missionary schools provide the right ambience for the middle classes to study in English medium for going abroad. It has been a fashion to reduce the missionary contribution only to conversions and give them a bad name and hang them. This comes largely from Hindu nationalists. There are of course those who realize the wider contribution of missionaries in the sector of education, health, development and of late their efforts to raise social awareness, legal awareness, and their fight for human rights and social justice. This has contributed to ushering in change among the tribals more than merely due to conversions. Indeed the future of the missionery contributions is not in the relief and service mode but in the rights mode.

By focusing on conversions alone the Hindutvavadis want to discredit the missionary contribution to overall change introduced by them through their interventions like education, health, and development. Hindutvavadis have replicated the missionary model in relief and service delivery. But they are unlikely to take to the rights mode. The missionary interventions go diametrically against the Hindutvavadis. Hindutvavad is nothing but resurgence of Brahminism or upper caste interests. These upper caste interests were under threat due to the secular democratic institutions which went against the interests of hierarchically ordered Hindu caste society. Those at the top of the hierarchy had power, privileges, perks, status and honor.

One cannot merely attribute the violence on Christians to these evangelical sects. It is also due to the Bhartiya Janta Party (BJP) which had no base among the tribals but wanted to get a foothold among Adivasis. After unleashing violence against Christians BJP won more seats in tribal areas for assembly elections. Not that the Congress did much for the tribals. It kept them in poverty and during the last forty years the tribals were increasingly marginated.

Critique of missionaries

Missionaries were singularly known to have ushered in modernity into India though it was not their primary aim. Modernity was ushered in mainly through education and health activities. Modernity was also ushered in by working on the consciousness of masses by raising their social, legal, and human rights awareness. Fight for social justice had engaged many early Protestant missionaries and then Catholic missionaries. The modern evangelical Protestant sects have little to do with either development, or social justice. They engage in a kind of mumbo jumbo which resonates with the tribals. Hardiman (2002) makes the following observation:

> In all this there was a dramatic reversal. Whereas in the past the missionaries had stood for 'civilization', it was now Hindus who accused Christians of being guilty of the latter, by duping credulous 'tribals' into conversion through what they depicted as trickery. It was argued that the missionaries should have confined their medical activities to the practice of 'modern' scientific bio-medicine.

Missionaries in the past fought against superstition while evangelical missionaries are spreading superstition or irrationality by having recourse to faith, healing and prayer rather than bio-medicine. However, Hindutvatadis fail to distinguish Catholic from Protestant missionaries and from among the Protestant missionaries the earlier main-line churches and the latest, the evangelical sects. They lump them into one. They display their ire on all hues of missionaries.

Christianization and Hinduisation

In Hinduisation or Christianization what the tribal stands to gain or lose is a question one must ponder. What is good for the tribal in his search for identity, cultural autonomy, integral development, without compromising his dignity? What has happened to the Hinduised tribals? There is a well documented case of Dublas, or Halpatis as they are known, who have largely become bonded labourers to the rich Patidar and Anavil Brahmins of South Gujarat. It is a case of a tribe becoming a caste and being placed at the lowest rung of Hindu society. They are the modern untouchables. A few other upwardly mobile tribals also Hinduise after being educated and securing employment in cities. They want to pass off as non-tribals for fear of ridicule from non-tribals. These must be distinguished from the large masses of marginalized tribals.

It is true that there have been and there are different types of missionaries. One cannot throw out the baby with the bathwater. The missionaries have also changed their ideologies and action. The tribal context in which missionaries entered the tribal areas, the interventions at the initial stage and later how they changed—from relief, charities to social work, and development to social action to rights and justice mode. Does Christianization answer the real issues of tribals? The perceptions and views referred to in this paper suggest a partial yes and no.

Sumit Sarkar has commented on the missionary question saying that for the earlier missionary social justice was not the main agenda of the missionaries but a fall out of their craving for conversions. But for the modern day missionary, barring the evangelical sects, social justice and liberation theology has become a key issue. The number of Catholic missionaries killed, murdered or harassed for their work for social justice is on the rise. Sarkar also comments that it is this brand of missionaries that the Sangh Parivar is mortally afraid of and not the converting variety, though their rhetoric is full of anti-conversion.

Missionaries and the state

Missionaries have shifted from a religious ideological stance to a developmental stance...religion to development...conversion to development over the decades. But the state, particularly the BJP in Gujarat, wants them implicated in ideological/religious issues. Christians are 0.42 per cent of Gujarat and Muslims are 11.5%. And yet Christians are more feared or powerful due to institutional spread. Legal awareness brought about among tribals by missionaries has been threatening to the vested interests including the state. The only way to attack the missionaries is through the ideological way, by implicating them in the conversion racket. It does not matter if the BJP in collusion with the state is actively Hinduising the tribals. The state here has got paranoid about Christians. They have unleashed a hate campaign and violence against them by burning churches 12; vandalizing churches 14; physical attacks 17; harassments of all kinds in the tribal areas of Gujarat during 1997-1999 (Lobo and Macwan 2002:10 ff). The BJP promised an anti-conversion law against the Christians and has enacted the same in 2003. While this may satisfy the gullible masses it will not satisfy the tribals whose issues are not religious but related to livelihood, employment, education, income generation and survival.

Conclusion

For nearly three months we intensely toured the tribal areas of Gujarat, visiting some fifty villages talking to several hundreds of men and women. Despite rhetoric to the contrary, their economic condition spurred by the ecological degradation has increased at least five fold in the last five years. Displacement (direct or indirect) due to dams, quarries, land alienation, deforestation, transfer or resources of tribals to non-tribal hands, has led to ecological degradation and misery for the tribal people. Not only masses of tribals are found unable to find sustenance in their degraded habitat but also their labour is exploited by vested interests. This has led to waves of seasonal migration in tribal areas. Child labour is rampant and on the increase. Attaining the objectives of universal primary education, as promised in the 93rd Constitutional Amendment, is a far cry. Even child labour in the carpet industry, something that has been declared hazardous, is quite common. Those from the education ministry see the low levels of learning of these children when they come to seek admission in our schools at the secondary level. The average food security of most tribal households from their own crop production has been reduced from 90 days to about 70 days a year. Water has become extremely scarce, thanks to the continuous degradation of forests and the washing away of the top-soil.

The Christian missionaries have dedicated themselves to producing citizens who are secular through their schools. The emphasis they place on developing cognitive skills and a questioning attitude in their students is indeed good. This perhaps is more dangerous than converting a few to Christianity. The Hindutva forces are more worried about the secular education or 'the secularists' than religious conversions. It is to contain their secular character that they are given the label of conversionists. Coming to conversions, one must reflect seriously if the converts have changed their socio-economic status after conversion. Quite often it remains unchanged. Only a few individuals manage to come up. There is individual mobility and not societal mobility. Religious conversion has helped some of the tribals who were marginalized due to the policies of the state. It is this margination that Christians need to fight both at the ideological and empirical level. The BJP government is diverting the minds of Church personnel by engaging them in only religious issues, so that they have no time or interest to empower the tribals in a systematic manner.

REFERENCES

Deliege, Robert

1985 *The Bhils of Western India,* Delhi: National.

2002 *Directory of Baroda Diocese 2000.* Baroda: Bishop's House.

Garriz, D.M.

1984 'Twenty years of growth (1953-73)'. *The Ahmedabad Missionary,* No. 555, June.

Ghurye, G.S.

1959 *The Scheduled Tribes.* Bombay: Popular Prakashan.

Hardiman, David

2002 'Christianity and the adivasis of Gujarat'. In Ghanshyam Shah *et al.* (eds.) *Development and*

Deprivation in Gujarat. Delhi: Sage Publications.

Lal, R.B.

1998 'Tribal situation in Gujarat'. In Vidyut Joshi (ed.) *Tribal Situation in India*: 57-82. Jaipur: Rawat Publication.

Lobo, Lancy

1991 "Christianisaton process among the tribals of Gujarat: An overview'. *Indian Missiological Review*, 13:3:39-57.

2002 'Adivasis, Hindutva and post-Godhra riots in Gujarat'. *Economic and Political Weekly*, Nov. 30: 4844-4848.

2002 *Globalization, Hindu Nationalism and Christians in India*. New Delhi: Rawat Publications.

Lobo, Lancy and Jayanti Macwan

2002 *Shoshan ane Atankni Aagma Adivasio* (in Gujarati). Vadodara: Centre for Culture and Development.

London Missionary Society

1914 *Battling and Building Amongst the Bhils.* London: The Church Missionary Society.

Naik, T.B.

1956 *The Bhils: A Study.* Delhi: Bhartiya Adimjati Sevak Sangh.

Pathy, Jaganath

1998 'Impact of development projects on tribals'. In Vidyut Joshi (ed) *Tribal Situation in India.* Jaipur: Rawat Publication.

Punalekar, S.P.

1998 'Growth with contradictions: Tribal situation in South Gujarat'. In Vidyut Joshi. (ed). *Tribal*

Situation in India: 285-304. Jaipur: Rawat Publication.

Sardar Patel Institute of Economic and Social Research (SPIER)

1987 *Gujarat's Economy in 2000 A.D.* Ahmedabad: S.P. Institute of Economic and Social Research.

13

Changing Aspects of Kinship Among Kondhs

Sukant K. Chaudhury

Is kinship a relevant topic to study today? Indian society is marching ahead in the 21st century with the forces of modernization and globalization. It is said that the non-kinship ties, formal relationships and complex organization constitute the structure today. However, for tribals, it seems things are different. Tribals in India are a part of the wider society. Despite the processes of globalization and modernization, Indian society has retained its core structure and values. Social scientists have started saying that structural changes are initiated in India but they do not have a wide reach. The tribals are no exception to this process. Thus, even today, the social structure of simple or tribal societies cannot be understood without its kinship structure (Parkin 1997). However, these societies are also confronted with the forces of many processes like modernization, urbanization and industrialization, etc. Against this background, this paper attempts to understand the structure and dynamics of Kondh kinship, and links of kinship organization with other related institutions such as marriage and family. It also focuses on the fluid areas where the individual manipulates their structural rules to maintain the ideal structure.

The Kondh constitute one of the largest tribes in India both in terms of population and the area of habitation. They number about 10 million, which is the seventh largest in India in terms of tribal population. They inhabit mainly Phulbani, Ganjam, Koraput and Kalahandi districts of Orissa and two districts of Andhra Pradesh: Visakhapatnam and Srikakulam. Among all these districts the majority of Kondhs live in Phulbani district. The Kondh are known by many names: Kondh, Kond, Khand, Kandha, Kond (Thruston 1909 and 1987). Patrilineal descent is the rule among them. The clan, *gossi,* has remained less important for them these days rather for all practical purposes *mutha*, a political unit, is relevant (also see Bailey 1960 and Boal 1982). The Kondh practice monogamy. Traditionally they are shifting cultivators as well as plain cultivators. Their economy mainly rests upon cultivation and forest (minor forest produce). There is some internal differentiation found among them and on the basis of which three sections of Kondhs are found: Dongria Kondhs, Kuttia Kondhs and Desia Kondhs. This differentiation mainly pertains to their economic pursuits and habitation (Chaudhury 1993). The present paper is based on a study conducted among the Desia Kondhs in three villages: Gressingia, Kilakia and Baudi in G. Udaygiri Block of Phulbani district (Chaudhury 1999).

The descent groups

The existing literature on Kondh has varied opinion on the nature of descent groups among them. Observers such as Friend-Pereira, Niggemeyer, Bailey and Boal have reported the existence of clan among them. The local term for clan has also been differently termed by these authors and others, for instance: Risley calls it *gochi*, Niggemeyer calls it *gossi*, whereas for Bailey it is *gossi*. Risley (1891) found 50 *gochi* or exogamous septs of a territorial nature and each *gochi* was divided into sub-septs known as *klambus*. Russel and Hiralal (1916) found

32 exogamous septs that were localized and took their names after the names of their villages, titles and nicknames. Further, the septs were divided into sub-septs as Bachhas (calf), Chattra (umbrella), Hikoka (horse), Kelka (king fisher), Onjaka (monkey), Manding (earthen pot) and Kadam (a kind of tree).

According to Friend-Pereira (cited from Ferreira 1965), the Mal Kondh of northern section are more primitive than the plain Kondh. The former are divided into communes or confederacies and septs or sub-septs. Further, each commune consists of a few territorial areas known as *mutha*. A few communes Friend-Pereira finds are the Chhota Paju (or Chhota Padki), the Tin Pari (or Bargocha), the Bengrika, the Ath Kombo and the Tin Kombo. The Chhota Paju (or Chhota Padki) commune consists of six *muthas*, which form three pairs of sub communes. Each of these six exogamous *muthas* has families of various stocks, each with a different totem, and the six *muthas* together form an exogamous unit. In this commune (Chhota Paju), out of eleven stocks, seven have totems – namely the elephant, the cudgel, the clarinet, the cane, the chameleon, the potter's hammer, and the kettledrum. The Bengrika commune has two *muthas* – Bhetimendi and Tuniamendi. Likewise other communes have many *muthas* that in turn consist of many stocks and also their totems.

Further Friend-Pereira (*ibid*) says that the Kondh have a series of exogamous circles extending from the smallest unit to one of truly stupendous magnitude. However, the actual exogamous circle is the commune within which marriage is strictly forbidden. The exogamy of Kondh is based on real or fictitious blood relationship between the members of various stocks, constituting the commune, but is always subject to the wider totemic circle of prohibition that lies outside the limits of the commune (cited from Ferreira 1965:150).

As said earlier, the Kondh are divided into various communes which in turn consist of several *muthas*. At times, some *muthas* combine together to form sub-communes. Ideally speaking, *muthas* are exogamous. Each of these *muthas* further consists of several totemic and exogamous groups which Friend-Pereira calls 'stocks'. Even though he recognized several circles of exogamy, he gave primacy to the rule of exogamy at the level of commune. Therefore, he treated commune as the ultimate exogamous unit regulating marriage among the Kondhs, but he ignored the potential flexibility inherent in the ideal structure of marriage rules which he called the "series of exogamous circles". Bailey (1960) noted two types of clans: dispersed and localized: the former is significant only in the kinship system and the latter is a political unit. According to him, the modern *mutha* is a territorial group and not a clan.

Niggemeyer concluded that the Kondh (or Kui-speaking tribe) were originally made up of different tribes, all of which need not have been totemic. Among the Kuttia Kondhs there are 14 patrilineal exogamous clans (or *gossi*) in which membership depends on a belief in descent from a common ancestor. However, according to him, the village has acquired greater significance than the clan (cited from Ferreira 1965:151).

According to Boal (1982), *gossi* is made up of a number of lineage groups, which had greater importance when warfare was common. But the devastation caused by the Goomsur war has changed the emphasis from loyalty to the whole clan to the lineage (or *kutum*). All lineage groups within a clan consider themselves as descendants of a common ancestor and therefore agnatic kin (Boal 1982:17). Pradhan's (1990) observations on the Kondh clan is different from others. According to him, the Kui term for clan is *klambu*, which represents the patrilineal descent group. He calls *gossi* the territorial unit of a descent group or a village, *gossi* is an exogamous unit. He says:

> A settlement (*gossi*) is established following a further split of a group and is named after the founder. Such a segment may probably be termed as a minimal lineage. The maximal lineage, the *klambuka* is exogamous. Several such *klambu* form an endogamous sub tribe (Pradhan 1990).

The above discussion on the views of different authors on the Kondh descent groups has tremendous confusion. However, the information gathered from the field regarding the descent group is as follows: *Gossi* is the term used for the clan, which is exogamous in nature. The members of a *gossi* are related by blood and used to stay in a definite territory. *Klambu* is a generic term for the lineage. A *klambu* is purely exogamous in nature. Finally, *kutum* is a domestic group or family and not a lineage as referred by Boal.

The Kondh tribe is divided into three sections, Desia or Maliah, Dongria and Kuttia. Each section of the Kondh tribe is further divided into several totemic exogamous clans known as *gossi*, which include all those members who have descended from a common mythical ancestor. Therefore, a sense of fraternity exists among the *gossi* members. It operates on the principle of patrilineage; new members are also recruited on the same principle. A Kondh woman enjoys a marginal place in the patrilineal kinship structure. Before marriage she is a part of her father's *gossi* and after marriage she becomes a part of her husband's gossi. In both the cases her membership to *gossi* is marginal. Ideally speaking, a *gossi* regulates marriage. Members of a *gossi* are not permitted to marry each other. Violation of such marriage rules were treated very seriously in the past. At an ideal level, *gossi* functions as a ritual unit. All members who stay nearby attend the periodic ritual of worshiping the *gossi* ancestor as well as the *Darni Penu* (earth goddess), thrice a year. Traditionally, members of the same *gossi* helped each other at the time of exigencies and crises. They also helped each other at the time of cultivation if extra labour was required.

However, the functions of *gossi* are gradually losing their relevance due to population expansion and migration. Earlier, members of the *gossi* used to live in closed proximity. Due to pressure of population and job opportunities outside, the *gossi* became dispersed. Therefore it became too difficult to maintain the *gossi* relationship among its members in the changing economic and ecological scenario. Today, *gossi* has become a symbolic group where each member feels attached to the group, which never assembles. The younger Kondhs are even unable to identify the role of the *gossi*, which it used to play in the traditional society.

Each *gossi* is further divided into several *klambu* or lineage, which is an exogamous group and thus regulates marriage. The members of the *klambu* are related to each other through a single male ancestor who lived not more than five to six generations ago. *Klambu* operates through the principle of patriliny. Traditionally, *klambu* used to be the property-owning unit. Gradually the property got divided into various *kutums*, hence now *klambu* has only remained as a ritual group. Members of the same *klambu* perform the *gossi* ritual together and also worship the *Darni Penu,* the clan totem and the founder of the lineage. Earlier, each *klambu* had a well-defined territory. Currently its association with territory has also lost its relevance. In the past each Kondh village used to be inhabited by a single *klambu*, but now the members of different *klambu* inhabit the same village.

Principle of descent and its operation

The Kondhs follow patrilineal rule. Exclusively the physical ties of fatherhood determine descent among them. However, the practice of adopting a child is prevalent. Normally, a Kondh would adopt a child from his lineage only. Thus, a person acquires the membership of a descent group through the physical ties with his genitor and the pater assumes significance in those cases where the genitor is not the pater. This is true in case of an adopted child. Here kinship may not be synonymous with genetic relationships.

Problem arises in the case of an illegitimate child, born to unmarried woman. In earlier days, this was not uncommon, as unmarried people used to have intimate ties in youth dormitories. Normally in this case, the boy who impregnated the girl was bound to marry her, and if he did not, the girl's family admonished him and the girl's father's lineage used to severe its ties with his family and lineage. Subsequently, when the girl married another boy, the latter was asked to keep the child. If he refused, the girl's family used to keep the child. Thus, three alternatives existed: (i) when the genitor married the girl, the child acquired full membership of the genitor's lineage; (ii) when a man other than the genitor married the girl the child was adopted by the former and thus acquired the full membership of the pater's lineage; and (iii) when the girl's parents kept the child and the child was informally accepted by the girl's parent's lineage but was not given full rights. If the girl's parents formally adopted the child then it acquired the full rights of the girl's parents' lineage. Such a thing usually happened when the child happened to be a boy. Bhandari (1992:54) in his study of Mishing of Assam, observes:

> there are societies which are patrilineally organized, yet some of the links in a descent system may actually be through the women, which implies that principle of physically determined patrilineal descent is neither exclusive nor absolute.

This holds good in case of the Kondhs as well.

Ancestor worship and the adopted son

Ancestor worship (*pideringa-laka*) among the Kondh is very popular and performed with great care and devotion. Held annually, it is a religious belief based on the cult of agnatic ancestors who are worshipped and propitiated regularly. All the male descendants must worship their ancestors for their own and their family members' welfare and prosperity. In case such rituals are not performed, it is believed that misfortune would result. Further, it is believed that agnatic ancestors keep a vigil on their descendants; hence worship of the real ancestors is an essential part of the Kondh belief system. In most cases, where the genitor is the pater, the son performs the ritual. Problem arises in the case of adopted son. When the adopted son is from the pater's lineage, he performs the ancestor worship. The illegitimate adopted child is not allowed to perform the ancestor worship.

Kin and affines

The Kondhs make a clear distinction between the kin and the affines. The kin belong to one's own lineage and clan, whereas the affines are drawn from different lineages and clans. The Kondh treat their affines with great honour.

After marriage, a wife maintains her relationship with her agnatic group, but at the same time she becomes a member of her husband's natal group. This indicates that though a woman after her marriage maintains effective kinship ties with her agnates, her filial status and ritual bonds are terminated from them. She is fully transferred from her father's jural authority and comes under her husband's jural authority. Thus the politico-jural bond between a woman and her father and agnate siblings are severed after her marriage. Hence the principle of full incorporation of women into their husband's lineage after marriage, and the adherence to patrifiliation as the basis of the membership of descent groups make the Kondhs a strong patrilineally organized society.

Marriage among Kondhs

The institution of marriage is significant in the life cycle ritual of Kondhs. A life bachelor or spinster is inconceivable among them. The lineage would continue only through the birth of a child and is possible only through marriage. Children born out of wedlock are not recognized. Hence, marriage is considered essential for continuation of descent group. Laxmidhar (key informant) says:

> Marriage is a blessing from *Darni Penu* (Kondh's Earth Goddess); it does not mean only sexual gratification, but also means fulfillment of life. Through it men and women share domestic responsibilities, besides children born to them become an economic asset to the family.

Owing to patrilineal rule, the Kondh say that through the marriage ceremony, the adolescent woman goes to a man, i.e., in other words, the man has to bring a woman with her consent. When the girl attains puberty, she is consciously nurtured for marriage. She is not allowed to move around freely and have male friends openly. She is asked to do all household works, like cooking, cleaning, thrashing and grinding cereals and pulses, stitching leaf plates. Expertise in household work is considered to be a good qualification of a girl for marriage.

Rules of marriage

The Kondhs have a series of exogamous rules of marriage. They are clan exogamy, lineage exogamy, village exogamy and *mutha* (meaning 'fist') exogamy. All the above exogamous rules are self-explanatory except *mutha* exogamy. In G. Udayagiri area where I did my work, twelve different *muthas* combined to form *baramuthaka* and eighteen different *muthas* combined to form *atharamuthaka*. The Kondhs of this area still hold it good to observe *baramuthaka* exogamy and *atharamuthaka* exogamy. Kondhs from above two can marry each other, rather it is imperative for a member of *baramuthaka* to choose a partner from *atharamuthaka* and vice versa. Adherence to this rule is uncommon these days. Out of the 223 marriages recorded in the three villages, 78 followed this rule. Rest 145 cases did not follow the rule. In the past five years, all the marriages that have taken place in the three villages have not followed the rule. In fact, it is very difficult to follow this rule because people today do not know the details of *mutha*.

Among the other rules of exogamy, village exogamy and lineage exogamy are widely practised today. Out of the 223 marriages recorded only seven did not follow the rule of village exogamy. Out of these seven cases, six belong to village Gressingia, and one belongs to village Kilakia. In Gressingia, Kondhs from other villages have settled down because of many reasons, and only in such cases village endogamy resulted. Lineage exogamy has been followed in all the cases. Regarding clan exogamy, people say that it is very difficult to ascertain about the adherence to this rule. Clan exogamy is subsumed under *mutha* exogamy. These day people do not remember about their clans. However, in all the 223 marriages recorded, there were only two answers to the questions of clan exogamy – either they have adhered to it or they did not remember.

The Kondh follow two important endogamous rules: tribe endogamy and sub-tribe endogamy. The former is self-explanatory, the latter means a Maliah Kondh cannot marry a Kuttia Kondh or a Dongria Kondh. Even today such inter-subtribal marriages are rare. The Desia Kondh or the plain Kondh are a little flexible in this regard.

There are a few cases of marriage with outsiders such as Pana (a scheduled caste living in the area), and some other caste Hindus (13 of 223). In all the thirteen cases, the Kondh girls eloped with the outsiders and have left their villages. The Kondh are very critical of such marriages. However, because of changes in attitudes due to adaptation to modern values, they have become flexible in such cases. Polygamous unions occur among Kondhs though not frequently. It will be clear from the following case:

> Nineteen year old Sita of Gressingia was studying at Kalinga Mahavidyalaya, G. Udayagiri (only college in the area). She was an undergraduate first year student. Her father was a farmer and who had changed his outlook and was having the aspiration of seeing his daughter doing a government job after her higher education. Sita used to visit the town frequently with her friends. Kishor, a government employee from Phulbani was frequently visiting G. Udayagiri on official tours. Kishor fell in love with Sita. He tried to lure her by presenting her small gifts regularly. He was meeting her regularly at the college and used to take her to his place. They developed intimate relation. Sita became pregnant and was frightened of her parents and villagers. Clandestine operations followed. Kishor eloped with Sita to Phulbani and settled her there in a rented house. After a few months Sita came to know that Kishor already had a wife with two kids, living at Baud, fifty kilometers away from Phulbani. Sita was shocked. However, she adapted to the situation since such polygamous unions were not uncommon in her village. Sita's parents became very unhappy. However, they accepted her after a few days. Sita said that the villagers were still not happy with her, but her parents were happy, since she had become economically well off and stylish, unlike Kondh women.

Monogamy is the normative rule of marriage among the Kondhs these days. Earlier for several reasons – in case the first wife did not bear a child or the first wife became physically disabled or in some case for economic reasons—polygamy was practiced, but it was not the norm. However, these days, if a man has more than one wife he is ridiculed. Marriages between kin are completely forbidden among them. Their neighbouring tribes such as the Paraja in Koraput district practise cross-cousin marriage but the Kondh do not have such a rule (Patnaik 1996).

Type of marriage

Out of the several types of marriage found among tribes of India, the Kondhs practiced many, such as marriage by elopement, marriage by capture, marriage by service, love marriage and arranged marriage. Marriage by elopement and capture used to be quite popular in the past, because of the rules of strict exogamy. The rate of such marriages has come down. Now, marriage by capture hardly occurs, whereas marriage by elopement occurs now with a low rate, particularly in cases of Kondh-Oriya marriages or other inter-community marriages. The practice of love marriage earlier resulted mainly from the dormitory system prevailing among them. Since the dormitory system satisfied the rules of endogamy and exogamy, the Kondh did not have any problem in allowing the partners to get married. Such socially sanctioned premarital unions culminated in marriage mainly because of two reasons: (i) when the girl was impregnated by a boy, or (ii) when both the boy and girl fell in love with each other. In case of the former, disputes often occurred. The girl's testimony was the main, and if the boy did not agree to it, and if girl's party (family and villagers) was convinced about the case, then fine was imposed on the boy (such as a communal feast with liquor or some cash). In such cases, the girl was given off to any boy on a lower bride price after she had delivered the child.

In the three villages that I studied, no dormitory was found. But it still exists in other Kondh villages. The old are nostalgic about the dormitory and took delight in expressing its functions to me. Dayanidhi said:

> Today, we are having many problems in getting a suitable match for our children, earlier it was a smooth process through the dormitory. Because of this problem, we are not able to follow the exogamous rules.

On the other hand, the young feel deprived of their participation in such institutions today. One informant told me: "old people enjoyed everything and nothing is there in our fate".

Arranged marriages are most common these days. In this case, both the parties negotiate on the match, dates, and prestations. In case of love marriages, the boy or girl makes the choice and it is followed by the usual procedures as followed in case of arranged marriage. The age at marriage has changed considerably over a period of time. Earlier child marriage used to be practised; now it has been stopped. The present age at marriage for girls is 18 to 20 years in remote villages and 20 to 22 years in urban villages. The average age for boys in remote villages is 22 to 24 years and 24 to 28 years in urban villages.

The marriage process

Suggestions for suitable match for a boy is taken from various sources: kin, affines, friends and acquaintances. The boy visits with his friends the girl's village to 'see' her and if possible to talk to her regarding her wishes in marrying him. If they agree, father, brother and other kin of the boy visit the girl's house and begin the negotiations. Once these people enter the house of the girl, they have to pay some cash (known as *solbanga*, these days usually ranging between fifty rupees and two hundred rupees) to the girl's parents, whether they like or dislike the proposal. The girl's parents provide proper hospitality. First, the parents ask their daughter about her consent. Here, if the negotiation becomes successful, the important item: bride price (*site kalu*) – which Kondhs call the *gati* ceremony – is taken up. The negotiation mainly pertains to the bride price. These days it ranges between two hundred rupees and a few thousand rupees. Besides bride price, some bullocks, brasswares and gold ornaments are also given to the girl's parents. If the negotiation becomes satisfactory, then all of them enjoy a drink, followed by food (mainly rice and chicken curry).

After the *gati* ceremony, the boy's party is given a warm farewell. After a few days (these days ranging between three months and one year), the boy's party, mainly consisting of the boy and his friends, bring the girl from her house. Then the nuptial ceremony takes place at the boy's house. If financial condition permits, then the boy's family throws a party in the form of communal feast to friends, relatives and villagers. Once the marriage is consummated, the girl's rights are transferred from her father's lineage to her husbands' lineage.

Divorce

Divorce (*kutenju*) among Kondhs is described in earlier literature in a superficial manner. Patnaik (1992:182) has synthesized all descriptions on divorce which is as follows:

> The Kondh women had every right to quit their husbands at pleasure, and this right was availed by some as many as eight to ten times. The right to divorce was mutual and was exercised on slight grounds. The ceremony performed to effect a separation consisted of splitting or breaking a straw into two pieces. This ceremony was not followed often. It was common for a wife to go back to her father's house by mutual consent or at the bidding of her husband. When this took place, her father had to return the whole of the gifts or bride-money, which the bridegroom had paid for his wife when the marriage was originally arranged.

The people contest this earlier version, because they say that divorce was not that easy. It could only take place when there were some valid reasons such as barrenness of the women, extramarital relations, non-payment of dues of bride price, continuous fighting between the couple, and so on. However, these issues were to be thoroughly discussed by the respective parties and then it used to culminate in divorce. An informant said that these day people have changed gradually as they do not go for divorce for such reasons. Only extramarital relations can lead to divorce. However, this opinion is not well founded, since one of the voluntary organizations at G. Udayagiri, Kalinga Mahasabha is looking after divorce cases and issues related to women. The organization had received as many as 350 cases in 1996 of abuse against women and other reasons for divorce.

Extramarital relations

Though premarital sex was not tabooed, adultery was prohibited among the Kondhs. After marriage, they mostly cherished conjugal fidelity. However, premarital freedom often led to extra-marital relations. In early writings, Kondhs have been described as having a lax moral character (Campbell 1864: 43). Majumdar (1965) wrote:

> premarital license was recognized in their society and virginity was not essential for their marriage. Their social traditions and usages made it possible for an indiscriminate mixing of the sexes before marriage.

But after marriage they are always expected to remain virtuous. They always looked down upon adultery. The belief is that adultery would annoy the Earth Goddess who in turn would cause drought and a devastating situation. In case of adultery, they used to propitiate the Earth Goddess by sacrificing a pig and breaking a large earthen pot filled with water at the house of the offender. It was believed that the curse would go, if these acts were followed by rain. Besides, the offender was asked to pay fine to the husband of the victimized women. In some other case the man was asked to give liquor and sacrifice a buffalo to be consumed by the villagers. Today, adultery is rare. In case of such incidents, large-scale arguments and fighting occurs between the husband and the wife. In case of a husband committing adultery, maximum time is given to him to abstain from such activities. If not, then the woman goes for divorce. In many cases the woman does not go for divorce and accepts the faulty husband as the reality.

Many cases that I came across clearly show that Kondh women adjust themselves with the errant husbands. This has happened mainly due to the influence of the neighbouring Hindu culture. The Kondhs' gender relations, pertaining to such adultery cases, used to be better than the Hindus. Among Hindu women, two important virtues are chastity and devotion to her husband. Such notions never existed among Kondhs. These days (particularly in the urban influenced villages of Kondhs) the people have accepted such values and therefore they do not go for divorce even for such serious acts on the part of their husbands. In the interior areas, the values have not changed much. If the errant husband does not change, then women go for divorce.

Changes in marriage rituals and practices

The notion of bride price needs to be discussed here. Earlier it was the only type of prestation, these days things have changed considerably. Bride price is relegated to the background. Dowry has slowly come into existence. People seek dowry from girl's parents, which must not have been thought ever by their ancestors. The notion of wife is unique for Kondhs i.e. a wife is purchased. However, under the influence of the neighbouring Oriya culture, and under the pretext of 'civilized behaviour' – which says wives are not purchased – educated Kondhs have started practicing the Hindu customs of marriage. The first thing to make its appearance is the dowry system. This will be clear from the following case:

> DP, 28 years old, of Gressingia is a highly qualified Kondh. He holds a Master's Degree and is working as a Government officer in Madhya Pradesh. He got married in 1994. His parents on his insistence tried

> hard to get an educated Kondh girl and who could also pay heavy dowry. Finally they got a match and as dowry, they got television, double bed, sofa set, dinning table, refrigerator, and one hundred gram gold ornaments besides other household items along with twenty five thousand rupees in cash. DP went in for an elaborate procession having bands and other paraphernalia, used in common Hindu marriages, to the bride's place for marriage. The bride's parents had called a Oriya Brahmin priest to perform the rituals in marriage. After marriage, DP came back with his wife in a decorated car and gave a grand reception party at his village Gressingia. The dishes in the party included meat curry, vegetable curry, *palao*, salad, *papad*, *khir*, and tomato sauce, besides a cocktail. People of Gressingia fondly remember the grand party.

The above case is not exceptional. On an average, each village has the honour (as they say) of having such marriages every year these days. Adapting to Oriya customs, though not with perfection, has become the cherished ambition of the educated Kondhs.

Family organization

Among the Kondhs, there is a distinction between family and household. Family (*kutum*) is the larger group or the joint group of many nuclear households (*ghar*). The husband with his wife and unmarried children constitute a nuclear household. After the marriage of the sons, separate households are established for them. The property continues to be jointly managed by the father and his sons. After the death of the father, the property usually gets divided among the sons. Thus, the term *ghar* always refers to one's family of procreation after marriage or the family of orientation before marriage. The unmarried Kondh boys and girls have their *ghar* membership in their natal group, which changes after marriage. For a Kondh woman, it is not only the *ghar* membership but also the lineage and clan membership which changes. But for a

Kondh man it is only the *ghar* membership, which changes after a few months of marriage, when the married son establishes a new house or *ghar* adjacent to or near his father's house and with a separate hearth.

The size of households among the Kondhs varied between one and more than nine members per household. In the three villages, a maximum of 53.3 percent households have three to five members whereas only 5.1 percent are large households. The average size of a Kondh household in the three villages is 3.8 members per household.

Interpersonal relationships

Among the Kondhs, the structure of interpersonal relationship is hierarchical based on the criteria of age, sex and generation. The juniors always respect the seniors by age and generation. Further, the elders get preference in any matter over the young ones. The males are always favoured to females, except in a few rituals. To a large extent they believe that women are subordinate to men.

The husband (*kuda*) and wife (*jama*) relationship is seen by Kondh as the relationship, which brings stability and endurance to the household, family, domestic group and to the community as a whole. The ideal relationship is characterized by love, intimacy, economic cooperation, care for children, care for kin, etc. Since they live in nuclear households, marked with privacy, the intimacy between them is often expressed. It is the only socially sanctioned relationship for sexual intercourse, except the cases where marriage takes place through youth dormitory system. Notwithstanding the pre-marital sex, marriage revitalizes the relationship between the boy and the girl in the sense there is a sigh of relief for both the husband and wife to have approved sexual intimacy. Being a patriarchal society, the husband is the chief authority in the household, both in the domestic as well as extra-domestic spheres. The wife's rights are transferred to her husband's lineage after the full payment of bride price. She is fully incorporated into her husband's group. Though the wife is subordinate to the husband, she plays a crucial role in the overall management of the household. Important decisions concerning the family affairs are to be taken by both.

There is a clear division of labour between the husband and wife. The husband looks after economic activities like ploughing, cutting trees, cleaning shrubs for shifting cultivation, house construction, working as daily wage labourer or working in some office on a permanent basis to maintain the family. The wife on the other hand is in charge of the household chores such as cleaning the house, cooking, looking after the children, maintaining the cattle shed, fetching fuel wood from forest, looking after the guests, drying up grains and other eatables, preparing leaf plates (*khalli*) and *ambula* (dry mango) to be sold in the market. The relationship between them runs into a rough weather due to misunderstanding, wife beating, extramarital relationship by either of the spouses or for that matter serious ill behaviour by the husband due to frequent drinking. These factors may also lead to divorce. Divorce can be initiated by each of the spouses. There is no bar on marrying a divorced man or woman. Unmarried man and woman can marry divorced man and woman. The wife does not address her husband by name. They practice tecknonymy, i.e. addressing wife as the mother of son or daughter or vice-versa.

The father and son relationship among the Kondh is of patrilineal structure. The relationship is crucial throughout their lives. The relationship is based mainly on three aspects: economic, ritual and jural. On the economic aspect of the relationship, they are never treated independently. The father is the owner of all landed property, house and other valuables till death. After the death of the father, the land is divided among the sons. Usually the father helps the son in establishing a new household after his marriage. To maintain the household, the son works with his father in the field. Thus, the son's household and the father's household is a joint productive unit, but separate consumption units. The produce is either equally distributed among the sons or some additional share is given to the large household. The situation is gradually changing these days: the landed property is divided among sons during the father's lifetime.

The economic relationship between the father and the sons is constantly nurtured since the birth of a male child. The birth of a male child is celebrated because he is an economic asset to the family. The young boys (right from the age of eight to nine years) start supporting their fathers in economic activities like going to the field with the father, doing small things like cleaning the fields, carrying light weight items like baskets or, for that matter, collecting minor forest produce and fuel wood. The boys continuously watch their father's hard work in the land: ploughing, sowing, harvesting, cutting trees, etc. It is clear that sons are motivated to do hard work like their fathers. At the age of fifteen they start ploughing. In fact the sons feel very proud when they use any implement for the first time in field. During his old age, the father is usually dependent on the sons.

Ritually, the son has many obligations to his father particularly after his death. All the rituals are transferred to the eldest son who performs the *videringa laka* (annual worship of the dead father's soul and other ancestors). It is very important since after the death, the soul moves around the village and constantly keeps a vigil on the son's house. The soul has to be appeased regularly through periodic worship. If it is not done, then the descendants will be afflicted with misfortunes like ill health, severe injury or death. The misfortunes are sometimes specific like having disease (fever and small pox), getting hurt in the forest or suicidal killing by oneself through some instrument. As the head of the family, the eldest son inherits all the rituals from the father – *kutum* worship, the forest goddess worship, the earth goddess worship, the *kedu puja,* etc. Finally, on the jural front, the authority of the house is entrusted to the father. The attitude of the father towards his son is always of domination till the son's marriage. The son is not expected to argue in a raised voice with his father. He is always expected to obey his father. However, in practice, there is often an argument between them. When the father turns old, the sons behave towards him in a different manner, sometimes making sarcastic jokes towards him.

Among the Kondh, the relationship between brothers assumes significance after the father-son relationship. It is manifested through economic, ritual and jural solidarity as well as the continuous conflicting situation. The relationship between brothers is of hierarchical nature. When the brothers are unmarried, the younger ones obey the elders sincerely. The elder brother is treated at par with the father particularly in the context of authority. When the elder brother starts going to the field with his father the younger ones take care of infants at home. In case of any peer group confrontation of the younger ones, the elder brother settles the issue. Often the elder brother controls the younger ones using force, both physical and verbal. After marriage, the relationship continues with the same vigour except for the fact that there may not be any physical abuse. On the ritual side, though the eldest brother performs the worship, the younger ones (both married and unmarried) cooperate with him economically and manually. After the father's death, the landed property is divided among the sons. The Kondh practice primogeniture in the sense that the eldest son receives some extra land to perform the worship or to take care of the old parents or widowed mother or father. The youngest son takes the possession of the father's house. Since the Kondh have a one-living room house, the youngest son after marriage constructs a separate house near the father's house. But after the father's death, he shifts to the father's house.

In contrast to the father-son and brother-brother relationship, the mother and son relationship is marked with emotion, affection and familiarity. The son is quite close to his mother particularly from his birth, till he goes with his father to work. The infant sons get more attention than the infant daughters in terms of food and care. In fact the son's total upbringing during childhood is fully dependent on his mother. The father hardly has any concern for his son's upbringing. Normally, a son is expected to obey his mother but the Kondh sons frequently disobey their mothers. During the marriage of a son the mother has an important role to play. The son usually confides first with his friends and next with his mother. If a son has already chosen a girl, he first informs his mother who helps him in arranging the marriage in consultation with the father and other senior males of the family. Though the mother and son relationship is not of joking, among the Kondh, the matured son usually cracks jokes with the mother, both inside and outside the house, in front of the father, by befooling her. The son performs a vital role towards his mother after the death of his father. The mother becomes totally dependent on her son. However, there are many cases where sons have deserted their widowed old mothers.

The father and daughter relationship is mainly characterized by protection and care of the daughter by the father particularly upto the former's marriage. At one time, the Kondh practiced female infanticide. There is a myth behind this practice. It is said that Donka Mallika, a Kondh, had four sons, of whom three had eight sons and the fourth had two daughters. The girls cohabited with their cousins as they could not find husbands. The other three brothers punished their father by depriving him of his share of property, and the guilty girls drowned themselves in a pond. After this incident, the three brothers reconciled with their father and as the dispute arose due to the daughters, they decided thenceforth to destroy the female issues and thus female infanticide as a custom came into existence (Sahoo 1989: 78). Besides this, there are other causes, like the marriage custom was a burden on them as women were virtually purchased through the bride price system. After marriage, woman had the right to leave her husband on some misconduct and go to another. In such cases the husband had the right to ask for the refund of bride price from the girl's father. Such cases repeatedly occurred and girls became a burden on the parents. Thus, the simplest way to get out of this burden was to kill the daughters.

However, the British government stopped this practice and now it has not been reported from any area but the parents are not very happy when a girl is born. On asking about such practices, the youth and extrovert elderly people protest with anger. However, the old and introvert ones confirm the practice. Against this backdrop it may be noted that a Kondh father always wishes for the birth of a son, and whenever a daughter is born he accepts her with an unpleasant mood. But gradually, the infant girl draws attention of the father in terms of affection. There is hardly any intimacy between the father and the daughter. The grown up daughter looks after her father when her mother is away. In case of the death of a wife, a Kondh man becomes dependent on his daughter for cooking and household maintenance. Even after the marriage of the daughter, she frequently visits her father; the father is pleased at the time of his daughter's marriage because he receives money and gifts as bride price.

The mother and daughter bond is a stronger one. Daughter helps her mother in domestic chores. The mother brings her up as well as teaches morality to the grown up daughter, besides training her in household chores. Sometimes the mothers punish the daughter for disobeying her. The daughter always takes the side of her mother whenever a drunken father beats the mother. On the other hand the brother and sister relationship is marked with amity and affection towards each other. The sisters respect the elder brothers and obey them. The elder sister takes care of the younger brothers. During the sister's marriage, particularly while choosing a mate, the brother performs a crucial role in selecting the mate. Even after the marriage of sister, brothers are quite concerned about the sister's well being.

The sister and sister relationship is a very close relationship marked with sympathy and cooperation. The sisters virtually become friends when they are in the same age group. They also maintain contact with each other after marriage. The grand parents and grand children relationship is marked with familiarity and joking. The grand parents who do not go to work spend their time with the infant grandchildren. Usually they sit in the middle of the street or under the shadow of a tree and play with their grandchildren. It is the duty of the grandparents to take care of the grandchildren whenever the parents are away.

Among the affinal relatives, the relatives who matter the most are brothers in-law (wife's brothers and huband's brothers), sisters-in-law (husband's sisters, wife's sisters and husband's brother's wife , mother's brother-sister's son, parents-in-laws, son-in-law, and daughter-in-law. The structure of this relationship will become clear from the following discussion.

The relationship between sister's husband and wife's brother is marked with respect and as well as joking. *Wibr* is an important affinal relative and when he visits the sister's place, the *SiHu* enthusiastically becomes hospitable. He cancels all his work and spends time with him. The same thing happens when *SiHu* visits his in-law's place. On the other hand the *YoBr*'s wife does not take the name of husband's elder brother. The husband's elder brother is treated at par with the husband's father. It is in fact an avoidance relationship. On the other hand, the relationship with the husband's younger brother is more cordial and joking. They often share vulgar jokes. The Kondhs have levirate marriage rule. The relationship between husband's sister and brother's wife is marked with friendship and affection as well as conflict. The BrWi treats husband's elder married sister with respect and closeness. Ideally husband's unmarried sisters see the elder brother's wife at par with the mother. An unmarried sister does less work and anticipates all the work to be done by the brother's wife. The relationship between mother's brother and sister's son is more of a formal nature because of the lack of continuous interaction between them. Only on ritual occasions do they visit each other. The *MoBr* represents the mother's family when the mother's father dies. He is more bothered about the *SiSo* welfare. The parents-in-laws and son-in-law relationship is marked with mutual respect for each other. The relationship between mother-in-law and son-in-law is that of avoidance. The father-in-law and daughter-in-law relationship is marked with avoidance. But in the absence of the mother in-law the daughter-in-law takes care of the father-in-law particularly in his old age.

The above descriptions of the nature of various relationships are not found in constancy and consistency. It is only the broad sameness of the nature of relationship, which is also ideal for the group, is being discussed above.

Changing patterns

Kinship has been the basis of social structure of simple societies. These societies are also confronting the processes of urbanization, industrialization and modernization. For instance, G. Udaygiri has been a town for about six decades. Therefore, the villages near the town are having a heterogeneous population. In Gressingia (4 km. away from G. Udaygiri) and Baudi (5 km away from G. Udaygiri), people working in G.Udaygiri have taken rented accommodation because the rent is cheaper. Besides, as already stated, the villages used to be a single lineage centered ones and today they have become heterogeneous with different part lineages living together. Kinship is in a total flux now. Impact of Christianity is dominant in the Kondh area. Within the same family one brother has been baptized and the other is not, and this creates interfamilial conflicts. The baptized ones are not supposed to perform/follow the Kondh religious rituals, but they still continue to practise them. Kinship is facing both the processes of fission and fusion. Fusion in the sense, the relationship within natal family continues to be stronger because of the modern communication methods. The joint family continues to be the joint property owning unit and joint ritual unit. As said earlier, the Kondhs always practiced natolocal households within the joint family organization. Those who are working outside their villages are in close touch with their natal family. They visit regularly depending on the proximity to the village. The money order economy (i.e. son sending money to the parents for the latter's livelihood) is also found among Kondhs. The sons and daughters visit parent's villages during life cycle rituals. However, visiting parents' house for religious rituals has become rare today. Parents are very proud of those sons who are working in government jobs. Clan has remained today only a ritual category, people do not even recall the names of the clan. On the other hand, lineage exogamy is still followed. For all practical purposes family and the extended kin group still remain as the social unit.

The institution of marriage largely remains traditional, except a few cases of inter-community love marriages, adultery and the practice of dowry. In this manner the modern forces have entered the people's mind, but integration of these with kinship and family structure has become vital today. Thus, we cannot analysis the Kondh situation in terms of structural change, but all changes are found only within the structure. They can be analyzed under organizational change. The choice and alternative used by members for maintaining the ideal kinship structure is clear. Extreme patriliny and adherence to exogamy rules are still there ideally but in reality it has become difficult to maintain clan and *mutha* exogamy though they still maintain village and lineage exogamy.

REFERENCES

Bailey, F.G.

1960 *Tribe, Caste and Nation: A Study in Political Activity and Political Change in Highland Orissa*. Manchester: Manchester Press.

Bhandari, J.S.

1992 *Kinship, Affinity and Domestic Group*. New Delhi: Gian.

Boal, Barabara M.

1982 *The Konds: Human Sacrifice and Religious Change*. Warminster: Aris and Phillips.

Campbell, Maj-Gen. John

1864 *A Personal Narrative of 13 Years' Service Among the Wild Tribe of Khondistan for the Suppression of Human Sacrifice*. London

Chaudhury, S.K.

1993 *Myopic Development and Cultural Lens: An Evaluative Study of Tribal Programmes Among Kondhs of Orissa*. New Delhi: Inter-India Publications.

1999 *Social Organization and Change: Contemporary Study of Kondhs of Orissa*'. Unpublished Ph.D. Thesis. Department of Anthropology: University of Delhi.

Ferriera, J.

1965 *Totemism in India*. London: OUP.

Firth, Raymond

1971 *Elements of Social Organization*. London: Tavistock.

Majumdar, D.N.

1965 *Races and Cultures of India*. Bombay: Asia Publishing House.

Parkin, Robert

1997 *Kinship*. Oxford: Blackwell.

Patnaik, S.M.

1996 *Displacement, Rehabilitation and Social Change: The Case of Paraja Highlanders*. New Delhi: Inter-India Publications.

Pradhan P.

1990 Economic Development and Social Change among the Kondhs. Unpublished Ph.D. Thesis. Sambalpur University, Orissa.

Risley, Sir H.H.

1891 *Tribes and Castes of Bengal*. Calcutta: Bengal Secretariat Press.

Russel, R.V. and Hira Lal

1916 *Tribes and Castes of Central Provinces*, Vol.III(G-Ko), London: Macmillan.

Sahoo, B.

1989 'The practice of infanticide among the Kondhs of Orissa': In Ray B.C. (ed.) *Tribes of Orissa: The Changing Socio-Economic Profile*. New Delhi: Gian.

Thurston, E.

(1909) 1987 *Castes and Tribes of Southern India*. New Delhi: Cosmo Publications: 356-419.

14

Land Alienation, Forest Rights and Displacement: Predicament of the Tribals in Jharkhand and Madhya Pradesh

K. Gopal Iyer

This paper highlights the current problems encountered by the scheduled tribes with regard to the land and forests which are the twin pillars of tribal economy. With the advent of the British rule the tribals not only started losing their lands but forests also became state property. The creation of 'Reserved' and 'Protected' forests during the colonial period considerably affected the tribal rights in such forest areas which had provided an important source of their livelihood. This policy was further extended during the post-independence period particularly due to the enactment of fresh legislation like the Forest Conservation Act, 1980 and legislations on wild life. The latter legislations displaced the tribals from national parks and sanctuaries and the tribals who have been cultivating the lands in the forest area for generations have been labelled as encroachers. Taking up the situation obtaining in the newly created state of Jharkhand and the undivided Madhya Pradesh as case studies, I have proceeded to chart the different dimensions of the rampant loss of tribal lands to them and its effect together with the denial of access to forest resources on the economic conditions of the large S.T. populations in these states.

The central ministry of environment and forests issued a circular on 3 May, 2002 for evicting tribals from 12.50 lakh hectares in different parts of India which has been reinforced by a Supreme Court judgment. This issue is taking the form of intense protest from the tribal groups particularly in Jharkhand and Madhya Pradesh. I have also examined the adverse impact of globalization in the two states. The new industrial policy of Jharkhand is inviting multinationals on a large scale to expand mining and industries which will result in further alienation of tribal lands. Similarly, the World Bank intervention in Madhya Pradesh in social forestry project is being strongly resisted by the various tribal groups.

Tribal land alienation in Jharkhand

The tribal land rights here are being viewed mainly in the context of various protective legislations which prevent alienation of tribal lands to non-tribals and restoring the alienated land to tribals. The alienation of tribal lands takes place both through private individuals and development projects. Tribals in Jharkhand constitute 29 percent of the state's population and 13 percent of the total tribal population in the country. In Ranchi and Singhbhum districts the tribals constitute 56 percent and 44 percent of the respective district's population; while in the districts of Hazaribagh, Palamau, Giridih and Dhanbad they comprise only 9.04 percent, 19.24 percent, 12.99 percent and 3.11 percent of the total population. Though there are thirty different tribal communities in the state, the more numerous ones are Santhals (25 lakhs), Oraons (13 lakhs), Mundas (10 lakhs), and Hos (7 lakhs). The overwhelming concentration of Santhals is in Santhal Paraganas, of Oraons and Mundas in Ranchi district and Hos in Singhbhum district of Chotanagpur region. Agriculture and forests are their principal sources of livelihood.

The introduction of zamindari system and market economy in the region not only brought the concept of private property but wrought havoc in the tribal economy. The traders, moneylenders, liquor contractors and the landlords grabbed tribal lands on large-scale during the 19th century. The tribals were pushed to the wall. It led to a number of tribal uprisings, e.g. the Kol rebellion of 1831-32, Santhal uprisings of 1855, and Birsa Munda rebellion of 1890-1895.

The series of tribal uprisings in the 19th century led the British to enact the Chotanagpur Tenancy Act 1908 and the Santhal Pargana Tenancy Act. It restricts the transfer of land from tribals to non-tribals. It permits alienation under certain circumstances, e.g. a simple mortgage or lease for a period of five years, a *bhugut bandha* (individual mortgage) for seven years and upto 15 years in case of mortgage with a registered cooperative society. It can also be transferred for charitable, religious, educational, industrial, and developmental purposes. The Act prevents alienation of Mundari Khuntkatti tenancy except in case of *bhugut bandha* mortgage of seven years or a *mukarrari* lease. Land transfers can also take place through the Land Acquisition Act. The non-tribals continued to alienate tribals from their lands through collusive title suits, *de facto* possession, transfers in fake and fictitious tribal name by marrying a tribal woman and so on. The Scheduled Areas Regulation in 1969 further strengthened the Act of 1908 relating to the restoration of land illegally alienated from the tribals. It restricts transfer of tribal lands to non-tribals and prevents possession where transfers have been effected through fraudulent and collusive means. It however, permits them to transfer lands in genuine cases to obtain institutional loans for agricultural development. The Indian Limitation Act has been amended and the period of limitation has been extended from 12 to 30 years. The amendment of

CNT Act in 1975 has put the onus of proving the validity of the title on the non-tribals. The first Scheduled Areas and Scheduled Tribes Commission (1962) had also recommended for a radical amendment to agrarian laws to completely prevent transfer of tribal lands to non-tribals, exclusion from jurisdiction of courts of law and restoration of the possession of lands with or without compensation in case of adverse possession with retrospective effect.

The alienation of Santhals lands to non-tribals dates back to one and a quarter century. The Santhal rebellion of 1855 was the direct result of massive alienation of tribal lands to moneylenders, landlords, and traders. In spite of this rebellion, alienation of tribal lands continued. The McPhersons Survey (1905-12) records that land sold between 1855-87 was 30,927 acres, from 1887-1905 it was 32,146 acres and 71,401 acres during 1905-1912, i.e. a total of 1.35 lakh acres was alienated between 1855 and 1912. Another 35,927 acres were alienated from Santhals between 1912-1932. These alienations continued in spite of the Santhal Pargana Settlement Regulation of 1872. In this Regulation the tenants had been assured not to be ejected except through due process of law. The Santhal Parganas Tenancy (Supplementary Provisions) Act of 1949 also reiterated the same provisions of security to tenants under sections 42 and 20. Yet the land alienation of the tribals continued unabated. The Santhal were forced to initiate land struggles between 1967 to 1979 for the restoration of land. The agitation successfully restored a big chunk of land from *mahajans*. However, the grabbing of tribal lands by the landlords continues even today. The tribals are reduced to the status of sharecroppers on their own land.

The Bihar Scheduled Areas Regulations of 1969 is of limited help to Santhals. This Regulation has put a time limitation for the restoration of land. It provides that if an intruder is continuously in possession of tribal land for more than 30 years, it is in the discretion of the Deputy Commissioner to let him remain on the encroached land on payment of compensation. This in practice is the liberalisation of the law. Previously no one could have intruded into the landed property of the tribals without taking the risk of being evicted. This provision has given him an option to remain in possession of the tribal land on payment of compensation.

The other kind of alienation is a recent innovation. This land loot is committed by the revenue officials. The anchal adhikaris have been entrusted with some responsibilities under the Bihar Land Reforms Act, 1950. The Act provides for homestead to such persons who are agricultural labourers or village artisans. They can be given lands in the rural areas for their homestead by the state. But, in this area this act has been completely misinterpreted by providing land for homestead to the well-to-do families, mostly government servants. In 1987-88, around 60 persons have been given land for dwellings by the circle officer, Dumka, alone. Many beneficiaries are wives of government servants. Of the total beneficiaries, 80 percent are women. This situation is similar in all the four district headquarters, six sub-divisional headquarters, and the block headquarters of Santhal Pargana region. Approximately 1000 acres of land has been settled by the circle officers under this pretext in Santhal Pargana. This has caused great resentment among the tribals. Scores of cases are pending in different courts and all of them have been pending for months, as stated in a 1988 batch IAS Probationer's report on Jharkhand movement. Several other studies point to the continuing process of land alienation of tribals during the post-independence period both to the private individuals and government projects.

Gupta's study (1960) in Dhanbad district is quite revealing. It points out that the extent of land alienation, through 145 cases of collusive title suits involved 92 acres of tribal land passing into the hands of non-tribals by adverse possession. Land alienation in seven anchals of Dhanbad district was to the extent of 195 acres which included registered deeds (since 1950) and court decrees. The acute indebtedness accompanied with land alienation agitated the tribal mind. Between 1974-76 there was a militant movement in the districts of Dhanbad, Giridih, and Santhal Parganas. Tribals in thousands forcibly harvested the crops from the alienated tribal land in spite of massive police mobilization. This was one of the major peasant movements of tribals in the post-independence period for restoration of alienated land (Iyer and Mahajan 1982: 180-187). The district administration of Dhanbad and Giridih had restored 2066-84 acres and 2378-42 acres of alienated lands during this period.

The Study Team of the Ministry of Home Affairs which made an assessment of the tribal situation in 1974 in Chotanagpur and Santhal Parganas observed numerous forms of land alienation in the region:

- *(a)* Legal transfer facilitated by casual and routine approach adopted by the authorities;
- *(b)* Benami transactions in the name of servants:
- *(c)* Transfers through collusive civil proceedings;
- *(d)* Transfers in the name of tribal women taken as wives or concubines by non-tribals; and
- *(e)* Informal transactions in which land remains in the name of original land owner but he is reduced to the status of a sharecropper.

The team also noticed the alienation of tribal lands in urban and industrial areas and observed that though the tribals have been dispossessed of their lands by due process of law but on average tribal did not know the use of cash, he was either deceived and cheated or he squandered the money and became penniless as well as landless.

Sachchidananda (1972: 177) and others have observed that in the wake of industrialisation, large-scale alienation of tribal lands took place in Ranchi, Hatia, Bokaro, etc., causing widespread resentment. Similarly, large-scale alienation of tribal lands have taken place due to construction of various dams. The Heavy Engineering Corporation, Ranchi, alone acquired 7479 acres of land, affecting 23 tribal villages and 3000 tribal families. Land has also been acquired in and around Ranchi for several other manufacturing concerns.

As a consequence of the construction of the Sindri Fertiliser Factory in the district of Dhanbad, 1228 acres of land belonging to tribals was lost. In the same way Bokaro Steel Plant forced tribals from 48 villages of Dhanbad district and 36 villages of Hazaribagh district to lose 29820 acres and 36080.73 acres respectively (Roy Choudhury 1964: 486-487). Further several irrigation projects in Chotanagpur area like Tenughat, Koil Karo and Subarnrekha have displaced the tribals from 97843 acres, 45112 acres, and 85000 acres respectively. The compensation was quite paltry and bulk of it was siphoned off by middlemen like speculators in land, pleaders, *munshis* and clerks.

Commissioner for SC and ST (1984) observes that displacement of tribals from their land due to its acquisition by the government for projects of national interest has been going on from the beginning of the first five year plan. While complete information of displacement of tribal families on account of projects is not available, the enormity and the extent of displacement of tribals from their lands may be judged from the report of the working group on development of S.T. during VII five year plan, which gives a list of 17 projects located in various states from which 43,338 tribal families were displaced. Even this list does not include many projects in the tribal areas. Of these, in six projects, all the displaced persons belonged to S.T. Project authorities were found to be indifferent to the task of rehabilitation, with the result that over a period of time this has given rise to serious problems and discontentment among the tribal communities.

Commission for SC/ST observes (1983-84) that big projects may be taken up when inevitable in the national interest and the rehabilitation of the tribals affected by the projects, should invariably precede the commencement of the projects, keeping in view the following principles:

(i) Land for land - affected tribals should be given land for habitation and cultivation.

(ii) Village for village - the entire tribal population in the affected village should be rehabilitated enbloc as a village on the periphery of the project.

(iii) The benefits flowing from the projects should go as far as possible to the displaced tribals.

The Commission observes that a large number of tribals who had received substantial amounts by way of compensation were exploited by unscrupulous elements in the area so much so that some of them had to take to rickshaw pulling for their living. This happened despite the fact that the compensation amounts were paid to them through post offices.

The Land Acquisition Act, 1894 continues to be inimical to the interest of the tribals. Commissioner for SC and ST (1987-89: xv) has observed that this law, in a way was functioning like an indomitable, inanimate instrument for the transformation of the agriculture based traditional system into a modern system and, in that process, snatching away from the poor all those natural resources which have formed the basis of their life so far. The Commissioner (1979-81) gives a comprehensive account of the causes of tribal unrest in different districts of Jharkhand. In the Santhal Parganas, large-scale alienation of tribal lands had been taking place right from 1972 and even after the enactment of the Scheduled Areas Regulations in 1969. The Santhal wanted that all those lands which were fraudulently recorded in the name of non-tribals during various settlements, should be restored to them. The tribals forcibly recovered their lands and hypothecated goods from the possession of non-tribal traders and money-lenders who charged exorbitant rates of interest from them, as a result of which they always remained economically sub-servient to the *mahajans*. Moreover, the tribal workers were paid wages, at rates much less than those prescribed under the Minimum Wages Act. The benefits of the development programmes undertaken for the S.T. too have not reached the interior of tribal areas.

In Singhbhum district the forest development corporation was cutting sal trees in the forest to plant teak trees in their place. The tribals considered the sal trees as sacred and useful and did not like the plantation of teak trees. They, therefore, felt highly agitated which resulted in the police firing in Ichachatu village (police station Goelkera) on 6 October 1978, resulting in the death of one tribal and arrest and beating of two tribals. To quote another case, thirty five Khuntkatti villages (areas where tribals were the first settlers) in the Saraikela sub-division were acquired by the government in 1899 and declared as reserved forest, without the payment of any compensation to tribals. The tribals who had then been awakened by the publication of a couple of books on the subject, were demanding that these Khuntkatti villages should be restored to them. Large scale alienation of tribal lands had taken place in spite of the Chotanagpur Tenancy Act, 1908 and the Scheduled Areas Regulations of 1969. This was the result of the various loopholes in the existing tenancy legislation. The tribals also felt that all the land at present, owned by the non-tribals according to the last Revisional Survey of 1924-29, actually belonged to them and should be restored to them. The effect of large scale alienation of tribal lands to non-tribals was being exploited by some political parties who were encouraging the tribals to forcibly get back the land.

Lacunae in the Santhal Pargana Tenancy Act, 1949

Under Section 70 of the Santhal Civil Rules, there is a provision for filing suits for arrears of rent by the landlords against the village headmen and by the village headmen against the *raiyats* (cultivators). As a result of such suits the *raiyats* and pradhans were evicted from their *jamabandhi* (owned) land. The amount involved in such suits was very small while the *raiyats* and pradhans were evicted from very big areas of land. The tribal leaders claimed that these lands were fraudulently alienated from them as these were non-transferable under Section 27 of the Santhal Pargans Regulation III of 1872 and should be restored to them under the Santhal Pargana Tenancy Act, 1949 and Scheduled Areas Regulation, 1969, the right of adverse possession never accrues howsoever long the possession may have been. According to a ruling given by the Patna High Court, lands alienated before 1949, i.e. the year when the Act came into force, could not be restored. As a result of this, all cases relating to the period before 1949 had to be dealt with under the provisions of Santhal Pargana Regulation of 1872 and no restorations could be made under the 1949 Act and 1969 Regulation.

Lacunae in the Chotanagpur Tenancy Act, 1908

(i) There were practical difficulties in the implementation of the Scheduled Areas

Regulation, 1969. Sometimes applications filed by tribals for restoration of alienated lands under Section 71-A of the Chotanagpur Tenancy Act were rejected on flimsy technical grounds by the trial courts. Furthermore, Section 49 of the Act permitted transfer of tribal lands to non-tribals for certain purposes and this provision was being exploited by non-tribals.

(ii) According to a ruling of the High Court, 'surrender' of land by a *raiyat* was not a transfer within the meaning of Section 46 of this Act. It was, however, claimed that almost all the 'surrenders' of *raiyati* lands by S.T. had taken place before 1947 when it was legally not necessary to obtain prior permission of the Deputy Commissioner. Hence, the *raiyati* lands of ST alienated to non-tribals via the zamindars could not be restored to the tribals under the Scheduled Areas Regulation, 1969.

(iii) The benefit of the amendment to the Limitation Act 1963 extending the period of limitation from 12 to 30 years in case of tribal lands did not accrue to the Bhuinhari and Khuntkatti lands. Moreover, this provision was not made applicable retrospectively, i.e., prior to February 8, 1969.

(iv) Tribal lands on a very large-scale had been alienated by the non-tribals in Ranchi town. However, restoration of alienated tribal lands in the municipal areas was not possible under the Chotanagpur Tenancy Act as decided by the High Court. This had the

effect of not only legitimizing and regularizing alienation that had taken place in the urban areas but also intensifying the process of further alienation of tribal lands.

(v) Under Section 46 (1) of the Chotanagpur Tenancy Act, tribal *raiyats* can mortgage their lands to get loans from cooperative institutions and banks for improvements in their agriculture. However, there is no such provision for Bhuinhari and Mundari Khunkattidars to mortgage their lands for this purpose, under Sections 48 and 240 of the Act respectively.

In pursuance of the above mentioned suggestions, the state government promulgated the Chotanagpur Tenancy (Amendment) Ordinance 1979 in November, 1979, in order to remove some of the above mentioned lacunae. Provisions of the Act were retrospectively made applicable to tribal lands alienated in areas which had been constituted into a municipality or a notified area committee or a cantonment. Further, members of the Bhuinhari family or a Mundari Khunkattidars tenants were vested with the rights to transfer by a simple mortgage his tenancy or any portion thereof, with a view to raising loan for agricultural purposes from certain banks, societies, etc.

Displacement and land alienation in Jharkhand

The foregoing account brings out that the basic phenomenon that affects the tribal people of Jharkhand historically and today is dispossession from their land. The displacement and land alienation also affects their cultural and political identity. They are uprooted from their culture, their values and through it from their identity. They are deprived of their hearth and home, their rights and are forced to get integrated and assimilated with the so-called "national mainstream". The alienation of the tribal land during the British period was both by the state and the individuals. The land alienation by the state represented alienation for the development purposes by the colonial government like opening of mines, construction of railways, etc. The land alienation to the private sources consisted of the nexus between the powerful rural elites, bureaucracy and the police force. The main culprits of land alienation were the landlords, moneylenders, traders and liquor contractors, who were later on added to by the migration of non-tribals particularly from North Bihar to Jharkhand area. Even during the post-independence period both forms of alienation and dispossession of tribals from their lands continued on a large scale. In the name of development and national interest a lot of tribal lands were acquired for what can be euphemistically called 'public purpose'.

Land acquisition and *eminent domain*

At present the land acquisition takes place in the name of development, which is based on the colonial principle of *terranulleu* and this principle was initially adopted by the white colonizers in occupying indigenous lands in Australia, New Zealand, Southern Africa and Americas. The judiciary in Australia however, declared this principle invalid in 1993. This principle under the term *eminent domain* is the basic and guiding principle in land acquisitions for 'public purpose' The concept confers on the state the right to define 'public purpose', which is the basic principle of the Indian Land Acquisition Act, 1894. The indigenous peoples demand the abrogation of the principle of *eminent domain* and restricting the meaning of 'public purpose'. They demand that displacement must recognize the historically established rights of the people over their livelihood including land, forests and other customary rights. Conservative estimates establish that the number of people displaced due to development measures such as setting up of industries during the 19th century was 35 million and between 1950 to 1991, 25 to 30 millions were displaced due to the construction of dams, mines, industries, wildlife and sanctuaries. The major portion of those displaced have not been rehabilitated (Fernandes and Paranjpye 1997). Table 1 and Table 2 show the total number of persons and tribals displaced due to various development projects between 1951-1990 all over India and in Jharkhand.

Multinational corporations in Jharkhand

The various structural and economic reforms recently initiated by the government in order to deregulate the Indian economy will have serious adverse impact on Jharkhand and its people. In line with these measures, in March 1993 the government of India announced with much fanfare a new National Mineral Policy designed to attract private and multinational investors for large expansion of mineral exploitation in the country. Foreign companies would be allowed cent percent equity participation in mining projects and restrictions would be removed on thirteen minerals previously reserved for the state sector. Since all these major minerals are mined mostly in Jharkhand the new mineral policy will have far reaching consequences for the environment and people of this area. The dominant mining companies of the world are now showing great interest in India, especially in Jharkhand. The White Industries of Australia and the Canadian Metchem Company have already taken up projects in this sector. The Piparwar Coal Project is being jointly run by the Coal India Ltd. (CIL) and the White Industries Ltd. The cost of the project is estimated to be Rs. 542.43 crores. The Australian business interests will make a substantial profit from this project.

The Rajmahal Coal Mining Project, one of India's largest open pit mines, is an ambitious hi-tech project in one of the country's poorest districts, Godda. Mét-Chem, a

Canada based multinational, serves as collaborator-consultant in this project. In a project worth Rs. 966 crores the charges made by Met-Chem, for consultancy service alone come to Rs. 105 crores. In effect, Met-Chem became purchaser, middleman, consultant and collaborator, a deadly combination as it proved. The indigenous people of Godda district have not benefitted from this great project. In fact, many have lost their homes and there is very little chance for them to get employment in the mines due to high-tech mechanization of the project. All this will have a tremendous adverse impact on the ecology and on the people of Jharkhhand. A 'coal mafia' has developed in the area and prostitution has come in a significant way to the villages where it was never a major problem. Anti-social elements have grown powerful. The visible beneficiary is the multinational Met-Chem that, by its own admission, is doing very well. While the multinationals and the commercial and industrial sectors will amass huge profits, a large number of indigenous people of Jharkhand will be driven out of their homelands and deprived of their sources of livelihood. Their lands would turn into wastelands due to wanton exploitation of the riches hidden in her womb. International environment pressure groups and human rights organizations, such as Mine Watch and Partisans, both based in London, monitoring global mining industry are watching with great apprehension the proposed entry of RTZ into India. These organizations have documented RTZ's recent involvement in the violation of indigenous people's rights. As a result of the new mineral policy, which encourages the entry of multinationals into the mining sector, there will be an unprecedented assault on the mineral wealth of the country by these companies whose only interest is to maximize their profits, whatever the eventual cost may be.

The entire Jharkhand area, rich in mineral, will be now thrown open for plunder and loot by these vested interests with the expansion of mining activities, especially with the opening of fifty new coal mines in the area to achieve the targeted production of 417 mt coal by 2000 AD. Land degradation, air, water and noise pollution will attain alarming proportions. It is estimated that the rate of degradation of land will intensify to 1,400 hectares a year or more. The existing agricultural and forest lands will shrink further with the eventual emergence of more wastelands. More and more indigenous people will be forced to move out of their hearth and homes to brick kilns, stone quarries, etc., in search of livelihood.

Land rights and land alienation in Madhya Pradesh

Madhya Pradesh has the largest scheduled tribe population in the country; 22.73 percent of the S.T. of the country live in Madhya Pradesh. There are 125 scheduled tribes in the state and their total populations is 1.20 crores. They are overwhelmingly located in the rural areas. There were 11 tribes having more than one lakh population. Numerically preponderant among them are Gonds (54 lakhs), Bhils (25 lakhs), followed by Kawar (5.62 lakhs). The other scheduled tribes with more than one lakh population are Baiga, Bharia, Bhatra, Halva, Kwar and Saharia. They have very low literacy rates, which was 10.68 percent in 1981. Female literacy was much lower (3.19%). The Gond constitute 44.63 percent and Bhil-Bhilalas constitute 20.90 percent of the total tribal population in the states.

Before the bifurcation of Madhya Pradesh into two states (Chattisgarh the new state) the total tribal population constituted 23 percent but after bifurcation it stands at 19 percent. The primitive communities among them like Baigas are virtually struggling for their survival. The tribals are numerically preponderant in a few districts—Dhar, Jhabua, Badwani, Mandla and Dindori—and there are 12 districts with 20 to 50 percent tribal population. The land and forests are the twin sources of their livelihood. They have also diversified into other occupations like casual labour in stone cutting and mines.

In March 1960, Verrier Elwin wrote:

> Throughout vast areas of tribal India, the last hundred years represent a melancholy history of encroachment, alienation and exploitation (India 1960).

Indebtedness and poverty are major factors in divesting tribals of their land. A study on tribes and tribal areas (Dube and Bahadur 1967) had stated that 73 percent of the tribals were cultivators, and 20.5 percent of these were classed as agricultural labourers. Tribal districts had poor soil, low productivity, growing inferior crops (like *kodon*, *kutki* and *manduva*) and had virtually no irrigation facilities. The *Human Development Report* (1998) indicates that there has been little change in this sceanrio as far as the status of agriculture in tribal life is concerned. In tribal districts like Jhabua and Bastar, two thirds of the tribals are self-employed. However, most of them were marginal farmers or agricultural labourers. Another remarkable feature for the agrarian sector is the remarkably slow rate of urbanization in the tribal districts. Seasonal migration in this region was not recorded or marked. Hence most tribal districts like Jhabua, Mandla, Bastar, Sarguja and Dhar show an urbanization rate between 1.6 and 2.9 percent. In the districts with the highest tribal population – Jhabua, Dhar, Mandla, Bastar and Sarguja—though tribals own most of the cultivable land the net sown area is very little.

The National Commission for Scheduled Castes and Scheduled Tribes provides adequate evidence of the problem of land alienation. The number of land alienation cases registered till June 1994 were 54,139. Of these, 54.67 percent were rejected and land restoration took place only in 31.50 percent cases. Though plenty of provisions existed against the transfer of tribal lands to non-tribals, the situation was quite dismal. Land ceiling laws were enacted and surplus land was distributed but the tribal beneficiaries received only a fraction of the total lands. Many tribals are forced to sell their bullocks and other equipment in lieu of debts. Non-tribals got whatever harvest the tribals received from their lands in return for money lent; thus the informal lending system took a heavy toll on tribal's access to land and resources, keeping them in perpetual debts leading to mortgage and ultimate loss of their lands. It must be admitted that alienation of land from tribals has also occurred significantly directly as a result of government policy.

Laws on land alienation

Even existing landholdings of the marginalized have been alienated, in spite of score of laws in force for maintaining the land rights of the marginalized *adivasis*. The first act to protect *adivasi* land from being alienated— the Land Alienation Act 1916— was passed by the Central Provinces and Berar (present Madhya Pradesh). Another law, the Madhya Bharat Scheduled Areas (Allotment and Transfer of Land) Regulation, 1954, (applicable to Madhya Bharat region only) intended to check the unwanted transfer of *adivasi* land and restrict transfer of their land to non-*adivasis* by way of sale, mortgage, lease or otherwise without the prior permission of district collectors.

Later on a number of legal provisions were incorporated in the Madhya Pradesh Land Revenue Code of 1959 to protect tribal rights on land and livelihood. Section 165 (6) of the Code imposed a ban on transfer of agricultural land owned by *bhumiswamis* belonging to a designated aboriginal tribe, to a person not belonging to a designated aboriginal tribe, without the prior permission of the collector, who must specify the reasons for giving such permission in writing. However, this did not deter land sharks. They misused the provisions of sections 169 and 190 of the Code to bypass the prohibition under sections 165 (6) and 165 (7). According to section 169, if any *bhumiswami* allows his land to be cultivated by others for a period of more than three years continuously, the rights of an occupancy tenant will accrue to them, who would then automatically become *bhumiswami* by virtue of section 190. These sections (169 and 190) were incorporated to prevent absentee landlordism and protect the interests of actual tillers of the soil. But these provisions were misused to facilitate illegal and exploitative transfers of *adivasi* land to non-*adivasis*.

A powerful effort to plug legal loopholes and to secure social justice to the *adivasis* was made by introducing sections 170 (A) and 170 (B) in 1976 and 1980 respectively. The amendment 170 (A) notified some areas of the state as 'predominantly inhabited by aboriginal Adivasis' and transfer of agricultural land held by aboriginal Adivasi to non-Adivasi was completely banned in such notified areas. The amendment gave sole power to the collector to decide on matters related to agricultural lands of *adivasis*. Section 170 (B) says that every person who on the date of commencement of the Madhya Pradesh Land Revenue Code (Amendment) Act, 1980 is in possession of agricultural land which belonged to a member of a tribe that has been declared to be an aboriginal tribe under sub-section (6) of section 165 between the period commencing on 2 October 1959 and ending on the date of commencement of Amendment Act, 1980 shall, within two years of such commencement, notify to sub-divisional officer in such form and in such manner as may be prescribed, all the information as to how he has come in possession of such land. Sub-section (2) of Section 170 (B) states that when any person fails to notify the information as required by Sub-section (1) within the period specified therein, it shall be presumed that such a person has been in possession of the agricultural land without any lawful authority and the agricultural land shall, on the expiration of the period aforesaid, revert to the person to whom it originally belonged and if that person be dead, to his legal heirs. Another amendment in section 170 (B) of the Code was introduced by the Land Revenue Code (Second Amendment) Bill, 1997. The amendment is as follows:

> 170-B (2A): If a Gram Sabha in the Scheduled Areas referred to in clause (1) of Article 944 of the constitution finds that a person, other than a member of an aboriginal tribe, is in possession of any land belonging to an aboriginal tribe, without any lawful authority, it shall restore the possession of such land to that person to whom it originally belonged. If Gram Sabha fails to restore the possession of such land, it shall refer the matter to the Sub-Divisional Officer, who shall restore the possession of such land within three months from the date of the receipt.

This is undoubtedly a significant amendment because it seeks to involve the gram sabha in restoration of land illegally taken from S.T. According to the latest available official data, up to September 1997, a total of 39,710 cases were registered under Section 170 (B) involving 45,729,792 hectares of land. Of these, 34.489 cases involving 41,963.053 hectares of land have been decided. In other words, 17 years after the legislation, 13.15 percent cases still remain pending in courts. Even lands of which possession has been officially restored to the original tribal landowners form only 12.65 percent of the total land under dispute. Disposal of cases tends to be slow, and a large majority of cases seem to have been decided mechanically in favour of non-tribals. That the legal shield could not protect the S.T. is borne out by the fact that all over India (India 2000) a total of 1,563,403.95 acres of land were alienated upto 1996. Of all the cases, 55.05% cases have been rejected, accounting for 61.32% of the total land. Till now 44.95% cases are pending before the courts for adjudication.

A 1983 study of eight districts by the Tribal Research Institute, Bhopal reported that of the 4,118 cases registered in these eight districts only 1,782 cases (43.20 percent) were disposed off. Of these, 1,140 cases (64.5 percent) were decided against the tribals. The study gives the example of Majholi, Narayanpur and Bijapur sub-divisions of Bastar district in which although a paltry 17, 16 and 19 cases were registered respectively, not one had finally been disposed off. The trend has not substantially altered till the present day. Implementation is weakest at the stage of restoring physical possession to the original tribal landowners. It is clear that even according to official figures, of a total of 16,149,997 hectares of land decided in favour of tribals, possession of 5,787,55 hectares (35.8%) has not been restored (Table 3).

Reasons for land alienation

Following are the reasons for *adivasi* land alienation, despite the radical provisions of Section 170 (A-B).

(i) In most sub-divisions, cases under section 170 (B) of the Code have not been registered. This is in defiance of the mandatory responsibility given to the SDO under section 170 (B) with regard to the holdings of agricultural land, which on October, 1959 were owned by notified aboriginal tribals, and which on October, 1980 were in the possession of non-tribals. This required firstly a thorough comparison of the record of rights for the two years 1959 and 1980,

and secondly a survey of holdings which are in the name of tribals but are actually in the *benami* possession of non-tribals. Many a time cases of land alienation are not registered by tribals themselves under duress of influential people in league with the administration.

(ii) A close scrutiny of many of the cases decided in favour of non-tribals shows that disposal of the lands has been frequently in contravention of the interest of the tribals.

(iii) Implementation is the weakest at the stage of restoring possession to the original tribal landowners. According to official figures, disputes about the ownership of a total of 16,149.997 hectares of land were decided in favour of tribals, but possession of 10,362.440 hectares (64.17 percent) has not been restored. A study by the Tribal Research Institute, Bhopal in 1983 revealed that in a majority of cases they did not secure actual possession because of threats and violence by non-tribals in possession of the land, and delays in implementation of the orders with the complicity of local revenue functionaries.

(iv) The second set of problems relates to the nature of our legal system, which, even in the context of sensitive and pro-poor legislation like this tends to be strongly weighted against the tribal poor. The Code restricts litigation to a single appeal, but non-tribal litigants easily get around this restriction.

The first significant study to assess the impact of the protective legislation specifically in the context of

Madhya Pradesh was taken up by the Tribal Research and Development Institute, Bhopal in 1973. The area of study was confined to the major tribal districts of Jhabua, Sarguja, Shahdol and Bastar. The focus of the study was on the extent of legally alienated land and causes thereof. Besides, one village study was also taken up in each of the four districts to fathom the problem of *benami* transfers. The most important conclusion of the study was the discovery that while one part of Section 165 (6) of the MP Land Revenue Code, 1959 prohibited transfer of land from aboriginals, the latter, part of the same section permitted it under certain conditions. All other clauses in the interest of the aboriginals seemed to be over-shadowed by this and transfer of land from the tribal to the non-tribals was a regular feature. Despite progressive and imaginative legislation to protect tribals from land alienation, both legal and illegal transfers continued, as a result of chronic indebtedness. Non-tribals often resorted to *benami* transfers to circumvent the laws and got collusive decrees passed by the civil courts for declaration of their title for the land belonging to tribals, which was illegally in their possession.

Displacement due to dams

The construction of Narmada dam has displaced a large number of tribals from their traditional land. Even the recent Supreme Court decision has affected their interests adversely. The permission to construct the dam up to 90 meters has brought more tribals within the ambiance of displacement, "the death warrant for the Valley". It comprises 30 large dams, 135 medium dams, and 3,000 small dams. One such high dam on Narmada is the Sardar Sarovar (SSP) which is being built in Baruch district of Gujarat. This dam will create a reservoir that will submerge over 24 villages and the forests, lands and homes of over 2.5 lakh people in Gujarat, Maharashtra and Madhya Pradesh. It will deprive a large number of tribals of their livelihood. The total number of people to be affected by the SSP will cross ten lakhs. Their rehabilitation has become a major problem. The government of Madhya Pradesh claims that there are no lands for the rehabilitation of displaced persons. The families whose lands have been submerged due to the reservoir have been dispersed to forty different sites and they have received uncultivable, water logged, and fragmented lands and in many cases no land. Many of these rehabilitated families have fled back to their original villages. The preparation for rehabilitation is awfully inadequate. In spite of the very strong and sustained movement of the Narmada Bachao Andolan (NBA) led by Megha Patkar and her team, the Narmada oustees are facing a grim scenario. The unhelpful attitude of the central government and Madhya Pradesh government to properly rehabilitate them has placed the question of livelihood of lakhs of tribals at stake. The tribals have been trying to resist these anti-people measures. The NBA has been a non-violent and peaceful movement and it has forcefully raised the issue of sustainability of big dams and has severely criticized the existing development paradigm.

Big dam controversy

The big dam controversy first of all involves 'interference with nature' argument: The argument is that rivers represent a natural regime. The interference is dangerous and must be avoided. The recent attacks are on specific projects, e.g. Silent Valley, Tehri, Sardar Sarovar, Narmada Sagar, etc. The environmental impact attributable to large dams includes the loss of agricultural and forest land, displacement of people and livestock, dislocation of wild life and loss of rare species of flora and fauna, problems of public health, loss of vegetative cover, and water logging and salinity in the command area. Large dams also invite the dangers of seismic activity.

The World Commission on Dams (WCD)

The WCD has pointed out that social impact includes livelihood and health of the affected communities and there is usually an improper assessment of the impact; all over the world dams have displaced four to eight crore people. The most vulnerable have been the indigenous and tribal people. The WCD recommends that the best possible choice is a combination of small and large dams. According to WCD the priorities in this regard should be: (i) giving public acceptance for a development decision and protecting interests of the affected groups; (ii) comprehensive option assessment of needs through participatory process; (iii) examining the capacity of providing development benefits and the options for rehabilitation; (iv) sustaining livelihoods; (v) recognizing entitlement; (vi) ensuring public trust and confidence; and (vii) a sharing of rivers for peace, development and security. The most important contribution of the WCD is the inclusion of non-state actors such as affected communities as key decision makers. And that large and small projects, and the use of surface water and groundwater, have to be integral parts of an overall plan of land-use and water-use for a drainage basin or watercourse system as a whole.

Sardar Sarovar Project (SSP): Failed rehabilitation

The first submergence occurred in the satyagraha villages in Jalsindhi and Domkhedi, where NBA had held out against the SSP. Ironically, resettlement and rehabilitation of the project affected peoples (PAP) has not taken place at all in MP. The administration turned a blind eye to the havoc caused by the SSP as the waters were rising and the sluices closed on the people affected by the Mann dam. Rich standing crops were annihilated. The MP government has been totally indifferent to the problems of rehabilitation and resettlement of which

Jalsindhi itself is a stark example. This goes blatantly against the policies of the Narmada Waters' Dispute Tribunal (NWDT) Award, which accepts that basic amenities must be provided before resettlement and that people be resettled as communities. It also shows why the government is so keen to give cash compensation. It will be so much cheaper than land for land. According to the MP government policy, the cut-off date to prove right over the encroached land is 1987, due to which many PAPs cannot establish their right and are not included in the PAP list. In MP about 8,000 families in 70 villages were affected due to SSP.

Task Force Study in Maharashtra has stated that at least 1,000 families affected by below 85 metres dam height still need to be rehabilitated. The affected people are tribals who have been told invariably that some people have to pay the price for 'development'. Maharashtra, after the Task Force Study has at least up to a point admitted the problem though it is not standing firm. The NBA has, however, proved its non-violent character, its respect for life and its tenacity: *'Dubenge nahin, par hatenge nahin'*— We won't drown, but will not budge, (Ditrich 2002). The NBA has conducted detailed surveys regarding displacement and resettlement below the present 90 meters of height. It was found that more than 3,500 families in all the three states – Gujarat, MP and Maharashtra –are still to be resettled as per the NWDT award in MP. In Kukshi and Alirajpur tehsils, about 2,000 families remained to be resettled while in Maharashtra more than 1,061 families below the present 90 meters are still to be resettled. The oustees have been allotted lands, which are rocky, uncultivable due to water-logging, salinisation or grass. As things stand, the governments of Madhya Pradesh and Maharashtra have no cultivable land for resettlement, as per the NWDT provisions. If the PAPs are required to be allotted agricultural land and arrangement of land is to be made by the state, and the resettlement unit is to be a village it will be very difficult to adhere to the time frame for the resettlement of the PAPs as approved by the Narmada Control Authority (NCA). There are over 35,000 affected families from Madhya Pradesh alone and there is no possibility of land-based resettlement for them (Sangvai 2002).

Interpreting Narmada judgement

On October 18, 2000, the Supreme Court delivered its verdict in the Narmada Bachao Andolan case bringing to an uneasy close, one of the most important judicial cases in recent times. It has been criticized by several experts. Until recently, most of the opposition was focused on the SSP, which forms the subject of the Narmada case. The history of opposition to the SSP dates back to 1978, soon after the NWDT gave its award.

The NBA brought the case to the Supreme Court; in 1994 the case was filed as a public interest writ petition alleging violation of the fundamental rights of the various groups of persons who were to be affected by the dam. In response to these pleadings, in 1995 the Supreme Court stayed the construction of the dam at a height of 80.3 meters until further orders. In February, 1999, while the case was posted for final hearing, the court passed an interim order allowing the raising of the height of the dam by an extra five meters to 85.3 meters. Finally, after completing hearings of the case, in May 2000, the court delivered its final verdict allowing the construction of the dam to a height of 90 meters and thereafter to its full height of 138.6 meters, provided that every increase in height of five meters would require the clearance of the NCA, the body constituted to look into the issues of compliance with the provisions of the NWDT award. Though hotly contested, this order of the court was broadly based on the assumption that relief and rehabilitation had been and were being carried on as required under the NWDT award, that all environmental studies were completed and that all safeguards had been met.

The main objections to the continuance of the construction of the dam raised by NBA in its petition were as follows: (1) that adequate provision for rehabilitation of the families whose lands were submerged had not been made and since it was a condition precedent to the construction of the dam (laid down by the tribunal in its award) the dam construction could not go on; (2) that no environmental studies mandated by the Ministry of Environment, Government of India to be done *pari passu* with the construction of the dam while granting conditional clearance to the project had been made; and (3) big dams did not yield benefits commensurate with the investment made therein.

The majority decision in NBA vs. Union of India disappoints more because of the majority judges taking a very formal view of issues like rehabilitation or environment. It seems that the court was suggesting its withdrawal from the larger role which it had assumed in recent decades.

Cullet (2001) has questioned the Supreme Court judgement from Human Rights angle–displaced people's right to life including the right to live in a healthy environment, right to a house or right to food are very important considerations in the eyes of the Supreme Court. As noted, in the court's words the judgement is fundamentally about the human rights of displaced people. In practice, however, human rights are given surprisingly little place in the arguments of the court. However, rather than providing a full reasoned analysis of the human rights situation, the judgement focuses on the various administrative procedures put in place by the state to deal with the various issues arising from the SSP. This is rather surprising. One of the dimensions that has been left aside in the majority judgement is the question of participation by oustees in the development of the project, or at least in the planning of their resettlement.

NBA compelled the government of Maharashtra to set up two independent committees to assess issues of resettlement and the cost benefit aspects of the dam. The government agreed to set up a secretary level overview committee and a planning committee at ministerial level to prepare a master plan of resettlement. About the land rights of the 73 villages in Akrani tehsil, the government would take a positive approach and it would support the NBA's contention regarding giving the land rights in the Mumbai High Court.

It was the latest, though an indirect admission of the failure of the resettlement up to 90 meters of the dam and that there have been major problems over this. After a year of the majority Supreme Court verdict, it is now clear that, the court was wrong in assuming that resettlement had been completed up to the dam height of 90 meters and that there would not be any difficulty in the resettlement of the oustees beyond that. The court assumed that large dams in India have been beneficial and there has been no negative fallout. After the verdict, in November and December 2000, the Indore-based NCA officials conceded before the people from the Narmada Valley that the rehabilitation of the people up to 90 meters of the dam was not complete and no land was available. The Daud Committee Report of Maharashtra concluded that the resettlement of those affected at 90 meters is yet to be completed due to non-availability of land. Thus there have been violations of NWDT, state policy and Supreme Court order regarding the resettlement hitherto.

In Madhya Pradesh, the government has already declared that it has no land for resettlement. On August

6, 2001 at the time of the protest demonstrations by over 600 people in Indore, the senior officials of NCA admitted that the rehabilitation of the people falling under 90 meters (90m+3 humps) was not yet over. They made it clear that NCA had never given any permission to construct the dam above 88 meters, something which the Supreme Court has claimed to have been done by NCA. The people took out the Manav Adhikar Yatra in October 2000, and protested in front of the Supreme Court on December 13. On September 3, M.P. Police mercilessly beat up 800 protestors in Badwani injuring over 25 people who were refusing the cash compensation and instead asked lands for rehabilitation. There were forcible surveys in the Nimad villages in September-October 2001, which saw suppression of the people's resistance, and beating up of the protesting villagers. However, people are also resisting such attempts as was evident in a protest rally in Manavar on October, 13. The decision of 18 October 2000 has not ended the matter, but rather made matters worse. The governments are now using the verdict to go ahead with the submergence of the valley and displace people without rehabilitations (Sangvai 2001).

Tribals and forest rights

Madhya Pradesh and Chhatisgarh have 20 percent of the total forest area in the country. In M.P., 30.89 percent of the geographical area is covered under reserved, protected and unclassified forests. It has 11 major national parks and 31 sanctuaries which constitute 3.86 percent of the total geographical area and 11 percent of the total forest area of the state. It has 12658 joint forest management committees covering an area of 52.07 lakh hectares. It also has the largest number of forest villages (1346) in the country which were to be converted into revenue villages but the Supreme Court's decision in 1997 to evict the encroachers from the forest land has affected the process of conversion of the forest villages to revenue villages. The central government had issued an order on 3 May 2002 to evict the encroachers which has created a problem for the tribals who are located in various villages. Only 522 villages had been converted into revenue villages and in the remaining 824 forest villages the tribals are considered as encroachers on the forest land extending to six lakh acres. Similarly, the tribals located in another three lakh acres in the orange area will also be affected.

After the enactment of the Wild Life Conservation Act, 1972 and the Forest Conservation Act, 1980, tribals were ousted from the forest lands as illegal encroachers and a large number of tribals have been displaced from their natural habitat after the setting up of national parks and wild life sanctuaries. A social forestry project has been set up in MP since 1992 with financial assistance from the World Bank. It has displaced 4.5 lakh *Dalit* and *Adivasis* (*Indian Express* August 5, 2002). The Forest Conservation Act stipulates that no settled forest land should be regularized without prior permission of the central government. In this connection the government of MP had issued a document on 30 April, 1994 stating that there was controversy over ownership of 7,33,829 hectares of forest land. After scrutinizing the applications the government found that 1,77,902 hectares of land genuinely belonged to the tribals and in the rest 5,55,927 hectares they were to be evicted.

The Baiga, a primitive tribal group has been facing severe repression. In July 1990 in Luri the forest department started large scale displacement of Baigas in a violent manner. Houses of twenty two families were torched and tractors were used to destroy the standing crops. The cases against these 22 Baigas are going on. There are cases where some families have been displaced as many as thirteen times. This displacement of 1.4 million tribals (20% of tribal population) could have been avoided had the government regularized their land *pattas*.

Forest and tribals: Legislations a basic cause of irritance

The Wild Life (Protection) Act, 1972: This legislation is significantly different from the forest act in giving primacy to conservation over exploitation. It also seeks to justify curtailing legitimate daily/survival activities of forest dependent people from wildlife habitats, evicting them forcibly without proper resettlement and centralizing management of these habitats in the hands of a callous and irresponsive bureaucracy. It created the two major types of protected areas, national parks and wildlife sanctuaries in which it places a blanket ban on all human activities except tourism leading to considerable suffering for the local people, depriving them access to the forests which was their source of survival, leading to conflict between local people and forest authorities. It has also led to sharp decline in public support for conservation. It is thus affecting the survival of the forest dwellers and is also proving not strong enough to fight pressure from commercial and industrial interests.

The Forest Conservation Act, 1980: The legislation seeks to prohibit the diversion of forest land for non-forest purposes, and thereby protect forest from vested interests. It requires the states to take permission from the centre before denotifying forest land for other purposes. As a result villagers are routinely denied land for basic amenities like road and water supply pipelines and the forest and *taungya* villages are denied schools and health centres as well.

National Forest Policy 1988: This policy document acknowledges the dependency of local forest people on forest resources, the primacy of their basic needs for livelihood and survival over commercial and industrial interests. It recognized the need for a partnership between forest communities and the department through joint forest management approach (JFM). This is a sea change from the earlier forest policy, fifth five year plan document (1974) and the recommendation of National Commission on Agriculture (1976) which had equated forests exclusively with production of raw material for industry and ignored people's rights to forest.

JFM: Central and State Resolutions 1990: The decision recommending involvement of village communities and voluntary agencies in the regeneration of degraded forestlands was issued on June 1, 1990 by the central ministry of environment and forests. It was merely a government order with no force of law behind it. In compliance, however, because of threats to stop centrally sponsored projects, most states have passed resolutions, to introduce JFM. It is a positive step where state control had eroded traditional role of forest community in forest management completely. However, in areas where traditional forest management practices exist, JFM is undermining and commercializing traditional systems and bringing community protected forest under the control of the state forest departments. The instructions of the government of India issued in August 1990 for the first time acknowledged the fact that there are a number of disputed claims of the tribal people which it distinguished from encroachments. The land occupied by the tribal people should not be deemed to be encroachment but regarded as disputed claims to be amicably settled by the state and the tribal people, as detailed in these circulars.

Unsettled claims

(*a*) *Claims pertaining to forest settlement*: The first set of cases is referred to in the second circular. They cover disputed claims over forest land arising out of forest settlement. There are cases where the tribal people have been in occupation of the land prior to the formal process of the reservation of the forest started.

(b) *Claims pertaining to pattas leases/grants*: The second set of cases, dealt with in the third circular, relates to habitations and forest villages. A decision was taken by the government of India in the 1970s to convert all forest villages into revenue villages. This process was completed in some states, but remained incomplete in other states. With the coming of the Forest Conservation Act in 1980, the process came to a grinding halt. All habitations other than villages have been divided into two categories: (i) habitations of those people who may have encroached upon forest land for cultivation, and (ii) where the habitations may be regularized.

(c) *Lands under encroachment of the tribal people*: The next set of cases in the first circular relate to encroachment on forestland. These instructions broadly divide these encroachments into two groups, viz. encroachment before and after the enforcement of the Forest Conservation Act, 1980. The instructions clearly state that all encroachments prior to 1980 should be settled provided the land is cultivable and the person is eligible for allotment of lands. The post-1980 encroachments cannot be settled.

(d) *Evidence about disputed claims/encroachments*: A major point, which crops up in all disputes concerning land is about the evidence acceptable to establish the fact of possession and its duration. If the claims of the tribal people are to be determined on the basis of the record of other government departments, their claim may be as good as lost. It is the fact of possession of lands, its cultivation and actual reclamation in some cases by his ancestors, which is a common knowledge of the villagers and which should be the basis of his claim.

Displacement dilemmas of tribals in Orissa

In Kucheipadar village in tahsil Kashipur, district Rayagada in Orissa, a large tract of agricultural land belonging to tribals living in this village has been acquired by the government for Utkal Alumina International (UAIL). Most of the tribals refused to take the compensation money and are resisting eviction from their land. The matter came to a head when the government of Orissa in its intolerance and vengefulness issued showcause notices to four non-government organizations viz. Agragamee, Laxman Nayak Society, Ankuran and Weaker Sections Integrated Development Agency (WIDA) for 'deregistering' and banning for funds to them from various state departments and requesting the government of India to do the same

The Council for Social Development, New Delhi, had been receiving representations and information regarding the adverse effect of bauxite mining on the tribals and environment since the early 1990s. The Council decided to send a mission to study the situation at Rayagada with a view to assessing the ground realities and framing a policy package to defuse the situation and to safeguard the interest of the tribals. The mission visited five of the affected villages in Rayagada district, met state government officials – from the chief secretary to field-level functionaries during the second and third weeks of

January 1999. The team found overwhelming evidence of excessive use of coercive methods by the district authorities against the tribals and scheduled caste population affected by these projects. The district administration's reaction has been quite out of proportion with what the situation demanded. The team felt that:

> It was undesirable to use the local and special police to prevent the affected people *from* meeting and organizing them to express their grievances and voice their concern and opposition. Normally, the police have no role in this, unless specific crimes have been reported (CSD 1999:23).

The team was told by the highest level officers of the Orissa government that the government would not countenance any opposition to industrialization of Rayagada by anybody or any group and that the government was determined to 'teach a lesson' to the NGOs which were indulging in acts of incitement by organizing tribals against land acquisition. The government's coercive measures, however, produced contrary results. People became doubly determined to protect their land and forest resources. One of the most disturbing and worrisome phenomenon encountered was the scant regard shown by the Orissa administration to the laws and the Constitution so far as these relate to tribals. The districts of Rayagada, Koraput and Kalahandi are Scheduled Areas. In their single –minded pursuit of promoting the cause of the three large corporations, the state government had been grossly negligent in performing its constitutional duties to the tribals. The Provisions of the Panchayats (Extension to the Scheduled Areas) Act, 1996, provides for extensive powers to the gram sabha and panchayats in the Scheduled Areas. This law makes prior consultation necessary with the gram sabha and/or panchayats mandatory both in cases of land acquisition and preparing a resettlement and rehabilitation package for the affected tribals. There was no such consultation at any stage either for the purpose of land acquisition or for the RR package. The most unfortunate part of the situation is that there has been no transparency about these mining projects vis-à-vis the affected population. There has been no communication except conveying premptory orders regarding lands to be acquired and compensation to be given. With dissatisfaction spreading too wide and deep among the tribals due to inept handling of the situation by the administration, these NGOs are standing as a buffer between expression of dissent in a democratic form and open destructive militancy which is happening just across the border in Andhra Pradesh. Instead of appreciating that a conscious, articulate and rational population is a great national asset essential for democracy to take roots in the society, the administrators in Orissa are treating every dissent as defiance and every assertion as insurrection. The bureaucracy is so insensitive, obdurate and callous to people's needs and aspirations. The team in its report has demanded that the punitive action initiated against the four NGOs should be withdrawn immediately and criminal cases against numerous men, women and children taking part in anti-land acquisition movement should be withdrawn. The government should take bold initiatives to settle the dispute through direct negotiation and discussion, allay the genuine apprehension about livelihood by a generous package of resettlement and rehabilitation prepared through proper participatory process and try to heal the hurt already caused with appropriate conciliatory measures. The situation is tense but can be defused. Let the industrialization of Rayagada be a boon and not a curse to the tribals living there.

Samata vs. State of Andhra Pradesh and Others: A landmark Supreme Court judgement

The tribals in Borra panchayat of Vizagapatnam district who have inhabited these hills for centuries were denied title deeds to their own lands. On the other hand, mining companies were given leases since the 1960s on tribal's land and forest. The tribals of Borra had approached Samata a NGO working in the area for assisting them in obtaining title deeds. The first major company to enter the area was Birla Pericla, which is a subsidiary of India Rayon. The company was given a lease of 120 acres in a small interior village called Nimmalpadu for exploiting calcite, one of the principal raw materials for their sea water plant near Bhimla. Besides building up a strong peoples' movement, Samata took up a legal battle against the state questioning its rights to grant mining leases in the scheduled areas to private companies as the leases amounted to transfer of tribal lands to non-tribals.

A public interest litigation was filed in the High Court of Andhra Pradesh in 1993 on the grounds that the government was also a 'person' (non-tribal) and hence does not have the power to grant lands in a scheduled area to non-tribals. A stay order was granted and for the first time after independence, the tribals of Borra panchayat cultivated their own lands. In 1995 the stay order was vacated and the case was dismissed by the High Court. A special leave petition was then filed in the Supreme Court in July 1997. A historic full bench judgment declared that the mining leases in the scheduled areas were against the land transfer Regulations and therefore, null and void. The constitutional scheme which is sought to be enforced through this law is that the property of the S.T. or the immovable property situated in agency tracts (Scheduled Areas) may be protected and they may retain their original character and may continue to belong to members of the S.T. The highlights of the judgement (Samata 2000) were:

(*a*) Government lands, forest lands and tribal lands in the scheduled areas cannot be leased out to non-tribals or to private industries for mining operations.

(b) The issue which started as non-settlement of lands in reserve forest enclosures in Borra panchayat was addressed by the bench by directing the state government to immediately issue title deeds to tribals in occupation and ruled that government has no right to grant mining leases in the lands belonging to tribal people.

(c) Mining activity in the scheduled areas can be taken up only by the State of Andhra Pradesh, the State Mineral Development Corporation or a cooperative of tribals and that too if they are in compliance with the Forest Conservation Act and the Environment Protection Act.

(d) The Court recognized the 73rd Constitutional amendment and the Provision of the Panchayats (Extension to the Scheduled Areas) Act, 1996 by stating that the gram sabhas shall be competent to safeguard and preserve community resources and thereby reiterated the need to give the right of self governance to the tribals.

The state government was, therefore, directed to stop all industries from mining operations. The Court also directed that at least 20 percent of the net profits flowing out of the mining operations by the state should be set apart as a permanent fund for establishment and maintenance of water resources, hospitals and transport facilities by laying roads, etc. This allocation would not include the expenditure on reforestation and maintenance of ecology by the mining agency. In this context the apex court correlated such investments to the achievement of the constitutional objectives of social, economic and human resource empowerment of the tribals and 'peace and good government' in Scheduled Areas.

Conclusion

Summing up, it is seen that land alienation of the tribals in Jharkhand was the direct outcome of introduction of zamindari system and private property rights in land. The process of land alienation of tribals in Jharkhand was very intense during the 19th century which culminated in three major tribal movements. These movements led to the enactment of the Chotanagpur and Santhal Parganas Tenancy Acts which were landmarks in making provisions for preventing alienation of tribal lands to landlords, moneylenders, traders and other non-tribals. The exploiters were labelled by the tribals as *diku* which has a deep symbolic cultural meaning for them.

The process of land alienation nonetheless was continuous during the 20th century through informal sources. It was further accentuated during the post-independence period due to development measures such as opening of mines, industries, dams, etc. It had a tremendous adverse effect in the marginalization of the tribals accompanied with pauperization and proletarianization. The tribals were bled white which led to massive tribal protests between 1970s and 1990s. It raised the issues of rehabilitation, viz. land for land, and a comprehensive concept of social, economic and cultural ingredients of rehabilitation.

Land alienation through informal sources was also acute in Madhya Pradesh both during pre-independence and post-independence. The tribals in Madhya Pradesh, however, did not indulge in militant protest similar to their brethren in Jharkhand. This is a researchable question by itself. However, the acquisition of lands for development purpose during the post-independence period particularly for the construction of Narmada Dam has attracted major protests from the tribals in Madhya Pradesh. The NBA has drawn a massive mobilization of tribals and has raised the basic issues under the big dam controversy, challenging the existing development paradigm and questioning the basics of rehabilitation. However, the Supreme Court judgment of October 2000 which allowed construction of Narmada Dam beyond 90 meter had an adverse effect on the livelihood concerns of the tribals.

The data and discussions throw up quite a few definitional and basic issues connected with land alienation. The first and the foremost is framing a valid definition of the term 'alienation of tribal lands'. Does it include only the lands alienated from tribals by informal sources or lands acquired by the government for development as well? Furthermore, does an erosion of the forest rights of tribals represent a diminution of their land rights and whether the tribals inhabiting the forest for generations can be treated as 'encroachers'.

In the context of land acquisition for development, the consequent displacement of the S.T., a debate on the very principle of *eminent domain*, i.e. land belongs to the states and need for a restrictive definition resultant in the abandonment of the principle of *eminent domain* is called for. Other basic issues in view of the pauperization and misery caused by ill-planned acquisitions should be a people's right to know well in advance specific proposals of land acquisition and displacement and the need to take people's consent and gram sabha's consent before any acquisition and displacement. An explicit definition of DP/PAP which should go beyond landowners to include individuals and communities that depend for sustenance on land owned by others or on the common property resources is also urgently called for. Land for land should be the basic principle for compensation and rehabilitation for the landowners and compensation packages must take care of communities, and in order to provide them with better life-style after displacement the PAPs should be the first to be included as beneficiaries for jobs and other project benefits. Effective rehabilitation should be mandatory and in advance of dislocation. It has to be ensured that the displaced people are resettled as individuals and communities that depend on land owned by others or the common property resources, customary rights and women's rights.

ACKNOWLEDGEMENT

This is a revised text of the D.N. Majumdar Memorial Lecture delivered at the XXIII Conference of the Indian Social Science Association at Mangalore on 12 January 2003 while receiving the D.N. Majumdar Medal (2003).

Table 1

Estimates of displacement by various development projects in India–1951-90 (in lakhs)

Type of project	*All DPs*	*No. of tribals displaced*	*Percentage of tribals displaced*	*Percentage of tribals not yet rehabilitated*
Dams	164.0	63.21	38.5	75.0
Mines	25.5	13.30	52.2	75.0
Industry	12.5	3.13	25.0	75.0
Wildlife Sanctuary/ National Park &	6.0	4.50	75.0	78.0
Others	5.0	1.25	25.0	80.0
Total	213.0	85.39	40.0	75.0

Source: Fernandes (1991)

Table 2

Tribals displaced in Jharkhand due to development projects

Name of the project	*Year of displacement*	*Area from which displaced (hectares)*	*Population displaced*	*Percentage of tribals displaced*
Mithan and DVC	1957	10719	93900	NA
Panchet	1959	15327	10000	NA
Icha	1965	4268	30800	80.00
Chandil	1965	17683	37600	87.92
Koel-karo	1980	17764	66000	88.00
Masan Reservior	1964	4498	3700	31
Central and Eastem Coalfield	1981-85	150300	32709	NA
Bokaro Steel	1967	1018	12847	NA
HEC	1958	9200.	12487	NA
Netarhat Pilot Project Field firing Range*	1993	112287	104617	85.2

Source: Fernandes and Thukral (1989); *PUDR (1993)

Table 3

Settlement of adivasi land alienation in Madhya Pradesh

Number of *Adivasi's* land alienation cases registered so far under section 170 (B)	39,710
Area alienated by the above cases	45,729.792 ha
Number of cases in which restoration of *Adivasi* land was ordered	14,395
Percentage of cases decided in favour of *Adivasi* land owners	41.73%
Area of alienated land ordered for restoration to *Adivasis*	16,149.97 ha
Percentage of alienated land ordered for restoration to *Adivasis*	35.32%
Area of alienated land restored with physical possession	5787.557
Percentage of physically restored area out of total land ordered to be restored	35.84%
Percentage of cases still pending after 17 years of the enactment of law (170, A) &(170, B).	13.15

REFERENCES

Areeparampil, Mathew

1995 *Tribals of Jharkhand: Victims of Development.* New Delhi: Indian Social Institute.

Cullet, Phillippe

2001 *Economic and Political Weekly,* May 5.

Council for Social Development (CSD)

1999 *Report on the Visit of a Team of the CSD: Rayagava and Bhubaneswar, January 11-18, 1999.* New Delhi: CSD.

Ditrich, G.

2002 'Sardar Sarovar Project: Braving the rising waters', *Economic and Political Weekly,* 37:38: 3878-80.

Dube, B.K. and F. Bahadur

1967 *A Study of the Tribal People and Tribal Areas of M.P.* Bhopal; Tribal Research and Development Institute.

Dubey, S.N. and Ratna Murdia (eds.)

1977 *Land Alienation and Restoration in Tribal Communities in India.* Bombay: Himalaya Publishing House.

Fernandes, Walter

1988 *Forest, Environment, and Tribal Economy.* New Delhi: Indian Social Institute.

1999 *The Land Acquisition (Amendment) Bill 1998.* New Delhi: Indian Social Institute.

Fernandes, W. and E.G. Thukral (eds.)

1996 *Development, Displacement and Rehabilitation.* New Delhi: Indian Social Institute.

Fernandes, W. and Vijay Paranjpye

1997 *Rehabilitation Policy and Law in India: A Right to Livelihood.* Pune: Econet, and Indian Social Institue.

Garg, Anil

2001 *Forest Dwellers—The Victims of Negligence of Government Administraion.* Baitul, Madhya Pradesh.

Gupta, Satya Prakash

1960 *Tribal Indebtedness and Land Alienation in Dhanbad District Ranchi,* Mimeographed. Bihar Tribal Research Institute.

Iyer, Gopal and N. Mahajan

1982 'Agrarian movement in Dhanbad'; In N. Sengupta (ed.) *Fourth World Dynamics.* Delhi. Authors Guild Publications.

Jha, P.K. (ed.)

2003 *Land Reforms in India: Issues of Equity in Rural Madhya Pradesh.* New Delhi: Sage.

Mukhoty, Gobinda

1978 *Singbhum Today: Exploitation and Protest.* Delhi: PUCL.

Narmada Bachao Andolan

2000 *People vs. Verdict.* Mumbai: NBA.

Narmada The Struggle for Life, Against Destruction. Baroda: NBA.

Peoples' Union for Democratic Rights (PUDR)

2001 *When People Organize; Forest Struggles and Repression in Dewas.* Delhi: PUDR

1993 *Netarhat in the Line of Fire.* Delhi: PUDR

India, Government of

1960 *Report of the Committee on Special Multipurpose Tribal Blocks.* New Delhi: Ministry of Home Affairs.

1962 *Report of the Scheduled Areas and Scheduled Tribes Commission 1960-61,* Vol. 1. Simla: Government of India Press.

1974 *Report of the National Commission on Agriculture, 1976, Part IX – Forestry.* New Delhi: Ministry of Agriculture and Irrigation.

1979-81 *Report of the Commissioner for Scheduled Castes and Scheduled Tribes.* Delhi: Manager of Publications.

1982 *Report of Committee on Forest and Tribals in India.* New Delhi: Ministry of Home Affairs, Tribal Development Division.

1983-84 *Report of the Commission for Scheduled Castes and Scheduled Tribes.*

Sixth *Report.* Delhi: Manager of Publications.

1986-87 *Report of the Commissioner for Scheduled Caste and Scheduled Tribes.* Delhi: Manager of Publications.

1987-89 *Report of the Commissioner for Scheduled Castes and Scheduled Tribes.* Delhi: Manager of Publications.

2000 *Annual Report 1999-2000 – Ministry of Rural Development.*

Madhya Pradesh, Government of

1989 *The Madhya Pradesh Human Development Report.* Bhopal.

Roy Choudhary, P.C.

1963 *Bihar District Gazetters – Dhanbad.* Patna: Bihar Secretariat Press.

Sachchidananda

1972 'Tribal situation in Bihar'. In K.S. Singh (ed.) *Tribal Situation in India.* Simla: IIAS.

Samata

2000 *Surviving a Minefield – An Adivasi Trimuph.* Hyderabad: Samata

Samuel, J., G. Prakasam and P Bedi (eds.)

2001 *Land for Life: Promise and Performance of Land Reforms in Madhya Pradesh.* Pune: National Centre for Advocacy Studies and Ekta Parishad, Bhopal.

Sangvai, Sanjay

2002 'Narmada Displacement: Continuing outrage', *Economic and Political Weekly,* 37:22: 2132-34

Sengupta, Nirmal (ed.)

1982 *Fourth World Dynamics: Jharkhand* Delhi: Authors Guild Publications.

Sharma, B.D.

2002 *Draft Industrial Policy of Jharkhand: 2001 X-rayed.* Delhi: Bharat Jan Andolan, Sahyog.

Singh, K.S. (ed.)

1972 *The Tribal Situation in India.* Simla: Indian Institute of Advanced Study.

1982 *Tribal Movements in India,*Vol. 2. New Delhi: Manohar.

1982 *Economics of the Tribes and Their Transformation.* New Delhi: Concept.

15

Primitive Tribes in Southern Region: A Case Study

P.K. Misra

All right thinking people have rejected branding some people as primitive. Therefore it becomes necessary to clarify as to how this term came into existence in the modern Indian context. Soon after India became independent it took upon itself the task of development of its tribes. There were many problems in this task, like lack of scientific information about them, protecting them from exploitation, giving legal recognition to their rights on land and forest, and also in developing appropriate strategies and plans for their development. In this regard, the most important step that was taken was to adopt the policy of reservation for the weaker sections of the Indian population. The tribes identified under this policy are called scheduled tribes. They are constitutionally entitled for protection and development, which is popularly known as positive discrimination. For their protection and development various plans were drawn and launched. Various committees and commissions were appointed to review the development among the scheduled tribes. Apart from many other things these reviews indicated huge differences in the levels of socio-politico-economic situation among the scheduled tribes. It was argued that in a situation like this a general plan of development may not suit all the scheduled tribe populations. These reports repeatedly drew attention to the problems of the backward groups among the scheduled tribes. On the eve of the fifth five year plan formulation, the issue of backwardness among the scheduled tribes was critically reviewed. It was pointed out that a distinction be made between those who were poor because they lacked resources and those who were in pre-agricultural level of technology. The latter may not necessarily be poor but may suffer on account of their limited wants, limited technology, also denial of their historic rights on the forest resources, and in not getting adequate returns for their products. In order to protect and develop appropriate plans especially for such groups, they were labeled as primitive. The first task in this endeavour was to identify such groups.

In order that they could be identified without prejudice it was felt necessary that there should be a minimum definition of primitive groups. The ministry of home affairs, government of India, organized a workshop to evolve such a definition (Sinha and Sharma 1977). It was decided that the groups, which were small, subsist on pre-agricultural economy and were pre-literate be called primitive groups. Of course it was cautioned that all people in the so-called primitive groups might not be at the same stage of economy. It was also emphasized that in many cases ethnographic records of such communities may be hopelessly outdated. Further, it was pointed out that a proper understanding of the situation of these communities would require a historical perspective. Sinha in a seminal statement about the development of the primitive tribes said:

> The basic question is how to bring the process of science and technology within the social control of the participating groups. Education has an important role in bringing about the process of modernization within their social and cultural

> outlook. The new world in which they have to participate and live has to be explained to them in commonsense terms. The research studies have to present the essential information both in qualitative and quantitative terms so that they can form the basis for programming development and influencing the process of change (1977:4).

In the above statement Sinha sets the yardstick to measure the development among the primitive tribes. His emphasis is on education, science, technology, and modernizing the outlook of the primitive groups. He stresses that the process of change has to be explained to them and should be based on scientific information generated by the researchers. Thus in the following discussion, the above standards set by Sinha will form the bases of assessing what is the present situation among the Jenu Kuruba, a group identified as primitive in southern region of India. In order to provide an understanding of the process of change, I will briefly compare their situation with the Kadar and the Cholanaikan[1].

The Jenu Kuruba

The Jenu Kuruba, a scheduled tribe, were once mainly a food gathering people. Their main concentration has been in the Mysore and Kodague districts of Karnataka. Formerly they lived inside or on the edges of the forests. Now most of their settlements except a few have been shifted out of the forest. The few, which are in the forests, are in the process of being relocated.

My first acquaintance with the Jenu Kuruba began when I carried out a field study among them of three months beginning from January 1967 (Misra 1969). In 1974, I carried out a quick survey of the Jenu Kuruba settlements in Heggadadevana Kote taluk of Mysore district, Karnataka (Misra 1977) to assess their economic situation. Again in 2001 we conducted a field study to prepare their socio-economic profile (Misra *et al.* 2001). In

2002 we made survey of a few settlements of the Jenu Kuruba to study the state of education among them (Misra *et al.* 2002). The programme of providing education to the Jenu Kuruba children through ashram schools (tribal residential schools) has been going on among them for almost four decades. Therefore it was appropriate to assess the impact of this crucial programme on their development. In between I have been visiting their settlements and have tried to keep myself informed about them.

The Jenu Kuruba, as their name implies, are known as honey collectors. They mainly made their living by food gathering. They practised shifting cultivation but that was on a limited scale. Now however that situation has drastically changed. Forests have been protected. The government of Karnataka declared 6439.26 hectares of forest under Rajiv Gandhi National Park. As a result of this declaration any human activity inside the forest was declared illegal. On the river, Kabini which flows through the heart of these forests and was the major sources of water and food for the Jenu Kuruba, a dam was erected. As a result of which vast areas of forest, which were the foraging area of the Jenu Kuruba, were submerged in the backwaters of the river Kabini. The settlements of the Jenu Kuruba, which were inside the forest, and that of the peasants in the neighbourhood were relocated. Much before these modern developments took place the farming communities of the neighbourhood and coffee planters encroached upon a lot of land in and around the forest ejecting the Jenu Kuruba from their habitats and pushing them deep inside the forest. Those lands were converted into agricultural lands. In between 1967 and 2002 the population of other communities has enormously grown. Road and transport links have phenomenally increased. As a result of these developments not only the traditional mode of subsistence of the Kuruba has been completely shattered but the shy and withdrawn Jenu Kuruba have been brought face to face with other populations who are technologically far more advanced and have vested interest in enhancing their control over the resources which were once the sole preserve of the Jenu Kuruba. This point is of great significance, which will become clear with a brief description of their erstwhile life-style.

The Jenu Kuruba settlements were scattered, at times a hamlet may be a furlong away from the other. The membership of a settlement remained in a flux owing to frequent migration of individuals and families from one settlement to the other. Their migrations were on account of a variety of reasons, such as search of resources for subsistence, disputes and disagreements between the members of a family and so on. In other words the ties with the settlement they inhabited were feeble. The 'we-feeling' in terms of settlement or the whole group was almost absent. Cooperation was noticed only within the members of the nuclear families otherwise it appeared they were highly individualistic. The Jenu Kuruba marriages generally took place by elopement, giving little scope for any group activity. The Jenu Kuruba observed very few rituals and whatever they observed remained confined to the members of the family. The mechanism of social control was by observing self-restraint. They did not have any council to settle their disputes or give any direction on any activity. Disputes were resolved at individual level. Withdrawal from a conflict situation was not only their standard technique but also a strong philosophical principle of their life (Misra 1970).

Subsistence

In 1967 I found that the Jenu Kuruba, though poor, were not a totally dependent population. Even at that time the forest department and forest contractors employed most of them on daily wages. Yet a substantial amount of their food came through collection in the forest. Their employment even as a daily wage worker gave them license to move inside the forest. Most of them had continued to live in and around forest.

The indigenous knowledge of the Jenu Kuruba about the forest, its animals and resources was fabulous. They could remain inside the forest for days together. They knew when and what could be extracted in the forest in a sustainable manner. The Jenu Kuruba particularly enjoyed the collection of honey. They had their own classification of different species of bees. They seemed to know their behaviour, their ferocity and their vulnerability. They knew exactly when they should go for the collection of honey of different varieties. They made elaborate plans before going into the forest for honey collection . Honey collection was teamwork and each member of the team was allotted a specific task. Since it was not always possible to climb tall trees or reach difficult rock crevices they either made scaffoldings or climbed the neighbouring trees to reach the desired spot. They made use of bamboos, creepers, leaves to make ropes and other devices for climbing, storing etc. Removal of honeycombs and bringing them down safely without much loss of honey were difficult and skilful jobs. They often made pulleys to bring down the honeycombs. Collection of honey from deep inside the forest was not only hazardous but an activity which required tremendous skill, courage, teamwork and ingenuity. Besides, the sting of the bees one has to face and compete with other animals who were also on the trail of honey. Honey collection required expertise in climbing trees, quick reflexes, a supple body, and ability to innovate in an emergency. For deep inside the forest no other help was available or possible. For their skills and indigenous knowledge of the forest wealth they were most sought after by the forest department and private contractors for the works in the forest. At the time the forest used to be leased to the private contractors for extracting minor forest produce (MFP). This scheme was disastrous both for the forest resources and the Jenu Kuruba. The forest contractors were heartless and had no scruples. They behaved as if they owned the forest. They extracted as much MFP as possible; always much more than the permits allowed them. They were merciless in their behaviour towards the Jenu Kuruba. They would often beat them if they found they were consuming what they had extracted or had not delivered the entire produce to them. The only way the Jenu Kuruba could save themselves from the cruel punishment of the contractors was by hiding themselves in the forest. They were so good in this art that the Jenu Kuruba could be hiding just a few feet away from the searching and greedy eyes of the contractors yet remain unnoticed. They surfaced only when it was no more possible to subsist on the resources of their hiding place. The officials of the forest department also always ill-treated the Jenu Kuruba. Their services were taken whenever they wanted. In return they got very little or nothing.

In 1967 there were numerous programmes for their development but the results were indifferent. Education programme was run in a casual manner. In any case, none of the development programmes were made keeping in view the specific needs of a food gathering tribe, their skills and their indigenous knowledge. Above all, the development agents treated the Jenu Kuruba with disdain and utter contempt. They were told in many ways that they were not good, were utterly lazy, and had no worthwhile social or cultural practices or knowledge. They were just like animals. They needed to be changed thoroughly. Such attitude of others about them made them more withdrawn, shy and isolated. They also developed a very low esteem about themselves and their capabilities.

In 1971 when I made a rapid survey of the Jenu Kuruba in Heggadadevana Kote taluk of Karnataka I found that their situation was very grim. The process of shifting the peasants and the Jenu Kuruba had already started owing to the construction of the dam over Kabini. The few hundred families of Jenu Kuruba who were still residing in the forest were not covered by any development programme while others who were shifted to new settlements were living in an entirely different atmosphere. I had written:

> Hitherto, their interaction with the peasants was minimal and they were heavily depending upon forests, but now the Jenu Kuruba of the settlements like Karapur and Udboor are completely cut off from the forests. Having no anchorage and being the weakest, their situation is bound to weaken them further. They have no spokesman of their own, and there has been no effort from any quarter to mobilize them (1977:124).

The employment survey, which I conducted then, indicated that on the given days, an overwhelming majority of them remained unemployed. The Jenu Kuruba had no savings. The day they did not get work either they had to starve or survive on *genasu,* an inferior type of tuber. Frequent starvation and insufficient food was clearly visible from their very weak physique.

The educational programme, which is so crucial for development, did not receive the kind of effort, which was required. It hardly made any serious impact on their lives except that on account of free meals in the schools so many children were saved from starvation.

In the study of 2001 we noted that the habitat, dwelling, dress pattern and economy of the Jenu Kuruba had completely changed. They increasingly made use of consumer goods in their daily life. No human settlements were allowed in Rajiv Gandhi National Park area, the erstwhile area of the Jenu Kuruba. The few families, which still resided in the forests, were being relocated.

Most of the Jenu Kuruba were wage earners working for the forest department in their various seasonal projects and plantation. There were some families who had received land from the government but they could hardly make them productive. This issue I had discussed in my paper of 1977. The same factors were still applicable. It is indeed very difficult for the kind of experience the Jenu Kuruba have about cultivation to make their small plots of land productive and also fetch them enough for their subsistence. That is why instead they find it easier to work on daily wages. The lure for daily dose of *arrack* (country liquor) is another factor, which attracts them to daily wage. To be a successful farmer it is essential that one should be able to save and systematically plan for future crops, keeping an eye on the market. The Jenu Kuruba neither have such abilities nor it is possible for them to save anything.

Now for collection of minor forest produce the Jenu Kuruba have to acquire licenses from the government. Since the forest is very much depleted, collection of minor forest produce has become a more time consuming activity. They occasionally do resort to it but basically for market. Fuel collection is one of their major activities for which there is a great demand in the neighbourhood.

Relocation of settlements, new economic activities, participation in development activities brings the Jenu Kuruba in interaction with different people. They have been taken out for sight seeing tours and so on. These interactions certainly have brought many profound changes in their outlook, values, etc., but their economic situation is so grim that they cannot afford to make any deviation from what they presently do or take any fresh initiative. One of the impacts of modern development on them has been that their identity got consolidated which I would like to argue has made them further weak as 'class'. In 1967 I had observed that the 'we' feeling among them was weak and membership to a settlement or residential group was fluid. That is no more the situation. In a caste and community ridden society the Jenu Kuruba have been put into their slot and their identity as a Jenu Kuruba has consolidated. Others identify them as the Jenu Kuruba and they have to identify themselves as Jenu Kuruba to derive the benefit of various development grants. Being identified as a primitive tribe entitles them for some special grants from the central government, which members of other scheduled tribe do not get. Even in classroom situation the Jenu Kuruba children sit separately. They in contrast to other children get stainless steel eating plates, umbrellas and higher allowances for meeting their daily expenses. Day in and day out they are identified as the Jenu Kuruba. As a result, the other populations particularly the Betta Kuruba, another scheduled tribe of the region who are also poor but not identified as primitive resent the favours granted to the Jenu Kuruba. Thus, a kind of animosity has developed among the two scheduled tribe groups. In the political arena where the numbers are important this makes both of them further weak.

In spite of the fact that educational programmes were started more than four decades ago, the literacy level among the Jenu Kuruba has remained very low. There are very few Jenu Kuruba who have reached the higher secondary education level. Drop out rates have remained almost total (Misra *et al.* 2002). They have not been able to acquire any new skills, either. In other words the Jenu Kuruba are left with hardly any other option but to sell their labour, expert knowledge and skills in the forest. The beneficiaries of their expertise have been the peasants, the planters, the forest department, the welfare agencies, smugglers of timber and poachers. It is an irony that in spite of various welfare programmes and ever increasing budget allocation for their development, the condition of the Jenu Kuruba has gone from bad to worse. It is difficult to imagine as to how they would be able to survive as a group.

The Kadar

The case of the Kadar of Cochin is very much similar to that of the Jenu Kuruba. Even at the time when Ehrenfels worked among them in 1947 (1952) most of them gathered forest products not for self-consumption only but to give to the forest contractor. Ehrenfels wrote that forest administration determined the life of 'this once exceedingly free and independent forest tribe' (1952:8). Forest department auctioned the exploitation of the minor forest products to the private contractors on a biannual rent. The contractor knew how to create new needs among the Kadar in order to induce them to collect more and more valuable forest products for them. The new things, which the Kadar required, were rice, chilies, aluminum vessels, ready-made garments, opium, *arrack,* etc. Previously the Kadar collected honey for self-consumption but in the new economy introduced among them they gave it to the contractors. Besides their territory was found suitable for the construction of a huge reservoir for the purpose of irrigation and electrification. Not only they had to migrate from their habitat but also in the new location they came in contact with a large number of outsiders. Ehrenfels observed:

> the outsiders continuously referred the Kadar as uncivilized. The Kadar were exploited in more than one ways. Though the Kadar were brought to the new habitats, the idea of settledness had not settled in them. Individual and small family groups move so frequently from one place to the other that the very idea of a permanent residence, carries little weight in Kadar thought (p. 127).

He also observed that in the traditional Kadar society, the position of women was equal and strong but as a result of contact the position of Kadar women went down. Earlier the Kadar women used to move freely to collect minor forest produce but with the coming of outsiders, Kadar women were often molested. They stopped going out of their houses. They did not participate in economic activities. The outsiders also imposed the concept of patriarchy order among them.

The development story of the Kadar is not much different from that of the Jenu Kuruba. There is any number of schemes but their reach has been superficial. In both the cases the people had to be relocated owing to the construction of a dam on the rivers that passed through their erstwhile habitats. In no way they were beneficiary of the mega projects though they not only lost their homeland but also resource of food.

The Cholanaickan

The Cholanaickan are another classical food gathering primitive tribe in the southern region. The Cholanaickan live in the caves of the forest areas of the Malappuram district of Kerala state. The Cholanaickan remained virtually unreported till 1973. After a journalist reported them a study was conducted by Mathur (1977). Later on Bhanu conducted a detailed study on them (1989). The Cholanaickan inhabit different territories in the rain forest in an area of about 89000 acres. Their population was just about 205 in 1979. The rain forests are dense and rich in fauna and flora. The Cholanaickan have been able to survive so far because the terrain they live in is extremely difficult. Leeches, wild animals, reptiles, ants and extreme humid weather makes the life so difficult that even the greediest of the greedy would not like to go there. Yet the long arm of the modern economy had reached the Cholanaickan even in 1978. Though they lived in caves in most difficult circumstance they collected minor forest produce for the market. A significant change that had taken place in 1979 itself was that the system of leasing out the collection of MFP to contractors was given up. A Girijan Cooperative Society was found which controlled the collection and sale of minor forest produce. Of course it saved the Cholanaickan from the unscrupulous contractors but even in 1979 nobody had a clear idea as to how to utilize the profits the society generated for the meaningful and sustainable welfare of the Cholanaickan.

The literacy was nil among the Cholanaickan and they had no other skills other than foraging in the forests. The demographic situation of the Cholanaickan has been grim. The census figures show a downward trend. Bhanu pointed out that there was high disparity in sex ratio. Many young Cholanaickan men could not find mates for themselves. Over years their diet pattern has significantly changed. From the Girijan Cooperative Society they get rice and other food items in exchange of the MFP they bring to it. The gathering of tubers and roots, hunting and fishing activities over years have decreased considerably. They look anemic. They have also been victims of many diseases; some are owing to the increasing contact with the outside world. The development programmes initiated among them have not produced any significant results. 'The Cholanaickan are facing a severe threat of extinction' (Bhanu 1989; 163).

There is some commonality between these primitive tribes except in the case of the Cholanaickan who continue to live in their habitat. The forest in their habitat continues to be rich in fauna and flora.

I may now highlight some of the factors responsible for the present situation among the selected primitive groups of the southern region.

1. The development programmes have been far from what Sinha envisaged they should have been. There has been no attempt to bring

science and technology within the social control of the participating groups. In all the three groups education programmes have been very weak. The new world has remained peripheral to them. The outside world, if at all, has been exploiting their labour and expert knowledge of the forest.

2. As they are small in number, in political terms they do not count for much in the regional or state political scenario. They cannot exert any pressure on political system.

3. They were never a hostile population. They always believed that the conflict could be resolved by withdrawing. Now a situation has come when there is no place to withdraw, and this principle of theirs makes it easier for others to exploit them.

4. While the dominant society has always been interested in the resources of their habitats, their skills, etc., they never received a genuine respect for their way of life. For the dominant society they have been 'junglee', needing reform. Their way of life had no meaning for them. This is indeed a crucial and difficult point. There is enormous gap in the scientific and technological levels and values of the two societies. This gap cannot be bridged easily but at least the modern society should be able to restrain itself from grabbing their resources and provide for them gentle programmes for their development.

5. The legal protection given to them is scuttled. In this regard Kerala experience is instructive. In 1975, the Kerala legislature unanimously

enacted the Kerala Scheduled Tribes Act, the purpose of which was to restrict transfer of lands and restoration of alienated lands to them. This act had a mission to redeem land to those members of scheduled tribes who were dispossessed. But this act proved to be a deception. It was not notified for years. In the meanwhile non-scheduled people settled in the scheduled tribe areas and encroached upon the land including the forest areas. The forest dwellers were disowned. The government did not implement its own law. The settlers, large in numbers and well organized under various political flags could not be dislodged. Meanwhile so many cases of land alienation were brought before the courts. The government of Kerala simply dragged its feet. Ultimately the Kerala High Court ordered peremptory compliance of the provisions of the Act that is to restore the land to the members of the scheduled tribes under it. Instead of implementing the orders of the High Court, the Kerala government brought out a legislation as an amendment largely sapping the original law. This case clearly shows firstly, that a political clout is absolutely necessary for the largesse of the state to flow. Second, there is no social passion to protect the weakest of the weak, in this case the food gatherers. The development programmes are just there to merely clear the conscience of the establishment and not for implementation in letter and spirit.

NOTES

1. As per the Census of 1981 the population of the Kadar was 2267 and the population of the Jenu

Kuruba was 33743. The population of the Jenu Kuruba in 1971 Census was 6656. The sudden increase in their population is owing to the enumeration of non-scheduled communities claiming the status of the Jenu Kuruba. This is yet another problem of this primitive group. The Census of 1981 does not even record the population of the Cholanaickan.

REFERENCES

Bhanu, Anand

1989 *The Cholanaickan of Kerala*. Calcutta: Anthropological Survey of India.

Ehrenfels, U.R.

1952 *Kadar of Cochin*. Madras: University of Madras.

Mathur, P.R.G.

1977 'Cholanaickan of Kerala'. In S.C. Sinha and B.D. Sharma (eds.) *Primitive Tribes: The First Step*. New Delhi: Government of India, Ministry of Home Affairs.

Misra, P.K.

1969 'The Jenu Kuruba', *Bulletin*, XVIII, 3. Calcutta: Anthropological Survey of India.

1970 'Economic development among the Jenu Kurubas', *Man in India*, 50, 1.

1977 'The Jenu Kuruba'. In Surajit Sinha and B.D. Sharma (eds.) *Primitive Tribes: The First Step*. New Delhi: Government of India.

Misra, P.K. *et al.*

2001 'A socio-economic profile of Scheduled Tribes in Rajiv Gandhi National Park, Nagarhole.' Unpublished Project Report. Forest Department, Government of Karnataka, Mysore.

2002 'The state of education among the Jenu Kuruba.' Unpublished Project Report, Institute of Development Studies, University of Mysore, Mysore.

Sinha, Surajit and B.D. Sharma

1977 *Primitive Tribes: The First Step.* New Delhi: Government of India, Ministry of Home Affairs.

16

Habitat, Society and Development in Ladakh

Paramita Majumdar

The peaks of snow mountains on bright mornings part the dense clouds and soar into the skies. Beneath the skies like a world submerged, lies a lost kingdom-Ladakh. Part fantasy, part reality...Ladakh, is where, the forces of nature conspired to render a magical realist landscape.... A landscape of extremes.... Desert and blue waters...burning sun and freezing winds, glaciers and sand dunes... a primeval battleground of the titanic forces which gave birth to the Himalayas (Singh 1989).

At an altitude of 9000 feet at Kargil to 25170 feet at Saser Kangri in the Karakoram, Ladakh has been referred to as the Moonscape region for its rugged beauty, red rocks, sea deep gorges and barren rocky mountains. It is totally isolated from the modern world. It is still faithful to ancestral customs where life is characterized by intense spirituality. Rich traditions of Mahayana Buddhism still flourish in the purest form in this region, which has often been referred to as Little Tibet (Bhasin 1992; Carr-Harris 1995; Bigelow 2001).

Physical characteristics

Ladakh, the 'land of many passes', is situated between two of the world's mightiest mountain ranges, the

Himalayas and the Karakoram. It borders Pakistan, Tibet and the Kashmir Valley, and consists of India's two northernmost districts, Leh and Kargil. The region consists of huge mountain masses, that represent the anticlines and the longitudinal valleys of the Gilgit, the Shyok, the Indus, and the Jhelum, the synclines of the main Himalayan folds. The main river of Ladakh is Indus, which follows in a northwest direction between Ladakh and Zanskar ranges. It is joined by several major rivers like Zanskar, Suru and Shyok before it reaches Pakistan.

The continentality in association with height, imparts the Ladakh region a character akin to the cold highland type. Altitude, which varies from place to place, is the main factor affecting local climate. Because of thin atmosphere, the radiation and insolation are extremely rapid resulting in extremes of temperature. The summer temperatures rarely exceed about 25°C while in winter the temperature touches as low as minus 30 degree. This results in freezing of all conceivable water resources. Surprisingly, though the thin air makes the heat of the sun even more intense than at lower altitudes, it is said that only in Ladakh can a man sitting in the sun with his feet in the shade suffer from sunstroke and frostbite at the same time. The great Himalaya lying to the south, forms a barrier to monsoon in this area. Due to this reason, Ladakh is an isolated cold desert region. Wind velocity in the afternoon and night is of high order resulting in heavy soil erosion with dust storm and snow blizzards, which make life very difficult.

Historical characteristics

For close to 900 years, from the middle of the 10th century, Ladakh was an independent kingdom, its dynasties descending from the kings of old Tibet. Its political fortunes ebbed and flowed over the centuries, and the kingdom was at its greatest in the early 17th century under the famous king Sengge Namgyal, whose rule extended across Spiti and western Tibet up to the Mayumla beyond the sacred sites of Mount Kailash and lake Mansarovar. And gradually perhaps due to the fact that it was politically stable, in contrast to the lawless tribes further west, Ladakh became recognized as the best trade route between the Punjab and Central Asia. For centuries it was traversed by caravans carrying textiles and spices, raw silk and carpets, dyestuffs and narcotics. On this long route, Leh was the halfway house, and developed into a bustling entrepot, its bazaars thronged with merchants from far countries.

Ironically it was this lucrative trade that finally spelt the doom of the independent kingdom. It attracted the covetous gaze of Gulab Singh, the ruler of Jammu in the early 19th century and in 1834 he sent his general Zorawar Singh to invade Ladakh. There followed a decade of war and turmoil which ended with the emergence of the British as the paramount power in north India. Ladakh together with Baltistan was incorporated into the newly created state of Jammu and Kashmir. Just over a century later, this union was disturbed by the partition of India; Baltistan becoming part of Pakistan while Ladakh remained in India as part of the state of Jammu and Kashmir.

Resources

Howling winds, cold night and frigid winters with temperatures dropping to –50°C one might imagine, is hardly the ideal conditions for life, but even here nature has been able to create a diversity of plant and animals life whose ability to economize and optimize resources is itself a strategy for survival. The small streams, the scorching sunlight, the mineral resources, precious stones all add to the potential for achieving regional development and overall growth.

In the eastern extremity of the Trans-Himalaya, the Zanskar and the Ladakh ranges fade away into the southern margins of the Tibetan plateau. Here begins a huge, brackish marsh and lake ecosystem which houses water bodies like Tso Morriri, Hanle and Chushul—home to some very threatened fauna, the best known being the black-necked crane. The three wetlands, namely, Tso-Morriri, Tsokar and Pangong Tso are believed to be the most important breeding site for waterfowl in Ladakh and represent the only breeding ground of bar-headed geese (*Anser indicus*) in India and the only breeding ground for the globally threatened black-necked crane (*Grus nigricollis*) outside China. In addition, this region also supports some of the most endangered species of mammals such as kiang, snow leopard, lynx, Himalayan blue sheep, etc. Among domestic animals are the famous shawl goat, two kinds of sheep, of which the larger (*huniya*) is used for carrying burdens, and is a principal source of wealth, the yak and the *dzo*, a valuable hybrid between the yak and common cow. Though the environment here appears harsh and inhospitable, a wealth of animal life exists. The largest number of wild sheep and goats in the world, are for instance, found here.

The landscape is characterized by a distinct lack of natural forests, the vegetation being primarily sparse alpine steppe, showing a high degree of endemism (only found locally). Along the riverbanks and valleys in Ladakh, some greenery does exist with willows, poplars, wild roses and many herbaceous plants and shrubs having colonized the land, and even extended up the mountain slopes. Most of the vegetation is, however, stunted. Recently, the government has given subsidies for planting trees such as willows and poplars, which are used for firewood and building.

Despite the extreme climate that limits the growth of natural resources such as trees and crops including herbal plants used for traditional medicine, Ladakhis have been traditionally using local herbs as cure for various ailments. A large number of medicinal herbs are found naturally growing in the mountains. In recent years there has been an increasing demand for such herbal medicines. As a result more and more herbal plants are harvested, but in an inappropriate way, resulting in depletion of many important herbs. The problem is compounded by lack of awareness among the herbal practitioners known as *amchi* as most of their knowledge of traditional medicine come from their parents and their practice emphasize only the treatment part. There is a great need for training to identify, collect and store herbal plants. Some of the herbal plants are becoming quite rare due to inappropriate harvesting, so there is also an urgent need to replant and preserve some of these plants. Laurent Prodié, a French anthropologist and ethno-pharmacologist, is attempting to reintroduce traditional *amchi* medicine to the Ladakh region (Laurent Pordie 2000). Such a reinstatement of *amchi* skills should not only revive and perpetuate the tradition but also, in doing so, improve the healthcare in one of the world's least hospitable environments. As Laurent Pordié himself says:

> Modernisation has brought a sense of individualism and a breakdown in the traditional system of help between families in the villages. The Amchi medical system is suffering because it is based on a strong sense of community, which is now declining.

As the government initiatives have failed to provide an adequate substitute for the traditional system, with drugs too expensive, knowledge scarce, and hospitals and clinics being few and far between and the *amchis* no longer passing their skills from father to son, Ladkhis have neither the traditional nor the Western medical systems to rely on. The standard of health in the region has suffered as a consequence, with the region having one of the highest infant mortality rates in India.

Within a radius of 100 to 200 metres of Leh there are centers of gold-mining industry, which apparently only require scientific development to render it enormously productive. Here the surface soil has been for many centuries washed for gold by bands of Tibetan miners, who never work deeper than 20 to 50 feet, and whose methods of washing are of the crudest description. The Ladakh arc (range) includes different units, and the structurally lower one consists of hornblende, oligoclase, biotite, epidote, minor quartz, rutile and sporadic muscovite and garnet—the precious stones.

Though the winter is brutally cold, there is constant and very intense sunshine throughout the year in Ladakh. The availability of renewable energy resources like hydro, solar, wind and geo-thermal, makes the region ideal for renewable energy based on decentralized power generation. The Ladakh Ecological Development Group, a local NGO, has developed numerous energy-saving technologies like hydraulic pumps, solar room-heating systems, water heaters and cookers as well as photovoltaic power for lighting and small wind turbines for electricity production. This work has helped to generate something of a renewable energy revolution in Ladakh. Many of the technologies have now been taken up on a large scale by government and other voluntary agencies. By introducing such techniques, the dependence of Ladakhis on imported and expensive fuels have been reduced. At present hydro and solar energy play an important role in power generation and rural electrification in Ladakh (Kingsnorth 2000). Solar ovens are something exciting and modern for the Ladakhis at present.

In India, seabuckthorn fruit (maritime shrub, *Hippophae rhamnoides,* with orange berries) grows in the cold deserts of Ladakh, in Lahul-Spiti areas of Himachal Pradesh and in some parts of Arunachal Pradesh. The fruit grows wild and as of now, very little quantities have been processed. An Indian company with the active support of Defence Research and Development Organization pioneered the processing of seabuckthorn fruit to manufacture fruit juice and fruit nectar (Mittal n.d.). The product has already caught the fancy of the younger people and also finds favor with the intelligentsia. The company has plans to manufacture seed and pulp oil, down stream products for cosmetics, pharmaceutical and food nutrition applications as well as cosmetics (Kaul 2002).

Settlements in Ladakh

Ladakh is the most sparsely inhabited part of India. According to 2001 census, 195407 Ladakhi population lives in very remote villages and hamlets, most of them with no road access. Donkeys, ponies and yaks are used to carry heavy loads to the villages, though people themselves often carry goods on their own backs, sometimes for several days of walking. Many villages get completely cut off from the outside world for more than five months each year, due to heavy snowfall on the high passes that give access to them.

Leh district has the distinction of being the largest district area-wise, in India (45110 sq. kms) with second lowest density at three persons per sq. km., after Lahul and Spiti in Himachal Pradesh which has the lowest density of two persons, per sq. km. Leh the main town of the region is dominated by Sengee Namgyal's nine-storey palace, a building in the grand tradition of Tibetan architecture said to have inspired the famous Potala in Lhasa, which was built half a century later. Above it, on Namgyal Tsemo, the peak overlooking the town are the ruins of the earliest royal residence at Leh, a fort built by King Tashi Namgyal in the 16th century. Within 10km radius of Leh, Saboo a charming village with a small gompa, nestles between two southward stretching spurs of the Ladakh range.

The approach to a Buddhist village is invariably marked by *mani* walls which are long chest-high structures faced with engraved stones bearing the mantra *om mane padme hum* and by chorten, commemortive cairns, like stone pepper-pots. Many villages are crowned with a gompa or monastery which may be anything from an imposing complex of temples, prayer halls and monks' dwellings, to a tiny hermitage housing a single image and home to a solitary lama.

Kargil (2740m), the second town of Ladakh, is situated on the Suru river just short of its confluence with the Dress-Shingo. It is also the headquarters of Kargil district. A quiet town today Kargil was once witness to the most hectic bartering among traders of different faiths and nationalities. Hunderds of caravans carrying silks, ivory, carpets and precious stones to and from China, Turkey, Yarkand, Afghanistan and India, passed through the town. Several caravanserais, now rendered dangerous due to years of disuse, can be seen in and around Kargil. Apart from these two small townships, people mostly live in rural areas, in the beautiful villages—Silmo, Garkone, Shergol, Mulbekh, Lamayuru and others.

People and society

The faces and physique of the Ladakhi and the clothes they wear are akin to those of Tibet and Central Asia. The original population may have been Dards, an Indo-Aryan race from down the Indus. But immigration from Tibet, perhaps a millennium or so ago, largely overwhelmed the culture of the Dards and obliterated their racial characteristics. In eastern and central Ladakh, today's population seems to be mostly of Tibetan origin. Further west, in and around Kargil, there is much in the people's appearance that suggests a mixed origin. The exception to this generalization is the Arghons, a community of Muslims in Leh, the descendants of marriages between local women and Kashmiri or Central Asian merchants. A brief ethnographic account of the scheduled tribes in Ladakh is contained in the Appendix.

Some features of the culture of Ladakh, for example its egalitarianism has always been brought into focus. Here the womenfolk can be seen interacting with unrelated men and doing business rather than confining themselves to the homes like in the west. People do not waste anything in Ladakh—it may be wood, it may be stones, it may be grass, it may be water, they take care of everything.

The Ladakhi believe implicitly in the influence of gods and spirits on the material world, and undertake no major enterprise without taking this influence into consideration. The lamas are the vital intermediaries between the human and the spirit worlds. Not only do they perform the rites necessary to propitiate the gods—in private houses as well as in the gompa temples. They also often take on the role of astrologers and oracles who can predict the auspicious time for starting any enterprise, whether ploughing the fields, or taking in the harvest, arranging a marriage or going on a journey—and advise as to the auspicious way of going about it.

Of the secular culture, the most important element is the rich oral literature of songs and poems for every occasion, as well as local versions of the *Kesar Saga,* the Tibetan national epic. This literature is common to both Buddhists and Muslims. There are various monastic and other religious festivals in the Buddhist areas, mainly in the winter. During summer archery and polo are played. Open-air parties and dances are held alongside.

Economic life

The Ladakhi economy has always been primarily agricultural. In itself this is remarkable, as Ladakh's landscape is supremely hostile. Under snow for more than half the year, dusty and dry for much of the rest it is a place of climatic extremes and unforgiving soils. But what makes Ladakh so special is, or was, its economic independence. Though Ladakh has been invaded by outsiders from the Sikh emperors to the British, its local farming economy has always remained in the hands of its people. Its isolation allowed it to develop a remarkable rural economy, uniquely adapted to an unique environment. Farming is small scale; traditionally, each family owns a few acres of land, and their whitewashed mud houses are grouped together in villages whose size varies according to the availability of water. The land is irrigated by a system of channels, which funnel water from the melted ice, and snow of the mountains (Gupta and Tewari 2002). The principal crop is barley, the mainstay of traditional Ladakhi food. In the valleys there are orchards, and up on the high pastures, where not even barley will grow, people husband yaks, crows or sheep. Draft animals, especially the ubiquitous *dzo,* play a central part in the farming economy.

In order to get the best from this harsh landscape, systems of cooperative labour sharing have developed; Ladakh's traditional farmers have always known that to survive they need to work together. But for many years now the fate of Ladakhi farming has been largely out of their hands. The emerging process of economic development has more to do with capital, entrepreneurship and infrastructure.

Since the setting up of the army base in Ladakh in 1962 and the opening of the region to tourism in 1974, the economy of the region has undergone significant changes. The external interventions, while leading to a marked improvement in the economy, have caused concern regarding the sustainability of the economic development that the region has seen. Ladakhis have lost interest in traditional agriculture. Their traditional barely fields are being replaced with vegetable cash crops and their *dzo* with power tillers. The feeling is that with power tillers productivity will go up. Then people will be able to keep jersey cows instead, which produce more milk. But power tillers rely on outside input for fuel and parts. Jersey cows are not adapted to high altitudes, and as for productivity—studies have shown that Ladakhi traditional agriculture is among the most productive in the world.

The economy of Ladakh today is dependent largely on the government, particularly army and tourism . The army and the government provide direct employment, where local residents are either presently employed or retired and are receiving a pension. There are about 1500 local residents being recruited to the Ladakh Scouts. Additionally the army also provides temporary employment to local residents as porters to reach difficult areas such as the Siachen and for materials movement. These recruitments provide for an important part of the wealth coming into the system. The army porters earn up to Rs. 60000 per annum over a 3-4 month period. The army also procures some local produce which is, however, limited to a few large farmers. While reportedly there are village committees for this aspect, they largely serve as a conduit for the payments. Issues of matching the army demands and requirements such as quality, and range of produce remain to be addressed.

The army's development programmes such as Sadbhavna in the Turtuk region was observed and the interventions had deployed about Rs 2 crores over a small region with a population of about 3000. The activities of Sadbhavana include primary education, secondary and tertiary healthcare, community development and empowerment of women. The direct contribution of the programme to the local economy caused through hiring of ponies/porters, purchase of local produce, business to local flour mills and engagement of local labour. The programme appears to have had a positive impact on the local residents as observed during the visit both in terms of increased trust in the army through increasing involvement of the local residents in the programme. A concern, however, remains on the extent of dependency being created with the external intervention.

During the past 27 years, tourism activity has had a substantial growth (J&K. n.d). The tourism arrival in 1989 was the highest, but it has declined subsequently. Ladakh tourism attracts more international tourists than domestic. However, this pattern is changing with increased flights into the region. Though tourism generates various economic benefits such as rentals for land and residence for tourist accommodation, taxi operation, shops and sales in Leh, some sales of local agricultural produce and handicrafts, much of the economic benefit is not actually accruing to the local residents. Most of the shops in Leh are owned/operated by people from outside and much of the employment in the hotels goes to people from Uttar Pradesh and Bihar.

From observations and discussions with the local people it appeared that much of the tourism potential is being exploited by external agencies. This is happening at two levels. The first is the exploitation of Ladakh tourism by agencies from outside. This is being addressed to some extent as indicated by the LAHDC that all investment in the region is being done with local partnerships. At another level, much of the tourism in non-urban areas such as in Nubra valley, the local residents have marginal benefits on account of nominal rentals and some revenues from running taxi services. Both these aspects, when applied with the need to strengthen the local economy would need to be addressed to ensure that local capital is reinvested to create greater local economic value and thereby a stronger local economy.

An aspect of development is the extent of local savings that is being reinvested in development activities in the local area. This is significant and a clear indicator of external dependence and sustainability. The credit deposit ratio as obtained from the bank in Nubra valley is Rs. 2.1 crores and about Rs 30 lakhs. This indicates that there is a need to be able to channel the savings in the area to create economic activity that can create an extent of self-reliance in the region. In addition to the local entrepreneurship and capital, the need for basic infrastructure is essential for local development. The important aspects of infrastructure are transport, energy and telecommunication.

The transport infrastructure in Ladakh is characterized by terrain limitations that could pose a potential hurdle to economic development. In the Nubra valley (Tiger village), it was observed that the connectivity to Diskit was limited to two buses a week. This often leads to overcrowding of buses. Further, while the present system of limiting taxi carrying capacity by the local tourism association ensures even distribution, this could be relaxed for local transport (say within the Nubra valley) to supplement the public transport while also providing some local economic benefits. Further, much of the transport is also used for communication where villagers need to travel to nearby villages to be able to communicate, indicating the potential for better telecommunication facilities.

Energy is an integral part of all development processes. Therefore based on the sources available, energy is required for lighting, heating, cooking, and industrial use. Ladakh, being located at a high altitude with long and severe winters requires a substantial amount of energy for heating purposes. Predominantly an economy based on agriculture, Ladakh has very little industrial activity and that too concentrated around the urban areas. Therefore it is important to effectively and extensively harness the local resources such as solar and hydro both to stimulate economic development as well as to derive the associated environmental benefits. Ladakh is blessed with up to 325 solar days in a year with an average day length of 14 hours. The solar intensity is up to 1Kw/m2. Due to this fact solar energy could be the most reliable source of energy, especially for rural and remote areas of this hilly terrain, in a cost effective manner. This potential has been recognized and solar energy is being developed and used for the last ten years. But for sustainability of such system, it is essential that local people be trained to manage all aspects of the system. This not only ensures timely and effective handling but also helps reduce costs substantially.

A potential of about 105 MW has been identified in the district from hydro. However, there remains the constraint of demand creation and the reliability of the system. An aspect that can help further development and increase economic efficiency is the presence of telecommunications. For Tiger village, the nearest public telephone availability is in Diskit and this further isolates the area while making aspects such as emergency medical assistance and help a problem. It would be worthwhile to explore whether wireless in local loop (WLL) technologies could be set up and operated at the Nubra valley and other remote/inaccessible valleys initially as an internal network.

The issue of development

Ladakh has been dramatically transformed by 'development'. Over the last few decades things have changed very fast. Until the 1960s the region was virtually ignored by the world and the rest of India. All that changed when the Chinese invaded Tibet in 1950, going on to launch an attack on Ladakh in 1962. In the mid-1960s Ladakh's isolation was broken once and for all with the construction of a trans-Himalayan road linking it to the subcontinent. Then things really began to change. The Indian government pursued an energetic policy of drawing

Ladakh into the Indian economy. In 1974, it opened the region to foreign tourism. Gradually the modern cultural invasion changed Ladakh through tourism, compulsory schooling, highway development, movies, imports of inexpensive barley and wheat, and new retail stores.

And today, as India throws its own economy open to the global market, that change is gathering speed here as well. Globalisation, tourism and politics are combining to produce a cocktail of communal tension, environmental destruction, social disintegration and economic breakdown that threaten to engulf this once stable and peaceful region.

A Ladakhi interviewed on the street in Leh, summarized the changes brought by development:

> People used to have peace of mind. They were happy and they used to help one another. These days there are motorbikes and things, there have been all sorts of improvements, but on the inside I don't see the same kind of happiness.

Tsering Dolkar, a Ladakhi farmer, lamented the loss of shared work on each other's farms that characterized traditional Ladakh. Now everyone was looking for paid jobs, and one could not get any help with plowing or harvesting without paying for it.

Development has affected young people, as they have been compelled to attend school to learn in Urdu and then in English, both foreign languages to Ladakhis. As a result 90 to 95 per cent of Ladakhi students fail their final school examinations. The effect is that they cannot go back to the traditional life and start doing farming and other things, They are rejected by the modern and they are cut off from the traditional. As Norberg-Hodge, a Swedish linguist and environmentalist, has observed (1986; 1991) that the the changes wrought on the Ladkhis over the last few decades have brought them a great sense of cultural inferiority. The combination of economic and psychological pressures led to a dramatic loss of self-esteem amongst people who had previously been emotionally healthy. A sense of shame developed about their traditions and their way of life.

But none of the NGOs in Ladakh are under any illusions as to the scale of the challenge they still face. A walk around Leh shows how far things still have to go. Tourism has become one of Ladakh's greatest problems as well as a source of benefits. Central Leh is awash with Coke stands, 'German Bakeries', trekking agencies, T-shirt shops and unshaven men shuffling around on street corners muttering 'you want good smoke?' More than half of Ladkh's tourist shops are run by non-Ladakhis, and few of them sell anything made in the region. Backpackers roar around the unpaved roads on hired motorbikes or sit in cafes complaining about the price of guest-houses. And Leh continues to grow. More and more impoverished farmers, their livelihoods destroyed or destabilized, drift in Leh to try and make their fortune from tourists and the urban economy, largely due to the pull of tourist dollars.

Traditionally, virtually everything in Ladakh was made from natural materials and reused and recycled. Today, rubbish bins have sprung up around Leh, but there is nowhere to empty them; litter is dumped on a mountainside on the edge of the town. Water is another problem. Traditional Ladakhi compost toilets used no water and rural Ladakhis knew that such a scarce resource must be used carefully. No such considerations are known to the tourists or the new generation of young urban Ladakhis who emulate them. Today compost toilets are being replaced with western style flush systems, despite the fact that Ladakh has no sewers. The new toilets, along with the increasing numbers of baths and showers are seriously depleting the amount of water available in Leh. As a result, much of the drinking water is now trucked in, across the mountains in government tankers.

Once can also hear how development has brought new health problems to Ladakh—incidence of obesity, diabetes, coronary artery disease and various cancers are increasing as diets and lifestyles change. But traditional Ladakh too had one of the highest rates of hypertension in the world, possibly caused by traditional salt tea. Similarly, much can be heard about the wonders of Ladakh's cooperative farming culture, but little about the caste system which has made the original tribal people of the region, the Mons and Bedas, the most despised people in Ladakhi society.

Therefore it is not that traditional Ladakh was perfect and should not change. It is the consumer culture that has been criticized for gradually destroying a culture that existed in relative peace and harmony for generations. The global capitalist economy bears the greatest blame for what has happened in Ladakh. It is global capitalism that seeks to turn every corner of the globe into a market place to be exploited, and every man, woman and child into a lifetime consumer of useless products. If this process continues, it may destroy a viable ecologically responsible culture.

APPENDIX

Scheduled tribes of Ladakh

Balti — Presumably the descendants of the Scythians (Shakas) they are a majority group among the Muslims (Shia sect) of Ladakh. They derive their name from their homeland. Baltistan. They speak in Balti among themselves and in Urdu with outsiders and write in the Arabic script. The Balti are short, below medium in height, oblong head tending to a round shape and a medium nose. Balti are differentiated on the basis of achieved social status such as the sheikh (priests), akhun (priest of lower order), hajji and saget. Agriculture is the primary source of livelihood.

Beda

Beda community of Ladakh is partly sedentary and partly nomadic and earns their livelihood as musicians, playing the flute and drums. They inhabit the cold desert regions at a high altitude, which has a heavy snowfall. Though the majority are Buddhists, a small section living in the Nubra valley is Muslim. They speak in Ladakhi and use the Bodhi script among themselves and Perso-Arabic with others. Beda have prominent cheekbones and broad and flat faces like other Ladakhis. The Beda families are of a mixed extended type and they prefer to have many children. A Beda girl is cherished by her family as she brings bride price.

Bodh

Bodh, also known as Ladakhi Bodh, Ladakshpa or Bdriksha live in the Zanskar and Nubra region. They belong to the Mahayana sect of Buddhism with the Gelukpa (yellow shirt), Drokpa (red shirt) and Naima sub sects. They speak in Ladakhi among themselves but converse with others in Urdu and Hindi. They can be identified by their prayer flags, caps, charms, amulets and the long plaits of the men. They are non-vegetarians who eat yak but fish is a taboo. Barley (*namdev*) and wheat are their staple food, mustard oil is the cooking medium and apricot oil is used to burn lamps in gompas. Alchoholic beverages (chang and arrakh) are drunk on festive occasions but tea, both salty (*gur gur*) and sweet (*limpton*) is drunk everyday. The joint polyandrous familial set up (*khangsoo*) is common though the spread of modernity is working in favour of a monogamous familial set up. The Bodh women participate in all socio-economic activities and are employed in white-collar jobs. Land is the primary economic resource and agriculture is the primary occupation, though some of them are landless. The subsidiary economic resources are handicrafts, fruit orchards, small scale industries, wood carving and transportation. The exchange of scarves (*khatak*) by the couple is an important ritual in a marriage. The major Bodh festivals are the Buddhist new year, the birth anniversary of Shakapa, Buddha Purnima and Dosmoche.

Broq-pa Also called Shin, they inhabit the high hills of Ladakh and speak in Shina, but with outsiders in Ladakhi and Urdu. The Broqpa are divided into a number of patri-lineages (*gatti*) which were exogamous in the past. These *gattis* play a role in re-locating economic resources like land and water and in regulating socio-cultural activities. Most of the Broqpa are Shia Muslims. The Broqpa women can be easily identified by the peculiar Dardic cap. They participate in all the socio-economic pursuits of the family. Their high status is indicated by the large amount of bride price (*mahr*) demanded by their parents and paid in cash to the wife. Pastoralism blended with trade was their traditional means of livelihood. It has now been replaced by agriculture and labour-intensive activities.

Champa/Changpa Also known as Fangpa and Phalpa (nomadic), the people have derived their name from the territory they inhabit, *chang* meaning north and *thang* meaning plains. Hence Champa or Changpa are the people of the northern plains of Ladakh. They inhabit an extremely cold area which is ravaged by snow storms and can be identified by their conical yak-skin tents (reboo) and a garment made of hide and wool by them. The Champa belong to the Dokpa sect of Buddhism and religion occupies a central place in their culture. Their staple food is barley (*tsampa*) and the meat of yak and wild horses (*kiang*). The major economic resources of the Champa are yaks and goats. Polyandry is permissible but with monogamy gaining favour it has become rare.

Dokhpa — Also known as Drokpa or Brokhpa meaning people of the meadow they are descendants of the Dards and have migrated from Gilgit. They are agriculturists who inhabit the villages on the banks of the river Indus. The Dokhpa wear a headgear and a gown, the former being decorated with flowers, beads, needles, ribbons and buttons. The men and women cover their body with goatskin, lined inside with fur. Roasted barley flour (*sattu*) is their staple food. Beef, cow's milk and its products, poultry birds and eggs are strictly prohibited. The village headman, *mokdam*, is also the village judge and leader. The Dokhpa follow the rule of endogamy. Monogamy and fraternal polyandry are in vogue.

Gara/Garba — Majority of the Gara/Garba tribe live in Leh and Kargil districts and are Buddhist by religion. Traditionally, the Gara are blacksmiths who make iron implements and supply them throughout the year to their clients for which they receive a fixed amount of grain from each family at harvest time. Their staple food is wheat, supplemented with barley (*grim*) and rice.

Mon — The Mon are the musicians and flute players of the Ladakh region whose villages are located along the river Indus. They are the ancient people of this part as is evident from the rock carvings and ruins still known as Mon-castles. The Mon live in nuclear and extended families and are patrilineal. Married women wear a long gown (*goncha*) and scarf (*firoza*). Bride price is paid among them in cash and kind. The Mon women help their menflok in agriculture, tending cattle, cooking for the family and spinning wool. During the sowing of crops, they sing *goru* songs and are paid for this too. After the harvest, the Mon visit the houses of the

	Ladakhi to provide *larango* music and are offered grain and salt. The Mon are not allowed to enter the house of the Ladakhi, but they accept food and water from their neighbours.
Purig-pa	The inhabitants of Purig or Kargil are known as Purig-pa. It is a mixed ethnic conglomerate of the Dard, Balti and Pot-riksha people.

Source: K.S. Singh (1994).

REFERENCES

Bhasin, M.

1992 *Cold Desert: Ladakh, Ecology and Development,* Delhi: Kamla-Raj Enterprises.

Bigelow, Bill

2001 'Learning from Ladakh,' *Rethinking Schools,* 15:4, Summer.

Carr-Harris, J. (ed.)

1995 'Mountains and people: A peoples' perspective from the Indian Himalayas, Sri Bhuvaneshwari Mahila Ashram'. Paper presented at the Global NGO Consultation on Sustainable Mountain Development, 22-25 February Lima, Peru.

Mittal, Devender Kumar

Seabuckthorn Fruit Processing the Indian Experience. Ladakh Foods Ltd.

Singh, K.S.

1993 *The Scheduled Tribes.* New Delhi: Anthropological Survey of India and Oxford University Press.

Kaul, Pummy

2002 'Last straw? Health drink players struggle to stay afloat', *Financial Express, The Indian Express,* New Delhi.

Kingsnorth, Paul

'Shadows in the kingdom of light.' *The Ecologist,* 30:8, November: 34.

Jammu & Kashmir

n.d. *Ladakh: The Land of Endless Discovery*. Srinagar: Jammu and Kashmir Tourism.

Norberg-Hodge, Helena

1986 'Appropriate technology and cooperative culture in Ladakh', *Eco-Action*, December.

1991 *Ancient Futures, Learning From Ladakh.* San Fransisco: Sierra Club Books,

Singh, R.L.

1989 *India: A Regional Geography*. New Delhi: UBS Publishers Ltd.

Pordie, L.

2000 'Reviving traditional medicine in Ladakh', summarised from information distributed by the Rolex Awards for Enterprise in October.

Gupta, R. and S. Tiwari

2002 'At the crossroads: Continuity and change in the traditional irrigation practices of Ladakh', Paper Presented at the 9th Biennial Conference of the IASCP, Winrock International India.

17

Continuity and Change: Social Institutions of the Tolcha Bhotia

Indu Sahai and Sameera Maiti

Society and culture, the human constructs par excellence, never remain stagnant, they are subject to growth, evolution and consequently change. Society is a process and changing equilibrium of present relationships. Thus, change with time becomes inevitable. These changes occur due to expansion of one's horizon or outlook and increase in awareness and education. Linton (1936) also states that the fundamental processes of culture change are concerned with the modification in knowledge, attitudes and behavior of individuals who composed a society. However, changes within institutions do not occur easily. As long as they fulfill human needs, changes are avoided. Consequently there are two types of processes operating simultaneously, those which sustain the old system and those which bring about changes in it. The first may be termed as conformity, or better still, continuity and the second as change. Again, it is a well known fact that external or outwardly elements of a society or culture change much faster and easily compared to internal or intangible aspects. The present paper tries to take note of changes if any, in social stratification and social institutions, notably in the institutions of marriage, family and kinship among the Bhotia.

Etymology of the label Bhotia, as per the earliest account of Atkinson (1882) on Himalayan tribes, is that:

> Bod, the native name for Tibet, corrupted by people of India into Bhot, has given rise to the name Bhotiaya for the border tribes between the two countries.

Thus, the term 'Bhotia' is employed to designate several different groups of people in the Himalayan and trans-Himalayan regions. In the districts of Almora and Garhwal, in the central Himalayas, the non-Tibetan borderland folk are called Bhotia, while outside these districts the Tibetans are often referred to by this generic name. In the eastern Himalayas, certain groups of people inhabiting the Napalese-Tibetan border regions, the Tibetans living in the vicinity of Darjeeling, and the inhabitants of Bhutan, are all referred to as 'Bhotia' in their respective region. To confuse the situation still further some of the eastern Tibetans also style themselves as 'Bhotia'. While all these are distinctly unrelated groups they seem to have one thing in common. They were all connected with some kind of a trade between Tibet and the region in which they live (Srivastava 1966). Scholars, from time to time, have divided the Bhotia into various sub groups with the inclusion of some and exclusion of others. The earliest classification was by Sherring (1906) who divided them into six sub groups - Shauka, Darmi, Jauhari, Tolcha, Marcha and Jarh, whereas the latest classification by Singh (1994) divides them into eight subgroups - Jad, Tolchha, Marchha, Johari, Jethora, Darmi, Chaudansi and Byansi. All these groups exhibit socio-cultural and religious variations, despite sharing a common ecology and generic name.

In Uttaranchal, the Bhotia are to be found in the districts of Pithoragarh, Chamoli, Almorah, Uttarkashi, and Nainital. Historical accounts inform that the Bhotia of the state are descendants of Kirat or the Mon Khmer who entered India from the eastern direction. The Bhotia inhabit the north eastern region of the state, locally known as *Bhot* or *Bhot Pradesh,* consisting of several valleys bordering Tibet. These valleys from east to west are - Byans, Chaudans, Darma, Johar, Dhauliganga (Mana) and Vishnuganga (Niti).

Although the Bhotia are a landowning community, their traditional occupation in the past had been trade. Their trade zone extended from Tibet in the north to the plains in the south. Agriculture, animal husbandry and cottage industry formed their subsidiary occupations. However, the Chinese occupation of Tibet and their subsequent invasion in 1962 led to sealing the border with India. This adversely affected Indo-Tibetan trade and the main sufferers were the Bhotia who were thrown out of their traditional trading economy. Thus, today they have taken to various occupations ranging from agriculture to cottage industry and from government jobs to government contracts.

The Bhotia claim to be of Rajput origin, although they are not able to put forward any proof for the same. The earliest record of this was made by Turner while working for the census of 1931. According to him, several tribal and lower caste groups found this opportunity most appropriate for putting forward their claims to a 'higher caste' and the Bhotia were one of them.

A special feature of the Bhotia is transhumance which involves their upward/northward migration along with animals during summer and downward/southward migration during winters. Consequently, they have two dwellings with all basic amenities in both summer and winter villages.

Given the fact that there exists considerable cultural diversity between the various Bhotia subgroups of the different valleys, the present paper is restricted to the Tolcha Bhotia who reside in villages of the Vishnuganga (Niti) valley in block Joshimath, district Chamoli. Data for the present paper is based on non-participatory observation and in-depth interviews carried out during field work in the lower valley of block Dasholi and Karnaprayag where the Tolcha settle during winters.

I

Like the other Bhotia sub-groups, the Tolcha too claim to be Kshatriyas of Rajput origin. However, lack of scriptural evidence clouds their origin in mystery. According to them, the term 'Tolcha' is derived from two words, *Tol* meaning salt and *jya* corrupted to *chha* which means tea. Thus, it means people who consume a lot of salted tea. However, it is also possible that since this community traded extensively in salt and tea, they derived the name. This is also because the word 'Marcha' is said to be derived from the words *mar* meaning *ghee* (processed butter) and *chha,* i.e., tea, whereas both the communities consume tea which contains both ghee and salt. Again, according to some others the term 'Tolcha' is derived from *talli* or *talla* which means lower area or valley and thus is used for those Bhotia who lived in the lower regions of the Himalaya, more near the plains.

The Tolcha share their valley with the Marcha, who also are found scattered in the lower valley in blocks Dasholi, Ghat, Joshimath, Karnaprayag and Nandprayag where they live during the winter season. As summers approach, these people migrate to higher altitudes and settle in the Dhauliganga (Mana) and Vishnuganga (Niti) valleys, both in block Joshimath. The Bhotia residing in Mana village in the Mana valley and Niti, Gamsali and Bampa in the Niti valley are the Marcha who among themselves speak a dialect of Tibetan origin, while the Bhotia living in villages like Jelum, Malari, Reni, Lata, Dronagiri, Kaga, Garpag and Jumna, all in the Niti valley, are the Tolcha who speak a mixed Garhwali dialect.

Since the Marcha lived in higher lands, more near to the Indo-Tibet border they show more Tibetan then Garhwali influence as is evident in their dialect and physical features which are more mongoloid. Further, although both the groups are followers of Hinduism, the Tolcha consider themselves ritually superior to the Marcha. According to the Tolcha, since the Marcha had closer links with the Tibetans and even intermarried, they speculate that the Marcha have eaten the *chaurgai* or Tibetan cow. Since the cow is a sacred animal for the Hindu, eating it made the Marcha ritually impure. It was due to these very reasons that the Tolcha and Marcha did not intermarry despite sharing a common ecology, territory and culture. In fact, dining or associating with the Marcha was considered an act of defilement, one that could lead to excommunication. However, things have changed today. Although till date the Tolcha and Marcha do not share common villages, intermarriages have started to take place and rules of commensality between the two groups no longer exist.

The Tolcha, among themselves, are divided into several clans and lineages which regulate marriage alliances and indicate ancestry, e.g. Bhandari, Rawat, Rana, Bisht, Kunwar, Negi, etc. Among these, the Bhandari and Rana are regarded as ritually higher to the rest. Apart from the Kshatriya, which includes the aforesaid clans, there are Harijan Bhotias too within this community. Also known as *shilpkaar* or *das,* these people are considered low, ritually impure, and are discriminated against in almost all spheres. They are considered untouchables, and the practice was reflected at a subtle level, primarily in thought process. The Harijan Bhotia belong to the artisan class and traditionally worked as tailors, carpenters, blacksmith, agricultural labourers and musicians who play the *dhol-damau* (drums) on festive occasions. Although, following of the traditional occupation has been weakened of late, it has not been weeded out completely. The prime reason for this is poverty and illiteracy common to all belonging to this section. Being a landless class, for years they have been living on the fringe of the society depending on the Kshatriya Bhotia for their sustenance. There exists a kind of *jajmani* system according to which generations of Harijan provide their services to their Kshatriya *jajmans* who in turn give them grains, clothes and money. Their condition continues to remain the same because, neither do these people have sufficient capital to expand their network, nor expertise and skill to compete with modern and cheaply available products.

Strong rules of commnensality are followed even today between the two groups. Houses of Harijan Bhotia are generally situated at the outskirts of the village or at a distance from houses of the 'higher caste' groups. In the Bhotia summer villages and a few large winter villages, like Deolibaggar, where they form a sizable population, the Harijans live at the outskirts forming a nearly separate cluster that is usually known as *Harijan basti.* Food touched or cooked by them is not eaten by others. Harijans are not allowed to enter the houses of the 'higher caste' Bhotia. They are made to sit in the verandah or courtyard and given food and drinks in utensils kept separately for them.

Although a few 'higher caste' Bhotia have a sympathetic attitude towards the Harijans, they dare not break the traditional rules of commensality for fear of the *devta's* wrath which can be manifested in the form of diseases or other problems. Thus, despite literacy being high among the Kshatriya Bhotia, superstitions still stand strong. The Harijans, on their part are conscious of their separate identity and try to imitate their higher caste counterparts in various respects. They too are strictly endogamous, and marry only among Harijans. Caste mobility is virtually impossible.

As of today, untouchability seems to be decreasing. The Harijan are becoming aware of their rights, but this process of transition is slow since they are not mobilized as a groups. A few individuals have managed to acquire scheduled caste certificates so that they may benefit from the various government schemes. This attempt has been made since they believe that they are not in a position to compete with the 'high caste' Bhotia for government benefits. Thus, a unique situation has arisin wherein there exists a caste within a tribe. However, despite their attempts to improve their lot, the Harijan Bhotia continue to be discriminated against due to poverty and illiteracy. The only way this condition can be improved is by educating them and providing them ample employment opportunities.

II

Coming to the second part of the paper, related with changes in the social institutions, it may be stated that social organization in tribal societies rests upon the kinship system to a great extent. Among the Bhotia too, kinship plays an important role in determining much of its social functions. The Bhotia are a patrilineal, patrilocal and patriarchal society. Maternal relatives, however, are not completely ignored and are given special importance during the life cycle rituals. Descent and inheritance are from the paternal side and therefore priority and importance is given to them. Only sons receive a share in the property, but if a widowed daughter lives with her parents, she too receives a share. The Bhotia traditonally followed the rule of primogeniture which is called *jethwad* here. Thus, the eldest son receives one *nali* land more than his other brothers. This practice is gradually being replaced with equal division of property among the sons to avoid any ill feelings.

Children are socialized from the very beginning to respect and obey their elders, specially the men of the family. Being a patrilocal society, girls have to stay with their husbands and their families after marriage. In the husband's house, women are supposed to keep their head covered as a mark of respect to the elders of the house. Among the Bhotia, as in most other Indian communities, avoidance is maintained between a woman and elder male relatives of her husband's family, specially with her father-in-law, brother-in-law and husband's maternal uncle or *mamsaura*. Women avoid coming face to face with, or speaking directly to these relatives. Touching any of them, even accidentally, is considered a sin that inflicts impurity and therefore taking a ritual bath and sprinkling of *gau mutra* (cow's urine) was essential for both the individuals. However, the rules are stricter, for the *mamsaura* who had earlier to pay the daughter-in-law a compensation and also visit one of the four *dhams* (religious places) apart from taking a ritual bath. This rule has been toned down and presently the *mamsaura* simply visits one of the local temples, pays a compensation and has a ritual bath if he accidentally touches the daughter-in-law. Joking relations are found present between a man and his elder brother's wife, his wife's younger brothers and sisters and between a woman and her husband's younger sister too. Such relations become conspicuous at the time of marriage and Holi. Teknonymy is practised among husband and wife, and couvade too is noticable. Certain restrictions are laid on a man during his wife's pregnancy since her stars are believed to be weak and she is vulnerable to evil spirits. Thus, he is not supposed to visit the cremation ground or shave his head if any family member dies, neither can he cut his hair or shave his beard. Earlier, these restrictions were applicable from the second or third month of pregnancy, but now it is followed only after completion of the seventh month.

The Bhotia have their distinctive pattern of kinship terminology which includes both descriptive and classification terms. A few classificatory terms tell us about regulations that are no longer in practice, for example, the term *mama* is used for mother's brother and father's sister's husband. Again the terms *didi* and *bhulli* are used for elder and younger sister respectively and also for wife's elder and younger brother's wife respectively. Such usage suggests the existence of marriage by exchange, and was confirmed by the Bhotia as the tradition of *saata* which is no longer in existence. Over the years, culture-contact has led to the replacement of Bhotia terms of address by urban Hindi terms, eg. 'papa' and 'mummy' in place of *baba* and *ija*. As such, in this context it can be derived that, although the kinship system has undergone certain changes in accordance with time and current needs, the essential structure remains.

III

Marriage, among the Bhotia, is considered a sacred institution and therefore solemnized amidst several ceremonies and great fanfare. As mentioned earlier, the Bhotia practice sub-group endogamy and clan exogamy. Traditionally, the average age at marriage was 16-18 years for girls and 19-21 years for boys. However, age at marriage has considerably increased here and today the average age for girls is 21-23 years and 25-27 years for boys. This shift in age can be attributed to education and awareness among the Bhotia boys and girls, both of whom desire educated partners. Further, they also wish to settle down only when the boy is well placed in a job with earnings enough to sustain a family.

Among the Bhotia, marriage proposals are sent from the boy's side. If the girl's family considers the boy suitable, the boy's and girl's horoscopes are matched before the final approval. If, one of the two does not have a horoscope, permission of the *devta* is sought. This is done by putting the question to a person who is temporarily possessed by a *devta.* Initially, girls had no say in selection of their groom and had to marry whoever was selected by the family. Neither were they allowed to meet the groom before marriage nor see him. However, this trend has changed and today a majority of the girls and boys are allowed to meet before taking the final decision. In fact, a few cases were noted in which the girls themselves rejected the boys since they were less educated or did not have a good job. Yet again there were also cases in which educated girls with government jobs were being forced by their parents to marry boys who were is search of jobs or preparing for competitive examinations.

Once the match is fixed, an engagement ceremony takes place which is followed by the marriage ceremony. Several changes has also taken place in the ritualistic performances and ceremonies related to marriage. To a great extent, the Hindu marriage performance has been adopted in totality. In dress, too, urban Indian clothing have been adopted as a preference over the traditonal bride and groom's attire. These changes, however, have not effected the structure of the institution. On the other hand, contact with non-Bhotia Hindus has brought about remarkable changes in Bhotia marriage transactions. Earlier the practice of giving bride wealth existed. In fact in many instances, it was the groom's side which had to shoulder the entire marriage expenses. Giving of dowry too existed, but it was a symbolic gesture of five utensils known as *bhana.* This trend seems to have reversed. Presently, although the demand for dowry does not exist, parents give their daughter all articles needed to set up a new household including expensive electronic gadgets like washing machines, T.V. and fridge. On their part, the groom's families have started taking the financial status of the girls family into consideration while selecting a match for their son. Bride wealth among the Bhotia, today, is non-existent, only a token amount of Rs. 1.25/- to 11/- is given as a *shagun.* This changed trend, if not controlled, may assume the evils it has in the mainstream Indian society.

The bond of marriage, being a sacred one, is considered unbreakable by the Bhotia and as such there is no provison for dissolution. In case of incompatibility, the two may separate. Monogamy is the prevalent form of marriage, but if a woman cannot conceive, her husband can take a second wife without leaving the first. The permission of the first wife, however has to be taken before the second marriage. This remains mostly in theory, since the wife is forced to adhere to her husband's wishes. Women, on the other hand, cannot remarry under any circumstance. Widow remarriage too is absent although a widower has the right to remarry. Earlier, a form of levirate existed under which, if the husband's family so wished, the widow could live on as the wife of the deceased's brother. However, no marriage ceremony was performed to solemnize this relationship. At present, the Bhotia tend to deny even the existence of such a custom in their past, because contact with the non-tribals has led them to consider it a shameful act (Maiti 2003). Marriages with lower caste Bhotia, Marcha, or non-Bhotia were strictly prohibited and flouters were ex-communicated. This strict attitude has undergone a change, specially after increased interaction with non-tribals. In fact, quite a few cases of Bhotia's marrying non-tribals and Marchas were brought to light. Now a days, marriages with Marchas, as stated earlier, are not considered wrong since the Marcha too are Bhotias sharing common socio-cultural, religious and economic traits. Marriages of Bhotia boys to high caste non-Bhotia girls are tolerated, but not easily accepted. On the other hand marriage of Bhotia girls to non-Bhotias even of high caste, or of a Bhotia to a lower caste person is still not acceptable under any condition. Thus, in the context of marriage it may be stated that though considerable changes have occurred over the years in the traditional pattern, these changes have not been strong enough to alter the structure of the institution.

All the three kinds of families—nuclear, extended and non-familial household units—can be found among the Bhotia. However, a predominance of nuclear families or non-familial units seems apparent on first contact. The main cause for this is migration of family members to far off places for jobs or studies. Moreover, the yearly transhumance seems to cause a division in the family. Such divisions, however, are only seasonal and present a wrong pricture of the type of family to those who do not probe further to get accurate information. Whereas a decade or so ago, the entire family used to migrate to summer villages, today only some members (usually the older ones) migrate during summers mainly due to insufficiency of education facilities available in these villages. This changing trend of migration creates a wrong picture of the family structure. Although, individualistic attitude has created quite a number of nuclear families here, it was noted that brothers tend to live close by, usually sharing a common courtyard. Family members living in distant cities collect at one place on various festive occasions and religious ceremonies. In fact, how so ever much the distance, the entire family collects at least once a year on some special occasion, and also visits their ancestral (traditional summer) village which they consider a *dev bhumi* (land of gods) to take the blessings of their *devta*. It is thus deduced that although need has forced the family structure to change, in essence they remain part of a joint family.

Division of labour among family members is glaringly disproportionate. Women of the house shoulder most of the workload in the family. They not only do all household work like cleaning, cooking, fetching water, cutting and collecting fire wood, looking after the children, etc, but also help out in the fields, kitchen garden and if need be, work as labourers too. In their free time, women in every Bhotia household weave carpets, shawls and other wool products, thus contributing substantially to the family income. Men, on their part, do not do any household work and idle away their free time gossiping, drinking and playing cards. As children too, girls are expected to help out with the household chores besides studying whereas boys are free from domestic responsibilities to concentrate on their studies. Socialization of children is mainly the task of women. Men help out when the child is sick, by taking the child to the doctor, and getting medicines, or when women are out working.

Major decisions were traditionally taken by the male members of the family without consulting the womenfolk. Today, although men are considered free to take decisions on their own, they generally consult the women on matters of importance. Thus, in this sphere relative importance has started being given to women which is a positive change. This, however, does not mean that Bhotia women are considered equal to their men. In the family, a woman's status is inferior to that of the men. She does not have the right to raise her voice against her husband, father, brother, brother-in-law or any elder member of the family. In fact, in this community a married woman's status rises only when she gives birth to a male child. Thus, although the Bhotia women contribute greatly to the community, they do not get the recognition due to them.

Summing up, it would be right to say that contact with non-Bhotias, education, developmental measures and a desire to acquire higher position in society have undoubtedly brought about changes in the traditional Bhotia social life. However, these changes have not been strong enough to influence all its attributes or elements. Although outwardly it may seem that the institutions of kinship, marriage and family have undergone several changes, an organized study indicates that these changes do not have the capacity of replacing the older structure completely or substitute them with a new one. The fact remains that in practice much of the traditional structure continues even today.

REFERENCES

Atkinson, E.T.

1882 *The Himalayan Gazetteer.* Delhi: Cosmo Publications (Reprint 1973).

Linton, R.

1936 *The Study of Man: An Introduction.* New York: D. Appleton-Century Co.

Maiti, S.

2003 'Political organization and customary laws of the Bhotia of Uttaranchal', *The Oriental Anthropologist,* 3 (2).

Sherring, C.A.

1906 *Western Tibet and British Borderland.* London: Edward Arnold.

Singh, K.S.

1994 *The Scheduled Tribes:* People of India Series. Vol III. Delhi: Oxford University Press.

Srivastava, R.P.

1966 'Tribe, caste mobility in India and the case of Kumaon Bhotias', in C.F. Haimendorf (ed). *Caste and Kin in Nepal, India and Ceylon:* Bombay: Asia Publishing House.

Turner, A.C.

1931 *Census of India 1931, Vol. XVIII United Provinces of Agra and Oudh.* Allahabad: Government Press.

18

Journey through *The Unquiet Woods:* Contested Resources and Protest Movement in Uttaranchal

Shalina Mehta

In a poignant statement, Guha (1994) drew the attention of social scientists to the neglect of environmental crisis in their discourse. He lamented that:

> environmental journalists, social activists and natural scientists made significant contributions to our understanding of the social implications of environmental degradation, by contrast social science community remained unaware.[1]

The concern was partially valid as Guha himself was one of the few forerunners of social science, arguing and augmenting the need for comprehending 'environmental crisis' in a holistic perspective.[2]

There is no denying the fact that post-independent India was in desperation to fulfill Nehru's dream of 'scientific temples of learning'—a construction of society that was rooted in western ideology and awed assertive statements of economic prosperity emanating from preliminary successes of industrialization. In the formative period of post-independent history, linkages between industrialization and quality of life were rarely questioned.

Mathematical models dominated development planning, and were guilty of ignoring biophysical realities.[3] One may suggest that preponderance of economic thought and the hold economists had on development planning minimized the urgency and importance of local voices and the arguments put forward by anthropologists and other social scientists, rooted in grass root realities. Attempts made by some scholars to bring to fore the ecological realities of deforestation, depletion of natural resources and resulting imbalances between nature and lifestyle were totally ignored by political leadership and dominant voices in academics and politics.[4]

Referring to the analysis of Bardhan (1984), Guha rightly points out that even Bardhan's acclaimed observations on ruling coalition in India comprising of three social groups namely industrial capitalists, rich farmers and bureaucracy failed to take cognizance of the importance of natural resources to Indian economy. It would be pertinent to argue here that the failure of economic, political and scientific leadership was primarily responsible for rampant destruction of India's vast natural resources. Greed combined with indifference and ignorance challenged the resilience of the 'unquiet woods' that echoed in people's movements in the last decades of the 20th century.

The term movement refers to 'persistent, patterned and widely distributed challenges to the status quo' (Darnovsky Epstein and Richard 1995: vii). The authors also go on to argue that social movements appear to be simultaneously spontaneous and strategic, expressive (of emotion and need) and instrumental (seeking some concrete ends), unruly and organised, political and cultural, that are not only challenging political systems and cultural status but also social order and social theory. Marx (1842) in his efforts at theorizing evoked realities of subordination and complimented it by a paradigm of 'solutions', that the exploited in the society envisage for their problems. Inherent in this theory of 'collective behaviour' is the necessity of collective perception of exploitation and a spoken agreement on envisaged solutions. Thus the logic explains—if a community perceives that 'cutting trees' or 'building of 'dams' is not about providing them jobs, water or electricity but is an extension of their aggravation, then they will organize themselves on principles of protecting existing *status quo*. In other words movements are on-going processes. What matters really is the impact that they generate and how successful they are in achieving, what Nadel may have liked to call the 'purposiveness' of their collective action?

It is important here to assert re-orientation provided to understanding and analysis of theoretical construction of 'movement' by social scientists, once they started unfolding the mystique of 'civil rights' movements. The non-violent disobedience or disregard of state sponsored legitimacies may add a fresh contour to the understanding of 'protest' It was this phase that brought forth:

> the rationality of disorder and disruption, the capacity for collective challenge inherent in cohesive communities, the intricate complexity of relations between leaders and followers, and the necessary interplay of spontaneity and organization' (Darnovsky Epstein & Richard 1995: x).

My purpose in this essay is not to define or rectify the concept of 'social movement' or 'ecological movement' or the concept of movement *per se*. I want to examine people's voices as they emerged through the colonial history to contemporary India. Guha's journey through the 'unquiet woods' (1991) was an attempt to locate 'chipko' within the broader context of ongoing peasant movements. My effort is to revisit and resource through the local histories—people's concerns, their perceptions and articulation of denials.

One of the expressed modes of representing denial is through 'protest'. The agent or the perceived perpetrator of 'denial' is projected either in symbols or through rendering in oral traditions. Prior to culmination in what one may describe as full throttle verbal frenzy, mass hysteria resulting in open conflict or violence, there is an underpinning of seething discontent. Failure to assess the magnitude of dormant discontentment or its denial often subjects state machinery to various push factors. Consequently, state fails to own up its responsibility, acknowledges impracticality of proposed policies and interventions and admits withdrawl. On the contrary it may also unleash tyranny, rampant violation of human rights and open condemnation of people's legitimate rights and just demands. My endeavor in this text is to read through unfolding of messages delivered through chipko and post-chipko movements in the state of Uttaranchal.

The state of Uttaranchal has recently been constituted out of the state of Uttar Pradesh. It comprises of the hill districts of Uttarkashi, Chamoli, Rudraprayag, Tehri Garhwal, Dehradun, Pithoragarh, Bageshwar, Almora, Champawat and Nainital along with the districts of Udham Singh Nagar in the terai region and Hardwar in the foothills. The state has a unique character as nearly 63% of the region is covered by forests and about 93% of the area is hilly, with only 7% of the area constituting the plains. The state is divided into 13 districts, 49 Tehsils, 95 blocks and 16,414 villages.

Revisiting chipko

Renderings in this section are deeply influenced and motivated by readings of Madhav Gadgil, Ramchandra Guha, Shekhar Pathak and various contributions made to *Yugvani*—a prominent monthly Hindi magazine published from Dehradun. My inspiration, however, are Gaura Devi and many other silent protesters whose contributions in generating might in their fight for their fundamental rights and for a better quality of life remain buried in the local histories. Sunderlal Bahuguna—crusader behind chipko movement—describes them as the marginalized people who kept the soul of democracy, the community spirit alive and are the last living representatives of participatory democracy.

Prasun (2001) is of special significance in this context. He was referring to demonstrations and protests against overhead cables of the capacity of eight lakh kilowatts that were being laid over Advani and Barni villages. The electricity department was busy clearing thick forest cover of sal and pine to facilitate laying of heavily loaded wires. It was the same forest cover that contractors wanted to cut and the people of Havelghat came out in large numbers and clung to trees to save them, evoking the spirit that is now popularly called the 'Chipko movement'. It was 1 February 1978. Government of Uttar Pradesh provided police cover to the contractor and 22 Nepali labourers to enable them to cut the trees in the earmarked zone in Havelighat. Villagers protested and came out in large numbers to save the trees that they believed were essential for their survival and livelihood. They organized themselves in groups and hugged the trees. The police stood still unable to take any action. People were charged. They had conceived various folk songs for the occasion. One of the folk songs implied that even if the axes fall, they would not be able to touch the trees as our bodies are going to provide a protective shield to the trees. If trees are to be attacked, we shall be sacrificed first. Come what may, we shall protect our trees at any cost.

It was this commitment to protecting their forest cover, that compelled the armed constabulary to withdraw from Advani village and the contract leased by the state government for cutting the forest cover was withdrawn.

The Advani village once again faced a similar challenge in the year 2001. This time it was in the name of development. The project implemented by the power grid is to provide electricity from Tehri Dam that is under construction. The electricity department decided to clear a stretch of 170 meters of thick forest cover for laying cables and wires. The villagers argued that the contractors in connivance with the officials of the power grid deliberately chose the thickest forest stretch for generating maximum profit by selling wood and other forest produce. Villagers were also apprehensive that when the actual cutting takes place the contractors are likely to violate the boundaries marked for cutting. A much larger portion of the forest may be destroyed to provide huge profits to contractors and officials involved in the deal.

The contract for laying cable was given to two companies-KEC and RPG. The forest cover to be cleared by RPG was much larger than what KEC was planning to clear. On 15 July 2001, residents of Advani village with the support of some activist of chipko movement organized a meeting in the village. The meeting concluded that the villagers would request the contractor to stop digging and if they did not comply, then the villagers would start filling the pits dug previously for installing electricity poles. The RPG suspended work immediately. But the villagers were not content with it as they feared that the company might get a clearance from the court and resume work again.

On 25 July 2001, a day celebrated in the memory of Shridev Suman, who sacrificed his life during 1978 chipko struggle, the villagers organized a five kilometre walk starting from Berni village and passing through Advani forest. The peace march concluded with a meeting and the volunteers vowed that if the power grid refuses to accede to their request to change the route of the cables, then the villagers shall follow the precedent set during the chipko movement and shall embrace the trees. They vowed that they would take the axe blows on their bodies and would not allow the trees to be axed under any circumstance. On 4 August 2001, villagers tied symbolic sacred threads of *rakhi* around trees. It was a historic moment. For the first time a ritual that had remained confined for centuries to the domain of individual relationships was evoked as a symbol of collective assertion and community spirit. Villagers with great gusto narrate the events of that historic day:

> On the *rakhi* day, 82 year old Bachni Devi along with lady sarpanch of Barni village, Sopna Devi, the head of Bhilgana development block-Beena Sajwan and an old activist of chipko movement, Sudesha Devi carried *rakhi* in a procession and tied them around all those trees that were earmarked for felling. What made the event acquire greater significance and political importance was the participation of the local Member of Legislative Assembly along with chairman of forest protection committee and various other community leaders who joined the local women and tied *rakhis* to the trees according support and wholehearted commitment to the cause. The popular folk song recited by the processionists asked the state to pay heed to the silent cries of the trees and protect them by tying sacred threads, symbolic of protection and love. It was an emotional appeal, addressing sensitivities of the officials, administrators and contractors.

From clinging to the trees to tying sacred threat of *rakhi,* these ecological 'protest and protect' movements provide material for fascinating sociology. It unfolds various dimensions of ecological movements that have hitherto remained either hidden or dormant in environmental discourse. Environmental movements for long have been classified as violent, non-violent; Gandhian Marxian; radical mainstream; deep shallow; mainstream grassroots, etc[6]. and various organizations supporting these ideologies are further compartmentalized in these constructed categories. The students of what is described as 'popular ecological resistance movements' assume a common precept to reconstruct these widely diverse collective social actions. The phrase 'popular ecological resistance movements' is inspired by Latin American social scientists that refer to 'non-middle class, peasant indigenous people and participants in underground economies' (Taylor 1995:2).

Guha while analyzing chipko and other ecological protest movements in Tehri Garhwal refers to indigenous traditions of 'dhandak'. He argues:

> 'dhandak' is representative of a type of 'rebellion', widely prevalent in pre-industrial and pre-capitalist monarchies. The dhandak is a sub-type of what one might call 'customary' rebellion; a form of rebellion that draws its legitimacy from custom and does not seek to overthrow the social order (1991:89).

Guha draws extensively upon Gluckman (1963) and Max Weber.[7] Gluckman in particular argued that 'customary rebellion' is seen central to coherence and persistence of a society, a functional safety valve that allows for the periodic constructive release of discontent.[8] Gluckman's model of oscillating equilibrium essentially discussed fluctuating balances and counterbalances within societies and their ultimate return to equilibrium. The fundamental argument examines catharsis within traditional peasant and ecological movements in what were previously the large state of Uttar Pradesh and a part of which is now called Uttaranchal. Unlike Marxian notion of rebellion these movements operated within the narrow confines of protecting their own interests and were not a challenge to the broader state order. Customs and rituals are time and again evoked for the protection of common community interests. It is often argued that:

> In the transition to capitalism it is peasants who have more frequently invoked custom, for it is they

> who stand to lose from their enclosure, state, forest management, or the mechanization of agricultural work (Guha 1991:92).

It is in this spirit that peasant women from Advani and Barni villages invoked the traditional custom of *rakhi* that was symbolic of brothers providing protection to more vulnerable female siblings. Indian history is witness to occasions when women have invoked the tradition to ask rulers to come to their rescue by invoking the spirit behind the custom.

What is peculiar and of significance is the fact that in the Advani episode, even men came forward to tie *rakhis* to the trees overriding inherent gender connotations. The trees symbolized the endangered and weak and women and men had to take collective onus for their protection. The wisdom that governed their action re-interpreted and re-located a cultural practice. It is this reinvention or reinterpretation that is critical to my understanding of social theory and principles that govern mobilization during protest movements. Guha has argued in a similar vein when he asserts:

> In Tehri Garhwal, several centuries later, custom was often the most effective weapon for a peasantry facing the onslaught of a 'modernizing' state. For 'the ideological struggle to define the present is a struggle to define the past as well. ....Customary rebellion is more appropriately viewed as shrewd and effective tactic used by peasants to exploit inherent ambiguities of the dominant ideology (1991:92,97).

Clinging to the trees, tying *rakhi* to them are gestures that provide legitimacy to a collective belief. The sentiment is invoked in the popular folklore that recollects blessings of forests, the fact that forests provide water, fresh air and soil, the basic necessities of life and the folk invocation concludes by saying that the day is not far, when Himalaya shall awaken in its full glory and the killer axe shall have no existence.

> *Kya hae jangal kae upkar; Mitti, pani aur bayar;*
> *Jinda rahane kae adhar; Aaj Himalaya jagega;*
> *Krura kulahada bhagaiga.*

This study provides an interesting complementarity between belief and fear. There is impeded rationality and rustic logic. The current resource mobilization theory facilitates our understanding of peasant movements related to ecology, livelihood issues, strategizing for joint forest management or even locating 'dhandak' in its historical context. Each of these movements is integral to social and political landscape. The leadership comprehends the finer nuances of local culture. It mobilizes support using powerful local symbols. The linkages between spontaneity of the protest and efficacy of organization behind it are rooted in local idioms. The involvement of the local MLA, the head of the forest protection committee and representation by local women leadership in the *rakhi* movement, construe cogent perception of dynamics of chipko and its aftermath, culminating in a sequence of similar events.

Impact of resource mobilization

The mobilization of resources in Uttaranchal through the colonial period to contemporary history may have moved from custom to confrontation but its impact is of vital interest in critical theory of social movements. Resource mobilization analysis examines movements as vehicles of reform in institutional structure and government policy. A movement's success is measured in terms of political outcomes; movement strategies and tactics are assessed in relation to what might be called instrumental criteria (Darnovasky, Epstein & Flacks 1995:xv). Placed in this context, I shall briefly examine the impact that the Rakhi Bandho movement had in Uttaranchal.

The revitalization movement for ecological protection marched ahead with the slogan, 'listen to the cries of the trees-protect them by tying *rakhis* to them'. The slogan made an emotional appeal and invoked tradition to involve people in organizing protest. Language is being used here as an effective instrument to create a new worldview. The message that was delivered through these articulations had the desired impact. The electricity grid responded to what one may call the 'war cry' of the local inhabitants. Immediate contact was established with the activists of the Chipko movement. They reasoned that in order to lay fifty meters of electricity cables, at least ninety thousand trees have to be removed. Nearly sixty six thousand trees of these were in the Raja Ji National Park alone. Raja Ji National Park is a protected forest zone and even the natives of the area are not allowed to cut grass or even remove fallen twigs from the protected forest. It was ironical that in the same protected ecological zone 90,000 trees were ordered to be removed in the name of development. Some local activists took the matter to the Supreme Court of India. The Supreme Court through an interim order stopped cutting of the trees till further orders. The fear of losing enormous forest wealth, still looms large in the thickly wooded region of Tehri Garhwal.

Two crucial points emerge in the listing of the above events. First relates to a total neglect of ecological concerns by development planners and second relates to dependence on legal recourse for temporary suspension of 'planned destruction'. Customary protest can initiate a process but it is not necessarily capable of achieving desired results. There is need for a second level of oganizational planning and mobility to achieve the desired objective.

It is important to locate the discourse on ecological movements in the context of development planning. This study makes the disconnect that exists between development planning and conservation more than apparent. Attention, may also be paid to deceit and how measures are taken to circumvent delays by making minimal projections of damages. For instance in this particular case, a survey was conducted by the forest department in the year 1994 and the number of trees counted for clearing was much less than the later proposed 90,000. While giving clearance to the project, the ministry of environment and forest did not even bother to examine the ground reality. Local activists argue that it is quite unbelievable that over a stretch of 170 meters, only 90,000 trees are being cleared. They believe that the number is likely to be much more. The chipko activists believe that between Tehri Garhwal and Agarkhal, more than one lakh trees are likely to be removed for this project. The activists also assert that the forest department has deliberately underestimated the loss of forest wealth. They have only counted adult trees, which are more than ten years old. The loss of other vegetation and the trees, which are less than ten years old is not even accounted for. The forest department has also argued that a massive re-plantation is already in place in the adjacent Hardoi forest to counter the loss of natural wealth in the Havelighat.

What emerges in this narrative is largely a question of ethics. The yardstick for determining ethical concerns is different for the planning at the centre for development and has entirely different meaning for smaller and regional players. For the local people it is primarily environmental degradation, quality of life and issues of livelihood that are critical. There is a whole range of social and personal concerns that each participant in the protest movement can envisage for himself and others in the area. The development planner is rooted in the philosophy of 'assumed technological excellence'—but the activist is facing challenges of survival and loss of his civilization that is anchored by nature. It is a conflict that any modern nation state is likely to confront in its aspiration for material well being.

In 1980 and 1981, the Chipko movement was able to curtail destruction of forest cover in the Havelighat and Himalayan region. The present protest in the Havelighat region is asking for the removal of ten electricity poles from Advani and the suspension of the project pursued by RPG that encroaches thick forest cover. It is interesting to quote some results from a study conducted in the USA. The study reported that 65% respondents owing some commitment to environmentalism supported the view that it would be better if people lived a simple life without too much technology. In the survey 65% of the respondents also argued that:

> if the price of a beautiful and health full environment is the cessation of further economic growth, it is a price worth paying (Mitchell 1980:347).

Unfortunately there is increasing void between the way committed local environmental activists perceive environmental concerns and the way environmental bodies like the ministry of forest and environment or other regional and local bodies involved in development and environment protection visualize the emergent needs.

The resurrection of chipko movement in Havelghat is a classic the 'soft technological thinking' that is articulated by those occupying positions in the decision making bodies. The argument is that electricity is crucial for development and to ensure that if a few thousand trees are to be crucified, it is worth the bargain. In the past ten to twelve years, every time I had a debate with people who mattered in the official echelons of forest and environment management, I have always received a dressing down for having oriental views. It is thus encouraging for me to record—however insignificant they may be—the continuous success stories that emanate from chipko and successive ecological movements. Success in this context is not necessarily measured by what people involved in these movements achieve, but what they inspire.

Prasun (2003) follows through what happened after Havelighat protest was launched in the year 2001. On 15 October 2001, the sub-divisional magistrate of the region convened a meeting of the power grid and representatives of the '*rakhi* bandho-pade bachao' movement. He reports that after prolonged discussions, power grid officials expressed their helplessness in altering the course of cables. The only conversion they were willing to offer was that instead of removing trees from 83 meters belt marked in 1994, they will now cut trees only on a belt of 36 meters. The surprising part of this discussion was that the central forest and environment ministry had already written to the Uttaranchal power grid authorities to utilize existing cables or to change cables that were passing through the forest belt in Narendra Nagar and Dehradun. But the power grid officials failed to mention that communication, and when activists confronted them with a copy of that letter which was supposed to be confidential, the officials had no worthy reply.

Sociological enquiry would reconstruct these events through a macro analysis. It will not only concentrate on examining matrices that look into appropriate technology concerns but also probe hidden factors pertaining to structures of economic and political relations and incursions of state and corporate power. As it is obvious, there were visible differences between the perception of the central ministry and the local managers within the power grid. Engagement of the corporate sector implementing the project with the local hierarchies is also visible. When power nexus is actualized it provides benefits to a few individuals, who act for their personal interests at the expense of hundreds of others and their immediate surroundings. In such situations local activists are left with hardly any choice. They either persist with the existing mode of protest, constantly wealing under moral pressure; or move public interest litigations believing in the fair judgement of the judges. The ecological protest movements in the Himalayan region have always operated within the structural principles of democracy and democratic institutions.

In pursuance of democratic and constitutional provisions, Jaiprakash Dabral from Advani filed a public interest litigation challenging the decision of power grid to cut trees in the forest region of Advani, Agarkhala and Kurala. A litigation on similar lines filed by officials of Raja Ji Park was already pending in the court. Fresh estimates worked out by activists and officials of Raja Ji National Park suggested that if power grid persisted with the present design, nearly five lakh trees were likely to be destroyed. The Supreme Court in a landmark judgement ordered that the overhead cables shall not pass through the national park, instead these cables would run parallel to electricity cables running from Rishikesh to Haridwar. They also advised the power grid to ensure that the procedure of laying cables has no adverse impact on the existing forest cover. The Supreme Court also ordered that the height of power towers should be raised from 43 to 60 metres. Prasun points out that despite these measures nearly 14,739 trees in the vicinity of Raja Ji Park will be sacrificed.

The narrative presented in this article is a sad commentary on how indifference of those entrusted with the task of providing appropriate technology fuel protest movements and, sometimes, ensuing violence. Irrespective of Supreme Court orders, the power grid failed to identify an alternative route for the remaining belt for which there were no specific directions. This resulted in a series of protests beginning 10 December 2002. A procession of villagers and activists marched to the offices of power grid carrying torches and ceremonial lights called *Bhailo.* Now the traditional slogan was revised and specific attack on power grid was launched. The folk songs created for the occasion said:

> Himalayas shall rise again and ensure that power grid is destroyed. If axes shine again, we shall embrace the trees; and to this they added—those wires running over our villages are a sign of impending disaster, stop it or we shall destroy it.

The procession marched from Advani to Rishikesh. It was for the first time that protest was launched on such a massive scale. To my enthnographic instinct, it was the element of folk culture and village solidarity that was most exciting. The protests were rhymed in folk tunes, and a folk dance called *Mandan* was organized on the occasion. The traditional symbolic lamps earlier lighted only on the occasion of Diwali were carried by protesters to send a message across conveying that brightness is not an attribute of electricity bulbs but the vision people have of their future.

The protest mingled with celebration and supported by a galaxy of local leadership was symbolic enough to shake the sleeping bosses of Uttaranchal power grid. The power of only this protest demonstration succeeded in making officials concede to drop plans of constructing a strip that was only 39 meters long and not 85 meters as was planned earlier. However, power grid employees were in for surprise, when on 7 January 2003, a high powered committee constituted by Supreme Court surveyed the belt and in its preliminary report endorsed the demands of the chipko activists and tentatively approved the alternative plan proposed by them. The plan was aborted as villagers living in Ganga Saagar refused to allow cables to pass through their fields. The ultimate plan proposed that instead of 85-meter long belt earmarked in the beginning for clearing, the clearing will now restrict itself to three belts of four meters width each. Their major achievement was that instead of thousands of trees initially marked for clearing, only 756 trees would be eventually chopped. The primary regret that activists had was that they were not able to divert the course of the 800 kilowatt cable that would finally pass through thick forest cover and pose a potential threat to the entire vegetation cover in the region.

Contested resources and power dynamics

Out of all the articles short-listed from *Yugvani* for this essay, two articles written by Prasun are used as basic resource material for understanding meanings attached to ecological debates in the local discourse. Prasun (2003) makes some explicit and certain other implicit statements. The article entitled in Hindi reads: *'Kya Chipko ka garbhpat ho gaya hai* ('Is Chipko aborted?')—the connotation is implicit. The former chipko activists believe that the success chipko had in its formative stage is not visible now. Prasun too concludes to this effect. He constructs two power centres—one being 'state power' that we may qualify here as 'legitimate power', enjoyed by the democratically elected government and its representative institutions, for instance law courts in this case. The other power that he talks about is 'power of the people' expressed in 'collective action' in the form of protest. Prasun's argument is that in 1978, it was 'people's power' that won because the provincial police was forced to withdraw from the scene. But, in this chapter of the Andolan the movement activists were forced to comply because of the judicial intervention. It is a matter of analytical importance for understanding the operational dynamics of a 'protest movement'. The protesters file public interest litigations to protect natural resources. At the same time they lament that because of judicial intervention 'people's power' was not able to exercise its desired control. According to Prasun, success achieved by the people's movement met its objective in 1978, because people's will ultimately ruled. The movement was however aborted in 2003 as people were not able to achieve what they desired at the outset of the agitation. Partial success in restricting the number of trees to be axed or minor diversion in the route of overhead cables was not enough from the point of the local people.

Protest movement and political ecology debate

The state of Uttaranchal has always had a special place in the environmental debate in India. Not only that 'the unquiet wood' (Guha 1991) is located in the region, India's renowned eco-feminist Vandana Shiva hails from the region and has written extensively about it. Guha in his analysis of chipko movement refers to it as a social movement. The format of his interpretation hinges upon 'interconnections' between chipko and different aspects of state interventions, scientific forestry in particular and, more generally the administrative policies followed by different governments—*it examines* changing relationship between the state and the peasantry—to this he adds the importance of changes brought about in the social structure because of 'money order' economy forcing heavy out migration and centrality of women in economic life *and establishes this as a* 'structural constant' (1991:152). With respect to enduring and organizational form of chipko, Guha posits three major questions—nature of leadership, the ecological clashes between different subcultures of the movement and the redefinition of the relations between sexes. Regarding goals mooted by the movement Guha outlines 'presentations to the state and the general public' with alternative strategies of resource use and social development and encompassing of other social issues (1991:153).

At this stage of the discussion, I want to introduce the concept of political ecology. Part of my understanding of the concept emanates from listening to, and reading through texts generated by Michael Watts. Political ecology seeks to understand the complex relations between nature and society through careful analysis of what one might call the forms of access and control over resources and their implications for environmental health and sustainable livelihood (Watts 2003). This notion is further elucidated by his argument that:

> nature is now deeply embedded in late twentieth century political identities; and is central to the new political ecology as a sensitivity to environmental politics as a process of cultural mobilization and the ways in which such cultural practices—whether science of 'traditional' knowledge or discourse, or risk, or property rights—are contested fought over and negotiated (2003:2-3).

To illustrate the concept Watts cites Blaikie and Brookfield's (1987:17) construction of the phrase 'political ecology', which combines the concern of ecology and a broadly defined political economy. Together this encompasses the constantly shifting dialectic, between society and a broadly defined political economy and also encompasses the constantly shifting dialectics between society and land based resources, and also within classes and groups within society itself: to appropriate these notions/concepts to Uttaranchal story, I want to borrow the following paragraph from Watts (2003).

> The work of Blaikie and Brookfield (1987), and their notion of political ecology (PE), can plausibly be taken as an exemplary formulation of PE perspective. In their view it contains three essential assumptions. The first is interactive, contradictory and dialectical: society and land based resources are mutually causal in such a way that poverty can induce, via poor management, environmental degradation which itself deepens poverty (p. 48). Second, Blaikie and Brookfield argue for

> regional or spatial accounts of degradation which link through "chains of explanation" (p. 46) local decision makers to spatial variations in environmental" structures (stability and resilience as traits of particular ecosystem in particular). Locality studies are, thus subsumed within multi-layered analyses pitched at a variety of regional scales.. And third, land management is framed by 'external structures', which in the lexicon of PE means the role of state (p. 17), the core periphery model (p. 18), and almost every element in the world economy (p. 68).

The history of political ecology is rooted in colonial legacy. Dolby (2003) and Li (2003) have argued that colonial ecological interventions, especially in deforestation and subsequently in forest conservation had more impact than the colonial rule. The argument further asserts that over the period 1670 to 1950, a pattern of power relations emerged in which the expanding European states acquired a global reach over natural resources in terms of consumption and that too, in terms of political and ecological control (cf. Dolby 2003). In political ecology discourse, it is frequently pointed out that the colonial legacy continues to flourish, even within well defined democratic systems (Dolby 2003:12-13). Neumann (1999) in a telling commentary demonstrates how local political forces administer the parks, forests and rivers, the population and their participation in commercial markets, contributing to reproducing the colonial pattern in post-colonial states. The story in Havelighat and Advani is very much in tune with these observations.

Guha in his analysis of various protest movements clubbed under chipko traces its defining movement in the events of 25 March 1974 in Reni. In his words it was then that:

> Chipko came into its own as a peasant movement in defence of traditional forest rights, continuing a

> century long tradition of resistance to state encroachment (1994:160).

While looking for a cultural space within which chipko is located, Guha reasons that persistence of community spirit is partially responsible for chipko's success. Otherwise the social fabric of the villages, the geographical spaces of chipko are experiencing intense transformation. The money order economy, 'underdevelopment of the hills', 'commercial forestry', 'exploitation of the woods by timber merchants', 'availability of the motorable road' and greater involvement of women in the economy resulted in social differentiation that were hitherto not known to the local communities. A fact that is repeatedly emphasized in Guha's and other ecologists' work from India is related to popular prevalence of 'ecological consciousness' among the local communities. The debate thus centers on shifts in state control and power dynamics in 'management' procedures. It also zones itself in domains that are articulated by local leadership.

Li in her work from Indonesia (2002; 2003) has clearly demonstrated that a concept of ecological movements based on a model that categorizes 'virtuous peasant' versus 'vicious states' (based on Bernstein 1990) neglects to specify the diversity of peasant interests, and positions them as pure subjects resisting power from outside. Nor does it account for the diversity of state projects, many of which are not intentionally vicious but aim to bring about some kind of development or improvement.

Let me try and re-contextualize Li's understanding and theoretical premise of political ecology debate in the ethnographic text of this essay. I would also like to incorporate articulations by local leadership and charisma associated with it as critical instrumentalities in structuring these 'protest movements'. Two articles by Prasun that form the ethnographic core of this analysis are representative on two accounts. Prasun who was one of the key members and motivators of the Chipko Andolan in 1978-79 (Guha 1992) in a reflexive discourse assumes that 'chipko is aborted' as they were not able to achieve total retraction of the state in the Havelghat contestations. He also embarks on an ambiguous discourse that he is disillusioned with the 'channels'—judiciary, state, representation—created for negotiation. These channels in his opinion deprive the protesters of their power of negotiation. In 1978, the potential of these channels was not appropriately conceived and the state was under immense pressure, which was largely generated by local level leadership. As a consequence, the state was forced to withdraw, leaving space to the community leadership to proclaim total success.

When we traverse through the unquiet woods and relocate sequence of events, protest emerges as the theme that local leadership successfully manipulates to establish a representativeness. Is this truly representative of the people's voices is a fact that is difficult to establish through any anthropological enquiry. What is significant is that through these protests a course for local ecological histories and a narrative for political formulations are chartered. Prasun's grievance is that if the judiciary had not interfered, the 2001-2003 protests would have reached its zenith as it did in 1978. There is melancholy in his writings that seems to result from a sense of loss of political supremacy, whose content is rooted in ecological concerns of the people. This interplay between ecology and politics and potentialities inherent in it in determining local political histories is crucial in understanding environmental dynamics along with the growth of the democratic processes that legitimatize 'protest'. It is another matter that those participating in the 'protest' draw their own yardsticks to measure success. For the leadership, the present phase of chipko was a partial success, but for an average participant there was a sense of satisfaction, as they believed that they had made the 'ruler'—the state in this instance—aware of their grievances. People also believed that by participating in demonstrations, they were able to assent their civic status and importance of their rationality and understanding of their immediate surroundings. But for those representing power grid it was a challenge to their expertise and 'better techno-economic' judgement and for the 'state' it was another political deterrent that had to be tackled. In this frame of analysis, even though environmental degradation is posed as 'movement goals', the agenda spans domains which are much larger than 'livelihood' or sustainable development. This was one of the reasons that at the outset, after prolonged deliberations that I decided to delete the qualifier 'ecology' from the title of the paper.

I am not even comfortable placing it in the ambit of 'peasant movement' as Guha has illustrated with remarkable dexterity. Application of epithet 'peasant' to a collectivity of rural and tribal communities who are primary producers and conform to the perception of a society stratified on economic classes and principles of state formation is problematic. But to debate 'who are peasants' or whether we can locate them within the confines of epithets used to define them is not part of the text of this essay. What interests me in Guha's analysis is the focus on 'moral religious sanction' that 'protest' has in this context; that is lighting of lamps, ritually lighted only on the occasion of Diwali, tying *rakhi* to trees by both men and women symbolizing 'moral protection' offered by the stronger of the species to its weaker siblings, performing ceremonial dances outside the office of the power grid, miles away from home—what may be described as alien and hostile environment—is an effective demonstration of how the leadership encashes twin edged sword of morality and religious sentimentality.

When I started exploring 'transnational agenda on environmentalism' with my colleague Pris Weeks (Weeks & Mehta 2001), we were taken in by WWF International's open agenda, espousing religious symbols and sentimentalities associated with the construct of 'sacredness'. I for one was somewhat surprised on being informed that the Vrindavan project of WWF had invited Asa Ram Bapu—a prominent religious leader from the region—to distribute *kadam* trees as part of its conservation programme. To my mind it was unprecedented. The field and central staff of WWF thought that the move was perfectly justified as it helped to achieve the desired objective. It is the similarity in the rhetoric of 'protest' and 'protect' movements generated at two polarities of management that is striking. What is significant in this debate is how 'rhetoric' is translated in legitimacies and transported under two apparently opposing contestations!

ACKNOWLEDGEMENTS

This research was assisted by a fellowship from the South Asia Program of the Social Science Research Council with funds provided by the Ford Foundation. I am particularly grateful to Itty Abraham and his team for putting together a great team of experts on the theme of "Contested resources". The meeting in Kathmandu helped in clarifying various concepts and constructs.

NOTES

1. Social scientists even now remain at the periphery of environmental management programmes. The responsibility may be partly theirs; partly the way issues relating to environment continue to be perceived in India. Science and economics together alienated the rationality rooted in philosophy of science and survival.

2. The title of the paper may appear incomplete to many. I debated and finally deliberately omitted the construct of

'ecological'/'environmental' from the title, retaining only 'protest' to convey the text of the paper. This deletion may be attributed to my understanding of Escobar's (1995) explanation that many of these movements were in no simple sense 'environmental' since they typically combined human rights, ethnicity/identity and questions of social justice.

3. Martinez-Alier remarked that none of the three major schools of economic theory-neo-classical, Keynesian and Marxian paid any attention to biophysical realities, Guha citing Martinez-Alier supports similar views (Guha 1994).

4. Contributions made by Singh (1976), Kumarappa (1931; 1938), Joshi (1986) Gadgil and Guha (1992), are some important works that were deliberately put aside by leading politicians and policy planners. Even Gandhi's minimalist approach to material goods was not appreciated by a class of leadership that was enamoured by 'consumption centered' industrial growth.

5. *Raksha Sutra,* a sacred band that binds a brother to his sister, and assures her life long security against all odds.

6. NSF Project Report (Weeks and Mehta 2001). In this report we discussed various heuristic schemes found in the literature to describe US and Indian environmentalist groups. We observed that Indian groups have been categorized according to ideological orientation (Gandhian, Marxists, appropriate technologists; anarchists); leadership (corporation run, NGO); Orientation (Conservation, Livelihood and Environment, Human Rights, Pollution, Health); and Volunteerism versus NGO. However, we did not borrow any one of these standard classificatory schemes as each of these schemes is historically and socially rooted and does not map onto each other.

7. Guha (1991:7) while discussing links between 'structure of domination and idioms of protest divides Uttarakahand between 1851-1949 into two distinct socio-political systems-the princely state of Tehri Garhwal and the colonial territory of Kumaun. Within these territories, he talks about prevalence of what Weber called 'traditional authority' and 'bureaucratic authority'.

8. Gluckman's famous analysis of custom and rebellion in tribal Africa is used as the heuristic tool by Guha to

understand the changing dynamics of peasant rebellion in Uttarakhand. Gluckman modified the functionlist model and assumed that ritual expression of conflict was ultimately responsible for bringing order in societies.

8. Rebellions are like revitalization movements. Revitalization movements in many instances may not remain religious in character but acquire a much wider meaning becoming social and political in character. Rebellions also like revitalization movements may become institutionalized and embrace many diverse actions, conflicts within its rubric.

9. In the context of Chipko, Watts, (2003) arguments are:

   Communities are to be understood in terms of hegemonies: not everyone participates or benefits equally in the construction of reproduction of the communities, or from the claims made in the name of community interest. And this is exactly what is at stake in the current political ecology work on the infamous tree hugging or Chipko movement in North India.

10. Smith (1986) defines the peasantry as a class of primary producers within a society characterized by the existence of social classes and state formation—within the category of agrarian peasantry itself there is considerable disagreement as to the exact defining characteristics of this social type, and the term is commonly used to refer to a wide range of cultivators whose relationships to the land (owners, tenants, share croppers) and to the market vary considerably.

REFERENCES

Bardhan, P.

1984 *The Political Economy of India's Development.* New Delhi: Oxford University Press.

Blaikie, P. and Brookfield

1987 *Land Degradation and Society.* London: Methuen.

Bryant, R. and Bailey

1997 *Third World Political Ecology.* London: Routledge.

Darnovsky, M., B. Epstein, and F. Richard (ed.)

1995 *Cultural Politics and Social Movements*, Philedelphia: Temple University Press.

Dolby, S.

1996 'The environment as geopolitical threat', *Eumene*, 3:472-96.

2003 'Resources and conflict: Contesting constructions of environmental security'. Paper presented at the Resources: Conceptions and Contestations Conference at Kathmandu, 4-12 January 2003.

Escobar, A.

1995 *Encountering Development*. Princeton: Princeton University Press.

Gadgil, M.

1983 'Forestry with a social purpose'. In Walter Fernandes and S. Kulkarni (eds.) *Towards a New Forest Policy*. New Delhi: Indian Social Institute.

Guha, Ramachandra

1983 'Forestry in British and post British India: A historical analysis' *Economic and Political Weekly*.

1991 *The Unquiet Woods: Ecological Change and Peasant Resistance in the Himalaya*. Delhi: Oxford University Press.

Guha, Ramachandra (ed.)

1994 Social *Ecology:* Delhi: Oxford University Press.

Guha, Ramachandra and Madhav Gadgil

1989 'State forestry and social conflicts in British India, *Past and Present*.

Gluckman, Max

1963 *Order and Rebellion in Tribal Africa*. Manchester: University of Manchester Press.

Joshi, P.C.

1986 'Founders of the Lucknow school and their legacy', *Economic and Political Weekly.*

Kumarappa, J.C.

1931 *An Economic Survey of Matar Taluka.* Ahmedabad: Gujarat Vidyapeeth.

1938 *Why the Village Movement?.* Wardha: All India Village Industries Association.

Li, Tania Murray

2002 'Local histories, global markets: Coca and class in Upland Sulawesi,' *Development and Change,* 33(3):415-437.

2003 'Layered landscapes of government and belonging'. Paper presented at the Resources: Conceptions and Contestations Conference, Kathmandu 4-12 January.

Martinez-Alier, J.

1989 'Poverty as a cause of environmental degradation'. Unpublished manuscript prepared for the World Bank (Latin American Division), Washington, D.C.

Mitchell, Robert Cameron

1980 'How "Soft, deep or left?" present constituencies in the environmental movement for certain world views', *Natural Resource Journal,* 20: 345-355.

Max, Karl

1842 'Debate on the law of thefts of wood', *Collected Works,* Vol. 1.

Nadel, S.F.

Foundations of Social Anthropology. London: Cohen & West.

Neumann

1999 *Imposing Wilderness.* Berkely: University of California Press.

Prasun, Kunwar

2001 *'Havelghatt main phir Chipko ki dastak'*, *Yugvani* (Hindi), 1(10):14-15.

2003 *'Kya Chipko andolan ka garbhpat ho gaya hai?'*, *Yugvani* (Hindi), 3(4): 14-16.

Singh, Narinder

1976 *Economics and Crisis of Ecology*. New Delhi: Oxford University Press.

Smith, C.S.

1986 *Macmillan Dictionary of Anthropology*.

Taylor, Bron. R. (ed.)

1995 *Ecological Resistance Movements*. New York: New York University Press.

Watts, M.

2003 'Political ecology'; Resource material for the annual conference on Resources: Conception and Contestations, Kathmandu 2-3 January.

Weeks, Pris and Shalina Mehta

2001 *'Transnational Environmentalism and In-country Environmental organizations'*. Report submitted to National Science Foundation. U.S.A.

19

Land and Agriculture among Scheduled Tribes in Maharashtra

B.B. Mohanty

Land is the pivotal property in rural India in terms of both income and employment. It is also the source of socio-political status and power around which socio-economic privileges and deprivations revolve. Though the members of tribes mostly reside in the countryside and derive their livelihood by working on land, they are the most disadvantaged groups in respect to it. Keeping in view their poor land ownership position that results in perpetual poverty and makes them vulnerable to social injustice and exploitation, systematic attempts have been made by the union and state governments to protect and promote their landholding position. Besides, efforts have been made to modernise their agricultural practices through various measures.

Following the national guidelines, the erstwhile state of Bombay and the present state of Maharashtra launched a package of land reforms for promoting the landholding position of the scheduled communities. Along with the legislative and allied measures for the improvement of landholdings, the government of Maharashtra has made elaborate and continuous efforts to boost agricultural production by bringing more land under cultivation, improving the quality and extent of irrigation, and inducing changes in the cropping pattern through expansion of cash crop cultivation, introduction of high yielding varieties (HYVs), adoption of new agricultural machinery and implements, etc. Apart from the general programmes of agricultural development, the state government has made special efforts through the Tribal Sub-Plan for the improvement of the landholding and agricultural practices among scheduled tribes.

In this context, it is imperative to analyse how far the collective impact of these measures has influenced the landholding and its use by the tribal communities, as it is of a major policy concern. Moreover, they constitute more than 9 per cent of the total population of the state with over 87 per cent of scheduled tribes living in rural areas with agriculture as the principal source of livelihood, as per the 1991 census.

There are a number of studies, which directly or indirectly deal with the land problems of scheduled tribes (Fuchs 1972; Kulkarni 1974; Patel 1979; Upadhyaya 1980; Rao 1987; Murdia 1975; Chakrabarty 1998; Mohanty 1997, 2000, 2001a). These studies have highlighted the problem of land alienation and the impact of land transfer regulations in the tribal areas.

A review of these studies reveals that a number of them were undertaken in the early phase of land reform measures. They largely confined their analysis to landholding position and ignored the aspects of agricultural practices. As most of them were conducted in other parts of the country their findings may not fit neatly into the situation in Maharashtra due to its different agro-climatic and socio-economic features as well as historical conditions. Though there are a few studies on scheduled tribes in Maharashtra, they have very briefly or tangentially attended the issues relating to landholding and agricultural practices (Nadkarni 1988). Studies involving an analysis both at the macro and micro levels are almost non-existent. Against this backdrop, the present study attempts to look into the aspects of landholding and agricultural practices of scheduled tribes in Maharashtra.

II

After Independence land reforms became a part of the planning process in the erstwhile state of Bombay and the present state of Maharashtra. Keeping in view the widespread agrarian discontent revolving around exploitative land and labour relations, some measures were also taken earlier by the colonial government. The important legislations were the Bombay Land Revenue Code, 1879, Central Provinces and Berar Act, 1939, Berar Alienated Villages Tenancy Law, 1921 and Berar Forest Law, 1886. But the reform measures launched in the post-independence period are more elaborate and comprehensive. They are the Bombay Tenancy and Agricultural Lands Act, 1948, the Bombay Tenancy and Agricultural Lands (Vidarbha Region and Kutch Area) Act, 1958 and Maharashtra Agricultural Land (Ceiling of Holding) Act, 1961. The major objectives of these legislations are: a) abolition of intermediaries, b) tenancy reforms; c) fixation of ceiling and distribution of surplus land, and d) consolidation of holdings. Despite inherent loopholes as reported by many studies (Dandekar and Khudanpur 1957, Shah and Sawant 1973; Mohanty 1999), many of these measures particularly the imposition of ceiling laws and the distribution of ceiling surplus land, have benefited scheduled communities. It is reported that as on December 1995, over 6,43,316 acres have been declared as ceiling surplus land of which 15 per cent has been distributed to the scheduled tribe beneficiaries (Mohanty 2001b). According to a more recent estimate (NIRD 1999), in the state as a whole, 7,29,644 acres of land has been declared as ceiling surplus as on 31 March 1999 and 76 per cent of this land has been distributed to the landless families. Of the distributed land, 17 per cent has been given to the scheduled tribe beneficiaries. Besides, a sizeable amount of land was also obtained and distributed among scheduled tribes through Bhoodan movement initiated by Vinoba Bhave. As on 31 March 1981, 88,462 acres of land were available for distribution through this scheme of which 15.80 per cent has been allotted to scheduled tribes (Commissioner 1980-81).

In addition to these, a package of specific measures has also been formulated to allot land to scheduled communities as well as to protect it from being transferred to non-scheduled communities. The Maharashtra Land Revenue Code and Tenancy Laws (Amendment) Act, 1974 provide for the restoration of agricultural land of a scheduled tribe person if it is illegally transferred to a non-scheduled tribe person, affected before 6 July 1974. The other legislative measures like the Maharashtra Restoration of Land to the Scheduled Tribes Act, 1974, Maharashtra Land Revenue Code, 1966 (Section-36), Bombay Tenancy and Agricultural Lands Act, 1948, Bombay Tenancy and Assignment Lands (Vidarbha Region) Act, 1958 and Hyderabad Tenancy and Agricultural Lands Act, 1950 contain provisions for restoration of agricultural land of scheduled tribes lawfully transferred to non-scheduled tribes by way of sale, mortgage, gift, etc. The government issued executive orders on 4 January 1961 for the disposal of land among scheduled tribes as the second priority. However, in the areas other than scheduled areas, they have been accorded only the seventh priority. It is reported (MRD 1999-2000) that, as on November 1999, 45,634 land alienation cases were filed in the courts. Though a majority of the registered cases were rejected and some of them were pending in the court, 43.70 per cent of them were decided in favour of the tribals.

The collective impact of these developments on the landholding position of scheduled tribes can be assessed by making an analysis of the changes in their operational holdings. However, as data on the operational holdings of scheduled communities are available only from 1980-81, it is difficult to assess the total impact of legislative measures because many of them have been implemented since the late sixties and early seventies. Nevertheless, an analysis of the trend of operational holdings will be useful in making the discussion on the aspects of land distribution more meaningful.

The size class wise information (Table 1) reveals that the operational holdings of the tribals have increased considerably over the years in terms of area as well as number. The number and area of operational holdings among the scheduled tribes increased from 6.02 per cent and 6.08 per cent respectively in 1980-81 to 6.69 and 7.32 per cent respectively in 1990-91. It may be noted that the scheduled tribes have witnessed an increase in the percentage of the large and medium operational holdings to that of the total large and medium holdings in the state.

Looking at the operational landholders of various size classes within the scheduled tribes, it is found that they mostly belong to the small and marginal groups (Table 2). More than 60 percent of the scheduled tribe holders belong to the small and marginal size groups. It is observed that there is an increasing trend of number and area of the marginal and small holders accompanied by a corresponding decline in that of the large and medium holders among them. The increase in the number of the small and marginal holders may be partly due to the division of large and medium holdings owing to family partitioning caused by population growth and partly to the allotment of small pieces of land through land reform measures.

On the whole, the share of land of scheduled tribes has improved and it seems they have acquired lands from other groups also. The landholding position of scheduled tribes can be considered good when compared to their demographic strength. Primarily due to the fact that scheduled tribes were not originally landless and a plenty of land was under their control the improvement in their land ownership status in the state can not be attributed to land reform measures alone. It is also due to the impact of strong movements of the tribes in some areas against the upper caste landed interests. The well organised agitation of tribals such as the Shramik Sangathan movement of the Bhils in Dhule and Gadchiroli districts against the alienation of tribal lands in early seventies and the Warli movement of Kolis in Thane district put mounting pressure on the administration to promote and protect their land rights. Apart from this, the impact of urbanisation and the effects of economic development also have enabled a section of them to buy land from the land market (Omvedt 1994; Mohanty 2001b).

Notwithstanding the signs of positive changes, scheduled tribes control 10 per cent of the area with a population of 9.3 per cent. Nevertheless, viewed in a comparative perspective, the state has shown a noticeable improvement over the years (Table 3). Though the position is not as good as in West Bengal, it is much better as compared to many other states. The better achievement of Maharashtra with regard to the improvement of landholding position of scheduled tribes has also been reported by many other studies (Nanekar 1968; Rao 1972; Rajasekaran 1998; Mohanty 2001a).

As land belonging to these communities is largely unirrigated, its use for agricultural purposes is dependent on rainfall. However, there has been a substantial growth of irrigated land over the years (Table 4). Area of irrigable land among scheduled tribes rose from 3.22 per cent during the period 1980-81 to 8.77 in 1990-91. The growth is higher among the medium and large holders. As per the

1990-91 position, there are minimum differences in the ratio of irrigated land among the size classes of scheduled tribes.

Looking at the land use pattern (Table 4), it is found that the net cultivated area has grown up to 94 per cent in 1990-91 as against 88 per cent in 1980-81 among the scheduled tribes. The growth rate is higher among the large holders possibly because of the decline in their total area. However, the percentage of net cultivated area is relatively higher among the marginal and small holders. This is understandable in view of their need to increase the farm income from their meagre holdings. More than 90 per cent of the cultivated area across the size classes comes under net sown area. However, in the case of the large holders it is considerably less. The proportion of uncultivated land and the land not available for cultivation shows a continuous declining trend and the percentage of total area under these uses is negligible across the size classes. It seems that the landholders of these communities are gradually expanding their cultivable area by making other categories of land cultivable.

The data on cropping pattern (Table 5) shows that the cultivators are largely food grain growers. More than 70 per cent of the gross cropped area is covered by the food grain crops. The smaller the land size, the greater is the area under food grains. Possibly due to lack of irrigation facilities coupled with economic constraints and limited skill and knowledge they fail to expand their area under capital-intensive and profitable cash crops. However, the large holders have shown signs of change. The low cropping intensity of 107.82 is found among scheduled tribes due to relatively less irrigation facilities and rough terrain. It is noted that cropping intensity decreases when the size of holdings increases. The aspects of landholding and use pattern among the scheduled tribes can be substantiated in more detail by analysing the situation at the micro level.

III

For examining empirically the landholding position of scheduled tribes and the nature of their agricultural practices at the micro-level, district Dhule which is known for its high concentration of scheduled tribe population in the state was selected. One taluka from the district, namely, Akrani was chosen for drawing the sample households. A sample of 50 households was drawn from various categories of landowning households (marginal, small, semi-medium, medium and large as defined by the agricultural census). However, there were only three scheduled tribe landholders from the large holding group.

The landholding pattern and agricultural practices of the sample scheduled tribe households are shown in Table 6. It is seen that the scheduled tribe households have acquired land mostly through inheritance. The allotment of land through land reforms is negligible. Only 3 per cent of their owned area can be attributed to these measures. Among the size classes, only the small and semi-medium holders have received around 10 per cent of their owned land as a result of land reform programmes. Moreover, none of the scheduled tribe landholders has been able to buy land from the open market. The large holders of this category have acquired a considerable portion of land through encroachment. It is reported that the encroachment on forest land is not uncommon in the tribal areas. Those who have relatively better economic position encroach these lands and make them cultivable by managing the *talathis* and local level revenue officials. As the tribals are mostly illiterate and unaware of the land laws, they accept the claims of the revenue officials. Sometimes these officials demand regular payment either in cash or kind.

Besides, due to the restrictions on land transfers from scheduled tribes to others, the incidence of land sales is not reported in the studied villages. However, in the tribal areas it is reported that though transfer of land through sale, mortgage or gift from the members of the scheduled tribes is prohibited, many of the tribal landholders have mortgaged their land with the non-tribal moneylenders under oral or informal agreements with some of the senior members of the village as witnesses who are often consulted in matters of special importance. The moneylender leases out the land to some of the cultivators of the same village or cultivates it himself using the available cheap *adivasi* labour force. The land remains with the moneylender till the loan is repaid and he cultivates the land in lieu of interest. Over 10 per cent of the land of the sample holders are mortgaged with the moneylenders and most of them are small and marginal holders.

Besides, an analysis of the changes in landholding position of the sample households over the last ten years indicates that excepting some improvement here and there, the overall landholding position of the scheduled tribe farmers has declined further. Of course, the reliability of these data is limited to the memory of the respondents. The lands of the scheduled tribes lack irrigation facilities since only 5 per cent land of scheduled tribes is irrigated. Therefore, their agricultural land use practices are mostly dependent on rainfall.

It was found that among the scheduled tribe farmers, 86 per cent of their total land comes under the plough. The marginal farmers of this category have put 98 per cent of their land to agricultural use. Though the semi-medium and medium holders have also a relatively higher proportion of cultivated area, the small and large holders have a considerable portion of area, which is not cultivated or not available for cultivation. The land not available for cultivation comes to 16.57 and 12.39 per cent of the total land of the small and the large holders respectively. It is attributed to the fact that these lands are barren, uncultivable and mostly covered by forests. The proportion of net sown area of these farmers is less, though the percentage is higher in the case of the marginal and semi-medium holders, it is considerably less among the large holders because 26 per cent of their cultivable land is reported as current fallow land. The current fallow land of the small holders is also not insignificant (8.7 per cent). A relatively higher proportion of fallow land among the tribals is primarily because they cultivate certain types of land every alternate year. The cropping intensity among these farmers is also low. However, comparatively greater cropping intensity is noticed among the marginal farmers, which is attributable to a higher proportion of their land under irrigation.

The cropping pattern of the landholders of various size classes of scheduled tribes indicates that they devote their cropped area almost entirely to food crops. Their agriculture is essentially of the subsistence level in which the family consumption is the guiding factor of production. Though there are differences across the size classes, they are minimal. Lack of irrigation facilities and working funds compels them not to go in for profitable capital-intensive crops such as sugarcane, cotton, etc. Even the higher landowning farmers are reluctant to cultivate these crops. Moreover, as the influence of the monsoon on land use is predominant, the cropped area is largely under Kharif crops. As a result, the agricultural activity is confined to a part of the year and the remaining period does not provide enough farm work. Another important characteristic feature is that the cropping pattern shows a high degree of diversity. This diversification is the outcome of subsistence type of farming combined with hazardous agriculture. The farmers grow many crops which are not very suitable or appropriate from the point of view of yields and consequently of farm incomes. Thus, considerable areas are misused.

The area under HYVs is largely confined to jowar, wheat, and tur. The scheduled tribe farmers are poorly equipped to carry out the agricultural production effectively. Modern agricultural machinery such as tractors, pump sets, etc. are not seen even with the higher landowning groups. The ownership of minimum agricultural implements such as ploughs is also inadequate across the size classes. The farmers due to their poor economic position find it difficult to apply high doses of agricultural inputs. The application of chemical fertilisers by these farmers appears to be low. The tribal cultivators mostly follow their traditional method of cultivation based on the application of indigenously prepared manure and pesticides. Also, the amount of pesticide used is negligible among scheduled tribe cultivators. The scheduled tribe farmers have failed to reap the benefit of better modern inputs due to their relative geographical isolation.

The lack of working capital is one of the major reasons that prevent these farmers from adopting extensively the new technologies and associated inputs, which would result in higher yields. The credit facilities provided by the formal credit institutions have not encouraged the scheduled tribe farmers much to go for the improved methods of cultivation and doses of agricultural inputs. Though the scheduled tribe farmers have taken loans from the formal credit institutions, their average as well as per acre quantum of loan is considerably less. The per acre and average loan of marginal and small holders, which is relatively higher, covers only 38 per cent of their cost of cultivation. Excepting the large holders, the farmers of remaining size classes are more or less indebted to the private moneylenders. The large farmers have kept themselves out of the debt burden of any kind because of their subsistence farming. Given the uncertainty involved in agriculture, they also do not like to invest more by taking loans from both formal and informal sources.

The collective impact of the lack of irrigation, working capital, appropriate instruments, etc. leads to under utilization of agricultural land, which ultimately has a negative impact on agricultural income and productivity. The overall per acre productivity of scheduled tribe farmers is 1.67. The medium farmers appear to be more productive than the farmers of other size classes.

IV

The analysis both at the micro and macro levels indicates that the scheduled tribes continue to be disadvantaged with regard to land. The agriculture of tribal farmers is mostly at the subsistence level due to the lack of irrigation, credit facilities and poor resource ownership. Therefore, a mere attempt to enhance the landholding position of these communities through land reforms is naïve without a concomitant improvement in their resources, skills and expertise for the effective use of their lands. In view of this, measures like introduction of some new crops consistent with the agro-climatic conditions and socio-cultural practices which could provide a relatively higher margin of profit, provisions to familiarise the farmers with the modern technology and inputs by improving their knowledge and skill through appropriate training, distribution of minimum productive assets and expansion of formal credit facilities may be considered for policy making.

ACKNOWLEDGEMENT

The paper is a part of the larger study, 'Landholding and Use Pattern among Scheduled Castes and Scheduled Tribes in Maharashtra' sponsored by the Ministry of Agriculture, Government of India.

Table 1
Operational holdings of scheduled tribes by size class (per cent to total holdings of the state)

Size class	*Number*	*Area*
	1980-81	
Marginal	5.12	5.42
Small	6.48	6.36
Semi-medium	6.38	6.22
Medium	6.37	6.29
Large	5.81	5.56
All	6.02	6.08
	1990-91	
Marginal	5.29	5.84
Small	7.35	7.38
Semi-medium	7.41	7.35
Medium	7.68	7.66
Large	7.59	7.18
All	6.69	7.32

Source: Agricultural Census Maharashtra State.

Table 2
Operational holdings of scheduled tribes by size class (per cent to total holding of the state)

Size class	*Number*	*Area*
	1980-81	
Marginal	23.85	4.06
Small	24.17	11.42
Semi-medium	26.04	23.07
Medium	21.46	40.95
Large	4.48	20.50
All	100.00	100.00
	1990-91	
Marginal	27.31	6.17
Small	31.62	19.19
Semi-medium	24.85	28.22
Medium	14.18	34.30
Large	2.04	12.12
All	100.00	100.00

Source: Same as in Table 1.

Table 3
State wise distribution of operational holdings of scheduled tribes (%)

States	*Number*		*Area*	
	1980-81	*1990-91*	*1980-81*	*1990-91*
A.P.	6.42	6.90	6.29	7.20
Bihar	7.54	7.80	16.25	16.10
Gujarat	10.92	11.00	8.05	9.10
Karnataka	3.71	4.90	3.47	5.00
Kerala	0.98	1.20	1.50	1.90
M.P.	25.11	24.70	24.84	25.20
Maharashtra	6.02	6.70	6.08	7.30
Orissa	27.58	26.60	29.90	28.70
Punjab	0.00	0.00	0.00	0.00
Rajasthan	15.36	15.40	8.53	8.40
Tamil Nadu	0.67	0.80	1.01	1.20
U.P.	0.16	0.20	0.28	0.30
West Bengal	7.08	7.30	6.59	7.00
All India	7.71	8.10	10.20	10.80

Note: Figures are in per cent to the total number and area operated of each state.

Source: Agriculture Census Reports. Figures for 1990-91 is taken from *Agricultural Situation in India.*

Table 4
Area under different land uses (%)

Size classes	*Net cultivated area*	*Total uncultivated land*	*Land not available for cultivation*	*Net sown area*	*Irrigation ratio (% to net sown area)*
			1980-81		
Marginal	91.41	4.38	4.22	97.04	9.26
Small	91.43	5.22	3.34	96.01	5.82
Semi-medium	90.35	5.64	4.00	94.06	3.74
Medium	88.24	6.73	5.03	92.39	2.19
Large	82.44	9.39	8.17	87.81	1.63
All	88.03	6.76	5.21	92.53	3.22
			1990-91		
Marginal	96.50	1.11	2.39	96.75	9.92
Small	95.93	1.55	2.52	96.23	6.79
Semi-medium	94.77	1.73	3.50	95.00	8.48
Medium	92.27	2.68	5.05	92.85	9.66
Large	89.58	3.55	6.87	85.14	9.83
All	93.61	2.21	4.18	93.48	8.77

Source: Same as in Table 1.

Table 5

Area under crops (% to gross cropped area) and cropping intensity in 1990-91

Size classes	*Total food grains*	*Oilseeds*	*Sugarcane*	*Fibre crops*	*Fruit crops*	*Vegetables*	*Cropping intensity*
Marginal	81.95	3.84	1.28	6.21	0.49	0.52	110.38
Small	75.22	4.85	1.05	12.79	0.37	0.38	107.41
Semi-medium	72.62	5.91	1.92	11.86	1.34	0.27	109.05
Medium	66.11	9.49	2.64	11.93	0.98	0.16	107.14
Large	65.56	11.13	2.74	7.68	0.42	0.12	105.82
All	70.86	7.29	2.30	11.26	0.87	0.26	107.82

Source: Same as in Table 1.

Table 6
Details of land and agricultural practices among scheduled tribes

Sr. No.	*Particulars*	*Marginal* N=12	*Small* N=12	*Semi-medium* N=12	*Medium* N=11	*Large* N=3	*All* N=50
1	2	3	4	5	6	7	8
1.	Average size of family	8.25	7.42	7.42	6.82	7.67	7.50
2.	Per cent of illiterate members	52.53	55.06	58.43	57.33	56.52	55.73
3.	Average size of family workers	2.33	2.58	2.33	2.45	5.33	2.60
4.	Agerage holding (in acres)	1.76	3.77	7.80	13.24	26.91	7.73
5.	Per cent of increase/decrease in average holding in the last ten years	–1.12	+15.64	+5.83	–7.86	–11.94	–3.01
6.	Per cent of land inherited	100.00	90.72	82.26	100.00	79.94	90.42
7.	Per cent of land purchased	0.00	0.00	0.00	0.00	0.00	0.00
8.	Per cent of land received through land reform measure	0.00	9.28	10.85	0.00	0.00	3.71
9.	Per cent of irrigated area to net sown area	21.50	0.00	6.13	4.79	0.00	4.91
10.	Per cent of net cultivated land to total land	97.87	76.23	88.19	90.09	77.04	85.70
11.	Per cent of uncultivated land to total land	2.13	7.20	8.68	5.75	10.58	7.44
12.	Per cent of land not available for cultivation to total land	0.00	16.57	3.13	4.15	12.39	6.85

Table 6 Contd...

1	2	3	*4*	5	*6*	7	8
13.	Per cent of net sown area to net cultivated area	100.00	91.30	98.79	95.43	73.95	92.09
14.	Per cent of current fallows to net cultivated area	00.00	8.70	1.21	4.57	26.05	7.91
15.	Cropping intensity	118.74	106.98	101.23	102.56	103.91	103.96
16.	Area under food grains to gross cropped area	98.78	93.47	88.12	89.57	95.82	91.26
17.	Area under cash crops to gross cropped area	1.22	6.53	11.64	6.39	4.18	7.04
18.	Per acre use of chemical fertilizers (Kg)	14.24	31.16	21.84	11.70	29.29	19.26
19.	Per acre use of pesticides (lit.)	0.01	0.00	0.01	0.00	0.01	0.003
20.	Per acre cost of cultivaiton (Rs.)	1688.38	1366.29	1145.15	930.16	933.93	1091.85
21.	Per acre loan (Rs.) from formal sources percentage of cost of cultivation	655.00	510.26	206.67	238.32	25.10	259.16
22.	Per acre loan (Rs.) from informal sources	537.02	192.88	41.21	39.94	0.00	88.65
23.	Productivity	1.81	1.82	2.15	1.29	1.36	1.67
24.	Per acre net income (Rs.)	1373.05	1118.87	1314.36	271.56	339.08	728.65

Source: Field survey.

REFERENCES

Chakrabarty, Gurupada

1998 'Scheduled castes and tribes in rural India: their income, education and health status,' *Margin,* 30, 4:100-30.

Dandekar, V.M. and G.J. Khudanpur

1957 *Working of Bombay Tenancy Act 1948: Report of Investigation.* Pune: Gokhale Institute Publications.

Fuchs, Stephen

1972 'Land scarcity and land hunger among some aboriginal tribes of Western Central India'. In K.S. Singh (ed) *Tribal Situation In India.* Simla: Indian Institute of Advanced Study: 367-73.

Kulkarni, S.D.

1974 'Alienation of adivasi lands, government not serious', *Economic and Political Weekly,* 9, 3.

Mohanty, B.B.

1997 'State and tribal relationship in Orissa', *Indian Anthropologist,* 27, 1: 1-17.

1999 'Agricultural modernisation and social inequality: Case study of Satara district', *Economic and Political Weekly,* 35, 26: A50-61.

2000 'Agricultural modernisation in rural Orissa: Land transfer and ownership pattern,' *Sociological Bulletin,* 49, 1-2: 63-90.

2001a 'Land distribution among Scheduled Castes and Tribes', *Economic and Political Weekly,* 36, 40: 3857-68.

2001b *Land holding and Use Pattern Among Scheduled Castes and Scheduled Tribes in Maharashtra.* Pune: Agro-Economic Research Centre, Gokhale Institute of Politics and Economics.

Murdia, Ratna

1975 'Land allotment and land alienation policies and programmes for Scheduled Castes and

Tribes', *Economic and Political Weekly,* 10, 32:1201-14.

Nadkarni, A.S.

1988 *Impact of Agricultural Development Programmes on Scheduled Castes and Scheduled Tribes Population in Maharashtra.* Poona: Gokhale Institute of Politics and Economics.

Nanekar, K.R.

1968 *Land Reforms in Vidarbha Region: An Inquiry into the Implementation of Land Reforms in the Vidarbha Region,* Calcutta: Oxford and IBH Publishing Company.

Omvedt, Gail

1994 *Dalits and the Democratic Revolution: Dr. Ambedkar and the Dalit Movement in Colonial India.* New Delhi: Sage Publication.

Patel, M.L.

1974 *Changing Land Problems of Tribal India.* Bhopal: Progress Publishers.

Rao B.J.

1987 *Land Alienation in Tribal Areas of Andhra Pradesh.* Warangal: Kakatiya University.

Rajasekaran, N.

1998 'Land reforms in Maharashtra: A regional analysis of development and change', *Review of Development and Change,* 3:2: 238-63.

Shah, C.H. and S.D. Sawant

1973 'Implementation of land tenancy laws in Western Maharashtra'. In S.H. Deshpande(ed.) *Economy of Maharashtra.* Pune: Samaj Prabodhan Saustha.

Upadhyaya, Ashok K.

1980 'Peasantisation of *adivasis* in Thane district', *Economic and Political Weekly,* 15, 52: A134-146.

20

Tribals, Anthropologists and Social Activists in India

Naresh Kumar Vaid

Tribals are sons of the Soil
They are *girijan*
They represent the lowest rung of the society
They must be uplifted
They must be brought into national mainstream

Or

There is nothing called 'tribal'
If at all there is, they get what they deserve
If they are not fit to survive, let them not

Or

They are Hindus, original but isolated
They deserve compassionate treatment
They must be made to realise their past

Or

It is our constitutional obligation to uplift tribals
If we release one rupee for tribals, only 6 paise reaches them

These are only some of the comments on tribals heard in the 'intellectual' circles of Indian society. But what is the truth?

> Our plans miscarry because they have no aim.
> When a man does not know what harbour he is
> making for, no wind is the right wind.— Seneca.

The Constitution of India has escaped, probably deliberately, the hassel of defining tribals. Here we don't talk about tribals but 'Scheduled' tribes. Even for 'Scheduled' tribes, article 366 (25)—that finds no mention in anthropological literature till date—defines Scheduled Tribes as:

> such tribes or tribal communities or part of or groups within such tribes or tribal communities as are deemed under Article 342 to be Scheduled Tribes for the purpose of this Constitution.

Even reference to Article 342 of the Constitution does not add to our wisdom because Article 342 prescribes only the procedure to be followed in the matter of specification of Scheduled Tribes.

The Annual Report (2001-02) of the Ministry of Tribal Affairs has for the first time identified the characteristics of 'tribal' communities as:

- *(a)* indication of primitive traits,
- *(b)* distinctive culture,
- *(c)* geographical isolation,
- *(d)* shyness of contact with the community at large, and
- *(e)* backwardness

That is all. The Ministry has not cared to define "primitive" (criterion 'a' above). Everybody, in one respect or the other, has some primitive traits!

All communities in India have distinct cultural traits (criterion 'c' above). Therefore some communities of Andaman and Nicobar Islands deserve to be STs.

Criterion 'c' and 'd' above are mutually related.

If we realize that India is basically rural till date, we should categorize India into India and Urban India. Here I mean India (and not Urban India) is backward (criterion 'e') and therefore all these people must be declared STs. Even most of the primitive tribal groups (PTGs) do not fulfill all these criteria.

The wise officials in the Ministry have taken up the task as routine. It is, therefore, understandable that over 10 million (may be more) of people deserving to be 'tribals' are still out of the list of Scheduled Tribes—included in 'Scheduled Castes', a category that is as vague as 'Scheduled Tribes'.

Even 53 years after the adoption of the Constitution, the government seems to have no clear vision of this top priority task. It can be gauged from some of the following random observations:

1. Large Area Multipurpose Cooperative Societies (LAMPS), their achievements and failures did not find mention in various annual reports of Ministry of Welfare and subsequently Ministry of Social Justice and Empowerment for half a decade. In the last two annual reports of Ministry of Tribal Affairs, the mention of LAMPS is there but not of their contribution.

2. The Commissioner for SCs and STs and subsequently National Commission for SCs and STs have highlighted several failures of government on the issue.

3. Crimes against STs were highlighted in annual reports of Ministry of Welfare. Subsequent such reports of Ministry of Social Justice and Empowerment, and now,

Ministry of Tribal Affairs have deliberately avoided these records. In the morning news on 12 August 2003, Radio FM 106.45 reported that of the 30,000 matters of atrocities against SCs and STs reported in the year 2000-2001, about 50% were yet to be disposed off. The Radio, however, did not mention how many cases decided went in favour of SCs and STs. The news was not covered by the so called national newspapers of Delhi. That shows the apathy of intelligentia towards their less equipped brethern.

4. In the last two consecutive annual reports (2001-02 and 2002-03) Ministry of Tribal Affairs has skipped the heading of 'number of beneficiaries' of government's schemes. This is happening at a time when the Ministry is being headed by a tribal himself. Is the Minister aware?

5. All the annual reports of the Ministry are a monotonous exercise and conceal more than what they reveal. Nobody can develop sympathy for tribals by going through such details.

Quite a lot has already been written in anthropological literature about apathy of administrative staff towards the task, and therefore we need not repeat it here.

> A want of necessaries of life, in peasants or artisans, when the seasons have been favourable, is a certain sign of defect in the Constitution or of criminality in administration.—Walter Savage Landor.

Since the inception of anthropology till a few decades ago, tribal studies were a hallmark of anthropological studies. In India as it evolved under colonial rule, the bearings of British social anthropology are explicit on the early developments of anthropology, at least upto independence. Subsequently, with the development of international interdisciplinary approach, we learned a lot from American anthropology. Upto 1960s several ethnographies of great importance saw the light of the day. Notable contributions to tribal studies from the legendary D.N. Majumdar to L.P. Vidyarthi have enriched anthropological literature.

These accounts are mainly ethnographic, some have contributed to anthropology conceptually and some have a great value in terms of applied anthropology. Many anthropologists have contributed to our understanding of tribal problems and impact of various governmental programmes while others have probed the impact of multinational activities as also of globalisation. In many of these studies suggestions have been made but these have either met the fate of dust or have fallen on deaf ears.

This reminds me of a situation in the early 20th century history of India when the pleadings of Moderates were of no consequence in influencing the British rule. Now when we claim to be independent (politically we are), political behaviour has not changed significantly while anthropologists have lapped up the role of Moderates.

> All mankind is divided into three classes: those that are immovable, those that are movable and those that move.—an Arab proverb

Without getting into debate about any precise definition of social activist or activism, I would contend that anyone who speaks about the issues concerning a social group, against injustice, for restoring justice and/or acts in that direction as a human being irrespective of his status in social, political or bureaucratic hierarchy, can be termed a social activist.

In that sense Nehru can be termed as the first social activist taking up the cause of tribals. On June 7, 1952, delivering a speech at the Scheduled Tribes and Scheduled Areas Conference, he had said:

> I am alarmed when I see ...... how people are anxious to shape others according to their own image or likeness and to impose on them their particular way of living. We are welcome to our way of living but why impose it on the others?

Remember, Nehru was not an anthropologist but he had the vision of an anthropologist. His acute observations on tribals culminated in his famous 'Tribal Panchsheel'.

While Nehru was an activist, more so in theory, Ambedkar was an activist in practise. Himself a victim of social injustice, he fought for social justice socially as well as politically. He was responsible for most of the clauses of social justice incorporated in the Constitution of India. It was social activism that to embarrass the Hindu orthodoxy, he embraced Buddhism.

Amongst anthropologists, Verrier Elwin can be included among social activists. He was single-handedly responsible for India's policy towards tribals during the first two decades after independence as also for Nehru's 'Tribal Panchsheel'. Though not in the same league, late P.K. Bhowmick's contribution as an action anthropologist for his work among Lodhas of S.W. Bengal through his Institute for Applied Anthropology and Social Action, can not be ignored. Similarly the contributions of K.S. Mathur of Lucknow in spreading the message of anthropology to the common man of Lucknow needs a special mention. Here, we must add that the term 'action anthropology' was coined by Sol Tax in 1950s, but as a practice it has not cut much ice with Indian anthropologists. If I am not mistaken, the contribution of 'practising anthropologists' has been much more than those in the academia.

Another example should suffice. B.D. Sharma, former Commissioner for SCs and STs, while in office, had the guts to remark:

> What should one say about a system in which the Constitution itself has bestowed on the President and the Governors unlimited powers for protection and welfare of the tribal people, yet they have not been able to save the people from exploitation and oppression of their own servants, and this historic task has been accomplished only by the Naxalite in some areas.

True to the spirit of social activism, he was with the tribals fighting for the cause of tribals (displaced because of the Sardar Sarovar Dam) immediately after retiring from his job. The names of Medha Patekar, Arundhati Roy, Rajendra Singh, Bharat Dogra, Anil Agrawal, Vandana Shiva and their ilk have become household names not because of their academic or family backgrounds but because of raising issues of survival for the lower rungs of society.

> It is error alone which needs the support of government. Truth can stand by itself.—Thomas Jaffereson.

Anthropologists in India are, in general, timid. They may do something for some definite returns but performing a thankless job of an activist is not only beyond them, they also consider it wastage of time. Social activism can not be pursued as a hobby. It is a way of life, value-loaded and idealistic. An activist shall not succumb to pressures and victimisation because he has clear goals. Bureaucracy has always been a hindrance and even antagonistic to his goals. It, with its colonial colours even today, sticks to rules, even at the cost of human dignity and development. Here, let me narrate my own experience.

Pawan Rana, a post-graduate in Political Science from the University of Delhi, hailing from a wealthy cultivator family of western Uttar Pradesh discussed the idea of forming an NGO with me in 1987 to work in Pithoragarh of U.P. (now in Uttaranchal). Subsequently, we formed an NGO, named it Experiments in Rural Advancement (ERA) and submitted a project to the central and state governments for funding of development in one of the most backward pockets of the district. We made our headquarters in village Pulla in the same pocket. As per rules, the recommendation of Collector, Pithoragarh was a must for the project (that related to providing safe drinking water) to be approved by the government. We sought an appointment with the Collector. Our conversation followed somewhat like this.

After preliminary introduction about ourselves and our NGO we requested him to act as per the merits of the project after going through all its aspects and if he had any queries he could call us back.

Collector	:	But I don't know you. How can I Ok your project.
Vaid	:	If administration reacts in this manner, then there will be no development.
Collector	:	You may be right but how can I Ok it without knowing you.
Vaid	:	What is the way out for you to know us?
Collector	:	How do I know? You tell me.
Vaid	:	You can know about us in three ways.
		Firstly, I am here for a week, I can keep coming everyday. We may develop some understanding in this period. Secondly, you can ask the local or tribal people and their leaders. (The district is inhabited by Bhotias in Munsiari and Dharchula tehsils).

Thereafter I had a deliberate pause.

Collector : And third?

Vaid : You tell me your batch. I may be able to name a few of your batch-mates—some common friends. You can know about me from them.

Collector : No, No. It never happens. Please don't waste your time.

The indication was clear. We moved out of his office.

The district administration subsequently told us that the project was not viable. State government had already spent over 20 lakh rupees for drinking water in the region, but in vain, while through our project we had demanded only Rs. 7.5 lakhs to do the job. On my return from Pithoragarh I communicated with people who mattered, and even complained. By chance or as reaction to my complaint, the Collector was transferred—not as a punishment—to the post of Secretary, Rural Development of the state. A person who could not understand development of a district, was made responsible for the development of the state. We can amply understand why U.P. is backward till date.

We however, completed the job successfully through a grant of only Rs. 5.00 lakh funded by another agency. The deficiency of funds was compensated by the community who provided free labour as well as boarding and lodging facilities for our workers.

A contrasting experience. A couple of years later we applied for our first major income generation project under income generation programme (IGP) for women to an NGO, Child Relief & You (CRY) with a budgetary estimate of Rs. 29 lakhs. We had put all our previous experience in preparing the project and expected to get full funds as estimated. CRY sent a team of experts to see the functioning of our NGO and to evaluate our project. Incidentally, the officials of CRY and myself travelled in the same bus from Delhi to Lohaghat and from there to Pulla but we were not familiar with each other.

On reaching Pulla by noon, CRY team visited various projects being undertaken by us and had a feed back about ERA from our workers as well as from the people. In the evening we sat to discuss IGP. The project was laid threadbare. They almost criticised each and every item of our project, especially the budget estimates. We had made serious blunders in our estimates by not including minor items but collectively that would cost heavily. They revised the estimates to over 37 lakhs and, to our utter surprise, recommended the project—then and there.

Ever since we have moved forward. We have received grants from WB, IGSSS, CRY, Danida and many more, but our experience with CAPART, country's own funding agency, has not been good enough to warrant a special mention. Yet the kind of support we have received makes me comment that there is no dearth of honesty and integrity in the world. If time permits, we shall be able to develop the whole region inhabited by 30,000 families in my lifetime.

A social scientist without being a social activist is nothing

Anthropologists have always claimed tribals as their constituency. Their understanding of tribals is, beyond doubt, much more than other academics and NGOs. Their recommendations for the cause of tribals may mean a lot to themselves, but who cares?

If my memory has not failed me, reservation for Other Backward Classes in jobs by V.P. Singh government in 1990 and subsequent anti-reservation stir in north

India was the only moment when Indian anthropologists felt socially concerned a bit and reacted as per their wisdom—though the reaction was so feable that it did not mean anything to the masses.

It may not be out of place to mention here that in 1960s when geologists were longing for recognition, they started a movement highlighting what they can do for the country. They did not rest till they got recognition (and have subsequently done a good job). Can we even imagine such a movement in anthropology—realising well that anthropology can contribute much more to human society than any other science or social science?

Indian anthropologists of the present generation seem to wake up after sun-set. Recently they kept sleeping when a separate independent section of Anthropology in Indian Science Congress was scrapped and merged along with Behavioural and Allied Sciences. Previously, they kept sleeping when the Union Public Service Commission revised the syllabus of anthropology for the Civil Services Examination and many outdated, even irrelevant, changes were made. They are even now sleeping when tribes throughout the country are crying wolf against globalization, privatization and marketisation and the forces unleashed through them.

It is a well-known fact that the Constitution made special provisions for tribals because it was felt that they were not in a position to compete with the much better equipped rest of India. Now they are being pushed into a far more uneven competition where they are pitted against the rest of the world.

It is, therefore, high time that anthropologists get up from their long slumber or they will have to opt for 'get up' and 'get lost'.

We will speak out, we will be heard,
Though all of earth's systems crack...—James Russell Lowell

ACKNOWLEDGEMENT

I am thankful to Nadeem Hasnain for 'provoking' me to write this piece.

21

Toda Social Structure and Change

R. Shankar and M. Thamilarasan

W.H.R. Rivers (1906) described life on the undulating plateau of the Nilgiri Hills in Southern India. The hills were visited by a Portuguese missionary in 1602, and have been invaded by Indian tribes on various occasions, but, at the beginning of the last century, the plateau and its inhabitants were absolutely unknown to Europeans. Of the various tribes inhabiting these hills, the Toda excited the greatest interest and this interest continues, partly because the people are so different from any other of the races by which they are surrounded, but still more because both they and their customs are so picturesque and in many ways, so unique.

Toda village and house

The Toda live in small villages scattered about the hills. The greater part of the plateau consists of grass covered hills separated by valleys, sometimes narrow, more often of wide extent. In every valley there are streams and in many places swamps. In the hollows of the hills are small woods, generally known as *sholas* and it is usually near these *sholas* that the Toda villages are to be found.

The Toda name for the village is *mad,* but this is now often replaced by the Badaga form of the word, *mand,*

and the latter word is used exclusively by the Europeans and others living on the hills. A *mad* usually consists of several huts. In some villages there may be only one hut, and the maximum number seen is six. At some places where there was formerly a village with dwelling-huts there is now only a dairy, but the term *mad* is still applied to the place at which the dairy is situated. The term *mad* is also given to the funeral-places of the Toda.

The daily life of the Toda

The daily life of the Toda men is largely devoted to the care of their buffalocs and to the performance of the dairy operations. As we shall see, much of the dairy work is the duty of certain men set aside to look after the sacred buffaloes and the sacred dairies connected with them. A large proportion, however, of the Toda buffaloes is not sacred, and their care falls on the ordinary Todas. The milking and churning is chiefly the duty of the younger men and boys but the older men also take part while the head of the family exercise a general superintendence.

On rising in the morning, the men salute the sun with the gesture called *kaimukhti,* and then they turn to their work of milking the buffaloes and churning the milk. When the dairy operations of the morning are over, the buffaloes are driven to the grazing ground, the people take their food and go about other businesses of the day. Some may collect firewood and procure leaves used as plates and drinking vessels; others may carry out any necessary tendance which the buffaloes require, or may go to fetch grain or rice from Badaga villages or from the bazaar. The chief men of the village may perhaps have to attend a meeting of the *naim*, or council, which holds very frequent sittings to adjudicate upon the many disputed points arising in connection with the intricate social organisation of the people.

The ordinary routine of the day is often broken by the visits of people from other villages, who may have come to talk over a proposed marriage or transference of wives; to announce some approaching ceremony; to discuss some business connected with the buffaloes, or perhaps, but probably rarely to pay a friendly call. Such a visit will probably give the opportunity of observing the characteristic Toda salutation. This is essentially a salutation between a woman and her male relatives older than herself.

Toda and social organisation

The fundamental feature of the social organisation is the division of the community into two perfectly distinct groups, the Tartharol and the Teivaliol. There is some resemblance between these two divisions and the castes of the Hindus. There is a certain amount of specialization of functions, certain grades of the priesthood being filled only by members of the Teivaliol. Further, marriage is not allowed between members of the two divisions, though some irregular unions are permitted; a Tarthar man must marry a Tarthar woman, and a Teivali man a Teivali woman.

The Tartharol are divided into twelve clans, which take their names from the villages. The Teivaliol are divided into six clans, or *madol,* taking their names from the villages. The villages of each clan are usually situated in the same part of the hills, though there are very often outlying villages far from the main group. At any one period of the year, only some of the villages of the clan are occupied. The people may move about from one village to another according to the need for pasturage, and the villages in the Kundahs and other outlying parts of the hills appear only to be visited during the dry season before the southwest monsoon sets in.

Toda's dairy organisation

The milking and churning operations of the dairy form the basis of the greater part of the religious ritual of the Toda. The lives of the people are largely devoted to their buffaloes, and the care of certain of these animals regarded as more sacred than the rest, is associated with much ceremonial features. The sacred animals are attended by men especially set apart who form the Toda priesthood, and the milk of the sacred animals is churned in dairies which may be regarded as the Toda temples and are so regarded by the people themselves. The classification of the sacred buffaloes is very different in the two divisions of the Toda people. The Teivaliol possess only one class of sacred buffaloes and these buffaloes are called collectively as *pasthir.* The Tartharol, on the other hand, have several classes of sacred buffaloes and they have properly no collective term for all of them, though they are often spoken of by the Teivali term *pasthir.*

Buffalo migrations

In certain seasons of the year it is customary that the buffaloes both of the village and the clan should migrate from one place to another. Sometimes the village buffaloes are accompanied by all the inhabitants of the village; sometimes the buffaloes are only accompanied by their dairyman and one or more male assistants.

There are two chief reasons for these movements of the buffaloes of which the most urgent is the need for new grazing places. During the dry season, lasting from about December to March, the pasturage around the villages where the Toda usually live becomes very scanty, and the buffaloes are taken to places where it is more abundant. Many of these places are in or near the Kundahs, where rainfall is greater than over the rest of the hills, and others and scattered here and there about the hills in spots where, owing to favourable conditions, the ground is less parched than elsewhere. In other seasons of the year it may happen that the grazing in the neighbourhood of a village becomes exhausted and it becomes necessary to take the buffaloes to another place.

The Toda gods

In describing the ritual of the dairy and the various ceremonies connected with the buffaloes, it has been mentioned that at certain times the prayer of the dairy or the prayer of the village is used. In these prayers there are references to various incidents in the lives of the gods, and many of the clauses would be unintelligible without a knowledge of these lives. It therefore becomes necessary to consider this branch of Toda mythology before dealing with the prayers in detail.

The typical Toda god is a being who is distinctly anthropomorphic and is called a *teu*. In the legends he lives much the same kind of life as the mortal Toda, having his dairies and buffaloes. The sacred dairies and the sacred buffaloes of the Toda are still regarded as being in some measure the property of the gods and the dairymen are looked upon as their priests. The gods hold councils and consult with one another just as do the Todas, and they are believed to be swayed by the same motives and to think in the same way as the Toda themselves.

The dairy ritual of Todas

This ritual is certainly of a religious character and though there is much in the nature of the dairy formulae which is uncertain, there can be little doubt that they are intercessory and that they bring the dairy operations into definite relations with the Toda deities.

It seems most probable that the general idea underlying the dairy ritual is that the dairyman is dealing with a sacred substance, the milk of the buffaloes. This sacred substance is to be converted into other substances, butter and buttermilk, which are to be used by the profane. At present, much of the butter goes to those who are not even Todas and are regarded by the Toda as inferior beings.

Todas purity and impurity

The idea of ceremonial purity runs through the whole of the dairy rites. Many of the details of the ritual, the purification of new vessels and of dairies revisited after a period of disuse, the ordination ceremonies of the dairyman, and elaborate ceremonies accompanying the making of new pep, all show a very deeply engrained idea than men and things have in themselves some degree of impurity, and that in order to be made fit for the service of the gods, they must be purified and sanctified by appropriate ceremonies.

As regards man, two grades of impurity are recognized: (i) the impurity of the ordinary man, which is perhaps an absence of ceremonial purity rather than actual impurity; and (ii) the special impurity which is the result of certain events especially of those accompanying birth and death. The impurity of the ordinary man does not prevent him from visiting the dairies of the lower grade, but it prohibits him from taking any part whatever in the actual dairy operations. With certain exceptions, he is rigorously excluded from actual contact either with dairies or dairymen of the higher grades.

Toda women and the dairy

Women take no part in the dairy ritual nor in the milking and churning operations which are carried on in the hut. It is said that at one time the women took charge of the buffaloes at the time of calving, but this is not the case now.

Women go to the dairy to fetch buttermilk, using an appointed path and standing at an appointed spot to receive it. Females enter dairies under two conditions only. They may enter the outermost rooms of those dairies which are used as funeral huts while the bodies of men may be lying. Here they may sit only on one side of the room, and only when the dairy operations are not in progress. Women also enter the temporary funeral huts of men which are called *pali* or dairies.

Funeral ceremonies of Todas

The funeral ceremonies of a Toda may be prolonged over many months. Soon after death, the body is burnt and the general name for the ceremony on this occasion is *etvainolkedr,* the first day funeral. After an interval which may vary greatly in length (two to three weeks), a second ceremony is performed connected with certain relics of the deceased which have been preserved from the first occasion. The rites on this occasion are more elaborate than at the *etvainolkedr.* The Toda name for this second funeral ceremony is *marvainolkedr,* the second day funeral. The final scene, in which the relics are burnt and the ashes buried, takes place before daybreak on the morning following the *marvainolkedr,* and this part of the ceremony is known as *azaramkedr,* the name being derived from the *azaram,* or circle of stones within which the final cremation takes place.

The funeral ceremonies have undergone some modification in recent times owing to the intervention of the government. Formerly it was the custom to slaughter many buffaloes at every funeral. This impoverished the people and was prohibited by the government about forty years ago, and since then the number of buffaloes killed at each ceremony has affected the second funeral ceremonies which, largely owing to this prohibition, are now much less elaborate and prolonged.

Todas and their changing life

Todas today live in small settlements known as *mod* but more popularly called *munds,* an anglicization of the Badaga term. The traditional Toda settlement comprises one to five barrel-vaulted huts, a buffalo pen and calf shed and occasionally a separate calf pen. Most hamlets have at least one dairy building, which looks just like the traditional dwellings; a few hamlets have up to three dairies. Surrounded by ample grazing land for the buffaloes, the settlement must also have running water and a *shoal* (*Nilgiri Copse*) nearby, the latter to supply firewood and in the past, building materials. But for more than a century, Toda hamlets have been undergoing change and many traditional huts have been replaced by front gabled wooden houses in the old Badaga style, side-gabled brick or stone building with tiled roof and concrete floor and other innovations. More recently to encourage modern house building among the Toda the government of Tamil Nadu has constructed in two showcase hamlets, 'model houses' in pseudo traditional style, half-barrel-shaped but made of concrete blocks on a poured concrete floor. Only the dairy huts remain virtually unchanged.

Several factors may account for the decline in pastoralism but probably the most significant is shrinking pasturelands. Afforestation of grassy slopes and flooding of valleys for hydro-electric projects by the government have consumed huge tracts, and the Toda practice of leasing land to cultivators has also diminished their former pasturage.

Traditional Toda society was so totally oriented — economically, socially and ritually — towards the buffalo that it is hardly surprising the people would resist such a thoroughgoing change. Their usual response to official inducements in the form of seed, tools and fertilizers was to sell these to others more enthusiastic about farming than themselves.

Conclusion

Even today buffaloes are still very important to the Toda, both for economic and ritual reasons. But modern Todas, some of whom own no buffaloes at all, do retain much of their traditional pastorally oriented social and cultural heritage, as we have seen. At the same time they are part of a complex modern society. Though dominated by the Hindu culture of south India as mediated through the Tamil language, this modern Nilgiri society is socially, culturally and linguistically heterogeneous. It is further characterized by a cash economy and by political affiliation with the state of Tamil Nadu and India. The individual Toda today has friends, acquaintances and business associates, not only among the indigenous hill peoples but also among the immigrant plainsfolk, and he is frequently involved with a number of government agencies: administrative, judicial, developmental and others.

The modern Toda seems fully to accept the efficacy of two parallel ritual systems: their own and that of the popular South Indian Hinduism, itself a variant of all India Hinduism. And there is nothing that is strange, at least in India, about this situation. Hinduism seldom converts in the manner of proselytizing faiths like Christianity and Islam, which generally demand that the individuals break with past beliefs and practices. It rather absorbs groups, often over long periods of time, first tolerating their reinterpreting past ideological and liturgical traditions. There is no need, then, to expect any sudden abandonment of the ritual aspects of Toda pastoralism. Today, with many a young Todas dressed no differently from the Tamilian majority, the truth of the matter is more evident to the casual observer than in the bygone years.

Always a small community, Toda today number about 1000 traditionalists. There are also a couple of hundred Toda Christians, mostly intermarried with co-religionists of other South Indian backgrounds.

The social structure as discussed above reflects the changing aspects of the social institutions of the Toda society. Thus, for example, the different kinship, religious, economic, political, and other institutions of a society may be said to comprise its social structure, as might such components as its norms, values, and social roles. The essence of this concept is those social relations which seem to be of critical importance for the behaviour of members of the society, so that if such relations were not in operation, the society could not be said to exist in that form. Structure is generally agreed to be one of the most important but also most elusive concepts in social sciences.

REFERENCES

Bahadur, K.P. *et al*

1978 *Caste, Tribe and Culture of India,* Vol. IV. New Delhi: Ess Ess Publications.

Breeks, James Wilkinson

1873 *An Account of the Primitive Tribes and Monuments of the Nilagiris,* Susan Maria (ed.) London: Indian Museum.

Malinowski, Bronislaw

1921 'The Primitive Economics of the Trobriand Islanders', *Economic Journal,* 31: 1-16.

Mandelbaum, David Goodman

1955b. 'The world and the world view of the Kota'. In McKim Marriott (ed.) *Village India: Studies in the Little Community.* Chicago: University of Chicago Press.

Natarajan, T.S.

1985 'Habitat of Todas'. In his *Tribal Habitats of Nilgiri District; A Profile.* Ootacamund: TRC, Tamil University (Mimeographed).

Rivers, W.H.R.

1906 *The Todas.* London: Macmllan Publications.

Sewell, W.H.

1992 'Theory of Structure', *American Journal of Sociology.*

Thurston, Edgar

1986 *Castes and Tribes of Southern India.* Madras: Superintendent, Government Press.

Walker, R. Anthony

1986 *The Toda of South India: A New Look.* Delhi: Hindustan Publishing Corp.

1998 *Between Tradition and Modernity and other Essays on Toda of South India.* Delhi: B.R. Publishing Corporation.

22

Globalisation in the Scheduled Areas

Samata and Mines

This paper analyses the problems of resource management and conflicts in the tribal areas in the light of the New Economic Policy (NEP) and processes of globalisation, particularly taking into consideration the provisions contained in the Fifth and Sixth Schedules of the Indian Contribution. These Schedules are specifically devoted to the protection of the millions of scheduled tribes concentrated in the Scheduled and Tribal areas recognized under them spread across the country. The Indian Constitution provided legal safeguards to these communities and all its policies regarding utilisation of resources, whether land, water or forests, were based on social equity rather than on market economy (Sharma 2000). The philosophy of decentralisation, community and customary practices under the system of traditional village panchayats formed the bases for the five-year plans of India. However, fifty years of constitutional safeguards to protect the scheduled tribes from exploitation has not saved them from losing their lands and livelihoods to non-*adivasis* as state's inclination to uphold and implement the laws was far from enthusiastic.

Until the nineties the country was guided by the socialistic model of development where the role of the state was clearly welfare and social justice was its fundamental mandate. As strategies of colonialism were defeated and led to revolts in most developing countries, the powerful nations restructured their global agendas through neo-imperial liberalisation philosophies. This process of globalisation has invaded India as well since the introduction of NEP of the nineties, which is a reversal of the welfare and socialistic essence of the Constitution to a great extent. It has ushered in an era of corporate, especially trans-national control of resources where the state is handing over the national resources to industries on the pretext that state has failed to deliver through its undertakings. In other words, industry has become the state and has been given the *carte blanche* to frame the educational, health, social, industrial, environmental, and legal policies, all leading up to the extremely urgent need for privatisation.

Conflicts over rights on land and other natural resources are arising out of swift changes in the context of NEP in India resulting in a shift in ownership and control over the resources and the means, methods and extent of exploitation. These changes are a direct influence of the industrial sector to steer the state away from the socialistic-democratic philosophy and to adopt a free market oriented approach. The paradigms of economic development are far removed from community needs and rights, particularly those of the *dalits*, indigenous people and other marginalised poor in the country.

The Scheduled Areas and their resources

The country has 67.8 million (1991 Census) scheduled tribe population, a substantial part of which lives in the areas recognised as the Scheduled Areas of nine states of Andhra Pradesh, Chattisgarh, Jharkhand, Himachal Pradesh, Gujarat, Chattisgarh, Madhya Pradesh, Orissa, Rajasthan and Maharashtra and in the seven north-eastern states. As per 1991 Census, 87.19%

of ST population depended on agriculture, either as settled and shifting cultivators or agricultural labourers or as collectors of forest produce. These figures corroborate their close association with land and forests as a means of survival, livelihood and a social way of life.

A very significant and alarming trend that is clearly upsetting is the depreciation in the percentage of ST cultivators from 68.18% as per 1961 Census to 54.50% in 1991 Census and an increase of agricultural labourers from 19.71% to 32.69%. This clearly indicates the alienation of tribal lands for various purposes like construction of dams, mining projects, setting up of forest based and other industries, notification of wildlife sanctuaries, construction of government infrastructure and encroachments by non tribals. The official figures for land alienation (Planning Commission 2000) report that the area alienated from tribals in all the states is 9,17,590 acres and those displaced between 1951-90 are 21.2 lakhs (39.4%).

Almost 80% of the forest and mineral resources of the country are found in the scheduled areas the exploitation of which has been the primary cause of land alienation among the *adivasis*. These areas, particularly the Eastern and Western Ghats are the catchments for a number of rivers which form the life systems for the large 'development' projects built during the 1960s and 70s. The diversity of natural resources available in these forests brought in two major stakeholders from the outside during this period — the non tribals who wanted to occupy the rich lands of the tribals and the state which launched its apparently public/national interest projects which were largescale and capital intensive causing millions of people, mainly *dalits* and *adivasis* to be uprooted from their lands.

The large projects were based on the Nehruvian philosophy of development where the voiceless millions living in the midst of these resources have to forfeit their livelihood for the progress of the nation. Thus the setting up of energy and hydro electric projects, public sector industries like mining, development of a network of roadways and railways in these scheduled and forest regions for the transportation needs of the industries and the expansion of government infrastructure were important vehicles of economic growth undertaken by the state.

By the nineties, the public sector had been heaped with the choicest of abuses and accusations for having failed to deliver much progress to the nation. The resources available in the scheduled areas were considered as having vast potential for exploitation and the NEP reflected a clear shift in the state's reverence to the private sector. The protective and welfare role so far played by the state suddenly began to shrink from the 1990s once the state decided to make these natural resources accessible to global and private powers. The subsequent changes in policies and laws or wherever possible, contravention of laws by the state in the scheduled areas has been the immediate consequence thereby exposing the remote tribal in an unknown hamlet to the fangs of globalistion.

Issues and questions relating to resources

It is true that the scheduled areas are a repository of rich natural resources and they hold most of the nation's wealth, whether physical, social, ecological, environmental, economic or aesthetic. The resources have been sustained over the centuries and maintained with little destruction more due to the social and cultural practices of the forest dwelling tribal communities whose systems of livelihood ensure minimum harm to the ecology. State perceptions of utilisation of resources are diametrically opposed to the *adivasi* worldview of resource exploitation and this divide has only widened further with the intrusion of globalisation's market oriented philosophy of development.

The experience of indigenous communities in other developing and underdeveloped countries outside India wherever globalisation has descended proves that indigenous knowledge systems, livelihoods, lands and forests have been brutally overridden by these forces. Experiences of all these communities have been gruesomely similar — that state transferred control over resources from communities and even from itself to industries and private institutions. The resources were exploited not because there was an urgent and immediate need for their utilisation and there was no long term or planned perspective to the utilisation of these resources. Commercialisation and commodification of resources became the primary concern without ensuring that the resources were available and sustained for optimal usage and for the majority's benefit. The experiences have further proved that resources conserved for millions of years were depleted beyond repair within a short period of globalised economies and that it has led to aggravated poverty of communities living in the areas of these resources while the industries and private institutions prospered enormously. This aggressive nature of resource exploitation has led to civil wars, strife, famines, political disturbances and violence in otherwise peaceful communities before globalisation took away their resources. Some of the scheduled areas in India have been a witness to such destruction mainly where mining projects and dams were built.

Population dependence and status of resources

As a result of increased pressure on the resources in the scheduled areas and the invasion of external populations particularly in the context of large projects like mining – which brought in migrant populations, big townships, tertiary sectors like trade and related activities for catering to the needs of the new populations in the townships, and new forms of economic activities – the *adivasis* have been displaced and pushed into the fringes of these areas while the natural resources were victim to largescale destruction directly for industrial purposes and indirectly by the new populations. The *adivasis* have been forced to shift desperately to other forms of unskilled labour like construction work, domestic service, vending, petty trade and even to prostitution.

The dependence of *adivasis* on the natural resources not only for their food but also for other domestic and health needs has been largely curtailed by these destructive consequences (Rao 1999). In the absence of any state support for fulfilment of their needs—basic amenities or medical services-their conditions of living have worsened to oppressive heights. The vast differences in consumption patterns of the *adivasi* communities and those of the new external societies who have no affinity to the land and its resources, has also led to the imbalance in utilisation of natural resources and further denial of the same to the ST.

While the state has displaced and uprooted *adivasis* from their natural way of life without a forethought, there has been no corresponding attempt to build up the literacy levels and skills of these forest dwellers in order to face the new economic situations. As a result they have ended up as debris in the globalised policies unable to access the resources which were their life sustaining forces or to compete with the mainstream society. Those absorbed in the new industries and projects are minimal compared to the extent of displacement and the in-migration of outsiders.

Legal and policy changes related to globalisation

In order to adapt to the globalisation processes ushered in at a feverish pace, the political powers and policy makers have made a complete reversal of the Indian Constitution where-ever people's rights and control over resources are concerned. In a globalised situation, it is the market and not community which is the focal player. It is centralisation of resources and decision-making, increasing communities' vulnerability to political vagaries and industrial interests. It is commercialisation of resources and profit gains to global powers and global corporates that is of crucial importance. As a result of such a political and economic ideology, the state as a social institution loses its role. The laws and policies are aimed not at social justice and social welfare but at maximisation of profits and maximum exploitation of resources. The Indian state after independence was carved under the socialist model where it had an important social responsibility to the backward and neglected communities. The laws framed under the Constitution were based on these principles. But, the new economic policy's primary goal is to redefine the role of the state and reframe laws to suit global interests.

Mining industries, power projects, dams and other industries projected as 'development' projects have been avariciously eyeing the abundant natural wealth. They take advantage of the poverty and illiteracy of *adivasis*, their inaccessibility to information and lack of political voice which helps in avoiding exposure of atrocities and violations committed by the industries in these remote areas to the world outside, and thus provides the opportunities for committing ecological havoc with impunity.

All laws and policies relating to the scheduled areas, the land transfer regulations, the forest act, the environment protection act, etc. are all under immediate threat of repeal, dilution or amendment. These laws clearly portray the need for protection of people and resources while the new policies call for exploitation of resources at the cost of people. These contradictions between law and policies are leading to industrial lobbying for amendment of the laws and even tampering with the Constitution. In the present context where good governance and transparency are being publicised by most state governments, it implies not effective administration and implementation for people's benefit but removal of bottlenecks hindering industrialisation and globalisation.

The Fifth Schedule under attack

One of the important Constitutional components, thus under attack of globalisation is the fifth schedule itself and the safeguards provided to the *adivasis*. As mentioned earlier, 80% of the country's resources are found in the scheduled areas, which implies that the fifth schedule has to be immediately nullified. The severe pressure and lobby from transnational corporates and financial institutions has unleashed a vehement denouncement of the state for all the laws related to the fifth schedule. The land transfer regulations operative in the scheduled areas are being diluted or amended by the centre and the state governments under the deceptive garb of bringing in economic development to the scheduled tribes.

Mining is one of the largest industries in India which is tending to be a serious threat to the areas protected by the fifth schedule. Most of the public sector mining projects and those areas proposed for future mining are being handed over to the private mining conglomerates with foreign direct investments. *Adivasi* movements against these projects have been questioning the legality of such mining leases as in Andhra Pradesh where bauxite, calcite and limestone leases were given to private industries. The Supreme Court's verdict (Samatha 2001) in the case of Samatha Vs the State of A.P. and others in 1997 that all mining leases to private industries in the scheduled areas were null and void, created a furore among the industry and political powers who are bent on selling away *adivasi* lands and mineral resources. Instead of amending its policies in the light of the apex court's ruling the state has started gearing up all strategies for dishonouring the judiciary and the Constitution. It appealed to the Supreme Court for a revision of the order. When this was struck down the ministry of mines at the centre circulated a secret document in July 2000 to the committee of secretaries stating that there was an urgent need to amend the schedule to allow mining industries to obtain leases in scheduled areas.

Clearly, the proposed amendment flies in the face of constitutional guarantees and safeguards to the S.T. and is in complete violation of the spirit of the fundamental rights. It is a clear indication that the new globalisation policies are steering the government towards finding ways of repealing the laws under the fifth schedule through legislative or judicial measures. The policies of several state governments, especially those undergoing structural adjustments ordained by World Bank and other global financial institutions have come up with new strategy papers where mining takes precedence over protection of the people and the forests where these resources are found in the scheduled areas.

Some of the state governments like Andhra Pradesh are pushing for parliamentary action for the amendment. The state government in its desperation to transfer tribal lands to mining companies in contravention of the A.P. Land Transfer Regulation act of 1959 has pressurized the tribes advisory council, the statutory advisory body on tribal affairs set up under the fifth schedule to pass resolutions for amending the law. Such negative signals from the government cannot be ignored cr taken under naïve assumptions that they are meant for the progress of the communities living in these areas.

The controversy over the sale of the public sector undertaking BALCO in the state of Chattisgarh to a private mining industry, Sterlite, stands out as a contradiction between law and the changes in policy decisions under the new economic policy. The constitutional provisions and the ruling of the Supreme Court in the Samatha case notwithstanding, the government has privatized the company inspite of stiff public outcry and justifies the sale on grounds of capital requirements. Keeping aside arguments of development and divestment of industries, the legal fact is that the state has become the primary violator of laws and the Constitution and this trend of state behaviour beyond law speaks of the alarming role of globalisation in policies relating to social sectors.

Changes to forest and agricultural policies and other laws

The state is finding back door means for transferring national properties like forests to industries as they contain vast potential for commercial activities like tourism, film and holiday industries, corporate plantations, etc. The dwindling forest resources have come under highly funded and publicized 'people's programme' like the joint forest management (JFM). The new global strategies of forest protection and regeneration in the scheduled areas in the name of decentralization and sharing of powers over forests with communities, has spelt disaster to the *adivasis*. Lands occupied by them for shifting (*podu*) cultivation and agriculture are being reclaimed by the government through such programmes. Corporate partnerships for raising plantations through the mechanism of JFM using jargons like community forestry are seen as imminent dangers to the forest policy and the Forest Conservation Act. In Andhra Pradesh the forest department issued an order in the year 2000 for entering into tripartite agreements with private industries and Vana Samarakshana Samithis for raising plantations. It was only after strong protests from NGO's and opposition parties that the government hastily withdrew its subversive tactics of privatizing forests in the name of forest and tribal development. (Samatha and Crynet 2001).

There is an inherent threat to the tribal way of agriculture and economic practices as the new 'visions' and strategies of many of the state governments and those of the centre are shifting their focus to corporatisation of agriculture. In the scheduled areas traditional methods of cultivation are contemptuously regarded by the government machinery and there is an invasion of new technologies of farming. Small landholdings are to be replaced by large corporate farming and local traditional crops are under attack from high yielding and genetically modified seed varieties and farmers are being pushed into shifting to cash crops and mono-crops which is totally contradictory to the diverse cropping pattern of the tribal communities which actually ensures their survival during national calamities like drought and provides a better balanced diet.

Most of these changes are being brought about by either the development projects from multinational financial institutions like IFAD and World Bank or through encouragement of agriculture based industries to provide loans, seeds and market linkages directly to *adivasi* farmers. It is tragic that the fifth schedule areas, which are the few regions in the country which have rich biodiversity of agriculture and sustainable organic methods based on selfreliant economy, are being wiped out with these new unsustainable systems. Without a proper knowledge and information of the new technologies and their impacts on their surrounding natural resources, the tribal farmers are coming under the noose of such transnational policies leading to indebtedness and even mass suicides as in the case of Andhra Pradesh.

People's struggles against alienation of resources

Thus in the scheduled areas, where people's problems have been neglected over decades and they have not been rehabilitated or compensated by earlier projects, the state is going ahead with new projects at an unimaginable pace. With this kind of development, it cannot rely on the proverbially short memories of people because memories are indelible actually. It is this blatant pandering to global forces and outright injustice to communities which is spearheading revolts, people's movements and protests from all corners of the scheduled areas in the country today. The S.T. have realised that conflicts between them and state cannot be resolved when private interests are projected as public national interests and people are forced to forego their rights over their resources.

The history of tribal regions is replete with revolts and rebellions whenever state policies violated the customary practices and laws of the people. The subjugation of *adivasi* cultures in the pre and post British administration have led to disturbances and violence in many of the tribal regions so much so that special laws had to be introduced hastily to contain the insurgencies. Right from the late 1770s starting with the revolt of the Paharia of Rajmahal Hills, the Kol insurrection in 1831-32, the resistence of Koyas, the refusal of Tana Bhagat to pay taxes and the famous Birsa Munda rebellion in Jharkhand and Kumaram Bhimu's revolt in Gondwana, the *adivasis* have shown their pride in resisting any destruction of their traditional laws and relations with the natural resources. Much as the nineties have become a decade of repression of people's rights over resources, it has also become the decade of people's movements fusing links and making their voices stronger and more assertive.

Kasipur block of Raigada district in Orissa has a predominant *adivasi* population who have been agitating against the joint venture aluminium plant of Alcan (Canada), Indal (India) and Norsk Hydro (Norway) called Utkal Alumina International Ltd since 1993. A strong people's movement called Pradrutika Sampadana Surakshya Parishad evolved out of the struggle for protection of lands and forests by the *adivasis*. The inability to suppress the movement led to a police firing in December 2000 when three tribals were shot dead. In Koel Karo, one of the longest drawn *adivasi* struggles in the country, the desperation of the state and the mounting pressure of the multinational forces to destroy the people's movement against the construction of the dam and to open up the scheduled areas for mining projects, is violently reflected in the police firing in January 2001 that left ten persons dead. In Anantagiri, the tribals who drove the Birlas, one of the biggest industrial houses in India, out of their lands and won a landmark judgement in the Supreme Court in 1997 have stirred up a hornet's nest by nullifying all private mining leases not only in their lands but in all the fifth schedule areas in the country.

In Jaduguda, Jharkhand, the adivasis are still struggling against the neo-liberal policies of nuclearisation. The fatal impact of radiation from uranium mining on the local communities, especially women, which the state is brutally trying to prevent the people from informing the world outside, is violative of all constitutional, ethical and social responsibilities. Corporate terrorism in Chattisgarh by large companies like Jindals have reached demonical proportions under state patronization. The adivasis and activists protesting against alienation of lands and forests to mining and other industries in this *adivasi* state are facing human rights abuses under the garb of industrial development.

In Mendha Lekha of Maharashtra where the tribals have defied state interference in their decisions over their lands, forests and water, there is a quiet revolution and assertion of the supremacy of the village institution. The government personnel connected with privatisation of the forests, commercialization of other resources and centralization of powers of liberalization are prohibited from entering their villages, thus standing steadfast to the customary practices of their forefathers. The Narmada Bachao Andolan has gained the widest publicity and has been the biggest people's movement in India in the last two decades. The movement has been one of the first to raise some fundamental issues of large development projects and people's, particularly those of *adivasis*, rights over their natural resources and their impact on livelihoods and forests.

There are thousands of such struggles large and small, in many corners of the tribal regions in India today. These symbolise the people's growing dissent towards state policies and the state's slavery to the global and multinational powers. The nineties have proved that the state has begun to play a dichotomous role in discharging its responsibilities vis-à-vis tribal friendly policies and laws. It speaks voluminously of the decentralisation, people's / communities' participation, transparency and good governance – all the terminology imported from international institutions. On the other hand, the state has also come up with some positive constitutional changes like the 73rd Amendment and the Provisions of the Panchayats (Extension to the Scheduled Areas) Act, 1996. However, these changes have lacked focussed relevance and earnest implementation as the economic policy aims at liberalisation of national resources and opening up of the scheduled areas and all natural resources to industries, private and foreign. The forests and natural wealth in these areas are the only remnants of national assets of the country and the communities living there and the decision to pass on this wealth into the hands of industries reflects the shortsightedness and the treachery underlying the new economic policy. It also speaks of the desperation of the debt trap that the country is viciously caught in for which the natural resources in the *adivasi* regions have to be sold out and the areas left barren. The sale of BALCO is the beginning of such a trend.

Adivasi movements are refusing to allow this to become a reality and are becoming more and more assertive. The isolated struggles of the earlier decades have learnt to forge linkages and grow into larger collective voices. They have realised that unless this strength is built, it is impossible to confront the globalisation forces. Indigenous communities from Asia, Africa and Latin America are also seen participating in building up this community of protestors and to bring in pressure on each other's countries and international institutions. And here one can conclude quoting the profound statement of an elderly *adivasi* village leader fighting the Indian multi-national, the Birla group:

> Companies are like monkeys. We have to keep a constant vigil and shoo them away to protect our crops and lands.

REFERENCES

Andhra Pradesh, Government of

Strategy Paper on Welfare of Scheduled Castes and Scheduled Tribes. Hyderabad.

2001 'Note on Demand no. XXXI', Department of Tribal Welfare 2001-2002.

2001 'Performance Budget 2001-2002', Department of Tribal Welfare.

2001 *Vision 2020, Swarna Andhra Pradesh.*

Furer-Haimendorf, C. von

1994 *Tribes of India: The Struggle for Survival.* Delhi: Oxford University Press.

ITDA, Paderu

2000 'Visakhapatnam District Report' presented at the meeting of the Governing Body, ITDA, Paderu, November 11.

Planning Commission, India

2001 *Approach Paper to the Tenth Five Year Plan.* New Delhi: Planning Commission, India.

Rao, K. Mohan

1999 *Tribal Development in Andhra Pradesh-Problems, Performance and Prospects.* Hyderabad: Booklinks Corporation.

Samata

2001 *Surviving a Minefield – An Adivasi Trimph.* Hyderabad: Samata.

Samata and Crynet (Visakhapatnam)

2001 *Joint Forest Management – A Critique Based on People's Perceptions*, Hyderabad: Samata.

Sharma, B.D.

2000 *The Fifth Schedule*, Volumes. I and II. New Delhi: Sahyog Pustak Kuteer Trust.

Thimma Reddy, M., K.S. Gopal, Raghav Narsalay and Mkinar Pimple

'Economic Restructuring in Andhra Pradesh – An analytical introduction to the Andhra Pradesh Economic Restructuring Project', Jointly prepared by Centre for Environment Concerns, Hyderabad and Focus on the Global South-India Programme, Mumbai.

23

Caste, Tribe and Peasantry in the Emergence of a People's Movement

D.R. Sahu

There have been many studies of tribal movements which focus on transformation, ideology, reform, development and displacement. Contemporary movement studies in India have made use of the notion of identity, action and community defence (Shiva 1988; Baviskar 1995; Patnaik 1998; Patel, 2001). These movements in India represent a range of collectivities which are oriented towards the 'grassroots' with new instruments of political action. The environmental movements with regard to the issues of dams, human displacement and resettlement effectively articulate ecological concerns. Chipko Andolan, Narmada Bachao Andolan, Anti-liquor movement in Andhra Pradesh, Anti-Silent Valley protest in Kerala, Anti-missile movement in Baliapal (Orissa) are examples of some social movements in recent times. These protests have not only questioned the development logic of the state but have also fought against the displacement of local people and their culture, symbols and habitats. In order to understand such movements, the details of the project particularly the area of its implementation and its approach to rehabilitation and the socio-economic structure of the community are very much essential. This paper makes an attempt to examine the movement against the setting up of the Missile Project at Baliapal, Orissa, from this perspective.

The project

The project, at an estimated budget of Rs. 40 billion (1.14 billion US dollars), was originally conceived in 1979 by the central government. The final decision for the project was taken in 1984 by the government of India based on the recommendations of scientific experts. The range was to be set up as a base for research, test and launch of India's tactical weaponry such as medium and large range missiles, rockets and pilotless target aircraft by the Defence Research Development Organisation (DRDO) under the ministry of defence, government of India. Indian Space Research Organization (ISRO) was also expected to use it for firing Polar Satellite Launch Vehicles (PSLV). It was to be spread over 350 kilometers of the Orissa coast in the north to Chilika Lake in the south. In the initial stage, 150-200 kilometer range missiles were to be tested and tracked with radar of the same range. The operational headquarters was to be established at Baliapal-Bhogari blocks, and the tracking station in the Niligiri hills, 35-km. west, which was, installed long back by the British.

The defence experts had technical and strategic reasons for selecting this particular site. Balasore coast is crescent shaped, Baliapal at its tip is ideal for the intensive monitoring required after a launch. From this site, missile could easily be test-fired on a horizontal trajectory into the Bay of Bengal or even further into the Indian Ocean without any fear of collision with populated islands or heavy sea traffic. Nestling on the east coast, the range was also said to be relatively free from the prying eyes of hostile neighbours or inquisitive air surveillance.

In addition, Balasore, as a district headquarter, has better infrastructural facilities and transport system, well connected to the whole country. The area has a firm soil which is conducive for a launching pad. Due to silting of ports in the east coast, there is not much of sea traffic and this area gets more number of sunny and clear days (300 days out of 365 days) as compared to Andamans' 200 to 240 days (*The Surya* 1987). Besides, an abandoned aerodrome at Rasgovindpur of the neighbouring Mayurbhanj district, which was prepared during the Second World War by the British, would facilitate the project.

The central government announced a land acquisition programme through state government involving 115-sq. km. for the test range and 45-sq km. for its safety zone. A total area of 160 sq. km. was to be claimed which would have affected a population of 71,102 comprising 11,609 families of 130 villages (*The Samaj* August 10 1984; *The Link* October 26 1986; PUDR 1988). Later on, the government revised the land requirement plan because of stiff resistance from all quarters and the revised proposal involved a total area of 102 sq.km. The revised plan claimed to affect only 54 villages (41 villages for the test range and 13 for the safety zone), 6484 families and a population of 40,793. The land to be acquired for the residential and administrative complex was claimed to involve no population displacement (*The Prajatantra,* August 9 1986; *The Link* October 26 1986).

The land acquisition programme of this project was conceptualised on the basis of three zones. The first zone was the central zone where the testing was to be done, the second was the safety zone, which was to remain as free area, and the third zone of 700 acres of land was only meant for residential and administrative purposes. In this area, land acquisition and displacement were to be almost total, and no cultivation was to be permitted. The safety zone fell in between the river Subarnarekha and the flood protection embankment known as *bhua bandha*. For this zone, 13 villages were to be displaced. While all the families in these areas had to move out to the rehabilitation centers, they would be allowed to cultivate agricultural land on lease basis even after its acquisition. However, the cultivators would have no ownership rights on the land, though they could cultivate it as temporary leaseholders on payment of prescribed rent to defence authorities. No private construction would be allowed in the safety zone and there would be certain restrictions on the movement of cultivators during notified periods (*India Today* August 31 1985; *The Link* October 26 1986).

Besides, government was to acquire the seacoast as well as the Subarnarekha river mouth, which were the sources of livelihood for a large number of fishermen staying in the area who were also to be displaced (*The Prajatantra* November 17 1985; *The Statesman* June 29 1986). Despite this displacement, fishing operations in the river mouth and the seacoast would be allowed as per the government instruction. However, the areas falling in the safety zone (including the Subarnarekha river mouth) and the seacoast would be kept under similar restrictions. Subsequently, the government announced a rehabilitation programme for the prospective oustees along with the revised land acquisition programme. Under this programme, the evacuees would be resettled and occupationally rehabilitated in the proposed model villages.

The protest

Many protests have been occurring for retaining access to natural resources and asserting cultural autonomy in India (Baviskar 1995). However, missile-testing centre as a 'development package' could not attract the people of Baliapal and Bhograi blocks of Balasore district and they protested against the project as they strongly felt that it, in fact, severely threatened their survival and their very identity.

Despite the persuasion of veteran political leaders for an alternative site for the missile centre, the defence ministry reiteracted that Baliapal is the most suitable site in the country. Finally, the defence ministry of India clearly set its sight on Baliapal and all speculations over the shifting of test range site was laid to rest after five years in July 1984.

J.B. Patnaik, the Chief Minister of Orissa, formally announced the government of India's decision to locate the missile-testing centre in Baliapal as development package to the people of the area in October 1984 as *puja veti* (gift). Earlier to this formal announcement, the people of Baliapal did receive information regarding the project through the word of mouth and knew about the survey of the area. One of the active leaders of this movement, Sasadhar Pradhan, revealed that local leaders including him presumed it initially to be a development package with many infrastructural facilities. Installation of the project was thought to be on the seacoast without any human or land displacement.

The district magistrate of Balasore made formal announcements for land acquisition to establish the missile range through various Oriya newspapers. This news became the precipitating factor for the agitation. Some educated people, particularly teachers, students and local youth formed an association to mobilise people against the project. Consequently, different political groups, rising over their ideological differences, joined hands on this issue. Gadadhar Giri, former member of Orissa state assembly took the leadership of the agitation. After mobilising support and solidarity from various groups, the local groups engaged in spearheading the agitation. A mobilisation process against the proposed missile centre by various political personalities and many voluntary organizations was initiated. The weekly markets in the villages were used as an important space for mobilisation activities.

During mobilisation phase, many prominent leaders organised and addressed a series of public meetings in many villages. Participation of the CPI (M-L) activists provided a militant turn to this movement under the leadership of Gananath Patra. Subsequently, people declared the proposed project area as the no-entry zone for government officials except the essential government officials, like doctors and health staff. Gates were erected on the three entry roads to the area. The gates could be perceived as the symbol of the movement and of security of the area and the people, their home and hearth, their past, present and future (*India Today* October 31 1985; *The Indian Express* February 7 1987). Furthermore the activists mobilised the people not to allow any outsider to enter the area and they advised the women there to blow *sankh* (conch shells) and beat *thalis* (metal plates) whenever any outsider was spotted.

March 2, 1986 was significant in the history of the Baliapal movement. The district magistrate, Balasore, along with other officers could manage to enter the barricaded area in the evening but within no time many *sankhs* were blown and thousands of people (including women and children) came out of their homes and cordoned the officials. The mob pressure was so high that they were made to get down from their vehicles and were forced to go outside the area on foot. Later on, the superintendent of police rushed to Baliapal with a large police force for their rescue. The activists released the sub-divisional officer on the condition of negotiating with the superintendent of police and to persuade him not to involve in a direct confrontation with the people. The police complied and did not attempt to enter the area. Later on, the officials apologised to the people for their action and went up to Baliapal block on foot. This incident was treated by people as the victory of 'people's power', which gave further impetus to the agitation.

The efforts by the administrative functionaries to enter into the area had mainly two purposes. First, that the officials could attempt to mobilise the support for the project and inform the people about the compensation and rehabilitation package. Second, the strategic mainstay, namely. the 'people's curfew', which was their symbol of strength could be broken which, in turn would lead to the loss of confidence among the people in themselves and in the leadership (Jena 1991). When all these efforts proved futile, the government resorted to repressive measures. Both Baliapal and Bhograi blocks were put under an undeclared economic blockade. The supply of essential commodities such as kerosene and edible oils, sugar, etc. was discontinued. The students were not even issued their caste and income certificates. Further, all the block level developmental activities including construction and repairing of roads, school buildings, etc. were also suspended. None was granted fresh loan by the cooperatives banks (Ahmed 1987; *The Telegraph* April 2 1987; *The Statesman* May 1 1988; *The Indian Express* May 15 1988). The government also obstructed the transportation of cash crops including *paan,* betel nuts, cashew nuts, groundnuts, coconut, fish, etc. (*ibid*). This was specifically aimed at hitting the interests of the upper and middle peasantry and the traders dealing in cash crops. They were the main targets for the government since they provided both leadership and resources to the movement. Economic blockade was adopted as counter strategy by the government to dissociate the people from collective action.

Historicity and the social structure

This movement can be understood in a holistic perspective in terms of its historicity and socio-economic conditions in the area. This area was one of the *Mughalbandi* areas during the Afghan period. During Aurangzeb's rule, Murshid Qulikhan I governed the area as Subedhar. A bigger portion of Midnapore of West Bengal was taken away from Jaleswar Sarkar of Orissa and in subsequent years, the river Subarnarekha was made the southern boundary of Bengal. Some of the older people of Baliapal told me that during the Mughal period, this area was used as a military base because of port facilities and sea routes. Geographically, Subarnarekha river merges in the sea here. The local people had vehemently opposed the construction of a coast canal by Britishers in 1855, as they would have to sacrifice their agricultural land. The coast canal divides the Baliapal block and Subarnarekha river divides Baliapal and Bhograi blocks.

People of Baliapal normally go to the adjacent district of West Bengal for shopping by simply crossing the Subarnarekha river by boat. Similarly people from West Bengal, particularly from Contai, Midnapore and Dantan come to the weekly markets in the villages of Baliapal for trading purposes through this short canal root.

Coming over to the demographic situation of Baliapal, it is a thickly populated block and has an area of 233.65 square kilometers with 24,716 households and 240 villages and 20% of its population belongs to the scheduled castes, and more than 5% are Santhal. (Table 3)

The staple crop in this region is paddy. Productivity levels are high due to the use of high yielding seeds. Since the area is vulnerable to natural calamities like landslides of river Subarnarekha and frequent change of its direction of flow on her way to merge in the sea, cyclonic flood and entry of saline water, many people of Baliapal depend heavily on fishing, especially in the coastal villages along with cultivation and agricultural labour. The production of cash crops (vegetables, groundnut, betel nut, cashew nut, coconut and most importantly betel leaves) has significantly enriched the economic position of the people.

As already indicated, the area is divided into two parts by the coast canal. Cash crops, viz., betel, coconut, groundnut, and cashew nut, are produced in the area nearer to sea and the other side is used for agricultural purposes. As such Baliapal block is situated on the crescent coastal part of north Balasore and is bordered by the river and the sea. Geographical factors have no doubt hampered the growth of settled cultivation in this area.

The frequent change of river belts and the receding aspect of sea force local people to resettle and sometimes the issue of resettlement leads to violent conflicts and legal disputes. Further, people from neighbouring areas— Ram Nagar, Saatmaile, Contai, Midnapore (all in West Bengal)– and refugees from Bangladesh have been migrating and settling down near this seacoast. Their settlement pattern has led to tensions over land rights. It may be noted that the 1934 land settlement was a dividing line for the people of Baliapal. Earlier to 1934 settlement, the average landholding size was not very high. Zamindari system was prevailing under the patronage of Jena family of Jamkunda village, Bhuiyan family of Chaumukh, Mohapatra family of Rupsa and Rai family of Dehurda. They used to collect taxes (one fourth and one sixth of total produce) subject to the quality of land and its produce.

People remembered that the first settlement known as Nijarat, was started in 1905, but the 1934 settlement changed the landholdings scenario and the average size of land holding decreased substantially. Unused coastlands were transferred to the village forest, locally known as *abadjogya anabadi.* Presently, Baliapal block can be identified with medium sized and small sized land holdings with very few large landowners. Average landholdings are between five to six acres (1991 Census).

The PUDR report (1988) revealed that during the colonial rule, permanent tenancy rights were not granted to the actual cultivators by the then zamindars. According to the local people, they had been granted rights over harvest of land (called *Amal Nama Patta*) by the zamindars but this was not recognised as tenancy by the Orissa land laws. Interestingly, the state has been accepting land revenue from them and on this basis the local people have been claiming their rights over the land. It was also revealed that the legal possession of government land is granted if the people have occupied it for at least 30 years and paid the taxes as per the land laws. Moreover, fishing is also an important occupation other than agriculture for the local people. As said earlier, cash crops like cashew nut, coconut, betel nut, peanut and betel leaf are the major thrust of Balaipal economy, especially in the seacoast areas, which have made that area relatively prosperous.

It is important to see the economic prosperity of the area in the context of people's resistance. The cultivation of betel leaves has made the area more prosperous. This prosperity has much relevance to the people's resistance in the area (PUDR 1988). Patel (1989) argues that the major changes in the economy of this area are a result of commercialisation of existing cash crops and agriculture by introducing groundnut in the northern parts and alternating with *til* (an oil seed) and rice and peanut in the southern part of Baliapal. As such, there is more than adequate supply of fresh water making irrigation redundant. According to her, introduction of the *paan* was not the only factor responsible for sudden prosperity of the poorer classes. Along with the growth of *paan*, cashew nut cultivation and fish also became an important marketable commodity. Coastal areas always depend on sea fish and it is always a part of their food culture because of its easy availability. Due to merger of Subarnarekha river into the Bay of Bengal, people of Baliapal have easy access to both sea fish and fresh water fish. As a native of this area, I have noticed that fish used to be a part of every day diet. Further, every house has a small pond within its boundary and whenever any guest arrives, immediately the guest will be offered green coconut water and fish will be trapped from the pond for food. The demand for fish in the neighbouring districts of Bengal has been increasing at a steady pace with supplies always low, especially after the diversification of certain types of fish for the export market. Orissa being the immediate neighbour and Balasore being the adjoining district soon started supplying the Bengal market. The nature of this demand led to the introduction of new technology. New kinds of nets could catch different types of fish and this led to the introduction of deep-sea fishing (*ibid*).

Caste, tribe and peasantry

For understanding the social structure of Baliapal, it is important to explore the iinkage between caste, tribe and economy, pattern of residence and local culture. Many castes and one tribe (Santhal) live in the area. The two villages selected for intensive study in the block (Table 1 and 2) have more than twenty-three castes and a few Muslims. Brahmins are at the top in the hierarchy and Raju, Khandayat, Barajia and Mahesh or Gola, all peasant castes, are found to be dominant castes. These four castes are considered as numerically, politically and economically powerful. Besides, they command more prestige than other castes groups in the area.

Other than these caste groups, there are Vaishnavites influenced by Sri Chaitanya, who spread *bhakti* movement especially in the eastern part of India. The people who belong to this sect are locally known as Vaishnav, the name derived from God Vishnu. Though they are not part of the caste hierarchy, over the years people of this sect have been identifying themselves as one of the Hindu castes. Vaishnavites are strictly vegetarian and do not plough like Brahmins. They propagate Sri Chaitanya's philosophy through *satsangs* and *bhajans*, lead a simple life and distinctly present themselves by making an anchor mark with the sandal wood paste *tilak* on their nose and both the arms and silently chant *Vishnu sahasra nama*. However, in course of time, they have also taken to agriculture, and subsequently, the cultivation of cash crops, but so far they have restricted themselves to vegetarian food and do not plough.

Jena (1991) has developed a ranking of the Hindu castes on the basis of local people's perception i.e. Brahmin, Vaishnav, peasant castes— Khandayat, Mahesh, Raju, Gaude, Sundhi, Teli, Tanti, Dhoba, Ketua, Barika, Radhi, Kumbhara and Kamara—all service caste groups and Kandara, Kodma, Mahuria, Kuranga and Domo-all scheduled castes. Hadi, Kandara, Kodoma, Mahuria, Kuranga and Doma are considered as untouchables for their menial work. However, the above caste groups are not considered under socially permitted caste group (*chala jeti*). There is a distinct social distance from the higher caste groups.

Nineteenth century records indicate that the Khandayat and Raju were traditionally peasant castes. Over the years, these caste groups were joined by the migrants from Contai, Midnapore and Belda areas of West Bengal, particularly Barajia and Mahesh or Gola castes. As already said earlier, in addition to acquiring tenancy, land settlements were made in the year 1934. Further, they had harvest land rights called *Amalnama Patta* declared by the then zamindars. Presently, these lands were cultivated particularly for cash crops (Patel 1989). For a long time, these dominant caste groups have remained as peasant castes. However, peasantry has been no more the monopoly of the dominant castes as non-cultivating castes particularly Brahmins, fishing communities, Vaishnavaites and even tribal people have entered into the cultivation of cash crops because of its low investments and high returns.

Looking at the life style of the people of the study villages, their food habits, housing pattern, and family rituals are quite distinct from the other rural areas of Orissa. Residential patterns are not strictly on the basis of caste except Domas, Panas, Keutas and Santhals. But there is a clear-cut distinction between socially permitted caste groups (*chala jati*) and socially distant caste groups (*achala jati*) and tribals (*adivasi*), though they do interact with the *achala jati* by maintaining a proper distance. However, all *achala jati* live in a cluster preferably on the outskirts of the village or periphery or roadside of the Dagara village. The cluster of the houses of these caste groups and tribals are known as *sahi* in the name of each caste groups such as Hadisahi, Kandarasahi, Santhalsahi.

Other than the above castes groups, there is one tribe (*i.e.* Santhal) who migrated from nearby Mayurbhanj district in search of work long ago. One Santhal family had settled in the study village on a small piece of land which was given by one of the villagers to take care of their cultivation during the 1920s. Now, there are 30 Santhal families in one of the study villages and they have been cultivating various crops including betel in their homestead land.

The migration of Santhals to this area has largely been determined by their growing numerical strength on the one hand and the pull factors of better wages and cash earnings. They have succeeded in adapting themselves and also added to the prosperity of the areas. The process of cultural change found among the Santhals of the area is in terms of their housing pattern. They have adopted the Hindu method of constructing houses with mud walls. Paddy straw has been used for thatching roofs. Some of them have also used tiles for roofing and equipped their houses with door frames having wooden bars and padlocks.

Their traditional occupations have changed. The people have accepted new ways of obtaining a livelihood. Other than agriculture, fishing has not only retained its earlier place in Santhal economy, but played a more important role because of the gradual acceptance of local culture of rearing fish in artificial ponds and fishing from Suvarnarekha river and sea. They have also started cultivating all kinds of cash crops. They have become bilingual due to contact with Oriya-speaking community but in their family interaction they use their own language.

Coming over to economy, the area has excellent natural resources to support a cash crop economy and it is known for growth of the market for the products. The specific nature of *paan* cultivation attracted the lower and non-cultivating castes, and this economic integration has strengthened the ideology of *Bheeta Maati.* The increased demand for *paan* led to the growth of trade and market. Consequently, the market forces facilitated caste-class dynamics and the ideology of *Bheeta Maati* and the crystallization of the agitation as well.

The peasant caste groups of the area initiated the cash crop production by encroaching on the common property land and the seacoast land. The *paan* cultivation was initiated by the outsiders, particularly by Bengali traders but consequently they were eliminated and replaced by the local traders. The local peasant castes found this cultivation more profitable in small patches of sandy land, since this cultivation requires intensive care and low investment. Upper caste peasants too were attracted to this production as a result of which the land consolidation process of local people was relegated to the background.

Consequently, production process increased the demand for agricultural labourers in the region and small cultivators and landless labourers fulfilled the demand. Gradually, they also started producing *paan*. Small cultivators produced *paan* in their homestead land and landless labourers produced by encroaching on the sea coast land. Similarly, migrant Santhal tribals also became *paan* cultivators. This production process also attracted the outside traders, particularly from Jaleswar and neighbouring areas. The spread of the market has led to the peasantisation process. In a way, the market forces brought many changes in the region particularly the people's quality of life and life style choices irrespective of their caste, tribe and class status. The sustenance of cash crop (*paan* economy) gained momentum due to the demand of this product in northern and western part of India. This production process empowered the local people economically and politically and their involvement in the protest became very much active. Further, these groups provided resources to the mobilisation process.

The land had been a major object of contention for the people of Baliapal. The natural resources of the area gave sufficient support to local people for a comfortable living including fishermen, small cultivators, agricultural labourers and Santhals. As soon as the organization took mass action, tribal community participated in many ways. One of the incidents of active participation was that the block development officer of the area along with some other officials, on the pretext of visiting some primary health centres, entered the area through the sea route by boat on December 7. The tribals, while fishing, spotted the official's boat. More than fifteen boats chased them and finally nabbed the officials' boat. Immediately, they communicated the news to villagers by beating the *madala* (drums), their traditional mode of protest (Majumdar 1947; Dutta-Majumdar 1956) and local people assembled on the spot. The officials were asked to go out of the area on foot up to ten kilometers (*The Samaj,* December 9, 1986).

The Santhals participated in every demonstration, but never encouraged participation in the meetings. Their emotional attachments to the sea and seacoast can be understood from the slogan they raised during protest.

E maati amara,
E samudra amara
Sarkar tume chali jao
(The land is ours. The sea is ours, government you go back.)

However, their active participation strengthened the collective mobilisation process and collective action. The people of the area did not leave any stone unturned to oppose the project through various mobilization strategies. Despite certain organisational crises the people of Baliapal collectively rose to the occasion, which led to the success of the movement.

Conclusion

The articulation of this ideology of *Bheeta Maati* brought out the economic, political, social, cultural and environmental dimensions of the protest movement. However, the ideology articulated by various fronts during the process of collective action focuses more on economic issues than cultural and environmental questions. The area, which was earlier divided into communities in terms of class, caste, gender and tribal identities, insiders and outsiders, peasants and political affiliation, closed ranks to form a community and succeeded in influencing the government to stop the project.

The political economy of the area contributed the needed underpinnings to the issues of struggles. The people outrightly rejected the compensation announced by the government. They further argued that government could never compensate for the socio-cultural life of the people. The fear of destruction of the socio-cultural fabric, economy and their resettlement in a new place strengthened the mobilisation process.

The mass character of the movement was also due to the support from major political parties. Their involvement facilitated the protest in terms of leadership, strategy and tactics. The lower caste-class groups and tribals participated more actively in *dharna,* rally and *gherao* than the upper-caste-class groups but the dominant caste peasantry had a complete control over the organization and decision making process.

Contemporary social movements have been termed as the new social movements but scholars are still debating how these are different from the traditional movements. New social movements are not based on traditional forms of class conflict. Their values are distinct from those of traditional movements and they embody a fundamental critique of modernity and rationality. The most important dimension of new social movements is that they belong to a 'different systemic location' from previous social movements (Melucci 1985). They are primarily cultural rather than political, bringing about social change through the transformation of cultural codes and collective identities. They are concerned with 'cultural reproduction, social integration and socialisation' and seek to defend the life world from encroachments by the system. The new 'politics' is about 'quality of life, equality, individual self realisation, participation and human rights' whereas the 'old politics' is based on economic, social, domestic and military security (Habermas 1981). The action primarily concerns civil society rather than the state.

The new social movements are class based, as are old social movements, but their base is middle class rather than working class. These movements operate primarily at a symbolic level. The movement is the message; the form taken by the movement is itself a challenge to dominant cultural codes and embodies different ways of understanding and relating to the social world. Social movements 'perceive' and 'name' the given society in new ways, ways that make visible previously invisible power relations.

Although these movements do not directly address the state or demand political power, one of their effects is to 'render' visible the power that lies behind the rationality of administrative or organisational procedure. 'Old' social movements were also involved in social transformation. They were the torchbearers of modernity and helped in mediating the transition from tradition to modern society by creating new individual and collective identities and new forms of politics. Now, however, they have become institutionalised and new social movements have taken their place. These new social movements occur at a distinct stage in societal development, involve new actors equipped with different orientations and identities and aim at achieving quite different ends as compared to the old movements. In addition, they take these older movements as a part of the other, a responsible party in the formation of the values and the institutions they react against.

In conclusion, it can be said that the Bheeta Mati is an issue based movement and it has participants from all strata of the community. It also does not demand any political power. The reinforcement of issues like sustenance of economy and home and hearth by the community, irrespective of caste, class and tribe affiliations made this movement a successful one. Finally, this people's movement can be interpreted as having the characters and perspectives of both 'old' and 'new' social movement.

Table 1
Profile of Dagara Revenue Village

Inhabited villages	3 (Hamlets)
Uninhabited villages	2
Total population	5576
S.C. population	600
S.T. population	1020
Households	921
Major occupation	Cultivation (paddy and all kind of cash crops and fishing)
Irrigated land	40.47 Acres
Unirrigated land	275.79 Acres

Block Development Office, Baliapal-2001

Table 2
Profile of Chaumukh Revenue Village

Inhabited villages	1
Uninhabited villages	2
Total population	5450
S.C. population	535
S.T. population	49
Households	994
Major occupation	Cultivation (paddy and all kind of cash crops and fishing)
Irrigated land	202.34 acres
Unirrigated land	1,011.72 acres

Block Development Office, Baliapal-2001

Table 3
Caste groups and tribe in the villages

Upper castes	:	Brahmin, Vaishneva, Karana, Khandayat, Raju, Mahesh, Gola, Gudia, Teli.
Middle castes	:	Gudia, Teli, Gauda, Barika, Radhi, Sundhi
Scheduled castes	:	Keuta, Dhobe, Tanti, Hadi, Kumbhara, Kamara, Kandara Pana, Kuranga, Madhuria, Bhumija.
Scheduled tribe	:	Santhal

REFERENCES

Ahmed, Farzand

1987 'Siege of Balasore', *India Today,* March 15.

Baviskar, Amita

1995 *In the Belly of River,* New Delhi: Oxford University Press

Dutta-Majumdar, Nabendu

1956 *The Santal: A Study in Culture-Change.* New Delhi: Manager of Publications.

Habermas, Jurgen.

1981 'Social movements', *Telos,* 19 (Fall).

The Hindu

1986 'Bandh in Balasore', December 6

1986 'Students oppose Missile Base in Balasore', December 11.

The Hindustan Times

1985 'Baliapal Project creates panic among villagers', August 28.

India Today

1985 'Orissa: Battle ground', August 31

1985 'Battle of the gods', October 31.

1986 'Resistance movement', June 15.

The Indian Express

1987 'Baliapal villagers vow to fight to finish', Feb. 7.

1988 'Baliapal blockade continues', May 15

1988 'Congress (I) hold rally at Baliapal without local leaders', May 18.

1991 'Stir against Baliapal range to be resumed', Oct. 21.

Jena, N.R.

1991 'Discontent, conflict and resistance in Balaiapal'. Unpublished Ph. D. Thesis, Chandigarh University.

The Link

1986 'Missile testing range to evict many', October 26.

Majumdar, D.N.

1947 *The Matrix of Indian Culture.* Lucknow: The Universal Publishers Ltd.

Melucci, Alberto

1980 'The New Social Movements: A theoretical approach', *Social Science Information,* 19.

Patnaik S.M.

1996 *Displacement, Rehabilitation and Social Change,* New Delhi: Inter-India Publications.

Patel, Sujata

1989a 'Baliapal, agitation socio-economic background', *Economic and Political Weekly* XXIV, 12, March 25.

1989b 'Agni, cyclone and Baliapal agitation', *Economic and Political Weekly* XXIV, 25, June 24.

1989c 'The Baliapal struggle and displaced communities', *The Times of India,* December 13.

1990 'Baliapal agitation: Leadership crises', *Economic and Political Weekly* XXIV, 23, June 9.

2001 'Community, identity and politics: Balaipal movement' In S.S. Jodhka (ed) *Community and identities: Contemporary Discourse on Culture and Politics in India*. New Delhi: Sage Publications.

People's Union for Democratic Rights

1988 *Bheeta Maati:* A Report on Baliapal Missile Base and People's Struggle. New Delhi.

The Prajatanta (Oriya)

1986 *'Baliapal basinka bisaḷ ganabikshoba'*, June 6.

The Samaj (Oriya)

1984 *'Kshepanastra ghati rupa rekha'*, August 10.

'Rastriya kshepanastra ghati: pooja bheti?', August 10.

1985 *'Baliapal kahinki?'*, April 19.

1986 *'Jaleshwar tehsildaranka gherao'*, December 9.

Shiva, Vandana.

1986 'Ecology movements in India', *Alternatives*, 9:2.

Singh, Rajendra

2001 *Social Movements, Old and New: A Post-modernist Critique*. New Delhi: Sage Publications.

The Statesman

1987 'Stiff resistance at Baliapal', April 10.

1988 'Blockade of Baliapal', May 1.

The Sunday

1986 'Facing the firing squad', June 1-7.

The Surya

1987 'People's war', January 13.

The Telegraph

1987 'Balasore lives in fear of stray missiles', June 7. or April 2 (49).

24

Situating Tribal Women

Nilika Mehrotra

Any discussion of tribal women in India should take into account the diverse and complex discourses on how this category has been constituted in social science. The first discourse positions tribes at the centrestage of anthropology. Objectification of tribe as the 'other', the 'exotic', pervades the concern, while the second questions the 'invisibity' of women's lives and their problems in tribal ethnographies. Feminist anthropology in the seventies, tried to correct the situation by focussing on women. Studies conducted on women in simple societies not only provided important insights in their lives but also enriched the theoretical understanding of gender relations. The third discourse raised the issues of gender and development, thereby viewing women as either active participants in conservation of their culture or helpless victims of the forces of globalization, culture change and modernisation.

Inherent in these discourses is the tendency to view tribal women as homogeneous having similar life experiences. The term tribal women itself is a pointer to the fact that it is ambiguous and has value mainly in terms of official discourse in India. In recent times, however, ethnic uprisings in tribal areas indicate how these official labels have acquired legitimacy in terms of the legality and boundary maintenance of these communities, thus tribal women have also come to acquire a legal and social status as a category. Sociologically, however, it is interesting to note the diversities among these women. In this paper I propose to raise certain basic, social, economic and political issues which create difficulties in understanding tribal women in social science literature, policy making and their implementation. The relationship of tribal women with the women's movement in India, and the changing economic scenario is being problematised here.

Ethnographic understandings

Women have always figured in monographs on tribal societies. Interest in them was translated in describing them as important social actors (wives, daughters, mothers, lovers, etc). Early monographs depict these women in 'exotic' attires and poses, and objectify them as things of beauty, sexuality and curiosity (Elwin 1943a and b; Majumdar 1950). Not much information, however, is given specifically on their activities, views and voices. Descriptions also do not detail women's work, though references are constantly made to their being hardworking. With the advent of anthropology of women, we now have some specific studies on them, which revolve generally around their roles and status. This literature points to the diverse roles played by women in clearly distinct cultural settings. What society expects of her is strongly determined by its norms and culture. Thus, right from Mead's classic work (1936), importance of culture has been established in privileging gender roles over biology. In India, the role played by factors, like region, neighbouring castes, and other communities, ethnicity and history and culture in the making of specific gender relations in a specific context is recognized. The idea of belonging to a tribal culture does not entail a particular lifestyle.

In the Indian context, tribal people engage in a variety of economic pursuits, like hunting and gathering Pulayas in the south, to professional agriculturalists like Ho and Oraons of Chotangpur region, to bureaucrats and professionals from tribes from the North East and Rajasthan. Contrary to the anthropological myth of relative isolation, tribals exist as a part of mainstream. A common similarity however, is that a large chunk of their population still reels under poverty, social backwardness, and illiteracy.

In tracing the history of writings on tribal women in India, we find that these descriptions do not take us very far. Inspired by the emergence of western women's movement in the late 1960s and 1970s, anthropology has paid attention to women's activities and lives. Interestingly, a major thrust was to map the status and position of these women vis-à-vis their men. Monographs on tribes concentrated mainly on their functions and roles. Simplistic structural functional approaches to understand women's status and role reduced these women as essentially complementary to men of their society. This sex role approach did not take cognizance of power imbalances and ignored the role of historical process (like colonialism, contact with other groups in the making and unmaking of gender equation).

Earlier approaches also propagated the view that tribal women were much better placed than their non-tribal counterparts. Such an idea was presumably based on the belief that tribes were not markedly stratified along gender lines. Gender relationships were seen as relatively egalitarian. Nuances of sexual inequality were not explored to the fullest. One of the major indicators of gender equality was assumed to be found in the amount of sexual freedom tribal women enjoyed. Autonomy in terms of choosing the spouse and easy access to divorce, remarriage, etc., were perceived as great markers of their 'liberation' or 'higher status'. Focus on autonomy in sexual life was essentially an upper caste perception which continues to plague the anthropological thinking even today.

Women and economy

One of the major contributions of this approach was to uncover the realities of women's worth unlike their counterparts in caste societies. Tribal women contribute substantially to economic activities, and the literature on tribal women deals with a variety of these activities. Apart from presenting interesting contrasts, the literature also provides a lot of data on the details of women's work. These studies also document the gradual deterioration of women's economic potential and declining status and attribute it to their contact with the outside world. Initially industrialization was seen as one of the major factors due to which tribal people have gradually been deprived of their habitat and subsistence economy. Migration of people to other areas in search of work was seen as a key factor exposing women and men to economic and physical exploitation. Other acculturative processes like modernization were seen to be playing havoc with tribals. Hinduization and Christianization have been said to be affecting the tribal value system. These new cultural values are seen to be imposing more restrictions on women in terms of the choice of mate/spouse, marriage practices, transition from brideprice to dowry, and withdrawal of women from work in the quest of acquisition of status.

Failure of land reform policies, indebtedness, land alienation force tribals to take up difficult jobs. Studies demonstrate that an unequal sexual division of labour perpetuated by modernization and technological development led to uneven effects on women. Boserup's (1972) pioneering study initiated debates on the role of women in economic development. Later more detailed studies came up on how modernization and capitalist intrusion led to the gradual decline of the domestic economy. Tribal economies in India were predominantly dependent on the household as a site of production, and women and men worked on an almost egalitarian basis and contributed to domestic economy. With modernization, however, the production was removed from the domestic sphere and women and men were forced to engage in other economic pursuits.

Some recent literature also discusses women's role in economy in relation to her rights in property, thereby her access to work and the ideological constraints which determine the first two. Marxist writings on this issue clearly assume the importance of women's economic contribution to the society as an important and sufficient indicator of her status. Some have gone beyond that, for instance, Kelkar and Nathan (1991). Literature on simpler tribal groups (like hunters and gathers, for instance Korwa in Central India) shows that in the absence of immovable property (like land), women have better position with respect to decision-making and control over income. In cultivation economies, women's lack of property rights marks her dependence on men.

Though women contribute substantially to economic production, they do not have direct rights over disposal of the produce. In shifting cultivation like in Orissa and North-Eastern states, women are in a far better position, as bulk of the work is performed by them and the societies allow them a say in the economic process. For instance, among the Bonda of south Orissa, division of labour was simple and based mainly on age and gender. They enjoyed a nearly egalitarian relationship prior to the incursions of 'modernization' (Nanda 1994). Women here also participate in selling and purchase of the produce, and they dominate the market place. Similarly, among Angami Nagas of Kohima district of Nagaland, though land was inherited patrilineally, women had a much better say in the distribution and consumption of the produce. They controlled the income, spending it mainly on domestic aspects (Mehrotra 1992).

In contrast, among patrilineal agriculturalist tribes like Hos, Santhals and Oraons, women are deprived of any rights in the property. Cultural sanctions also limit their access to work. This ideology further exposes women to forever depend on men in agricultural operations (Aggrawal 1994). Witch-hunting is one of the major problems in Chotanagpur where often older women are stoned to death by branding them as witches. Property disputes are said to be the major motives in most of such cases. Among tribals of Arunachal Pradesh like Indus and Thangsas, a switch from shifting to wet rice cultivation has led to a transformation in women autonomy and independence.

There is a substantial presence of tribal women in the Indian work force. According to the 1991 census, about 28.2% of tribal women were returned as main workers, clearly indicating the female work as essential to the maintenance of the household. The participation rate is higher in rural areas than in urban. Besides, around 13.1% were classified as marginal workers. These workers are mainly engaged in seasonal agricultural and plantation work. The industrial classification of tribal female workers shows that more than 90% of these workers are engaged in primary sector almost equally as cultivators or agricultural labourers, clearly indicating the dependence of tribals on land. Studies show that most of the tribal economies are still at the primitive stage of agriculture, and a large proportion of tribal female workers is engaged in agricultural activities. Heavy dependence on natural resources for subsistence economy exposes tribals to impoverishment in case of the depletion of forests. Large scale ecological destruction due to industrialisation in tribal areas of Bihar and Orissa has forced tribal men to migrate to towns or other areas in search of employment opportunities (Menon 1995).

In similar cases, industrialization is not the only factor affecting the lives of tribals rather many complex factors like modernization, land alienation, poverty, etc, intertwine to create a vicious circle which entrap them. Failure of land reform policies and incursion of modernization has affected tribal women adversely. Large scale migration of men and women to industrial areas and tea plantations has uprooted their cultural and economic base. Inequalities among genders which existed in the traditional culture get cumulative in such situations as the new capitalist order of which tribals become part, brings with it androcentric values and privileges for males.

Many scholars have documented the gradual deterioration in the women's domain of influence and rights in household. The patriarchal male ideologies of the employers get translated in terms of giving lower wages to women and harder and monotonous work rules. Industrial and agricultural labour though promising jobs to tribal women, also exposes them to worse kind of exploitation both in material and sexual terms. Outside contacts have also led to the habits of alcoholism and gambling among men which adversely affect the household economy and lead to wife beating and abondonment of women (Chatterjee 2003). Besides working hard as labourers, women are also found to engage in marginal farming, animal husbandry, fire wood collection, gathering of food products, as none of these activities is of permanent nature. Household chores and child care is also predominantly a woman's work. Thus, division of labour on gender lines remains grossly unequal in most tribal communities.

Tribal women and the state

Relationship between tribal women and the state has never been clear cut and straight. Article 14 of the

Constitution of India clearly grants equality between the sexes making it obligatory for the state to undertake steps to remove disabilities with which women suffer. On the other hand, women and men are allowed to have their affinities and loyalities to their respective communities and are even expected to be governed by customary (in case of tribals) and personal laws (in case of non-Hindus). Thus in case of tribal women, customary laws have paramount importance in conditioning their relationship with others in the society. The government of India in its special provision for the scheduled castes and tribes has recognised the scheduled tribes as a socially and economically backward class which requires special protection. Thus, special plans and programmes have been directed towards the uplift of tribals. Till very recently, tribal development policies in India failed to recognise its gender implications. Family continued to remain the focal point of the development programmes and gender inequalities within the family were not recognized.

For the purposes of planning, the category of tribal women has not mattered. Their interests are assumed to be taken care of within the tribal development programmes. Secondly, their interests are not seen as specific to them, as they are supposed to be benefitted by other special programmes launched for women, like that of special nutrition for pregnant and nursing mothers and children. In the sixth plan document, women and development slogan seemed to target rural women and their variety of anti-poverty programmes like IRDP, TRYSEM, NREP, RLEGP, DWACRA and the eradication of illiteracy through national literacy mission. Interestingly, the official discourse does not distinguish between the needs and capabilities of rural women including tribal on the basis of ethnicity, religion and region.

The national development strategy for women has undergone progressive changes through the phases of the five year plans. The approach changed from welfare-oriented policies in the early fifties to the production oriented approach in the seventies, to the emphasis on women legal rights and their empowerment in the early nineties (Nongbri 1998). Among various state sponsored programmes, education is one of the only programmes which has benefitted tribal women of a particular region, that is north-east India. Christian missionaries have played a greater role in spreading educational facilities than the state governments.

Various studies challenge the very base of tribal development as being male-biased and gender-blind (Bhandari 1990). They report that the benefits of development measures are unevenly distributed. A section of these people has cornered all the benefits. Educational and employment opportunities, provided through quotas and reservations, are also being cornered by the elite section of these communities.

Any discussion of tribal women and their relation to the development process needs to take cognizance of the special historical and cultural context which has contributed to women's bargaining power with regard to the benefits provided by the plans and policies. The question of development of tribal women is to be seen in the context of the debates over the history of their status of dependency and their subordination, and the reasons for their exclusion from mainstream development matrix. Tribal women's access to resources largely depends on the cultural and historical context and to the regions they belong. Even within the regions, issues like status and class cannot be ignored. Many studies tend to ignore the heterogenity among tribal groups with reference to land ownership, education, access to and utilisation of institutional resources. Punalekar's (1985) work on tribals of Gujarat clearly demonstrates the differential use and access of resources made by tribals living in the forest area to that of those living near road side area of the villages. There exists a clear division between the women of upper strata and that of the lower. The class divisions also explain the former's class proximity to political elite and life styles similar to that of non-tribals. Such stratifications based on wealth, status and class have been developing in the most tribal groups due to migration, urbanization and the availed opportunities of employment and education. Like other urban elites, educated tribal women in the north-eastern part of India have been freed from the erstwhile back-breaking agricultural work delinking drudgery from women's work. Many of them have now taken to white collar employment, while their poor counterparts serve them as housemaids.

Development as a policy has come for bitter criticism from all corners. State planned development has been seen as a destroyer rather than a benefactor of poor people (Bhandari and Channa 1996; Chaudhury 1993). Critics of development policy both at macro and micro level demonstrate the increasing alientation of poor people. Feminisation of poverty emerging in the 1980s symbolised the greater alienation of the Third World rural and tribal women (Singh *et al.* 1985). Changes in the agricultural sector, technological transplant and deforestation have been seen as critical in shaping the destiny of these people. Large scale migration of men leading to women shouldering the burdens of domestic economy, taking to begging and prostitution, are few such examples of women's losing control over their lives due to external forces. The forest dwelling tribals have become further marginalised due to forest policy which deprives them of rights over forest produce (Fernandes and Menon 1987). The women have to walk several kilometers to collect fodder both for fuel and selling purpose. On the other hand, large scale mining activities, hydro-electric projects and construction of dams have led to a decline in the resources of tribals and their displacement (Patnaik 1996) Structural adjustment policies in India have allowed multinationals to make entry into indigenous resource areas including those of tribal areas, rich in minerals, thereby depriving them of their habitat and subsistence base. Of late, many studies have documented the deleterious effect of such development policies and programmes on the lives of these women (Patnaik 1996; Chatterjee, 2003). Major problem areas emerging out of these are a threat to environment, health and nutritional status and the impoverishment of family economy. From national standards, these tribal health indicators are already much lower and in the wake of these programmes they further have to face specific problems relating to migration as evident in terms of frequent miscarriages and still births.

The gender blindness of tribal development policies fail to address the specific needs of women due to their heavy emphasis on fixation and achievement of quantitative targets. Tribal women's participation in the mainstream political life has been understood to be very marginal in Indian society. Relatively speaking, though tribal women enjoy far greater mobility in public life than their counterparts, these women remain totally cut off from the political process. The reasons for this virtual absence of their participation are to be examined in the nature of autonomy they have in terms of decision making in different areas of their social life. Despite their greater say in economic and social affairs, they are institutionally kept apart from the political institutions of the community. This marginalization is achieved through various restrictions on them. For instance, traditionally, women are encouraged to gender roles whereas men are encouraged to learn leadership qualities. Among the Angami Nagas, women of all age groups are proscribed to even come close to a sitting place (called *tehuba*) where all male political meetings are held and major decisions are taken (Mehrotra 1992). Almost all the customary laws discriminate against women in taking interest in the local politics. Very rarely do we find women as members of the local political bodies or having a direct say in village affairs.

In the political life of India, with the reservation ushering in education, jobs and political bodies, tribal women are gradually making an entry into the mainstream political process. Male dominance in the political structure of the society, however, restricts their movement in politics. For instance, till recently, in reserved seats for tribals, it was usually the men who were asked to represent different parties in the election process. A miniscule of women who are nominated or elected, essentially come from the political elite or are related to politicians. This scenario is not much different from what we see in the case of other categories of women in India. However, the question arises that despite their general greater autonomy and mobility, why do they lag behind in the most important area of social life? Among the north-eastern tribes also, customary laws prohibit women's active politicization. It is paradoxical that despite having very high education, women are not able to come out openly in the political process. Even in matrilineal communities like the Khasi and the Garo, men represent the political seats of power and women are sidelined (Nongbri 1998).

Promulgation of the 73rd amendment was a positive step in the direction of granting 33% of reservation for female membership in panchayat. This step could prove to be revolutionary as through it women who were traditional debarred from politics would be able to make their presence felt and rise above mere tokenism. Their presence in the statutory bodies like panchayat would enable them to inform and influence the decision at the village level. This amendment however remains problematic, since it chooses not to interfere with tribes of the north-eastern as they are perceived to have their local level customary governance. This is due to the assumption that tribal women do not have to suffer inequalities as their counterparts. Women's groups in Khasi and Jaintia hills have raised objections to this. The case is an important reminder of the fact that in the name of tribal customary practices, women's rights as citizen are being curbed (Nongbri 1998). On this question of women's political participation, the government of India makes no effort to distinguish between tribal women and men's political context and their aspirations. One of the objectives of the 73rd amendment was to empower women. The slogan of empowerment has become very fashionable in the official discourse. It has been coopted by the government from the vocabulary of development agencies but the issue of empowerment remains problematic and contentious, since it cannot be understood in terms of women's mere participation in the existing political structures.

Women's movement in India for last three decades has tried to divert the focus of attention to the problems of masses of Indian women. In much of feminist writings, women of all categories figure and the thrust is towards enabling them to fight against social-economic and political exploitation in the society. The feminist discourse in India largely makes a dichotomy between the interests of urban and rural women. They do not make a specific reference to tribal women. Their efforts are geared towards recovering the history of different women's participation in agitations, struggles and movements all over the country. From the colonial times, tribal women have been participating in the rebellion against the state in different parts of the country (Mitra 1984).

Documentation of tribal women's struggle against environmental destruction, for instance in Narmada Bachao Andolan or Chipko movement in the Uttarakhand region, is made popular but tribal women as a category is not taken note of. Women activists along with developmental professionals attack anti-women policy of the state extensively, nevertheless they too fail to recognise the specificities of gender and their problems in local, cultural and historical contexts. Of late, there is a pressure on women's movement to recognise the specificities along caste, tribe and religion and the role they play in the lives of women. It is not sufficient to accuse women's movement of being blind to these differences because it is through their creation of a gender-sensitive atmosphere that the government of India has taken note of the problems of women and moved in its policy from welfare to development towards the empowerment of women.

Given the diversity of tribal societies in the country there is enough evidence to demonstrate that development planning did not have homogenous impact on them due to the differences of social, cultural, geographical, regional and the economic aspects. Mere introduction of the components of gender in development planning would not ensure an equitable distribution of resources to women. In the recent years efforts have been made by development agencies in making the issues of tribal women prominent on the mainstream national agenda. The non-governmental organizations (NGOs), which work at the level of grassroots, have introduced a focus on gender in their strategies towards development. The addition of gender component is mainly dictated by the pressure of women's movement and the interest of international funding agencies to uplift poor women.

Since tribals form one of the most socially and economically 'backward' sections of the country, most of the development agencies are concentrating in tribal areas. In their programmes, they try to specifically address the problems of women as well as the community. Women are mobilized, their self help groups are being formed and through them community work is being run. Empowerment is seen as an important instrument in addressing the need of gender equality. The NGOs organize women around basic issues, like education, drinking water, credit cooperatives, land rights, dealing with corrupt officials, alcoholism and wife beating. Besides, these women are also engaged in various agricultural training and social forestry programmes. Camps and regular meetings organised on behalf of the NGOs bring women together and now a whole series of leadership is developing among them. Focus on the idea of development from below encourages women's participation in the village affairs, income generation and strategies for self sustenance. The case of Agragemee in Kashipur, a poor area of district Raigada in Orissa, is an excellent example of women taking over the leadership roles in their fight against social evils and rebuilding of the community. They have also been in the forefront in their agitation against installation of an aluminium factory in this area (Patnaik 1999).

Similarly, the Centre for Women's Development Studies launched development initiative in villages of Bankura district of West Bengal. It points to the fact that given the opportunities of defining their needs, they are able to overcome all obstacles, put their traditional knowledge to good use and even devise strategies for their own development (Mazumdar 2001). Similar stories of their struggle to restore their dignity and economic base against odds are being reported from different parts of the country. Empirically there are fewer connections between struggles of these women since their issues and nature of demands vary. Struggle for survival nevertheless emerges as the key issue. The issue of environment is not to be seen only in relation to political participation, rather it is to be understood in terms of the ability of women to intervene and transform the oppressive structures of the society.

These micro level strategies are political in nature since they have far greater implications for change.

On the other hand, women's movement also has to recognize the differences in the cultural context of various categories of women. Homogenization of interests creates problems in understanding why and how tribal women's strategies to survive and resist would be different from that of caste women of the same region. Internal complexities like status and class also need to be addressed. In the politicization of tribal women, the problem of identity is paramount. We need to have studies on whether these women recognize this category at all. Can an umbrella term like tribal women serve to promote solidarity between women of different tribes and classes? Identity formation is difficult in light of their individual relationship with the caste structure of the particular region and with others. Secondly, the rise of ethnicity would also hinder formation of an identity of sisterhood among tribal women. For instance, the rise of dalit women's movement in Maharashtra is an indicator of the fact that dalit movements of a particular region identify common issues and fight against them. Similarly, it is entirely possible to visualize tribal women's groups of the northeast having a similar agenda for action. However, the difference lies in the fact that dalit women of the other parts of the country may also identify with that of the former, but it is difficult to conceive of common interest articulation between tribal women of Chotanagpur with that of the north eastern region. Unlike dalits, tribals have been more variedly subjected to different social and historical processes of interaction with others. A ray of hope, however, is evident from active leadership tribal women have taken in local protests and movements. With the help of international organizations and the women's movements their issues are becoming visible. A poor tribal woman, Sumoni Jhadia's participation from Kashipur, Orissa in Beijing's

International Women's Conference is a case in point. Today, with globalization, such networks have become possible and increasingly protest discourses are assuming the language of human rights.

Conclusion

The above discussion clearly shows that the category of tribal women is marred with complex problems of definition, location and relationships both within and without. Traditional approaches of either treating them as 'exotica' or a homogenous category conceals the diversities within. On the other hand, particularizing them reduces the possibility of seeing and articulating their relationship with others, thus failing to consider them as citizens, participating in the democratic polity if the country. Other approaches of decontexualising them only as victims of development also negates the fact of stratification within the communities and their differential access to resources. Earlier, feminist approaches to see in them the source of understanding the gender inequality are also problematic in the light of their ongoing interaction with the outside world and their possibility of availing the opportunities in the educational and employment sector. Thus, opening of a democratic process, constitutional safeguards and capitalist intrusions have thrown open the boundaries of tribal communities and have given these women opportunities to be a part of the mainstream.

Rapid changes due to globalization are affecting them too and many of them are irreversible. The question is to see in what way, amidst sweeping globalizing forces, tribals emerge as specific individuals. I have not dealt here with questions like the negative implications of conversion politics, ethnicity and the identity politics that, however, threaten to be very volatile. Urgent researches are required in these contexts and their implications for the lives of tribal women. With the earlier approaches being unsatisfactory in understanding these problems, there is a need to recognize them as specific individuals rooted in historically and culturally specific contexts and also as active participants in socio-economic and political life of India. Thus, moving away from their objectification, their lives and needs require a much closer and finer appraisal.

REFERENCES

Aggarwal, B.

1994 *A Field of One's Own: Gender and Land Rights in South Asia.* Cambridge: Cambridge University Press.

Bhandari, J.S.

1990 'Gender issues in tribal development,' unpublished NIPCCD Report.

Bhandari, J.S. and Channa, S.M. (eds.)

1996 *Tribes and the Government Policies.* New Delhi: Cosmo Publications.

Boserup, E.

1970 *Women's Role in Economic Development.* London: George Allen.

Chaudhury, S.K.

1993 *Myopic Development and the Cultural Lens.* New Delhi: Inter-India Publications.

Chatterjee, Sonali

2003 'Economic Development and Changing position of Tribal Women'. Unpublished Ph.D. dissertation. University of Delhi, Delhi.

Elwin, V.

1943a. *The Aboriginals.* Bombay: Oxford University Press.

1943b. *Maria Murder and Suicide.* London: OUP.

Fernandes, W. and G. Menon

1987 *Tribal Women and Forest Economy.* New Delhi: Indian Social Institute.

Kelkar, G. and D. Nathan.

1991 *Gender and Tribe*. New Delhi : Kali For Women.

Majumdar, D.N.

1950 *Affairs of a Tribe: A Study in Tribal Dynamics*. Lucknow : Ethnographic and Folk Culture Society.

Mazumdar, Veena

2001 'Peasant women organise for empowerment: The Bankura experiment'. In Debal K. Singh Roy (ed.) *Social Development and the Empowerment of Marginalised Groups*. New Delhi: Sage Publications.

Mead, Margaret

1936 *Sex and Temperament in Three Primitive Societies*. New York: William Morrow.

Mehrotra, Nilika

1990 'Women's issues in Indian anthropology', *Eastern Anthropologist* 43: 2.

1992 'Angami Naga women: Some reflections on their status.' In S.M. Channa (ed.) *Nagaland : A Contemporary Ethnography*. New Delhi: Cosmo Publications.

Menon, Geeta

1995 *The Impact of Migration and the Work and Status of Tribal Women in Orissa*. Indo-Dutch Programmes on Alternatives in Development. New Delhi: Sage Publications.

Mitra, Manoshi

1984 *Women and Class Struggle: A Study of Tribal Movements and Women's Participation in Bihar, India*. Geneva.

Nanda, Bikram, N.

1994 *Contours of Change and Continuity: A Case of the Bondo Highlanders*. New Delhi: Sage Publications.

Nongbri, T.

1998 'Gender issues and tribal development,' RGCS Paper Number 47.

Patnaik, S.M.

1996 *Displacement, Rehabilitation and the Social Change: A case of Paraja Highlanders of Orissa.* New Delhi: Inter India Publications.

1999 'Proposed projects and emerging protests.' In D.K. Behera and G. Pfeffer (eds.) *Contemporary Society: Tribal studies.* Vol. III. New Delhi: Concept Publishing House.

Punalekar, S.P.

1985 'Tribal women in development mileu.' In J.P. Singh *et al.* (eds.) *Tribal Women and Development.* Jaipur: Rawan Publications.

Singh, J.P., N.N. Vyas and R.S. Mann

1985 *Tribal Women and Development.* Jaipur: Rawat Publications.

25

Conflict and Conflict Resolution in Natural Resource Management: The Case of Utilization of River Water in Harda (Madhya Pradesh)

Nadeem Hasnain & Aseem Hasnain

Managing conflicts in natural resource management is emerging as one of the key capabilities required for sustainable development in today's era of liberalization, globalization, and restructuring. Conflicts involving governments, their agencies, private sector and local communities generally arise because of disagreement over the use and control over natural resources. These conflicts, if not managed, can cause severe environmental degradation, threaten livelihood and disrupt social harmony. As Stephen R. Tylor (1999) rightly points out, conflicts over natural resources have always played a role in human society, but recent conditions have led to an increase in their intensity, public profile, and complexity. It is increasingly important to sort out new mechanisms and institutions to manage these conflicts and resolve them productively in the interest of both long term sustainability and short term economic feasibility.

In response to local natural resource management concerns of conflicts, many governments have introduced tenure reforms, decentralization of administrative authority, or organizational changes in resource management.

However, in order to understand the nature of conflict in natural resources it would be prudent to avoid any inter-sectoral comparisons. For instance, conflicts of forests can not be compared with the conflicts of water. "However, region specific ranking of resources could be developed. Conflict over water in Saurashtra (a water scarce region) was stated as more important than conflict over other natural resources as an example" (Singh & Sinha, 2003).

Identification of the source and causes of conflict are also critical for prioritizing conflicts. The understanding of history, culture and duration of conflict is necessary for identifying causes of conflict. Failure to respect the traditional rights of various communities at the local level may also lead to conflict. For instance, when forests are converted into sanctuaries or protected forests, local people or forest dependent communities who have been dependent on forest especially for minor forest produce suddenly find themselves deprived of their traditional rights. Moreover, as Pastakia (2000) points out, "In managing Common Property Resources, conflicts often occur because of differences over the usage of a particular resource. Differences arise because different stakeholders have different needs and perceptions. Failure to arrive at a resource use decision that satisfies all stake holders leads to conflicts. For instance, the shepherd's need for fodder would have to be balanced with the need of agricultural communities for crops. In the case of water, men's preferences for irrigation would need to be tempered with women's concern for drinking and other uses of water."

A proper understanding of the local social structure is very important to understand the nature and severity of conflict and to devise an institutional mechanism for conflict resolution. For instance, the social structure of a typical multicaste village is different from a tribal village. The caste hierarchy in a typical Indian village is usually used by upper castes to dominate the backward castes and scheduled castes to corner most of the natural resources available in the village. In tribal villages too, especially wherever tribal and non-tribal people live together in the same village, conflicts and tensions between these two segments may be observed. Moreover, a proper and adequate understanding of the pattern of interaction between human and natural resources is also critical to understand the nature of conflict. Thus, information on (i) the number and composition of stakeholders, (ii) the nature of the resources and its use, (iii) differential perceptions of the stakeholders, and (iv) institutional mechanisms, are considered necessary for analyzing conflicts in natural resources.

Going by the rapid growth of conflict situation in civil society, it is imperative that the complex dynamics of conflict situations and the ways to mitigate them peacefully need to be comprehended and studied. Thus, the strategic coordination among the civil society organizations both in terms of research and intervention programmes, which are relevant and feasible under the prevailing market situations, need to be developed to arrive at a cohesive policy for conflict resolution. As far as the approach is concerned, the holistic diachronic approach with emphasis on qualitative analysis seems to be the most appropriate. In the present paper, too, this has been used, employing observation, interview and focused group discussion as the primary tools of data collection.

II

The present study was conducted in six villages along river Samri that originates in Khandwa district and meets the mighty Narmada in Hoshangabad district of Madhya Pradesh. The chosen stretch lies in Khirkiya block of Harda district lying between Khandwa and Hoshangabad. The area is populated primarily by the fast changing Korku and Gond tribes alongwith some population of other castes mainly OBCs and scheduled castes.

This area has Basalat as the parent rock and hence black cotton soil abounds. The terrain is hilly and undulating resulting in heavily eroded surfaces. The groundwater level is low and the cost of extraction is high for most of the households. The annual rainfall is close to 1000 mm. The combination of black cotton soil, location of the ridge, deforestation and undulating terrain ensure that very little rainfall is absorbed to recharge the ground water aquifers.

The cluster of villages covered in the study is remotely located with poor roads and infrastructure facilities. These villages become almost inaccessible during the monsoon when only the bullock cart and the pedestrian trekkers can commute. The selected villages are on either side of the river and are hence, connected by this common resource. These villages and the residing communities are organically related to this resource in almost all aspects of their life cycle from birth to death.

The Korku form the numerical majority in the chosen villages with the Gond, Scheduled Castes and OBC households present in smaller numbers. In the Korku majority villages the other communities behave more or less like Korkus in matters of common decisions. The Korkus belong to the Munda family and are considered the 'most westward Munda speaking tribe'. The Korku are generally very gentle and straight. Their social skills are simple and make them susceptible to fraud and cheating. They are passing through the process of 'Hinduisation' and many of them now claim to be Hindus. The level of literacy and education among them is still quite low and finding an educated Korku beyond tenth standard is a hard task. The local economy is based on agriculture. Though landlessness among the Korku is low the quality of land in the chosen are is poor by the parameters of productivity. Irrigation facilities are limited to a few households. Since productivity is low hence most households migrate for wage labour to nearby irrigated areas twice every year. Off farm livelihoods are few and cattle and poultry do not contribute significantly to the household income. The role of forests in the local economy has reduced substantially as the area and quality of forests have deteriorated. In the past *tendu* leaf collection and non-timber forest produce added substantially to the household income. At present *mahua* flower is the only major non-timber forest produce gathered and sold by the community.

The river Samri is a tributary of the Kalimchak. It originates in Khandwa district and meets Kalimchak in Harda district about ten kilometers from the area of study. Samri used to be a perennial river till recent past but for the past decade it has been drying up latest by March very year. The river bed is now silted with sand, gravel and boulders that come from the ridge and mountains every year. The catchment area of the river is untreated and erodes in every monsoon. A faulty stop dam built in the chosen stretch has further compounded the problem. It has only two gates when it should have several. A fewer number of gates is responsible for the higher siltation rate as silt is unable to flow through the gates and hence piles up behind it. Sustained inflow of silt has drastically reduced the storage capacity of the river in the last about 10 years. The river flows turbulently in the monsoons and as late as November in good rainfall years. After this the flow reduces to a trickle by January. March onwards the flow stops and water is available only in natural depressions within the bed. By April, the number of water holes and the depth of stored water get further reduced and by the end of May water becomes a rare occurrence in the river. Only a few patches are left which are the sources of drinking water holes. These patches are highly protected as their value becomes immense to the local human population. Lately, as the handpumps and tap water are becoming sources of potable water, these patches are approaching a state of neglect.

The river water has the following uses:

(i) Drinking Water: This function has become less important now because of an increase in the number of open dug wells and hand pumps within the village during the last decade. This becomes important in the crunch season just before the monsoon when handpumps and open dug wells dry up. During this period, portions of the river bed are dug to obtain subsurface water for drinking purposes.

(ii) Domestic use and recreation: The river bank is used for washing clothes and for bathing as long as there is water either flowing or stagnant. Hand pumps have weaned away people from this use also. The river is also used for swimming and similar recreational activities as long as there is water deep enough for such purposes. These three uses generally continue upto February.

(iii) Cattle: The river is the most used source for drinking and grooming needs of the cattle. They are brought to the river twice everyday and for bathing usually once a week. Samri happens to be the biggest source of water and hence the only convenient place for cattle of the area. In the summers when the river dries up, it is the cattle who suffer and their owners who suffer indirectly. During draught years the cattle have to be relocated to water rich areas at a monetary cost of the owners.

(iv) Fishing: This activity is possible between September and February when water flows in the river. Small local fish and crabs are found though their availability is reducing increasingly. Fishing is not done on a commercial basis; rather it is for household consumption. It is done by younger people who see it also as a collective recreational activity using the indigenous fishing techniques and nets are seldom used.

(v) Irrigation: This is now the most voluminous and evident use. Diesel pumps and electric motors entered this area about a decade ago, though these are still not affordable for every household. But easier availability or credit, though at highly exploitative rates, have made it possible for relatively more affluent people. The owner-cultivators having land along the river (either legally owned or encroached) in all these villages use either diesel pumps or electrically operated motors to pump water from the depressions. There are also some farmers who, though distantly located from the river, have the financial resources to lay long pipelines and heavy duty pumps to extract scarce water for irrigation. Irrigation is required generally towards the end of Kharif season in September and during the whole of Rabi, i.e. November to January. In some cases, the cultivators go for a third crop (moong, lentil) during the summer which is an innovation in this region. The third crop is a potential source of conflict as it is the crunch time for water when it becomes the most sought after resource.

It is evidently clear that due to the forces of globalization and market, the overall policy environment for the agricultural sector is biased towards the hybrid, high grain yield, high input requiring crops, which are not suitable for a dry land area like the one in question. The local crops, namely sorghum, maize, pigeonpea and lesser millets, are slowly getting phased out because market support for these crops is very poor. These local crops have low water requirement and suit the local climate. This shift is directly having a bearing on the extraction of water for irrigating water-intensive corps like soyabean and hybrid wheat.

The national and state level water policies do exist, but not where the farmer operates. It is either in the mind of the development worker or in the files of the bureaucrats. Extraction of surface water from rivers, streams, ponds and from ground water aquifers continues unabated. The only limiting factor is the resource itself. Water resources lie chiefly in the domain of 'commons' and hence there is no common concern. Extraction depends upon some 'simple' rules—proximity of the user to the resources, availability of extraction technology and the guts to encroach on the commons. There is almost a total absence of norms and sanctions and hence a gloomy future lies ahead. Post 73rd amendment and the rhetoric surrounding it, rural governance is not in a happy state. There is definitely a feeling of achievement in terms of power to decide and run institutions but more definitely there is an increased confusion over the ownership of resources and penalties for the violators. The earlier active authority of the bureaucrat (*sahib*) is now absent and the newly empowered rural 'governors' have yet not become active. As per the prevailing ground realities, within the Panchayat, 'commons' are the end of the priority list because other direct and individual oriented benefits like rural development schemes and subsidies occupy the top of the list. This transitional period of confusion and neglect can bring about irreversible damages to such vulnerable 'commons' as rivers, aquifers and forests.

In light of the above discussion, when we try to make an analysis of conflict we find the following factors very important:

(i) Severity of conflict

(ii) Frequency of conflict

(iii) Number of stakeholders

'Severity of conflict' includes increasing intensity or levels of conflict. Damage and threat to human life may be the manifestation or result of the most severe conflict. Severity may also be measured by the extent of economic and ecological damages inflicted on the concerned parties. Frequency of conflict refers to the number of times a type of conflicts takes place annually during the last five years or so. Number of stakeholders may include the number of the conflict affected individuals and organizations. The nature of conflict in the area under study is understood largely during the peak summers when water is needed most by the cattle of all the villages.

There are a few villages such as Lafangdhana and Bheempura where the need of drinking water is also met by the river. During this period the situation heats up and the cattle owners and cultivators taking the third crop come face to face. Initially the cultivators do not pay much heed to this request and let the situation drift. Then mild requests and persuasive postures take threatening proportions. Usually, before social relations reach the breaking point the cultivators start showing gestures of reconciliation and balance is sought to be struck between the bare minimum needs of both the parties and the availability of water. In the absence of any enforcing mechanisms, the conflict could increase in severity but the strong tradition of harmony and bonds of ethnicity act as 'safety valve'. When water level goes below a healthy level there is real crisis for the cattle. The severity of conflict increases, heated arguments take place between the irrigators and the cattle owners. But still, surprisingly, no violence takes place. For the matter, violence has not been recorded so far.

Since communication is never severed between the cattle owners and non-irrigating villagers, and they approach the irrigators sometimes individually while some other times collectively whenever they come to the river with their cattle. No prior preparation for the deliberations is seen. Sometimes, when the cattle owners fail to persuade the irrigators not to extract excessive water they make a complaint to their village *panch* or *sarpanch* and ask him to talk to their counterpart from the offender's village. No effective dialogue takes place as the representatives of the Panchayat are generally inactive. In rare cases they have responded by taking up the case informally either with the offending irrigator or their counterparts in the offender's village. Solutions are not known to have emerged through this channel. Thus, in the absence of any institutional mechanisms for conflict resolution the complainant asks his friends or members from his extended family who happen to be related to the offender in some manner. These intermediaries are listened to as they are kinsmen. Thus the blood and marital networks are also harnessed. These do not guarantee conflict resolution immediately but prevent the conflict from escalating any further. Generally, what happens is that under such pressure the irrigator may stop at three rounds of irrigation instead of four. This definitely adds a significant dimension to the community based natural resource management. The Korku have a *jati panchayat* but there are hardly any cases where either the *jati panchayat* or the Panchayati raj institution have been formally asked to intervene in such issues or disputes.

The discontent decreases significantly after the summers, with the onset of monsoon but the bitterness remains. As the resource becomes surplus there is no problem of sharing during or immediately after the rainy season. The dispute is not clearly between the tribals and the non-tribals. Both the parties are generally tribal with only a few non-tribal on the offending side. The small population of non-tribals is usually better off than the tribals having their own open dug wells or bore wells for irrigation. Thus, it is more or less an intra-tribal conflict.

On probing the respondents about the possibility of community elders addressing this conflict, we got mixed response. Some of the respondents expressed the view that the traditional leaders could mobilize people across the villages to develop a common institution for managing the water resource but the majority of them had little confidence in the present, weakened, community leadership and its ability to handle such an issue. The lack of visibility of the incumbents from the panchayati raj institutions who actually have the mandate to ensure conservation and management of the resource compounds the problem. Madhya Pradesh government passed the Gram Swaraj Act in 2001 under which all natural resources have been given to the Panchayats for use, maintenance and management. Water bodies also fall under the ownership of village Panchayats. We spoke to the elected sarpanch in the chosen villages and several panchs, ward members and village secretaries regarding this new ownership regime. Almost all of them were unsure of ownership and the associated authority of the village Panchayat. They still think that the irrigation department is the legal owner and manager of these resources. Even the secretaries of the villages could not identify the responsibilities and authority of the village Panchayat vis-á-vis the maintenance of the river. Further, adding to this confusion is the fact that the river winds through several villages and hence there has to be shared to collective ownership also. There was no clarity on how river sections are to be divided and maintained among the villages. The presence of a large number of stakeholders will be a potential factor in future conflicts.

The above described and analysed case should not be taken lightly mainly because of the absence of any violence. This is clearly a case of 'latent conflict' and any such conflict provides a fertile ground for full scale 'manifest conflict'. The latent conflicts may also be described as implicit conflict. A variety of reasons may be cited for conflicts remaining latent, "such as fear, distrust, peer pressure, financial constraints, exclusion from certain disputing procedures and strategic and cultural reasons" (Castro and Ettenger, 1997). Because of their subterranean nature, it is difficult to identify such conflicts, leave alone document and study them. Not surprisingly, there is a dearth of empirical research on the subject and methods for analyzing latent conflicts.

REFERENCES

Buckles, Daniel (ed.)

1999 *Cultivating Peace: Conflict and Collaboration in Natural Resource Management.* Washington DC. International Development Research Centre (World Bank Institute).

Castro, A.P. & K. Ettenger

1996 *Indigenous knowledge and conflict Management: Exploring local perspectives for dealing with community forests disputes.* Rome. Food and Agricultural Organization.

Pastaki, Astad

2000 *Managing Conflicts Over Natural Resources.* New Delhi: Agha Khan Foundation (India).

Singh, R.K. & Vinay K. Sinha

2003 *Analysing Conflicts in Natural resource Management.* Bhopal. Indian Institute of Forest Management.

Tylor, Stephen R.

1999 "Policy Implications of Natural Resource Conflict Management" in *Cultivating Peace: Conflict and Collaboration in Natural Resources Management.* Washington DC. International Development Research Centre (World Bank Institute).

Serial - 18